# The Chosen

## Also by Avi Beker

*Disarmament without Order—The Politics of Disarmament in the United Nations*

*The United Nations and Israel—From Recognition to Reprehension*

*Jewish Communities of the World* (editor)

*The Plunder of Jewish Property During the Holocaust—Confronting European History* (editor)

*Jewish Culture and Identity in the Soviet Union* (coeditor)

*Arms Control Without Glasnost—Building Security in the Middle East* (editor)

*World Jewish Congress Jubilee 1936–1986* (editor)

*International Law and Foreign Policy* (editor)

*German Unification: A Jewish-Israeli Perspective* (editor)

# The Chosen

## The History of an Idea, the Anatomy of an Obsession

Avi Beker

THE CHOSEN
Copyright © Avi Beker, 2008.
All rights reserved. No part of this book may be used or reproduced in any manner whatsoever without written permission except in the case of brief quotations embodied in critical articles or reviews.

First published in 2008 by
PALGRAVE MACMILLAN™
175 Fifth Avenue, New York, N.Y. 10010 and
Houndmills, Basingstoke, Hampshire, England RG21 6XS.
Companies and representatives throughout the world.

PALGRAVE MACMILLAN is the global academic imprint of the Palgrave Macmillan division of St. Martin's Press, LLC and of Palgrave Macmillan Ltd. Macmillan® is a registered trademark in the United States, United Kingdom and other countries. Palgrave is a registered trademark in the European Union and other countries.

ISBN-13: 978-0-230-60048-5
ISBN-10: 0-230-60048-4

Library of Congress Cataloging-in-Publication Data

Beker, Avi.
    Chosen : the history of an idea, the anatomy of an obsession / by Avi Beker.
      p. cm.
    Includes bibliographical references and index.
    ISBN 0-230-60048-4 (alk. paper)
     1. Jews—Election, Doctrine of. 2. Judaism—Relations. 3. Gentiles. 4. Antisemitism.
    5. Holocaust, Jewish (1939–1945) I. Title.

BM613.B37 2007
296.3'1172—dc22                                                                 2007012083

A catalogue record of the book is available from the British Library.

Design by Scribe Inc.

First edition: April 2008

10 9 8 7 6 5 4 3 2 1

Printed in the United States of America.

To my late parents Aharon and Miriam
Who taught me on the gift and the burden of being chosen
And to my Song of Songs, Zvia

# Contents

# Preface

This book is not a personal memoir. Rather, to coin a term, it is a conceptual memoir. It is an attempt, based on cumulative life experience, to develop a frame of reference within which to understand the mysteries of the Jewish condition and the interaction, or rather friction, of the Jewish people and the rest of the world. I have devoted much of my professional career to studying these arenas of contention and friction. As a young member of the Israeli Mission to the United Nations in the late 1970s, I was astonished to learn how there, in the very heart of New York, the seat of the largest and supposedly most affluent Jewish community in the world, the institution representing the worldwide community of nations was, in fact, in the words of William F. Buckley Jr., "the most concentrated gathering of anti-Semitism since the days of Hitler's Germany." During my long career as a director of international affairs and as Secretary-General of the World Jewish Congress, I came in contact with world leaders and senior officials, as well as with Jewish community leaders from around the globe. I continued to be puzzled by the paradoxes and mysteries of Jewish-Gentile relations and was continually struck by the huge intellectual structure of faith, perceptions, and prejudice that lay behind many polite statements, feelings of appreciation, diplomatic ambiguities, and sometimes even expressions of envy or contempt.

Through my diplomatic work for Israel and the Jewish people, I have come to realize that my PhD in political science and international relations, and my years of university teaching and research, do little to illumine or solve this puzzle. The academic field of international relations is basically an elusive quest for a theory that, defined as a set of hypotheses postulating the relationship among variables, strives to make this, like other areas of social science, a semi-scientific field that can be rationally explained, analyzed, and even used to make some limited or general predictions. Moreover, this academic discipline can be used to help fair-minded people believe they can engineer the political conditions necessary to create a better world—something the Jews themselves, borrowing a mystical concept from the Kabbalah, call *tikkun olam* (repairing the world).

The lack of consensus regarding grand theories about world politics and history has led scholars to lower their expectations and exchange their search for theory for a search for so-called paradigms, which at most provide an example, model, or essential pattern in a particular field of inquiry. Even so, there is not much agreement among scholars, intellectuals, and diplomats about the real nature of world politics or the essence of the human motives that drive it. My own paradigm regarding the Jewish enigma was found in the halls of the United Nations and in corridors of power around the world in what was almost always a conceptual screen or filter through which people, both Jews and non-Jews, approached Jewish matters. It's not that I was blessed with divine revelation; rather, I gained the simple understanding that there was a hidden agenda, a self-imposed silence, a "political correctness" with which the concept of "the Chosen People"—which seems so irrational and atavistic—was regarded. Though this is, in fact, Judaism's defining concept, it remains the central unspoken psychological, historical, and theological problem at the heart of Jewish-Gentile relations.

References to and studies of the concept of "chosenness" are abundant in the endless literature on Jews, Judaism and anti-Semitism. However, not since the twelfth century has there been an attempt to explore this concept in the context of other religions, or to inquire as to the obsession that surrounds it. How have the Jews, of all people, come to represent at once the epitome of both the good and the odious? The priestly and the pariah? A source of envy and of enmity? A self-appointed or God-anointed people who are alternately emulated, merely acknowledged, or slated to be superseded by more worthy faiths or deserving nations?

These questions are not merely a matter for theologians. "Chosenness," a term that cannot be found in any dictionary or personal computer software program, a term that seems to have no historical significance in the postmodern era, nevertheless still informs new expressions of anti-Semitism and has a major impact on the Arab-Israeli conflict. Billions of people around the world entertain the concept of chosenness, but only the Jews—the biblical Chosen People—are censured for it. Why? Both Christianity and Islam are immune from this criticism, even though they have also, in turn, assumed the role of having been chosen by God and of superseding the Jews in this.

What is this chosenness? People from different backgrounds, in different centuries, gave different assessment of the nature and impact of Jewish chosenness. Both Maimonides (twelfth-century scholar) and Sigmund Freud regarded it as a cause of envy of the Jews, while intellectuals such as Arnold Toynbee and Josef Saramago regard it as a shrewd invention of the Jews themselves. More recently, Norwegian author Jostein Gaarder and Greek composer Mikos Theodorakis condemned and ridiculed the Jews' belief in their chosenness, even as several American presidents with Baptist upbringings view the Jews as God's people. It is amazing to note that Jews who were born centuries apart, and who lived very different lives religiously, such as Judah Halevi and Oscar-winning movie actor Richard Dreyfuss, have reached similar conclusions on the matter. Halevi, one of the greatest of the Jewish writers, poets, and philosophers of the Middle Ages (twelfth century), wrote the most all-encompassing work on the concept of chosenness, *The Kuzari*, in which he conducted a comparative analysis of Judaism, Christianity, and Islam. Hundreds of years later, Dreyfuss, a self-confessed secular, agnostic Jew, presented his own theory on Judaism: "I was one of those secret progressive Jews who believe that *We are the Chosen People. We are.* And even when that became not politically correct to say, I still do believe that."

Possibly the most outspoken public figure ever to address the concept of the Jews as the Chosen People was Benjamin Disraeli, prime minister of Great Britain during the second half of the nineteenth century, a converted Jew baptized by his father right before his *bar mitzvah* (at age thirteen). In his many books and speeches, Disraeli expressed strong views about the Chosen People, whose existence he regarded as "a miracle; alone of the ancient races."

In fact, chosenness forms a great divide between anti-Semitism and certain religious doctrines regarding Israel. There are only two groups, at opposing extremes, that refer openly and without constraint to the concept of Jewish chosenness: anti-Semites of all religions and types, and evangelical Christians who support Israel. Others may discuss it now and again in an indirect fashion, yet most of the time, it remains an *unspoken* issue. Even religious Jews, who refer to the concept countless times during their daily prayer and in their study of Torah, the prophets, and the Talmud, avoid a straightforward discussion of the implications of the concept of chosenness for matters of policy and relations with the outside world. The central role of Gentile Zionists, particularly evangelical Christian supporters of Israel, in shaping public debate and affecting policy regarding the "restoration" of the Jews to their homeland, remains a neglected field of inquiry.

The concept of chosenness has been and still is the driving force behind Jewish-Gentile relations. It is central to understanding the admiration and, more pointedly, the envy and hatred the world has felt for Jews at many of history's major crossroads: by Greeks and Romans in ancient times; by Christians and Muslims at the birth of their religions; by Crusaders in the eleventh century and Spanish Inquisitors in the fifteenth century; and by the Nazis in the Holocaust. In the twentieth century, German race theorists proclaimed the unique superiority of the Aryans. "We are God's people," Hitler declared. The German fuehrer regarded the Jews as an obstacle to Aryan chosenness and consequently decided that they had to be liquidated because, as he put it, "there cannot be two chosen peoples. We are God's choice." Even today, Jewish chosenness is the force that drives the virulent anti-Semites in the Islamic world and the more sophisticated anti-Semites of the liberal left.

While Christian churches (of most all denominations) began to speak in recent decades about their Jewish roots and even refer to a common American "Judeo-Christian" heritage, the opposite process has taken place in Islam. Although the Jewish roots of Islam are significantly deeper in theological terms, and even more conspicuous in the Quran than the New Testament, Islamic clergymen and political leaders have engaged for the last half of the century, and particularly so in recent years, in a project of obscuring it or even redacting those connections. The supersession doctrine, which explains why Christianity has replaced Judaism as the Chosen "New Israel," is far more central to Islam than

Christianity, and failure to recognize this centrality means failure to understand what has become the most crucial element in Islamic anti-Semitism today.

This book attempts to set the historical record straight—for Jews and Gentiles alike. It analyzes the concept of "the Chosen People" as it appears in the Old and New Testaments, the Talmud, and other rabbinic sources; the Quran and Hadith; and as expressed by the church fathers. All were reluctant to examine in depth what the concept of chosenness really means: For many Jews, "chosenness" means responsibility, a sense of universal mission. Why, then, does it continue to dominate the never-ending campaign against the Jews? For indeed, throughout history, Jewish chosenness has led to unprecedented persecution, suffering, and catastrophe. The apologetic and sometimes ostrich-like approach of the Jews to this concept should be rejected. Instead, it should be recognized as a pillar of Judaism, the most important paradigm for today's worldwide religious reawakening. Without recognizing its centrality in shaping the perceptions of both Jews and non-Jews, we cannot fully understand Jewish history and the world's attitude toward the Jews.

Some argue that the Jews invented their theory of chosenness. However, it is clear that this "invention" gave birth to two other monotheistic religions, which are practiced by billions. G. K. Chesterton, a renowned English writer of the early twentieth century, succinctly stated his anti-Jewish bias, "How odd of God to choose the Jews. . . . Not so odd the Jews chose God." Yet in so stating, Chesterton, like many others, proves why the concept of chosenness is at the heart of the mystery of Jewish existence, and the best paradigm for comprehending the paradoxes of that existence.

*Avi Beker*
*Jerusalem and Washington DC, Winter 2008*

# CHAPTER 1

## Confronting the Issue of the Chosen

For you are a people holy to the Lord your God; the Lord your God has chosen you to be for Him a treasured people above all the peoples who are on the face of the earth. It was not because you were more in number than any other people that the Lord set His love upon you and chose you for you were the fewest of all peoples but it is because the Lord loves you, and is keeping the oath which He swore to your fathers.

—Deuteronomy 7:6–8

The Jews rule the world by proxy. . . . They must never think they are the Chosen People.
—The prime minister of Malaysia, Mohammad Mahathir, October 2003[1]

Billions of people around the world define their religion, their nation, their tribe, or even their sports teams as the Chosen ones. This is natural: nations and religions alike tend to regard themselves as special. The 1.2 billion people in China see their country as the "center of the universe," which is the meaning of the Chinese word for China. Another 3.3 billion people who belong to the two largest monotheistic religions, Christianity (2 billion) and Islam (1.3 billion), believe that they are the Chosen ones of God. Other nations such as India (with another billion citizens), Spain, Germany, France, Britain, and the United States also believe in their Chosen legacy.[2] All like to entertain the Chosen concept, but only the Jews—the biblical Chosen People—are censured for it. In this book we will try to examine why this is so.

\* \* \*

The Chosen People is a term that elicits different reactions from different people. It can evoke pride or arrogance, embarrassment or hatred, devotion or confusion, apologetics or shame. The enemies of the Jews frequently invoke the Chosen concept, while the Jews are reluctant to mention it, and it is even denied by some of them. The apologetic approach coupled with the justified fear of possible anti-Semitism leads to confusion even in internal Jewish discussions. In our post-modern world, which is supposedly less religious and with fewer prejudices and ignorance, there is a widespread perception among religious and secular Jews alike that Jewish behavior is motivated by the "Chosen factor." Whether this is true or not is of little importance. It is the perceptions that matter, and often perceptions are stronger than reality.

Jews are hated because they are different—strangers, even when they are completely assimilated. Sometimes they are hated because they are successful. This kind of hatred is common to many other peoples. But the Jews are endowed with something else: they view themselves and are viewed by others as the Chosen People and are both envied and despised for it.

The amazing thing is that both Christianity and Islam are immune from criticism even though they also assume the role of having been Chosen by God. The Covenant between God and Abraham marked the beginning of the Chosen saga of the Jewish people. At the same time, those who criticize the Jews for behaving like a Chosen nation regard themselves as the children of Abraham who received the same promises from God. The Chosen concept is central to all three great monotheistic religions, but only the Jews are condemned for continuing to claim the title. This is because of a combination of antipathy, hypocrisy, cynicism, and deep jealousy. Could it be that the roots of both Christian and Muslim anti-Semitism lie in the struggle over the Chosen appellation?

In his book *Moses and Monotheism*, Sigmund Freud referred to the Chosen concept as one of the motives for anti-Semitism: "The deeper motives of anti-Semitism have their roots in times long past; they come from the unconscious, and I am quite prepared to hear that what I am going to say will at first appear incredible. I venture to assert that the jealousy that the Jews evoked in other peoples by maintaining that they were the first-born, the favorite child of God the Father, has not yet been overcome by those others, just as if the latter had given credence to the assumption."[3]

Freud may have been right in harnessing his own contribution to mankind, the "unconscious" motives of hatred, in his analysis. But he is wrong in blaming the Jews for evoking this hatred. The fact is that neither Christianity nor Islam, as we will see later in this book, denies that the Jewish people were Chosen by God; on the contrary, this is a central tenet of the dogma of both religions. Indeed, according to their own religious beliefs, it is accepted that the Jews were the first to introduce monotheism to the world. This is documented in both the Old and New Testaments of the Bible as well as in the Quran. Similarly, it is agreed that the Jews introduced the concept of an omnipotent, righteous, and holy God to mankind. In the Jewish view, this is part of their mission. But morality can be taxing, and there are people who prefer not to hear the message.

"Chosenness" is used here in the broadest sense and covers most aspects of Jewish-Gentile relations. Sometimes it lurks in the background and even in the unconscious, if we adopt Freud's theory, but it can nevertheless be detected and identified. Everything that is part of the unique condition of the Jews and reflects the complexity of attitudes toward them is part of the Chosen saga. This is why chapters of this book deal with the theological divide, the myths about the Jews and their separateness, the dispersion of the Jewish people, attitudes toward Israel, the issue of Jerusalem the Holy City, differing (sometimes double) standards in international law, the economic dimension, and the suffering of the Jews as expressed in the long history of anti-Semitism and in the unparalleled horrors of the Holocaust.

Chosenness is an all-encompassing term that covers different dimensions of the unique condition of the Jews. It deals with biblical tradition in both the Old and New Testaments, and the Quran and how these works deal with the concept of the Chosen People. Chosenness in the Bible also refers to the "Chosen" or "Promised" Land and the Chosen City, Jerusalem, all of which continue to be a critical part of the conflict in the Middle East. Chosenness is also the fundamental reason behind the uniqueness and separateness of the Jewish people wherever they live, in whatever age, in different cultures, in dictatorships, or in democracies. It includes the biblical mission of the Jews to act as a "Light unto the Nations," in the words of Prophet Isaiah (42:6), and to deliver a special moral message whether in religious or in secular life, whether as rabbis or as antireligious revolutionaries. We will illustrate how even Jews who had distanced themselves from their religion, and sometimes had actively fought against it, were still imbued with this sense of a special mission to "repair the world" (*tikkun olam* in Hebrew).

Chosenness sometimes lies behind the myths about Jewish conspiracies and perceived Jewish power and is the prime source of hatred toward Jews. The infamous *Protocols of the Elders of Zion* (see Chapter 5) is a good example of this. Chosenness also provides the pretext for the double standard that is so often prevalent in the deliberations of countless international organizations and in the reports and commentary by the media and intellectuals, aimed at Israel and the Jews. In the United Nations and many human rights bodies, Israel is treated as the Chosen Pariah. Chosenness brings with it the unique historical suffering of the Jews in the guise of anti-Semitism and, in its wake, attempts to deny it, to relativize it, and to link it to countercharges against Israel of Nazi-like crimes. Denial of anti-Semitism is part of an attempt to discredit the uniqueness of the Holocaust.

## Attacks on the Chosen

The revival of anti-Semitism at the beginning of the twenty-first century[4] highlights the fact that the concept of the Chosen People stands at the center of a modern form of the medieval disputations between Jew and Gentile. The use of disputation is not confined to extremist hate literature or esoteric Web sites, to street demagogues or preachers in mosques, but it can be heard from the mouths of heads of states, parliamentarians, leading intellectuals, writers, and journalists. The revival of anti-Semitism came as a shock to many—Jews and non-Jews alike—and it has now become increasingly clear that anti-Semitism masquerading as anti-Zionism is not simply a debate about the policies of the State of Israel, which is certainly not immune to criticism, but rather a reversion to classic old-fashioned anti-Semitism. This time, however, it comes in the shape of a mix of extreme Islamism and the intellectual left, both adopting the classic anti-Jewish stereotypes historically preached in Christianity and Islam. In this sense the new anti-Semitism is reverting to the ancient rivalry over the Chosen label, about who killed Christ and who betrayed Mohammad, and is the crucial element in a volatile mix of anti-Israel and anti-Jewish hostility. The alliance against the Jews uses Israel as the pretext for old-fashioned enmity toward the Chosen People.

Review and analysis of contemporary attacks against Israel demonstrate how central are those deeper motives of anti-Semitism—the old enmity against the Chosen. Many intellectuals and completely nonreligious people are using the Chosen concept and other related anti-Semitic stereotypes in their criticisms of Israeli policies. People like the renowned Greek composer Mikos Theodorakis and the Portuguese Nobel laureate Jose Saramago were using in their anti-Semitic attacks against Israel images taken from the Chosen. In 2004 Theodorakis spoke about Israel as the root of the world evil and about the Jews who control the world finances and the media. In Theodorakis's mind, all this has its origins in the Jewish "arrogance" and fanaticism of their biblical forefathers and the thought that they are the Chosen People. To make himself even clearer, Theodorakis, who had witnessed how Greek Jews were taken to their death during the Holocaust, admitted that his grandmother told him that "the Jews were the ones that crucified Christ." Saramago concentrated his attack on the suffering of the Chosen, which he accused the Jews for appropriating for themselves. While attacking Zionism for its "monstrous" idea that the Jews are the Chosen People, Saramago rejected the Jewish position that Israeli atrocities cannot be compared with Nazism and blamed the Jews for using the Holocaust as their bleeding banner (see Chapter 5).

France, because of its history and since it hosts the largest Muslim community in Europe, has become not only the major battlefield in the violent attacks against Jews but also in the war of ideas against the Chosen. The Jewish intellectual Alain Finkielkraut grappled with the paradox of how the Europeans who are haunted by the Holocaust now focus their blame on the Jews again. In Finkielkraut's words, France has become a country where synagogues have been burned, rabbis assaulted, cemeteries profaned, and very few Jews can dare to wear a *kippa* (a small cap, sometimes rendered *yarmulke*, worn at all times by Orthodox Jewish men) in some neighborhoods. "Every day, another intellectual denounces Zionism as a crime," he testifies, and Israel is becoming the target of anti-Semites. There is more old than new in this process: "Western discourse now accuses the [C]hosen [P]eople of believing themselves superior to other nation and of rejecting the gospel of a common, universal identity. Perhaps it is really the ancient condemnation of the Jew—for his worldliness, his particularism, his exclusivity, his national egoism, his closed fraternity—which, under the increasing burden of the Nazi trauma, is living a new youth, reveling in its flashy modern clothes."[5]

Because of its history, geography, and demography, Europe has again become the major arena of religious confrontation and anti-Semitism. With the presence in their countries of millions of Muslims, most of whom are recent immigrants, Europeans are ill-equipped to deal with what has been termed the "New Anti-Semitism." An incident in a Norwegian school in February 2004 is a good illustration of the new lines of confrontation and of the reemergence of old religious symbols. In the town of Kristiansand, Inge Telhaug, a teacher at the local adult education center, a government institution, was informed by the principal that he could no longer wear a half-inch-wide Star of David around his neck. The principal argued that the many Muslim students at the school could deem the Jewish symbol a provocation. Telhaug, who is not Jewish, hired a lawyer to defend what he regards as a violation of his freedom of expression. He said that he wanted to wear this small piece of jewelry, which he generally wore tucked under his shirt, since, "I see it as the oldest religious symbol we have in our culture; because without Judaism there would be no Christianity."[6] In Western and mostly secular Scandinavia, far, far away from the Middle East, the religious triangle of Jews, Christians, and Muslims failed dismally to find a way for cultural symbols to coexist. Is this despite or because of the common roots of the three monotheistic religions?

The scope of the hatred crosses cultures and religions. Among Muslims there is a growing tendency to adopt the stereotypical semantics from classic Christian anti-Semitism. The Muslim-Arab world has become the most dangerous propagator of Nazi-like hatred of Jews and the largest distributor of hate literature. It is easy to find references to the Chosen concept in hate-filled pamphlets and to hear Arab accusations that the Jews killed Jesus and betrayed Mohammad. The irony is that, according to the Quran, Jesus did not die on the cross, but a substitute (Judas) died instead. Christians, on the other hand, are regarded guilty by Islam of the unpardonable sin of shirk, which means to assign partners or companions to Allah.

\* \* \*

Even the September 11, 2001, attack on the Untied States is used in anti-Semitic rhetoric with the assertion that the Jews control the United States and orchestrated the attack to incite anti-Muslim sentiment. Saudi Arabia—from which fifteen of the nineteen terrorists responsible for the attack on the World Trade Center and the Pentagon had come—shamelessly claimed in official statements by the Saudi minister of the interior, Prince Nayef bin Abdul Aziz, that Israelis and the Jews were behind the attack.[7] This grotesque absurdity was reprinted in the media worldwide and appears in books in the West as well as throughout the third world. The Arab world's obsession with alleged Jewish power is widespread. In 2002, Egypt—which signed a peace treaty with Israel more than twenty years earlier—aired a forty-one-part television movie based on the *Protocols of the Elders of Zion* and Syria broadcast a similar production on the "Chosen Jews" that included old-fashioned blood libels, such as the Jews using Christian children's blood in the manufacture of Passover *matzot*.

The former prime minister of Malaysia, Mohammad Mahathir is a good example of the new anti-Semitism, which is new only in some characteristics and which adjusts to specific political realities. However, this new anti-Semitism is ancient in its content, mythology, stereotypes, virulent hatred, and irrationality. Mahathir's statement, quoted at the head of this chapter, contained a juxtaposition of vicious hatred as well as, paradoxically, grudging admiration for the Jews. His statement, made at the opening of the Organization of the Islamic Conference summit meeting in October 2003, combined jealously, frustration, and animosity. At the conclusion of his speech, leaders from the fifty-seven countries represented gave him a standing ovation. According to *New York Magazine*, "[n]ot since Hitler has a head of state had the gall to take off the rhetorical gloves with such zeal."[8]

Mahathir stated that Muslims have achieved nothing in more than fifty years of fighting Israel. Characteristically in his new anti-Semitism, he used the terms "Israel" and "Jews" interchangeably. He said, "They survived 2000 years of pogroms not by hitting back but by thinking. They invented Socialism, Communism, human rights and democracy so that persecuting them would appear to be wrong, so that they can enjoy equal rights with others." Mahathir noted that six million Jews out of twelve million were killed in Europe and that today, "Jews rule the world by proxy. They get others to fight and die for them. . . . 1.3 billion Moslems cannot be defeated by a few million Jews."[9] In his reply to a series of protests, he revealed the deep psychopathologic anti-Semitic motives behind his remarks: "They [the Jews] must never think they are the Chosen People."[10] After the speech by Mahathir, the foreign minister of Yemen also informed the press that "[t]he Israelis and the Jews control most of the economy and the media in the world."[11]

As we will see, the dispute between the Jews and Islam today has become more and more influenced by old Christian prejudices against Jews. The Islamic import of anti-Jewish teachings was accelerated with their growing frustration in the Chosen struggle over control of the holy places in Jerusalem and the humiliation Muslims feel as a result of their inability to remove the presence of a sovereign Jewish state from the Promised Land (a term that appears in the Quran).

In the United States, the year 2004 marked the opening of the most ancient wound in Christian-Jewish relations with the release of Mel Gibson's film *The Passion of Christ* (see Chapter 3) recounting the last twelve hours of Jesus' life, which focuses on the transfer or the displacement of the Chosen designation, according to Christian theology, from the Jews to Jesus and His followers. Jewish leaders pilloried the controversial film while at the same time most American Christians hailed it as "the best recruiting tool for 2000 years."[12] The film harks back to the origins of the Chosen rivalry, reviving the charge that it was the Jews, rather than the Romans, who were responsible for the crucifixion of Jesus. Gibson makes the movie as authentic as possible: the cast speaks Aramaic and Latin, and the movie contains some of the most brutal and graphic violence ever shot on film. In one controversial scene—that was subsequently cut—the Jewish high priest invokes a future curse on the Jewish people by declaring, "And the whole people said His blood be upon us, and upon our children."[13]

This quote is seen as the ultimate admission of the collective guilt of the Jews. It is a central statement that has affected Jewish-Christian relations for centuries and has served as the justification for endless pogroms and persecution. It has turned every Jew at all times and in all places into a "Christ-Killer." It was not the Jews who tried and crucified Jesus; nevertheless, because of this charge, millions of Jews were abused, tortured, and murdered over the course of two thousand years. The charge has become the backbone of Christian "displacement theology" sometimes also referred to as the "supersessionist doctrine" (see more in Chapter 3) because it justifies the *raison d'être*, repeated throughout the Gospels, that the followers of Jesus have replaced the Jews as the "People of God." The refusal of the Jews to accept the new doctrine and to agree to convert is a crucial challenge because it comes from those who are acknowledged to be the *original* "Chosen of God."

Many people are unaware of the extent to which the Chosen concept dominates the modern vocabulary of Islamic anti-Jewish propaganda. It is to be found everywhere in the Muslim world, including in the more "moderate" countries. For example, on November 29, 2003, in the *Daily Star* of Bangladesh, a Dr. Abdul Hashem wrote that the Jews "claim exclusivity as the 'Chosen People of God' and the right to the 'Promised Land,' all [of] which are biblical myths." This is a typical self-contradictory Islamic reaction as the Quran itself refers to the Jews as the People of the Book, the Chosen People by God in their Promised Land, so that in Islam itself it is not a myth but rather an established religious assertion (see Chapter 3). However, as we will see, Muslims contend that the Chosen role moved to Islam later in history.

The fact that a modern, educated head of state such as Malaysia's Mahathir feels comfortable uttering ancient and malicious charges to attack the Jews at a public forum is incredible enough. The weak European and even American reaction demonstrated how such attacks can easily become accepted *façons de parler* in the new century. Ten days after his statement and the resulting criticism, Mahathir reiterated his claim that the Jews control the world. Mahathir held power for twenty-two years and was known for his provocative statements against Jews, always leavened with a coating of sophistication so as to be more politically correct. Nevertheless, he engaged in classic anti-Semitism and even circulated the anti-Jewish tracts *The International Jew* and *The Protocols of the Elders of Zion*. He banned the Holocaust film *Schindler's List* and accused the Jews of manipulating the world's financial markets.

Professor Jomo K. Sundram, an economics professor at the University of Malaysia, explained that by criticizing the Jews, Mahathir was attempting to bolster his credentials among Malaysia's Islamic community. He needed to do so to compensate for his attacks against the Islamic religious leaders for not bringing their people into the modern world. Sundram explained that "[a]nti-Semitism is the kind of thing you do to establish your ostensible Islamic credentials.

Mahathir does this because his Islamic credentials are so weak, and because he spends so much time attacking the *ulamas* [Muslim clerics]. He was saying, 'In case you think I am anti-Moslem, here is some anti-Semitism.'"[14] Mahathir is a shrewd politician, and he understands the potential power of anti-Semitism, its political implications, and the added value to be earned by engaging in incitement and demagogy by using the term "the Chosen People."

## Setting the Record Straight

This book is not an attempt to present a theological case for any one particular Chosen People, although we will draw upon religious texts of Judaism, Christianity, and Islam to learn about the origins of the conflict. It is an attempt to set the historic record straight for Jews and Gentiles alike. A review of the attacks against Israel, and later against the United States as it moved toward the war in Iraq in 2003, shows how the anti-Semitic *Protocols* enjoyed a revival. This primitive czarist forgery about how a "cabal"* of Jewish elders supposedly control the world, provided a fashionable word to explain how a "Jewish Cabal" (an expression used recently by a British member of parliament and an American congressman in 2003) was pushing the United States into war.

Both Jews and non-Jews are reluctant to examine in depth what the Chosen concept is really about and why it continues to underline the never-ending campaign against the Jews. The present book is an attempt to present a summary of Jewish sources on the concept of the Chosen: its origins, its evolution, and its different interpretations among religious and secular Jews. We also look at it from the perspective of Christians and Muslims who claim to have assumed the title of the Chosen People, as well as from the point of view of those who ridicule the concept. This book attempts to fill the gaps in knowledge concerning the role that the issue still plays in Jewish-Gentile relations.

Islam and Christianity differ on many theological issues and the Quran and the New Testament provide texts and doctrines that are often at variance. However, there is a striking similarity in the attitude to the Jews in both texts. In both, one can trace the unfolding stages of the rivalry with the first Chosen People. Both acknowledge the Jewish sources of their religion, their attempts to convert the Jews, the formal recognition of the Jews as the first Chosen of God, the claim that the Jews sinned and were cursed—all common beliefs that finally culminate in Judeo-phobia and anti-Jewish rhetoric.

Is the doctrine of the Chosen People ethnocentric and arrogant? If indeed, one nation was Chosen by God to set an example for the rest of the world, does it mean that other nations are less moral? Can one nation claim moral superiority? The book will explore this question and provide references to traditional sources on the subject.

Some Jews are apologetic about and minimize the Chosen factor in Judaism. This is a misguided approach because it is clear that the concept of the Chosen

---

*The historical source of the word is from seventeenth-century Britain.

People is central to Jewish belief. However, deeper understanding of the Chosen concept shows that there is no need to apologize. The collective memory of the Chosen includes both the act on Mount Sinai of receiving the Ten Commandments and also the litany of curses that appears later and will befall the Jews should they fail to uphold the responsibilities of the Chosen. The words of the Prophet Amos demonstrate the burden and the price: "You only have I known of all the families of the earth, therefore I will punish you for all your iniquities."[15] From a historic perspective this is a heavy burden indeed. That is why many Jews have conflicting emotions about their role as the Chosen; they would prefer to be treated as a normal people. At the same time, all Jews take pride in the extraordinary contributions of the Jews to world culture, science, and civilization. It is no surprise that, in the face of persecution and hatred there are Jews who would prefer to escape from the Chosen role and feel less haunted and hunted. This is the case of Tevye the Milkman, the central character in Sholem Aleichem's story, which, transformed for *Fiddler on the Roof*, became a hit musical throughout the world. Tevye turns to God and appeals to him: "I know, I know. We're your Chosen People. But, once in a while, can't You choose someone else?"[16]

For the Jews, chosenness means Jewish responsibility, a sense of universal mission and accepting more than their fair share of suffering. Chosenness does imply better behavior or lack of evil, and the treatment of the Jews by their own prophets as well as by God demonstrates this. Chosenness does mean accountability for wrongdoing, and the corollary is punishment and suffering that exceeds all proportion. The Holocaust, the acme of anti-Semitic hatred and Jewish suffering, has become another arena of the same struggle. The Muslims, with some help from the West, deny the uniqueness of the Holocaust in two ways—one with a built-in contradiction: on the one hand they deny that the Holocaust actually took place, while at the same time, they accuse Israel of committing similar atrocities against the Palestinians. One can see how Holocaust denial thrives alongside the wish that it had actually been more successful. The assaults on Israel at the beginning of the new century are characterized by the unprecedented use of comparisons between the Jews and the Nazis; between the Holocaust and the Palestinian *intifada*. The Jews are portrayed as the "New Nazis" not just in the Arab press but sometimes even in the Western media. The attack on Israel is an attack against the Chosen.

There are various areas of contention. The battlefield is vast and spans the globe: it is about Israel, about Jerusalem, about religion, about the economy and globalization and international law. Jews cannot deny that the Chosen concept is religiously, historically, and culturally central to Judaism. At the same time it is critically important that students of anti-Semitism, whether Jew or Gentile, pay attention to the origins and perhaps the atavistic sources of anti-Semitism. This can clear the air and provide an important base for combating Judeophobia.

Since Judah Halevi in the twelfth century there has been no serious comparative work by a Jewish scholar on the concept of the Chosen and its impact on the three monotheistic religions. Halevi's study is in the style and language of the disputations of the Middle Ages, which were basically a theological debate on which religion is more authentic. It is surprising that despite dramatic changes in the Jewish condition after the Holocaust and following the establishment of the State of Israel, there has been almost no effort to reconsider in a comprehensive way, the subject of the Chosen in Jewish-Gentile relations. Following Vatican II and the Nostra Aetate of 1965, which, in addition to annulling the collective guilt of the Jews for the crucifixion of Jesus, referred to the Jews as the Chosen People, the need for such a review becomes clear.

It seems that Jews and Gentiles are still entangled in the old myths and constraints. For many Jews in the Diaspora, the issue of the Chosen People is seen as controversial, polemic, and provocative. In Israel, as part of the Zionist philosophy, there was a clear attempt to escape the fate of the Chosen and the mentality of the Diaspora so as to move toward being a "normal" nation in the Jewish homeland. The characterization of chosenness was left to the Bible, the Talmud, and the liturgy. While many non-Jews refer to the Chosen People, few are truly familiar with the Jewish sources and even less so, the taking over of the role of the Chosen—first by Christianity and then by Islam. Whether they like it or not, the Jews are still looked upon as the primary Chosen People. Daniel Bell, an American sociologist, wrote in 1946, "The Jews *are* a [C]hosen [P]eople, if not by God, then by the rest of the world."[17] Sixty years later Justice Ruth Bader Ginsburg of the Supreme Court provided the same rationale: "[W]hen you are a Jew, the world will look at you that way; and this is an heritage that you can be proud of. And then, too, it's something that you can't escape because the world won't let you."[18] The Gentile attitude to the Chosen People has usually been derogatory and on many occasions it adopted expressions of venomous hostility making the Jews a pariah people. However, there are also frequent expressions of admiration and appreciation for the contribution of the Jews to the values of mankind.

It is about time to put the issue squarely on the table and confront it as the most sensitive component in Jewish-Gentile relations and as the basic reason for anti-Semitism both now and throughout history The method of analysis is not conventional as we turn to religious texts so as to understand contemporary political and even legal aspects of Jewish-Gentile relations. The issue of the Chosen is not restricted to scholarly theological argumentation but enters every kind of debate: whether on politics, economics, law, globalization, or violence in the streets. Nonreligious people, who may well be atheists or left-wing secularist intellectuals, have no hesitation in harnessing the religious context of chosenness for their attacks against Israel and the Jews.

## The Big Divide

Chosenness is the big divide in explaining anti-Semitism and in formulating the religious doctrine toward Israel. There are only two groups, on the opposing extremes, that refer openly and without any constrains to the concept of Jewish chosenness: the anti-Semites of all religions and the evangelical Christians who support Israel. The rest may discuss it sometimes in a circumvent fashion, but most of the time it remains *the central unspoken psychological, historical, and theological problem at the heart of Jewish-Gentile relations.* Even religious Jews who refer to the concept endless times in their daily prayers, or in their studies of the Torah, the prophets, and the Talmud, avoided a straightforward discussion of the implications of the Chosen concept on matters of policy and relations with the outside world.

Christian and Islamic anti-Semitism are related to the contention that they have replaced the Jews as the Chosen People. This displacement is stated openly, and it is a basic element in the theological development of both religions. Today's Islamists are not only driven by the concept of Jihad or by incitements quoting anti-Jewish references from the Quran but also by their own vision of chosenness and supersession (the *caliph* is the successor, and the *Khalifah* is the world single state that will rule all Islamic lands and subjugate the rest of the world to Allah). Even self-described moderates and liberal Muslims agree that Muslim teachings unequivocally state that Islam supercedes and cancels out all previous revelations by God. Sayyid Qutb, the Eqyptian ideologue of Islam who was executed by President Gamal Abdul Nasser in 1966, denied the concept of Arab nationalism saying that "God's real [C]hosen [P]eople is the Muslim community, regardless of ethnic, racial, or territorial affiliation of its members."[19] Today's radical Islamic commentators have developed a new and a deadly twist to their displacement theory. In addition to the supersession theory, which is very similar to Christianity with its elements of anti-Semitism, they have added a new slant to it: that the Jewish Bible in its extant form is not authentic, but rather was distorted and corrupted by the Jews in their efforts to prove that they are God's people and that Palestine and Jerusalem belong to them.

Analysis of the Quran's text reveals, against the conventional wisdom, that supersession or replacement theories are even more central and significant in Islam than in Christianity. The clash of Islam with modernity and the series of defeats dealt to the armies of several major Arab powers by the small Jewish state reignited the built in tensions within Islam involving its foundational principles of theological origin and religious authenticity. The same Jews who opposed the gestures of Mohammad and were doomed, according to Islam, to dispersion and humiliation, were returning to their Promised Land, to the places from which they worshiped God before the Islam's conception. These Jews, who are according to the Quran "apes, despised and rejected,"[20] had become an inescapable political fact secured by an unbeatable army. The return of the Jews to what used to be their land—a land conquered by Muslim armies and therefore seen as given by Allah to his followers—served as a poignantly distressing reminder of their pre-Islam status as Chosen. Existing tradition and commentary within Islam could not reconcile this new reality; the recourse to hatred and anti-Semitism (which has a solid, vast base in the Quran) was a natural outcome.

The "humiliation and disgrace" of Islam by foreign powers to which bin Laden referred in his videotape of October 7, 2001, must be taken mainly in the context of the *Khalifah* vision of supersession. For Islamists who regard the West and America as their main enemy in their campaign for a global Islamic state, Zionism is not a matter of territorial or ethnic dispute but a shattering challenge to their claim to chosenness and a caustic reminder of the Jewish origins of Islam (see Chapter 3). An increasingly prevalent trope among Muslim religious leaders today emphasizes the claim that "Islam is the religion chosen by Allah for all humanity."[21]

For the Vatican and other Churches the supersession theology was the major obstacle in dealing with the reestablishment of Jewish sovereignty in the land of Israel. An independent Israel confronted the Catholic Church with one of the its greatest challenges, shattering years of theological belief based on the humiliated and dispersed position of the Jews and the loss of its Chosen title (Chapter 7). It took the Vatican about one hundred years since its flat rejection of the Zionist idea and a revolutionary transformation of doctrine regarding the Chosen in order to present a more pragmatic approach that, though it did not abandon the essence of supersession, would allow it to establish diplomatic relations with the Jewish state. But this view is not supported by all Catholic leaders and churches, and it is rejected outright by groups such as traditional Catholics.

On the other hand, the admiration by other Christian groups to the Jews and in particular their political support for Zionism and the State of Israel is based to a very large extent on the Chosen concept. The most critical divide between America's and the rest of the world's attitudes to the Middle East lie in the differences that their publics attach to the Chosen concept and the way they interpret its meanings to foreign policy. Many political observers and analysts underestimate the extent of religion's influence on American politics and fail to draw the links between theology and foreign policy. In the Library of Congress in Washington, DC, which is America's oldest federal cultural institution and the largest library in the world, there is a conspicuous recognition of the Jewish contribution to civilization. In the self-acclaimed "unparalleled treasure house of the world's knowledge and America's creativity"[22] the central architectural monument emphasizes the impact of Judaism on America and mankind. The domed ceiling, stretching 160 feet above the floor of the Main Reading Room in the Jefferson building, represent the different dimensions of *Human Understandings* in a huge painting by Edwin Blashfield (1898). The Jews (*Judea*) are depicted as those who contributed the idea of religion to mankind, and the pillar on the ceiling inscribes in Hebrew letters the injunction from Leviticus 19:18: "Thou shalt love thy neighbor as thyself."

At every crossroads of historical changes and decision making on the Middle East since the early nineteen century, Christian Zionists were very much involved in inspiring, acting, and lobbying for the restoration of the Jews in their historical Promised Land. As shown later in this work American Protestantism today has moved substantially to an evangelical theology that represents a sea change in the attitudes toward the role of Jews in modern history and in Christian redemption. Evangelists still believe in their own chosenness and attach great importance to their duty to spread their Christian values throughout the world, but they no longer subscribe to the age-old Christian supersessionist and displacement doctrine that refuses to recognize the viable existence of the Jewish people and, particularly, its Chosen status. These churches believe that the Jews continue to be favored as God's people, and some of them even renounce supersessionism and affirm that the Jews have a valid way to find God within their own faith. When so many Americans regard the Bible as the word of God and almost half Americans believe that the land of Israel was given to the Jewish People by God, the Middle East conflict gets an important dimension, which cannot be ignored. A poll taken by the Pew Research Center (the leading nonpartisan polling organization in America) in July 2003 found that 37 percent of Americans describe themselves as a "born-again" or evangelical Christian. Two-thirds of Americans regard the Bible as the word of God, and one-third says that it should be taken literally, word for word. Forty-four percent of Americans believe that the land of Israel was given to the Jewish people by God, and 36 percent believe that that the State of Israel is a fulfillment of the biblical prophesy about the second coming of Jesus.[23] When 86.3 percent of fundamental evangelical Christian respondents agree that the Jews are still the Chosen People,[24] the policy implications cannot be dismissed. For Evangelists the continued existence of the Jewish People and its return to its Promised Land is a proof for God power in history. Evangelists, more than most of the Jews, regard God's first act of chosenness toward the Jews in his words to Abraham: "And I will make of thee a great nation" a matter of policy. Literally they also read the following words of God: "And I will bless them that bless thee, and curse him that curseth thee,"[25] as a clear directive by God for U.S. officials that is based on the Chosen covenant with Israel and implying that God will bless America if the United States blesses Israel.

Charles Murray, an American Gentile and a scholar, has tried to develop a theory on the Jewish extraordinary intellectual skills to explain their outstanding and disproportional contribution to science and the advancement of mankind. He focuses his argument on the "Jewish Genius" (the title of his article) on their system of education and religious studies as an evolutionary process that he traces back to the period before the first century BCE, before the destruction of the Second Temple. His heroes include the Jewish sage Joshua ben Gamla, who issued an ordinance in 64 CE mandating universal schooling for boys at the age of six. Murray goes back to Moses, who propagated God's commandments, which were intertwined with intellectual complexity and required intense learning and deep insight. But despite his "evolutionary" theory Murray admits at the end, "I take sanctuary in my remaining hypothesis, uniquely parsimonious and happily irrefutable. The Jews are God's [C]hosen [P]eople."[26]

The apologetic and sometimes ostrich-like approach to the Chosen concept should be rejected. Without recognizing its centrality in shaping the perceptions of Jews and non-Jews alike, we cannot fully understand Jewish history and the world's attitude toward the Jews. In the final analysis there is no better explanation for the particular strength that has made the Jews different and kept them intact despite two thousand years of dispersion and persecution. As history shows, the Chosen factor is also part of the mission of the Jews and their contribution to mankind. Most Jews and non-Jews would agree (even if they prefer not to say it aloud) that for better or worse, the Jews are different, set apart, and a "People that Stands Alone."[27] There is no better expression for this mystery than the concept of the Chosen.

# CHAPTER 2

# How Were "The Chosen" Chosen?

You have distinguished the Lord today to be a God for you . . . and the Lord has distinguished you today to be for Him a treasured people.
— Deuteronomy 26:17–18

Then [Moses] took the Book of the Covenant and read it in the hearing of the people, and they said: All that the Lord has spoken, we will do and we will be obedient!"
— Exodus 24:7

For it is written [in Exodus] that "they stood at the foot of the [Sinai] mountain" and Rabbi Dimi bar Chama said: this teaches us that the Holy One, Blessed be He, tipped the mountain and positioned it over the Jews as though it were an overturned vat and told them if you accept the Torah, all is well—but if not your burial will be there!
— Talmud, *Avodah Zarah* 2b

How exactly did the Jewish people received their Torah, which so dramatically marked them off from all other peoples then and now? Did they make a conscious decision to accept the holy book from God's hands; did they do so out of their free will? Or were they selected for this honor (and burden); was this an offer they could not refuse? The two sources quoted above present diametrically opposed interpretations of this seminal event. The biblical account conveys the enthusiasm with which the Children of Israel embraced God's word and thus became the Chosen People. Jewish commentaries emphasize the immensity of this decision, taken at the foot of Mount Sinai. It was, they say, something the Jews alone undertook, of all the nations that might have, demonstrating the special qualities that uniquely qualified them for God's service. The talmudic source, however, tells us that the choice was imposed from above, that the Jews had no alternative but to accept the sacred word—upon pain of death. While the first interpretation emphasizes the Jewish people's avid hunger for the divine connection, the second focuses on the heavy yoke that being Chosen laid upon them.

How are we to understand these two approaches? Which is considered more correct? Are they truly contradictory, or is there common ground between them? Are there, indeed, other interpretations as well? As a starting point to exploring these questions we might say that for the Jewish religion the idea of chosenness is axiomatic. No theme in the Old Testament is more fundamental than that of the Covenant between God and Israel, that a people was Chosen and that they responded to the call in many ways and for so long. Judaism, its history, and its religion cannot be understood without focusing on the concept of the Chosen. It is hard to conceive Jewish identity in its various forms and throughout the ages without the Jewish claim to chosenness.

Since within Judaism the Chosen concept is axiomatic, the rabbis did not feel the need for extensive commentary. The Bible paints a vivid picture of how the Covenant originated and how it was confirmed and reconfirmed, and the sages for the most part are content with the biblical exposition. Even Maimonides (Rabbi Moses Ben Maimon, known as the Rambam) does not list chosenness in his compilation of the Thirteen Principles of Faith.[1] But, also because the concept is so axiomatic, interpretations are complex. Often they seem at odds; sometimes they are mysterious. But always they go right to the heart of what it means to be Jewish.

All the rabbinic commentaries are based on the biblical narrative, so interpretations are always anchored in the world of the patriarchs and prophets. But at the same time the rabbis saw the Bible not just as a sacred document from the past, but as a living instrument that illuminates the present. Consequently, interpretations often reflect Jewish-Gentile relations at the time of their writing. These belong to the genre of commentary known as *midrash haggadah*. *Midrash haggadah* (often called simply *midrash*) refers to nonlegal elements in the rabbinic literature, for example, legends, allegories, expositions of history, philosophy, and folklore. *Midrash* is not the law (*halakah*), but it is central to an understanding of the context and environment in which the sages developed their worldview, in our case their view of what it means for Jews to be the Chosen People. The interpretations reflected in these legends illustrate how involved and multidimensional the Chosen concept is in Jewish tradition. Let us start by considering our two apparently contradictory versions of how the Jews came to be Chosen.

### "We Will Do and We Will Be Obedient"

The Chosen process in the Bible starts with Abraham and the patriarchs in Genesis and reaches its culmination at Mount Sinai. In Exodus there is a dialogue, an offer, and a process. God calls to Moses from the mountain:

> Thus shall you say to the House of Jacob, and tell to the people of Israel. You have seen what I did to the Egyptians, and how I bore you on eagles' wings and brought you to myself. Now, therefore, if you will hear my voice and keep my covenant, you shall be my own possession among all peoples, for all the earth is mine. And you

shall be to me a kingdom of priests and a holy nation . . . So Moses came and called the elders of the people, and set before them all these words that the Lord had commanded him. And all the people answered together and said, 'All that the Lord has spoken we will do.'[2]

This pledge is confirmed and repeated later: "Then he took the book of the covenant and read it in the hearing of the people, and they said: 'All that the Lord has spoken, we will do and we will be obedient!'"[3]

The declaration "We will do and we will be obedient!" is a cornerstone of the Jewish people's faith in God and their commitment to Him without reservation. It is this commitment, this Covenant, that sets the Jewish people apart from others, so "We will do and we will be obedient" functions as both a vow of faith and a declaration of separateness. However, the process of choosing was mutual: God chose Israel only, not other peoples, and Israel chose God:

> [Moses] said: When God revealed himself to Israel to give them the Torah, He also revealed himself to all nations. First He went to Esau's people and asked them: "Are you willing to take the Torah?" And they asked: "What is written in it?" He told them: "Thou shall not kill." They refused. Then He went to the people of Amon and Moab and they asked the same question . . . and God told them that it is written: "Thou shalt not commit adultery" and they refused. He went to the Ishmaelites and they refused because of the commandment, "Thou shalt not steal." And there was no nation that God did not approach but all refused. And then He came to Israel; They replied: "We will do and we will be obedient."[4]

The verse from Deuteronomy at the top of this chapter shows that the process was mutual: God chooses Israel, and Israel (as distinct from the other peoples) chooses God. There is another midrash that speaks to the same idea, this one on Numbers (*Bamidbar Rabah*): "Why did God choose Israel?" it asks. "Because Israel has chosen Him and His Torah." Many Jews regard this notion with some degree of discomfort because it implies that Jews set themselves above others. But this discomfort deflects attention from the fact that the Torah and its Ten Commandments were indeed absolutely revolutionary. This set of laws and moral standards did differentiate the Jews from the surrounding peoples, while the concept of one omnipotent God, which was the basis of it all, was perhaps the most singular development in mankind's entire spiritual history. As Abba Eban, the former foreign minister of Israel, put it, "What was born in Sinai was a concept as revolutionary as the wheel, an idea as influential as the plow—the idea of hope and progress and the stubborn belief that human life can be improved."[5] Nothing distinguished the Jews more than their laws and their faith, which contrasted so sharply with the beliefs of the peoples among whom they lived.

Written during the early years of Christianity, these midrashim reflect an era of confrontation and persecution at the hands of both pagans and Christians, a time when it was especially important to confirm the distinctive identity of the vulnerable Jewish community. Professor Ephraim Urbach explains[6] that the talmudic emphasis on offering the Torah to many nations was an attempt to demonstrate that there was nothing arbitrary about the choosing, that it was not a forced imposition but the outcome of a reciprocal process. Later talmudic comments to this effect were part of the fourth-century conflict between Christians and the Roman Emperor Julian, who reverted to paganism. Julian (known later as "The Apostate") maintained that Christianity was a religion of trickery. He argued that Christian claims to have taken over the Chosen title from the Jews had no validity, no more than Roman claims to the title would have, and that Romans had never been vouchsafed an opportunity to be Chosen; they received neither the Torah and the prophets like the Jews, nor a purported Messiah like the Christians. In this atmosphere the talmudic scholars felt the need to demonstrate that there was not one among the myriad nations that God did not ask if they wanted to receive the Torah, with all the implications stemming from their refusal.

Maimonides, perhaps the greatest postbiblical Jewish figure, wrote in his "Epistle to the Jews of Yemen," (*Igeret Teiman*) that indeed prophets were sent to both Ishmael and Esau, as descendants of Abraham, but they rejected the Torah and the commandments. In his epistle, Maimonides tries to strengthen the resolve of the Jews of Yemen in the face of persecution, and he tells them that Jews believe in a God whose laws were given through Moses and that these teachings were

> intended to constitute us as an entirely distinct people. The chosenness was not due to any inherent worth of ours. Indeed we have been distinctly told so in the scriptures. But because our progenitors acted righteously through their knowledge of the Supreme Being, therefore we, their descendents, reap the benefit of their meritorious deeds. . . . My brethren, it behooves us to keep ever-present in our minds the great day of Sinai . . . you who were born in this covenant and raised in this belief. . . . For a whole people heard the word of God and saw the glory of His divinity. From this lasting memory we must draw our power to strengthen our faith even in a period of persecution and affliction such as the present one. My brethren! Hold fast to the covenant.[7]

Implicit in Maimonides' admonishments and the earlier teachings about choice is the recognition that the Covenant, however enthusiastically embraced, is exceptionally difficult to keep. In Exodus, immediately after becoming the Promised Nation, the Jews misbehaved, and their moral stature diminished. The Talmud emphasizes that at Mount Sinai, two events occurred: the Jews were uplifted to become the Chosen People, accompanied by the angels, while in the same place they sinned and were brought down again.[8] The Bible and later commentaries emphasize how demanding the task of the Chosen People is and how fragile the will to conform. Remaining God's Chosen requires the greatest effort; that is to say, the people must constantly exercise their will and make the same choice their ancestors made at Sinai.

### The Overturned Vat

In saying "We will do and we will be obedient," the impression is that the Jews had no alternative but to accept the Covenant. Not was there any suggestion that

God offered the Torah to other peoples, in this version of events. This interpretation created a double problem for commentators: After all, if the Jews were unwilling to agree on their own, did that render them less qualified for chosenness? And because they were forced, does straying from the commandments then seem justified? Moreover, how can any blame be attached to the Gentiles if they were never offered the role in the first place?

The Talmud even asks this question directly, positing an imaginary dialogue between God and the Gentiles. In this story, the Gentile nations come to God and complain that since they had not accepted the Torah they are under no obligation to observe its laws. God asks them, why did you not accept it in the first place? And the nations reply, "Master of the Universe, did you tip the mountain as if it were an overturned vat over us as you did with the Jews?"[9] In a similar vein, the late thirteenth-century commentator Rabbi Shlomo Ben Aderet (the *Rashba*) posed the question, Why did the Children of Israel have to go into exile for not observing the laws that they had never accepted of their own free will? As if anticipating this question, the Talmud, immediately after the midrash of the overturned vat, tells of the reaffirmation, some fifteen hundred years after Sinai, when the Jews in the days of Queen Esther finally accepted the Torah of their own free will.

In another talmudic tractate exploring the nature of the commitment at Mount Sinai, the two opposing approaches appear once more. Here too the rabbis say that if chosenness was imposed on the Children of Israel, then they could argue that since this was not done of their own free will God cannot blame them for violating the laws.[10] And here again the answer is that during the days of King Ahasuerus and Queen Esther the Jews reaffirmed their commitment. They "confirmed and undertook upon themselves and upon their seed."[11] This approach aims to explain that the Jewish people made this second affirmation while in exile, out of self-conviction, without the Temple and lacking all the miracles and revelations shown to them at Sinai.

Yet another dimension of the Jewish bonding with God is conveyed in the same tractate. This midrash tells about a certain Sadducee (rigorous proponents of free will, in opposition to the Pharisees) who tries to embarrass and heap scorn on the people because they made fools of themselves by accepting the Torah before actually seeing it. According to the midrash, the Sadducee comes to Rava, a renowned talmudic scholar, interrupts him in the middle of study, and tells him, "You are an impetuous people for you put your mouth before your ears. Why didn't you listen before accepting it [the Torah]?" Rava answers him patiently, "We, the Jews," he says, "are a wholesome people who love God and have faith in Him and know that He would never command the impossible from us. The people who attack us are devious and corrupt, and they project their own malevolent distrust on to others, assuming that they too cannot trust God." In the same passage, the Talmud says that because of their "naïve" acceptance of the Torah, God likened the Jews to the angels who are also totally submissive to His will.[12] The suggestion here is that the people's commitment at Sinai was neither forced nor the result of some rational decision—pure faith in God was the only operative factor.

In these various midrashim the sages examine the problem of chosenness from various angles and try to resolve the different interpretations, each interpretation with its own set of psychological and moral implications. In particular the sages were concerned to determine how free will and determinism worked themselves out in this most fundamental decision of the Jewish people.

The same juxtaposition appears in the tractate *Yoma* (87b), clearly revealing how the two meanings create a living tandem. This midrash concerns another renowned scholar, Rabba, who started his prayers on Yom Kippur, the holiest day of the year, by reciting, "You have chosen us above all the peoples; you have loved us and found favor in us; you have exalted us above all the tongues, and you have sanctified us with your commandments." But immediately after doing so, he moved on to confessional and penitential prayers, emphasizing the helplessness of human beings facing God. These then, are the two sides of the Chosen: the privilege and the burden.

Many of the myths concerning the Jewish concept of their chosenness are simplistic and freighted with negative implications. But the actual talmudic discussions embody a complex and spiritually rich amalgam that emphasizes both the significance and also the often painful responsibility of the Chosen. In the words of the historian R. Travers-Herford, "If it was an honor and a privilege to have been so chosen, it was full of danger and exposed the bearer of it to the ill-will and jealousy of his fellow men."[13] In so many ways, the selection was a terrible burden as well a grace. It was, writes Maurice Samuel, "a divine destiny reluctantly assumed, everlastingly repudiated, everlastingly reclaimed."[14] In this sense chosenness determined the ongoing moral dynamics of the Jewish people, just as it determined so much else about their essential identity.

## The Meaning of the Chosen

The concept of the Chosen occupies a central place in Jewish tradition and liturgy. The Torah, or Jewish prayer book, adopted many references based on the biblical texts concerning the concept of the Chosen People. When a Jew is called up to read the Torah, he recites the blessing, "Blessed art thou, O Lord our God king of the universe, who has chosen us from all peoples and hast given us thy Torah."[15] This blessing is recited in the daily prayers and is repeated in the reading of the Torah, twice during the week and twice on the Sabbath and during the festivals. The Talmud regards this blessing as supreme since it links together the choosing of Israel with its holy scripture, the Torah.[16] It is also important to note that the blessing ends in the present tense: "Blessed art thou, O Lord, giver of the Torah," as if to emphasize that the encounter on Mount Sinai between God and the Jewish people is a continuing process and that every Jew should feel as if he or she was actually present at the Mount.

From a religious point of view, the Covenant between God and the Jewish people is unbreakable, thus putting great responsibility and the resultant hardship on the Jews. They have to serve God and keep His laws, and in the process strive to perfect themselves and the world (*tikkun olam*). If they fail in these obligations they will be punished for their sins. It is clear to them that they are required to adhere to higher standards than those expected from other nations. In this sense, Chosen means to be separate and unique: "And you shall not walk in the customs of the nation which I am casting out before you. . . . I am the Lord your God who has separated you from the people. . . . [Y]ou shall be holy to Me, for I the Lord am holy and have separated you from the peoples, that you should be Mine."[17] While the Jews understand the burden implicit in chosenness, they also express their pride in becoming the Chosen. As Rabbi Akiva commented, "Beloved are Israel, for they are called children of God; for they were given a precious article; . . . My Torah. . . ."[18]

At the same time, Judaism rejects outright the idea that Jews are somehow personally or racially superior to others. The Jews were chosen not because of any personal merit but because they were ready to accept the Torah and commit themselves to serving God. The Torah states specifically that the Jewish people were selected not for their virtues but for their faults—"not for thy righteousness, nor for the uprightness of thine heart"—but because of their intransigence as stiff-necked people.[19] There is no call in Judaism to convert non-Jews, as there is in the great proselytizing religions. There is no faith-driven compulsion to assert Judaism's superiority. Chosenness does not imply hegemony over other nations, nor does it seek to impose the Torah on other peoples. On the contrary, there is an underlying acceptance of others as they are, the recognition that, despite differences, nations are capable of and deserve mutual respect. The prophet Micah, referring to the ultimate redemption, posits a famous pluralistic prescription: "Nations shall not lift up sword against nation, neither shall they learn war any more; but they shall sit every man under His vine and under His fig tree and none shall make them afraid."[20] In a similar vein, the prophet Isaiah envisioned the restored Temple as a sanctuary for non-Jews as well: "And the foreigners who join themselves to the Lord . . . these I will bring to my holy mountain, and make them joyful in My house of prayer. . . . For My house shall be called a house of prayer for all peoples."[21]

Chosenness implies distinctiveness, but not preeminence. And indeed Gentiles who conform to the seven laws given to Noah (or, Noahide laws) are assured a place "in the world to come."[22] Neither does chosenness embody any sense of racial superiority. Converts, for example, are treated as if they had been present at the encounter with God on Mount Sinai along with the rest of the Jewish people. The Torah says, "Nor is it with you only that I make this sworn covenant, but with He who is not with us here this day."[23] The phrase "He who is not here," refers to future converts as well as to the Jewish generations to come. The Talmud enjoins Jews not to embarrass a convert, nor treat him as a foreigner: "If he was a child of converts, one may not say to him, 'Remember the deeds of your ancestors [the Gentiles],' for it said, 'You shall not wrong a stranger or oppress him"[24] (*Exodus* 22:20).

Maimonides explains that under Jewish law the convert recites the same blessing to God "who selected us from among the peoples" and the blessing at the close of the Sabbath, "Blessed art thou O God . . . who separated . . . between

Israel and the nations," as well as the words, "Our God, and God of our ancestors."[25] The burden of the suffering element of chosenness is reflected in an important legal principle of conversion. The Talmud states, "When one comes to convert to Judaism, they [the rabbis, seating in the religious court] are to say to him: 'what benefit do you see in coming to convert? Do you not know that Israel is beset, downtrodden, lowly, distraught, and persecuted?' If he says, 'I know and I am not worthy to be part of them,' they are to accept him immediately."[26]

This absence of racism is also reflected in the halakic approach to Jews who converted to other religions. In Jewish law "a Jew remains Jewish even if he has sinned," so that converts to Christianity remain Jews. The late archbishop of Paris, Cardinal Jean-Marie Lustiger, was born to Polish-Jewish parents who immigrated to France. As a child during the Holocaust he was raised in a convent, and at the age of thirteen he converted to Catholicism. Lustiger takes pride in his Jewish origins. In interviews he always defines himself as a Jew who practices Christianity. In explaining this duality, he refers to the mission of the Chosen saying that "[f]or me, the vocation of [the People of] Israel is 'bearing a light unto the Gentiles.' I believe that Christianity is the means for achieving this."[27]

At the same time, Jews understand that while they may not discriminate against others, others often feel great anger toward them. Traditionally, the hatred felt by other nations is considered to have begun at Mount Sinai at the very moment when the Jews became the Chosen. The sages of the Talmud play on the words "Sinai" and "sinah"—"hate" in Hebrew. "Why is it called Sinai?" they ask. "Because from there the hatred against Israel descended . . . and from there the nations of the world received this hatred."[28] They recognize that chosenness brought, along with its distinction, the inevitable suffering that accompanies being an object of envy and hate, and that, consequently, suffering as well as pride is intrinsic to Jewish identity.

In his book, *Errata*, the Jewish writer and philosopher George Steiner argues that the moral code of the Jews, with its integral definition of God, lies at the very heart of anti-Semitism. Steiner, who is not religious, maintains that at Sinai the Jews introduced to the world a God who is beyond understanding and cannot be conceived and also introduced moral decrees that for their time were inflexible and unacceptable. The totality of the Ten Commandments—against murder, adultery, greed, setting up your own gods and idols, and so on, were too demanding, too all-inclusive, and too absolute. They call on man to overcome his ego, his natural instincts, his desires, and his freedoms. In doing so the Jews put tremendous moral pressure on the world, and the world responded with hatred and abomination and then with the urge to persecute the Jews, to make them pariahs, to shut their mouths, and finally to liquidate and destroy them. Without this bone-deep historical anger, Steiner reasons, it would be almost impossible to explain the persistence of anti-Semitism, especially after the Holocaust.[29]

Modern, self-confident Jews living in countries where they feel relatively insulated from anti-Semitism still tend to be uneasy and restless with the concept of chosenness. They understand the ominous historical implications of being

Chosen, and they reject the taint of some supposed innate superiority. They are more in tune with the kind of universalist sentiments voiced by the theologian Rabbi Abraham Joshua Heschel: "God is either the Father of all men or of no man. . . . It seems to be the will of God that there be more than one religion."[30] Many Jews who see themselves as part of liberal Western civilization are reluctant to emphasize the traces of Jewish particularism and ethnic separatism that seem to be implicit in the Jewish tradition. The Nazis' glorification of themselves as a "superior race" (the *Herrenvolk*), also helped erect a powerful psychological barrier against emphasizing a concept like the Chosen People, which seems so suggestive of ethnic exceptionalism.

American Jews generally have striven to integrate themselves into their surrounding society and have been ambivalent about characteristics that in the past separated Jews from others, even though they are aware that it is precisely these elements that have guaranteed Jewish survival over the millennia. The typical American Jew, says Professor Charles Liebman, seeks ideological positions that deny the existence of any tension between himself and his environment, and he needs, therefore, to cloud over and obscure some of the basic concepts of Judaism.[31] Chosenness, explains the historian Roland Eisen, has become in America "the most often blurred concept, and was reinterpreted with new definitions in America of the twentieth century. Jews could get comfort from being Chosen behind the ghetto walls, but they found it awkward to claim chosenness in the new Chosen Land of America."[32]

One group within American Jewry, the Reconstructionist movement, even took formal steps to drop the concept of the Chosen from its ideology altogether. Mordechai Kaplan (1881–1983), the founder of Reconstructionism, proposed a Judaism that rejected the concept of the Chosen People. He regarded Jewish chosenness as "anachronism" and as a dangerous idea that clashed with modern concepts of justice and equality and perpetrated a sense of "racial or national superiority." In that sense he also criticized the idea of the Reform movement that the Jews, because of their qualities, are entrusted with the mission of "Light unto the Nations." To claim that the Jews have "given mankind those religious and ethical concepts . . . smacks of arrogance," said Kaplan.[33] Following Kaplan's lead, Rabbi Ira Eisenstein, founder and former president of the Reconstructionist Rabbinical College, called for the elimination of the Chosen concept from the movement's liturgy and philosophy. He advocated humility and admonished modern Jews to avoid maintaining that "God gave the Torah to us and nobody else."[34] The Reconstructionist prayer book states candidly, "Modern-minded Jews can no longer believe . . . that the Jews constitute a divinely [C]hosen [P]eople."[35]

But even this outstanding exception of the Reconstructionist movement is gradually evaporating, and the text has been modified in new prayer books following discussions in the early 1980s. Members of the movement indicated clearly that the "Kaplanian position on the [C]hosen [P]eople might be *passé*."[36] Joseph Hayyim Brenner, a similarly minded, anti-religious Zionist writer (who was murdered by Arab rioters in Jaffa in 1921), wrote, "I would blot out from the prayer book of the Jew of our day the [words] 'Thou hast chosen us' in every shape and form."[37]

It is something of an irony that American Jews, who are tender about the Chosen People issue, have assimilated themselves into a society with its own strong tradition of chosenness. As rigorous, "purifying" Protestants, the Pilgrims and Founding Fathers believed that they had been especially selected by God as the new "Chosen People," superseding and replacing the biblical Children of Israel. Their new society, proclaimed John Winthrop, Massachusetts's first governor, would be a "City on a Hill," a divinely inspired model for the world to see and emulate. The Puritans, according to Winthrop, were the Chosen People of Massachusetts, like the Israelis the old. "The Lord thy God," Winthrop told his followers, echoing Moses' valedictory to the original Chosen People, "will bring thee into the land . . . and thou shalt possess it."[38] The Puritans' vision was later taken up in a secularized form by founders such as John Adams and James Madison and still animates America's view of its role in the world.

## The Chosen Pillars

The biblical tradition of the Chosen is based on the two individuals who received the Covenant from God: Abraham, the first Jew, and Moses, the first leader of the Jewish people. There are many other references to the concept by the prophets, but all of them derive from God's direct promises to Abraham and Moses. Abraham was the actual founder of Judaism and monotheism in an era so distant that its peoples could not even conceive of such an idea. God and Abraham's reciprocal Covenant was on a more personal level than the Covenant granted Moses (though God designated Abraham's Covenant for his descendants as well). But though separated by many hundreds of years, the link between the two Covenants is clear. They are twin parts of the same master plan for the Chosen People.

### Abraham

Both Christianity and Islam recognize Abraham's founding role as history's first believer in one God. Both refer to themselves as the "Children of Abraham." In Jewish tradition, when Abraham obeyed God's command to "Go forth," it was not only he but all of mankind that embarked on a new course. The great story begins with God's sudden, unanticipated announcement to Abraham (still "Abram." God changed his name only later), telling him to set out from his home. Abraham, for reasons the Torah does not tell us, hears and obeys, separating himself from his dwelling place and from the people he had lived among for so many years. "Go from your country," God tells him, "and from your kindred and your father's house, to the land that I will show you. And I will make of you a great nation and I will bless you and make your name great . . . [A]nd by you all the families of the earth shall bless themselves."[39] In that first command, and in Abraham's response to it, the concept of the Chosen People was born.

In the course of being Chosen, Abraham leaves his home and homeland, is circumcised, enters into a Covenant with God, and receives God's pledges concerning the Promised Land and the Chosen People. Adding to the biblical narrative, the commentaries tell us about ten trials, or tests of faith, that Abraham had to submit to before becoming the father of the Jewish people.[40] These tests show Abraham both as choosing and being Chosen; they illustrate the mutual nature of the Covenant. Abraham's status is confirmed only after he passes the tests— demonstrating that he has both the wisdom and the courage to make the right choices. Maimonides explains in his *Guide to the Perplexed* that God does not require the choosing and testing processes since He knows all future events. Instead their purpose is to demonstrate to the world how man should obey God. Abraham, in his faithful obedience to God's will in situations of extreme pressure, set a precedent and a lesson for the rest of humanity.[41]

Abraham was called *Ivri*, which is the semantic root of the "Hebrew people," derived from the word *ever*, meaning the "other side." From the very beginning, having been Chosen marks him off. It makes him different, a sojourner in alien and sometimes hostile lands. When he purchases a burial plot for his wife Sarah in Hebron, he tells the local Hittite inhabitants, "I am a stranger and a sojourner among you."[42] What Abraham means is "I am not the same as you. I may live among you, but I am different." Rashi (Rabbi Shlomo Yitzchaki, 1040–1105), perhaps the greatest commentator on the Bible and the Talmud, explains that this means that Abraham is both an alien from another land and a resident who has settled among people different from himself. Here then, at the very beginning, we see the Jew as an outsider, a prelude and parallel to the Jewish condition in the Diaspora.

Nachmanides (Rabbi Moshe Ben Nachman, 1194–1270), another great Jewish scholars of the Middle Ages who successfully defended Judaism at a historic disputation in Barcelona, Spain in 1263, laid down a rule that everything that happened to the patriarchs is a portent for future generations, inasmuch as the stories about them are both factual and allegories for the whole of Jewish history. Accordingly, Nachmanides considers the life story of Abraham and his travails as a microcosm of Jewish history: the Jew is fated to be an alien and a stranger, insecure in his surroundings, engaged in a perpetual search for the Promised Land, and practicing distinctive religious principles and following a moral code that presents a challenge to others.

Rabbi Joseph Dov (Baer) Soloveitchik, one of the great rabbinical scholars of American Jewry in the twentieth century, says that Abraham's situation among the Hittites gives expression to "the dual role that every Jew must play." On the one hand he must be a loyal citizen of his country and must pray for its welfare. But at the same time, as a Jew in this world, he is always an alien; his allegiance to God makes him so. Soloveitchik, who was born in Belorus, had undoubtedly heard accusations about Jewish double loyalty more than once. But he saw nothing either wrong or strange with his situation, which after all had been Abraham's as well from the moment he undertook God's service. "A Jew," Soloveitchik wrote, "must always be ready to be a lonely alien, resisting the culture that surrounds him and maintaining his unique responsibility."[43]

Paul Johnson, a noted non-Jewish historian, describes how the Jews' unique sense of history makes them the "only people in the world today who possess a historical record . . . which allows them to trace their origins back into very remote times."[44] That historical record began with the need to understand what Abraham did, how he did it, and what it meant for his descendants. In this sense Abraham's action of separating himself from others spurred the Jewish obsession to define themselves and record their story.

Abraham makes his decision out of his own will and vision, and once made he is faithful to his commitment, even at the expense of breaking his family and social ties. Declaring that there is only one God, he takes it upon himself to break his father's idols; that is to say, he is prepared to stand alone and apart from his family and from the universal beliefs of his time. An important dimension of Abraham's personality (and perhaps an essential component of the very nature of chosenness) is this exceptional courage. This quality is so powerful in him that he is not afraid even to confront God in making a stand for justice. The exchange between Abraham and God on the fate of Sodom and Gomorrah is unprecedented in ancient literature. Like a lawyer pleading in a court of law, he argues with God and asks, "Will You sweep away the innocent along with the guilty? What if there should be fifty innocent people within the city? Will you raze the place and not forgive it for the sake of the innocent fifty. . . . Shall not the judge of all the earth deal justly?" And so the argument continues and the stakes go down—forty-five, forty, thirty, twenty—stopping at ten. And Sodom and Gomorrah are destroyed only because not even ten righteous people could be found there.[45]

The debate between God and Abraham introduces another important element of the concept of the Chosen: the ability, even the obligation, to argue for justice and to exhaust all means available so as to save life. Their intimate relationship with God endows the Chosen with this special requirement to seek justice. Like Abraham before them, Jacob and Moses also found it necessary to argue with God. Courage, then, is not just a personal quality, as it might be for a warrior hero; it is a moral necessity, and it has a moral purpose. The role of Chosen bears with it not just the imperative for obedience but for moral action.

The role of Chosen marks Abraham spiritually. It also involves a physical marking. In Hebrew the same word, *brit*, means both circumcision and Covenant. All of Abraham's male descendants are to be marked in the same way as Abraham, bearing witness to their participation in the same Covenant to which Abraham committed himself. Abraham was seventy-five years old when he was circumcised. According to a midrash, God Himself was physically present at Abraham's circumcision and held his hand.[46]

The circumcision act, as shown later, would become the major barrier between Judaism and early Christianity. In Jewish tradition the Covenant of circumcision as it appears in the Genesis text made it clear that the blessing of children and the possession of the Land of Israel are depending on circumcision. The circumcision Covenant with Abraham is a strong act of chosenness aiming "to help the Jew ennoble himself and return to the spiritual state of Adam before his sin."[47] The text continues immediately to the promise to Sarah that she would give birth (at age ninety!), which is regarded by talmudic midrashim as another manifestation of the divine intervention toward the emergence of a new nation. This intervention becomes central in the narrative of the patriarchs and matriarchs as it unfolds in the book of Genesis since infertility is their common problem. As the leading contemporary Jewish orthodox commentary explains (based on talmudic sources) this is "God's way of proving that the Jewish people are not a natural phenomenon" and the way that Isaac is born, as well as the other patriarchs, "established the miraculous nature of God's Chosen People."[48]

"Abrahamic religion" has become a widely used term to designate the three major monotheistic religions, and each of the three regard Abraham as their first in line who revolted against idolatry and introduced the concept of God to their respected religions. For each religion the connection to Abraham is critical for its Chosen claim, and that is why in Christianity he is the early witness to the Trinity and that is why God's promises to him are not for the Jews but rather for the "True Israel" namely Christianity the supersessionist (see next chapter). The Muslims made, some say appropriated, Abraham as the first Muslim ("Our Father *Ibrahim*"), and the Quran introduces the concept of "the religion of Abraham" several times. A look at the world map shows how large is the spread of the Abrahamic religions. Though they are little more than half of the world's population (excluding China, India, and Japan) the arena of the contention for the Chosen title covers about 90 percent of the world's inhabited continents

For Abraham, the act of committing himself to the Covenant already bears within it the burden of suffering. Nothing illustrates this more dramatically than God's command that he must sacrifice his son Isaac. This *akeda* or "binding" is resolved thanks to a last-minute divine intervention, but the religious Jew understands from the story that conforming to God's requirements inevitably brings with it suffering and pain. This, the *akeda* indicates, is the lot of the future descendents of Abraham.

The story of Abraham is not just a study in ancient theology, but, as Nachmanides says, it contains within it the future codes of the history of the Jews and of mankind. It even has its bearing on the conflicts in the Middle East and in international relations. The former president of the United States, Jimmy Carter, wrote about his personal involvement in negotiating the historic peace treaty of 1979 between Israel and Egypt. He saw fit to call his book *The Blood of Abraham—Insights into the Middle East*. President Carter, himself a devout Christian, wrote that the scriptures are of critical importance for understanding the roots of hatred and bloodshed in the region. Carter recalled his discussions with President Anwar Sadat of Egypt and Prime Minister Menachem Begin of Israel, and he noted how both Christianity and Islam took the promises of God to Moses and his people and incorporated it into their religions. He writes, "To a remarkable degree, 'the Will of God' is the basis for both esoteric debates and the most vicious terrorist attacks among Jews, Moslems, and Christians. God's early promises and how they must be implemented cause conflict some forty centuries after the Patriarch Abraham fathered the Arabs and the Jews in the Holy

Land. . . . How could different believers be convinced by their reading of the same history that each was God's Chosen People?"[49]

### Moses

With Moses, Judaism emerged as a religion and the Jews as a people, a unique juxtaposition in itself. For the Jews, the struggle culminating in the Exodus from Egypt was not just a liberation from slavery, it was a crucial event in Israel's conception of itself as a nation as well as a religion based on the Chosen concept. The revolution in thinking is clear: prior to Moses there was no organized religion based on the belief in one God—and there was to be no other for another millennium and a half. In this immense time span Moses is *the* central figure. This is why he is of such towering importance, for Christians and Muslims as well as for Jews.

When God speaks to Moses He reveals and confirms the bond between Himself and the people He has chosen: "I am the Lord. I appeared to Abraham, to Isaac and to Jacob as God Almighty . . . and I established My covenant with the. . . . And I will take you for My people, and I will be your God."[50] And further, "Now therefore if you will obey My voice, and keep My covenant, you shall be My own possession among all peoples; for all the earth is mine. And you shall be to me a kingdom of priests, and a holy nation."[51]

The meaning of the story in Exodus is clear: freedom and liberation bring with it prodigious responsibilities. Here, in one of history's most profound dramas, we are brought to see that the decision to be free is not simply a personal choice with personal consequences. Freedom means keeping the Covenant, with all its obligations. We in the twenty-first century in the West are accustomed to thinking of freedom as something we enjoy as individuals who are not forced to endure arbitrary restrictions imposed by others. But Exodus reveals in stark terms that freedom is the farthest thing from a passive concept.

Being Chosen also means suffering. Immediately after their liberation from the Egyptian yoke, the Jews were confronted by the stringent demands at Mount Sinai. The Covenant with God binds the Jews to their faith and code of laws and makes them liable for punishment if they break them. "But if you will not obey the voice of the Lord your God which I command you this day . . . then all these curses will come upon you and overtake you."[52] Freedom, in other words, involves not just obligations, but fear and responsibility as well.

Many commentators suggest that Moses was selected by God to lead the Jews out of bondage precisely because of his different background. As a prince of Egypt, he was born and bred into Egyptian life and tradition. A midrash tells us that he was appointed by Pharaoh as a chamberlain over the palace, but at the same time the Torah speaks of him as a man who feels great compassion for his people: "Moses grew up and went out to his brethren and observed their burdens."[53] Rabbi Abraham Ibn Ezra, a biblical commentator in twelfth-century Spain, explains that this was a plan of divine conception, because only a person with an understanding of the royal mentality could later confront Pharaoh with the demand of "let my people go." It would have been unthinkable for a person living in slavery and in the conditions of humiliation of the Children of Israel to aspire to such a position.[54]

The Exodus from Egypt was not only a liberation from slavery. It became a universal metaphor for the attainment of human rights, freedom, and justice, again demonstrating the grip the ancient scriptural stories have exerted on subsequent history. The Exodus was the reaffirmation of the Covenant with Abraham, and it marked the beginning of the training process of the Hebrews towards chosenness. The biblical narrative provides an insight into the behavior of the Chosen People in a way that was not common in the chronicles of other peoples of antiquity. Unlike the records of other nations, the Bible does not engage in self-glorification. For example, contrary to the Egyptian inscriptions in praise of the almighty Pharaohs, the Children of Israel are under the continual scrutiny of a highly critical observer. Rather than being glorified, their special status exposes them to punishment and suffering. The Jews are depicted in all their fear, misbehavior, loss of faith, and betrayal. In crossing the Red Sea, they are not portrayed as a victorious nation triumphant because of their military prowess. Their survival is due not to their own merits, but only to God's protection: "Then Moses and the people of Israel sang this song to the Lord saying, 'I will sing to the Lord for He has triumphed gloriously, the horse and his rider He has thrown into the sea.'"[55]

The laws Moses received from God and taught to his people, give prominence to the concept of the Chosen in a variety of forms and statements that would later be incorporated in Jewish laws, liturgy, practices, and customs. The three festivals that commemorate the Exodus from Egypt would become central features in collective Jewish memory and its heritage of chosenness. Each of them marks a different season, creating together the yearly life cycle: *Pesach* (Passover), the spring festival, which also marks the early harvest in the land of Israel; *Shavu'ot* (Pentecost), the festival of the giving of the law, which marks the beginning of the summer and the main harvest; and *Succot* (Tabernacles), the autumn festival. Of them all, Passover is the most remarkable in the sense that it especially emphasizes the chosenness and uniqueness of the Jewish people.

The festival of Passover involves stringent restrictions on what may be eaten especially the strict prohibition of all leavened bread.[56] The festival focuses on the suffering of the Jews as slaves in Egypt and their miraculous deliverance by God, but it also contains reminders of later suffering in Jewish history under the Gentiles. The destruction of all leaven and the weeklong eating of *matza* (unleavened bread) is the crucial symbol of the holiday, which is why it is also known as the "Festival of Matzot." The thorough cleansing of any traces of leaven from the house symbolizes, among other things, turning away from the ordinary things of life; it makes the Jewish home even more different from other homes than do the year-long regular dietary laws.

Of all the holidays, Passover still has the most powerful hold on Jews all over the world. The observance of the festival and, in particular, its highlight at the first evening with the *Seder* (literally "Order"), the traditional service with the reading of the Haggadah and the festive meal, which is an intrinsic part of it, is replete with customs and symbols that dramatize the unique and peculiar Jewish condition. The Seder, which is attended by all members of the family, and the Haggadah give special prominence to children, and the dialogue with them emphasizes the special situation of the Jews and its continuance from generation to generation.

*Succot* is a seven-day festival in which Jews construct temporary shelters to commemorate the desert experience and God's protection. *Shavu'ot* commemorates the awesome event at the foot of Mount Sinai, with God's dialogue with Moses and the revelation of the Ten Commandments. These three holidays are marked by Jewish pilgrims from Israel and the Diaspora coming to Jerusalem and the Temple.

The special distinction of the three pilgrimage holidays can be found in their respective prayers, which stress the status of Israel as God's Chosen People. These are the national holidays of a people who were freed from Egypt (Passover), took refuge in the wilderness (*Sukkot*) and were given the Torah (*Shavu'ot*). At the center of the prayers on each of these holidays there is the declaration of the special status of the Jews as the Chosen People: "You have chosen us from all the peoples; You loved us and found favor in us; You exalted us above all the tongues and You sanctified us with Your commandments."[57] The same language appears also in the blessing over the wine (*kiddush*), which is recited in each of the festivals in synagogue and at home around the dinner table.

The other holiday associated with the Exodus is the weekly Sabbath, which was instituted in the desert even before the Jews came to Mount Sinai.[58] Moses admonishes the Israelites to "[r]emember that you were a slave in the land of Egypt and the Lord your God freed you from there. . . . [T]herefore the Lord your God has commanded you to observe the Sabbath day."[59] Sabbath is a reminder to the Jews of their chosenness, their being set apart, mirroring in its way God's setting aside the seventh day. Like the revelation on Sinai, Sabbath, with its injunction to rest and revere God's creative work, is another Jewish contribution to mankind, to social justice, and to spirituality. "The Sabbath," God tells the people, "is a sign between Me and you throughout all the ages so you may know that I, the Lord, have consecrated you."[60]

The Exodus from Egypt under Moses' leadership was an act of separation, a prelude to the forty years of nation building in the desert before the people were permitted to enter the Promised Land. Like Abraham, who had to leave his homeland and wander before he was worthy to receive the Covenant, so Moses had to lead the Children of Israel and separate them from their previous existence. Maimonides explains that the Children of Israel had to experience these forty years so as to rid themselves of the slave mentality of Egypt before becoming free men and women in the Promised Land.[61]

The revelation in Sinai has many facets: it demonstrates the human potential to choose between good and evil, to break free from hopelessness and continuing disaster, to fulfill the divine purpose through peoples' own actions, and to show compassion through rest from labor. In short, humans were now able to be responsible for their own future. The revolutionary nature of all this for ancient times can hardly be exaggerated. The same can be said for our own times, over three thousand years after the event.

Moses was the key player in shaping the nature and destiny of the Chosen People, its laws, festivals, and national perceptions. He is the father of the prophets, a colossus in terms of leadership, and as such he is remembered in the Sabbath prayers: "Moses rejoiced in the gift of his portion, that you called him a faithful servant . . . when he stood before You on Mount Sinai. He brought down two stone tablets in his hand."[62] Even before the Christian era non-Jews recognized Moses as the man responsible for introducing the Jewish concept of God, which was so unique and different. The Greek historian Hecataeus wrote about Moses in about 300 BCE: "He had no images whatsoever of the gods made for them, being of the opinion that God does not have human form; rather the heaven that surrounds the earth is alone divine."[63]

Moses is revered, but in Jewish tradition his role is carefully modulated (he is "a faithful servant") because of the rabbis' concern that he should not appear somehow superhuman. The Bible and subsequent commentaries emphasize his human nature and even weaknesses. This is also evident in Jewish oral law, where Moses, although greatly respected and admired, is very human. The Talmud, for example, refers this way to the act of giving charity: "The man who gives charity in secret is greater than Moses our teacher"[64] This modest depiction of Moses stands in decided contrast to the heroic fashion in which the seminal figures of other peoples tend to be depicted, including the founders of the other two great monotheistic religions, Jesus and Mohammad.

Moses' role is made clear in the Bible and in other sources, which emphasize that he faced Pharaoh by himself while the elders of the people, stayed behind. It is because of his personal courage and leadership that he alone was found worthy to ascend Mount Sinai while the elders had to wait below. But the extraordinary fact is that on the Seder evening, when every Jewish family comes together to retell the story of the Exodus from Egypt, Moses is mentioned only once and indirectly at that. The text of the Haggadah, which elaborates on every aspect of the liberation of the Jews, including the plagues visited upon the Egyptian people by Moses, virtually ignores him.

There is a clear Jewish message here to other religions, particularly to Christianity. The text of the Haggadah was compiled in several stages, starting from the days of the Second Temple and extending well into the Christian era. It seems certain that part of it was affected by the rivalry and disputation with the Christians at a time when the Church was developing its own texts and doctrines on the "New Israel"—the assumption of the "Chosen" title by Christianity.[65] In this period the authors of the Haggadah were determined to highlight the unique relationship between God and the Jews as the Chosen People. The Haggadah thus tries to demonstrate that it was God himself who redeemed the Children of Israel—without any intermediary. This is emphasized in the text, which says, "And the Lord brought us out of Egypt, not through an angel, and not through a seraph, and not through an intermediary, but the Holy One, blessed be He in his glory and with His own being."[66]

There is a deliberate effort here, which is substantiated by the Bible, to show that the miraculous intervention was performed directly by God. Omitting Moses from the Haggadah constitutes a pointed message, conveying the fact that Judaism, unlike Christianity, does not have God-like surrogates. As repeatedly emphasized in Jewish tradition, the Exodus portrays the collective experience of the Children of Israel, not the miracle working of a transcendent leader. Jewish people as a whole were both Chosen and made their choice. Jewish tradition contrasts sharply here with both Islam, which focuses on the revelations of God to Mohammad, His Prophet, and Christianity, which centers on the narratives of Jesus, God's son.

### Judah Halevi—Promoter of the Chosen

Judah Halevi (1075–1141), one of the greatest Jewish scholars of the Middle Ages (second only to Maimonides), wrote the most all-embracing work on the concept of the Chosen, as part of a comparative analysis with Christianity and Islam. Halevi dedicated his book, *The Kuzari* as well as many liturgical poems to the axis of the God of Israel, the Chosen People, and the Chosen land. This triumvirate was, in his view, the ideal, the mission, and the essence of Jewish existence.

From an early age, Halevi followed the great confrontation between the two major religions, Christianity and Islam. He was a young man when the Crusades got underway, and he moved from his birthplace of Christian Toledo to Cordoba in Muslim Spain. This was an era in which both Christians and Muslims claimed to have inherited the role of the Chosen, and the Jews were persecuted by both. Both had large armies at their disposal, and they attempted to prove their chosenness in the battlefield and by conquest, while Jews like Halevi could only watch from the sidelines. In their humiliated condition, lacking sovereignty and a military force, the Jews could only resort to spiritual and philosophical channels and tried to retain their title of the Chosen People through an intellectual exercise.

*The Kuzari* is an apology for Judaism at a time when the Jews were, according to Judah Halevi, a tragic and persecuted people. The subtitle of the book is, "In Defence of the Despised Faith,"[67] and Halevi was engaged in its compilation for twenty years. Written in Arabic, the book argued that the entire Jewish people was endowed with a special religious aura, first given to Adam, and then bequeathed, through a line of Chosen representatives, to the people of Israel.

*The Kuzari* is based on a legend that appears in several historic records about the Khazar people (an independent Turkic nation in the Caucasus region of today's southern Russia, between the seventh and tenth centuries CE), who converted to Judaism under King Bolan. The king began to study the origins of the three religions, following a dream in which an angel told him that "God appreciates his intentions but not his deeds." King Bolan invited a secular philosopher, a Jewish representative (Halevi), and representatives of Christianity and Islam to his court, and after a long exchange he determined that Judaism is the true religion.

At the outset of his examination, the king did not want to see the Jew because of the humble condition of the Jewish people, but when he realized that Judaism lay at the origins of the other two religions, he summoned Halevi to state his case. Halevi takes the bull by the horns and explains the roots of the theological rivalry: the concept of the Chosen. He focuses on the dual approach by which both Christianity and Islam call upon their Jewish heritage: They base themselves on it and claim that they are the rightful successors (a proof for their contention is that they are fighting in and for the Holy Land), and at same time, they hate and persecute the Jews, perhaps because of the Jew's temerity in holding on to the title of Chosen.

Judah Halevi was a strong religious Zionist (long before the term was invented) who regarded the redemption of the Land of Israel as a central imperative for world Jewry, a credo that he himself practiced. At the same time, he regarded the Diaspora as an important element in the Jewish mission, to be a "Light unto the Nations" and to disseminate the ideas of monotheism and the values of Judaism. The purpose of Jewish history according to Halevi is to bring humanity to accept that the world was created by God; the miracles as well as the suffering of the People of Israel serve as the proof for it.[68]

Judah Halevi's most famous poem, "My Heart is in the East" combines, all the elements of the Chosen saga: the contrast between the life of plenty in the Diaspora and the strong imperative to move to Zion with the resultant fate of the Jews caught between the two new contestants for the mantle of the Chosen: Christianity (Edom) and Islam (Arabia):

> My heart is in the East, and I am in the uttermost of the West,
> How can I taste what I eat, how can I enjoy it?
> How can I fulfill my oaths and vows, while yet
> Zion is in the hands of Edom, and I am in the chains of Arabia?[69]

The Jews, maintains Halevi, are the Chosen People for good or for bad: "Israel among the nations is like the heart among the other organs of the body—it is exposed to more ills yet it is healthier than the rest."[70] The Jewish people's special relationship with God and their observance of the Jewish laws lie at the core of the existence of the Chosen People. Rational laws are important for every society, but the illogical laws are crucial for keeping the links between Jew and God, whether in Israel or in the Diaspora. Those unique laws of the Jews are the reason for their separateness among the nations, and the laws keep them apart as "[a] people that dwells alone," otherwise they would be fated to disappear. The persecution and the suffering, the dispersion and the oppression cannot be seen as proof that the Jews were deserted by God but rather as their educative burden and task that was their lot as the Chosen nation.

Exile, according to Halevi, is part of the divine plan to disseminate the values of Judaism and to provide a guiding light for other nations. Suffering helps the Jews to improve their position with God. Unlike Christian doctrine (see next chapter), Halevi regards exile as part of God's divine design for the Jews and not as a proof of the abandonment of the Jews. Israel remains the Chosen People as it represents the original religion that was given at Mount Sinai as revealed by God: this is the axis of world history and human experience. The reality of being Chosen made the Jews special and different: "For God chose them for himself to be a people and a nation distinct from all nations of the world."[71]

Judah Halevi is unique. Not so much in his commentaries on the Chosen that also appear in other sources, but rather in his monumental work that amassed all the arguments and presented them in a concentrated form. Other commentators like Rashi or Maimonides, do this more selectively, in a more rational approach lacking the Kabbalistic, sometimes mystical, additions of Halevi. Halevi, which provides a "generic account of [the] election" of the Jews, causes very much discomfort for modern liberals.[72] Some sources share the premise of Maimonides that it is solely the Torah which gave rise to the uniqueness of the Jews, and not any qualities related to a Jewish gene pool, as argued by Halevi.

The philosopher Baruch Spinoza (1632–77) could not decipher the chosenness conundrum. As one who had rebelled against religious authority and was excommunicated from the Jewish community of Amsterdam as a result, he regarded the concept of the Chosen as a barrier, and he rejected the traditional doctrine of selection by God. Spinoza explains that "the Hebrew nation was chosen by God before all others not by reason of its understanding nor its spiritual qualities, but by reason of its social organization."[73] He stated that the Jews still exist because they choose to live separately, and this brings down hatred upon them, and in a vicious circle it is this hatred keeps them apart as separate community. However, he admitted that there is something mystical in the Jewish existence, even for those who are not religious. Spinoza maintained that "[t]hese Jews might cease to believe in God but they will cling to circumcision and all their separatist rituals."[74] Professor Arthur Hertzberg concludes, "This rationalist [Spinoza] is saying that the Jews will defy logic, and he is right. Generations of modern non-believing Jews have adhered to their Jewishness for reasons they themselves cannot articulate."[75]

But it seems that Spinoza did not desert the Chosen concept and he would use it in a pre-Zionist prophecy. The Jews, he said, may once become again a nation in the full sense of the term, including the idea of the Chosen: "I would not hesitate to believe that they will one day, given the opportunity . . . establish once more their independent state, and that God will again choose them."[76]

Nine hundred years after Halevi, Rabbi Samson Raphael Hirsch, who struggled to maintain Orthodoxy in the mid-nineteenth-century age of emancipation and enlightenment, attempted in a somewhat apologetic manner to emphasize the sense of the Jewish mission in fulfilling the role of the Chosen People. Hirsch, unlike Judah Halevi, did not dwell on the special qualities of the Jews but limited their role as Chosen only to the mission that they are required to perform. With reference to the blessing in praise of God, "[w]ho selected us from all the peoples and gave us His Torah," Hirsch explains that God has chosen Israel to disseminate, study, and observe the Torah. "The historic significance of Israel among the nations stands and falls to the extent that we cultivate the Torah and keep our faith in it. The moment that we stop doing so and do not observe it, we forfeit our role among the nations."[77]

The universal mission of the Chosen is a concept that often attracts more support among rabbis of the Reform Movement for Progressive Judaism, the world's largest organized Jewish religious group in the world. Rabbi Abba Hillel Silver, a Reform rabbi and a leader of the Zionist movement in America in the mid-twentieth century, presented a strong defense of the Chosen concept. Jews may be a Chosen and even holy people, he said, but this does not make them morally immaculate, racist, or superior. Their mission is to increase holiness in the world while remaining separate and distinct from heathen people. "Holiness is not an accolade of self-glorification but a hard discipline of self purification." [78]

Prime Minister David Ben Gurion, was another example of a secular promoter of the Chosen concept. According to Ben Gurion, who often used the term Chosen, the Covenant between God and the Jews is an original concept making the two parties equal. There was a universal Covenant between God and Noah and then came the Covenant between God and Abraham, which led to the Covenant with the Children of Israel given on Mount Sinai. In the view of Ben Gurion, the role of the Jews according to the Bible is not just in respecting crucial human values of justice, truth, peace, and fraternity, but, as we have seen so often, also determining the mission of the Jewish people to be Isaiah's "Light unto the Nations."[79]

## The Song of the Chosen

It must have been a difficult decision for the Jewish sages to include the Song of Solomon (Song of Songs) among the twenty-four books of the Hebrew Bible. Orthodox commentaries explain that it is one of the most complex books of the Scriptures—not because it is particularly hard to understand but because it is so easy to misunderstand. No other book seems so out of place in the biblical canon, "not only because it is a love song but because it is a love song of uncommon passion."[80]

It is clear that there was a tendency among the Jewish sages to remove the Song of Songs from the Bible. It was only by the intervention of Rabbi Akiva, the leading religious authority at this period, that the book was left in. Rabbi Akiva instructed to keep it, determining that "[a]ll of the books [of Scripture] are holy, but *Shir HaShirim* (Song of Songs) is the holy of holies."[81]

The Song of Songs is the love story of the Chosen, a tender and moving poem that is regarded in the tradition as an allegorical rendering of the love between God and Israel. Popular Orthodox commentary explains that the prophets frequently compared the relationship between God and Israel to that of a loving husband angered by a straying wife. Since Israel is destined to suffer a series of exiles, the Song of Songs nostalgically recalls "Israel's former status as God's beloved Chosen."[82] Less traditional interpretations refer to it as "the most secular of all the books of the Bible," and "the most erotic text in the Jewish tradition."[83]

The Song of Songs overflows with sensuality: "O that you would kiss me with the kisses of your mouth!" it begins. "For your love is better than wine. . . . Draw me after you, let us make haste," and far more. The unfolding love story tells of the lover choosing and coveting the Chosen. It speaks of courtship and marriage. "Go forth, O daughters of Zion, and behold King Solomon, with the crown with which his mother crowned him on the day of his wedding day, on the day of the gladness of his heart."[84]

The allegorical interpretation here, agreed on by Midrash, Kabbala, Zohar, and Rashi, understands "his mother" as signifying "His (God's) nation," as in, Israel. (In Hebrew, the word *ima* [mother] is related to *uma* [nation].) "When Israel accepted the Torah [becoming the Chosen] she becomes not only the mother of her own children, but the spiritual mother of all mankind."[85] When the lover describes his beloved the images are so erotic and bold that it is easy to understand why the sages might have objected. "Behold, you are beautiful, My love, behold you are beautiful, your eyes are doves behind your veil. . . . Your breasts are like two fawns, twins of a gazelle that feed upon the lilies."[86] Rashi, following the midrash, explains that "the two breasts" refers to Moses and Aaron who "nursed" the Children of Israel, twins because they are equal.[87]

The song asks, "How is your beloved better than another, O fairest among women?" The midrash and Rashi both declare: This is how the heathens question the Jews about their God—is He so superior to other gods that you are ready to be burned and tortured for Him? The verse, "My beloved has gone down to his garden, to the beds of spices, to pasture his flock in the garden and to gather roses," means allegorically that even when the Children of Israel are in exile, God is still with them. The Jews in exile, says a late nineteenth-century commentator, are as a "rose among thorns." God accompanies them in their exile, and on the day of redemption he will pick the roses.[88]

Another verse speaks to exile: "I am black yet comely, O daughters of Jerusalem. . . . Do not gaze upon me because I am swarthy."[89] In traditional Jewish commentaries this is an exchange with the nations (the daughters of Jerusalem), who condemn Israel because her "Husband" (God), abandoned her due to her sins (swarthiness). Rashi explains that here Israel tells the nations, "I am blackened in consequence of my own deeds, but I am comely by virtue of the deeds of my forefathers. Although I sinned with regard to the Golden Calf, I have compensated for that misdeed by the merit of having accepted the Torah."[90] As always, Rashi draws a parallel with the Chosen concept—the acceptance of the Torah after it was rejected by the other nations. Other commentators have their own interpretation: "Do not think that God has rejected me utterly: He still loves me because of my merits. And when I repent, He will grant me atonement for my sins 'Though your sins are like scarlet, they shall be as white as snow.'"[91]

It is perhaps worth noting that Christian scholars posit that this passage is actually testimony to the transfer of the election of the Chosen. In this definition, there are two Covenants: one at Mount Sinai, which was given to the Children of Israel, and the second, given in Jerusalem to the Church.[92] The literature on this exchange is vast, and there are many instances where it focuses on the replacement of the Chosen. What is common to both the Jewish and the Christian commentators is their agreement that the Song of Songs is an allegory, and the rivalry between the commentaries is so critical precisely because Rabbi Akiva identified this book as the "Holy of Holies."

Whatever the controversies, the crucial point for us is that the various Jewish religious authorities harness this unusual love story to describe the unique relationship between God and the Jews, through down-to-earth human language, dealing with the very act of mutual Choosing: how God seeks and finds the Jewish people with the Torah, and the consequent exile, redemption, and burden of love and suffering.

It is interesting that God's name does not appear in the Song of Songs. Maybe this is because of its allegorical nature, or the intent to keep God's ineffable name out of the earthy descriptions. Nevertheless the commentators, beginning with Rabbi Akiva, are convinced that the treatment of the Chosen concept is part of the continuing love story between God and His people, inasmuch as God moves to exile together with Israel. "How beloved is Israel before the Holy One, blessed be he; for wherever they were exiled the *Shekhinah* ["Divine Presence"] was with them."[93]

In a different commentary, this time from the Talmud, the sages compare sensual love between a married couple to the intimate relations between God and His Chosen People. The approach here is realistic as well as erotic, recognizing that love between a husband and wife is often intense at the beginning but then declines. The Talmud compares the love of a couple in their early days with the love between God and Israel in the desert, immediately following the revelation on Mount Sinai: "There was a man who used to say: 'When our love was strong, we could sleep on the edge of a sword; now that our love is waning, a bed of sixty cubits is not wide enough for us.'"[94]

The allegorical idea is clear: during the period in the wilderness, God and Israel could meet in a small space on the top of the ark in the portable sanctuary. During this period of great love there was no need for a larger space. Later, in Solomon's temple, the dimensions of "God's abode" grew significantly, and finally after the destruction of the Second Temple (because Israel sinned and became estranged from God), no temple would be able to accommodate God. The husband and the wife in this analogy will no longer be in love, and they will feel uncomfortable even in a bed of vast proportions.

\* \* \*

The Song of Songs is recited in the synagogue on the Sabbath of Passover, connecting its theme of chosen love with the drama of God and man choosing each other at Sinai. In the story of Abraham, the Bible tells of the personal Covenant between God and the first Jewish patriarch. In Exodus it relates how the Covenant came to be sealed between God and the nation. In the Song of Songs the idea of chosenness clothes itself in the intimacy and longing of lover and beloved. There could be no more powerful a portrayal of the passion with which the Jewish people held to the Lord their God. But they were not the only ones who claimed to be God's beloved. In the course of time bitter rivals emerged to challenge their role as the Chosen.

# CHAPTER 3

# The Gentile Replacement of the Chosen

Thus the Moslems, as well as the Christians, accept, in principle, the Jews' belief in the divine inspiration of the Torah and the consequent belief in the Jews' special status as the recipients of this divine revelation. . . . The Jews' present-day importance, celebrity, and discomfort all derive from the historic fact that they have involuntarily begotten two Judaic world religions whose millions of adherents make the preposterous but redoubtable claim to have superseded the Jews, by the Jewish God.

—Arnold J. Toynbee[1]

The Christian kneels before the image of the Jew, wrings his hands before the image of a Jewess; his Apostles, Festivals, and Psalms are Jewish. Only a few are able to come to terms with this contradiction—most free themselves by anti-Semitism. Obliged to revere a Jew as God, they wreak vengeance upon the rest of the Jews by treating them as devils.

Rabbi Moritz Gudeman, Chief Rabbi of Vienna, 1907[2]

References by non-Jews to the Chosen People tend to vary from hostile to factual and sympathetic. The struggle over the special character of the Chosen stands at the very core of Christianity and Islam—both claiming that they inherited the designation from God after the failure of the Jews to satisfy His demands. Neither religion denies Jewish chosenness but rather seeks to appropriate the title for themselves. Both religions regard the Jews as living testimony to the early revelation and election of the Chosen, but at the same time they scorn Jews for not converting, for continuing to maintain that they are the Chosen, and for continuing to live as a separate and different people. Both Christianity and Islam claim that they are correcting the damage done by the Jews to the Covenant between God and Abraham. Both refer to Abraham, to Moses, and to the Bible as the sources of their own beliefs. Both Saint Paul and Mohammad wished to claim Abraham as the father of their new religions since he lived according to his belief in God before the adoption of the Mosaic code of laws. Mohammad could even claim Abraham, the father of Ishmael, as a predominant symbol of the Arab people.

In the early days of both Christianity and Islam, the two religions made great efforts to win over the Jews. Both adopted tenets from the Jewish scriptures with the additional claim that they had now assumed the mantle of the Chosen. When they realized that the Jews would not convert, they made certain changes in their religious codes. Only after the death of Jesus did Christ's followers abolish Jewish laws. Christians did away with the rite of circumcision, changed the observance of the Sabbath from Saturday to Sunday, and finally abolished all the other Jewish laws. Mohammad tried to win over the Jews by asking his adherents to direct their prayers to Jerusalem for sixteen months, and he observed Yom Kippur, the Jewish Day of Atonement. Martin Luther, who broke away from Catholicism to create the Protestant Church, sent cordial and welcoming messages to the Jews, expecting that they would convert to his purified form of Christianity. After their refusal he launched his vicious campaign of anti-Semitism. Christianity and Islam have similar origins.

* * *

"Like Christianity," says historian Paul Johnson, "Islam was originally a heterodox movement within Judaism which diverged to the point where it became a separate religion, and then rapidly developed its own dynamic and characteristics."[3]

## Christianity and the Chosen

The early Christians adhered faithfully to Jewish laws. Jesus himself warned His followers, "Think not that I have come to abolish the law and the prophets; I have come not to abolish them but to fulfill them. For truly I say to you, till heaven and earth pass away, not an iota, not a dot, will pass from the law until all is accomplished. Whoever then relaxes one of the least of these commandments and teaches men so, shall be called least in the kingdom of heaven; but he who does them and teaches them shall be called great in the kingdom of Heaven."[4]

In the Acts of the Apostles we read how Jesus' disciples observed Jewish laws (*halakah*): they prayed in the Temple, observed the dietary laws, and maintained the practice of circumcision. "Unless you are circumcised according to the custom of Moses," the author of Acts writes, "you cannot be saved."[5] On January 1 many Christians celebrate the *Feast of the Circumcision of Our Lord* (mainly Eastern Orthodox Churches and few other groups including Traditionalist Roman Catholics), which marks the consent of Jesus to practice Jewish Law and is considered by them as a holy day. Nevertheless, in their long-term effort to assert Christianity's ascendance over its Jewish past, the various Christian churches attempted to conceal or downplay the fact that Jesus was an observant Jew. Only in the twentieth century did more and more Christian historians, including senior Church representatives, begin to agree with Rabbi Arthur Hertzberg's formulation that "the religion of Jesus is Judaism and the religion about Jesus is Christianity."[6] In 1985, the Vatican addressed the "Jewish roots of Christianity" starting with a clear statement: "Jesus was and always remained a Jew."[7]

It was Paul, for all practical purposes the founder of Christianity, who made a conscious and, in the event, historic decision to turn the new faith away from its Jewish origins. After failing to attract Jews to the belief in Jesus as the Messiah, Paul turned to the Gentiles as the primary pool of potential converts. Preaching to new audiences, he no longer insisted on observance of the laws as a condition for joining the community of believers.[8] Instead Paul developed a fresh approach to Jewish law and changed the focus of the new religion from action and observance to faith.

In his Letter to the Galatians, Paul declared, "Christ redeemed us from the curse of the Law."[9] To the Roman church, he wrote, "For we hold that a man is justified by faith apart from the law."[10] Paul, who was presenting the new faith of Christianity to tens of thousands of new followers, proposed a novel doctrine, which maintained that with God becoming incarnate in Jesus, the basis of the Torah was nullified. According to Paul Johnson, "God's plan had changed. The mechanism of salvation was now the New Testament, faith in Christ. The covenantal promises to Abraham no longer applied to his present descendants, but to Christians: and if you are Christ's, then you are Abraham's offspring, heirs according to promise."[11] This why the New Testament is called the New Covenant based on a passage from the Old Testament: "Behold, the days are coming, declares the Lord, when I will make a *new covenant* with the house of Israel and the house of Judah, not like the covenant that I made with their fathers on the day when I took them by the hand to bring them out of the land of Egypt, my covenant that they broke, though I was their husband, declares the Lord."[12]

Paul, like Jesus, was a religious Jew, a Pharisee, who worked as a tent maker. At first, he tells us, he not only opposed the supporters of Jesus, he persecuted them. But after Jesus appeared to him in a vision he reversed his stance and commenced preaching to the Jews about Christ. In his travels in Asia Minor, he would first preach in the synagogues of the cities he visited. Some of these synagogues kept a special side room for non-Jewish God-fearing people—those who had accepted the God of Israel but were not yet mentally ready to take on full observance of the laws. It is likely that Paul preached to these groups, which may suggest his initial motivation for breaking away from the Law. Soon, though, he was preaching to all the Gentiles. To them he proposed a faith without the complicated Jewish rituals and observances, a new covenant, not etched in stone but engraved on the hearts of men and women. Jesus, he preached, died on the cross in atonement for the sins of mankind.[13] Since that was so, the old methods of atonement and conformity to God's will had now been superseded.

The early Christians accomplished a highly sophisticated transition from the old faith to the new. While they differed with their Jewish forbears on the fundamental nature of God's presence in the world, they agreed on practically everything else. From Judaism they took the Pentateuch, the prophets and later writings, with all the ethical and moral precepts involved. They adopted the concept of the

Sabbath (albeit changing the day) and feast days. As Church ceremony developed they incorporated incense and burning lamps, the psalms, hymns and choral music, vestments and prayers, priests and martyrs, the readings of the sacred books, and the institution of the temple and synagogue (now transformed into churches).[14] Maimonides refers to early Christians as those who "founded a religion similar to ours."[15]

In the course of time, the Old Testament with its images and stories ingrained itself in the culture of the Christian West. Michelangelo's *David and Moses*, his Sistine Chapel ceiling, Handel's *Judas Maccabeus*, Rossini's *Moses in Egypt*, Verdi's *Nabucco*—the list of Old Testament inspired art is virtually endless. Likewise, the great Jewish themes of revelation and liberation have been essential sources for Europe's artists, writers, philosophers, and theologians from early times through the present day.

Christianity ingested Judaism almost whole, turning it into one of the basic building blocks of European culture. But at the same time, the Church found it necessary to stamp the old religion as null, void, surpassed, and of no further consequence. The destruction of Jerusalem and the Temple by Titus in 70 CE was taken by the early Church as a dramatic demonstration that God had abandoned His Chosen People, and Rome's decision to leave the city in ruins was supported by Christians who believed the destroyed city should serve as a perpetual sign that God's Covenant with the Jews was now likewise ruined and dead.

But although the Romans had demolished Jerusalem and Paul had nullified the Jewish Law, the concept of the Chosen People retained its hold on the religious imagination. But it was the Church that now claimed the Covenant as its own. From the time of Abraham Jews had been the Chosen People, but now, Christianity's founders declared, God's new people of faith, the followers of Jesus had inherited the special bond. Chosenness became a cardinal pillar in Church doctrine.

Christianity argues that Jesus has replaced the role and mission of the Jews. The Church claims to be "Israel after the spirit" and the heir to role of the Jews as the elect. Christians refer to the "Holy Church," and the congregants, having received the flesh and the blood in Holy Communion, are referred to as "the Sons of God"[16] and the "Chosen People," using the same terms as those originally bestowed in the Old Testament on the Children of Israel by God: "But you are a chosen race, a royal priesthood, a holy nation, God's own people that you may declare the wonderful deeds of Him who called you out of darkness into His marvelous light."[17] As Conor Cruise O'Brien explains "The *real* Chosen People are no longer the Jews but all those—of whatever language, culture, or nation—who know themselves to be redeemed by Christ's sacrifice on the Cross. That is the new covenant, which the older covenants are there to prefigure."[18]

From the second century the Christian literature claims that God had himself rejected the Jewish people and that the Church has completely taken over the position of the elect or Chosen People. This was not just a change in tone but rather becoming a central pillar of Christianity: the theology of supersession (sometimes called "replacement theology" by critics). This new doctrine had a two-fold theology that was intimately interdependent: (1) the belief that only Christianity is the fulfillment and continuation of the Old Testament and (2) that the Jews who rejected Christ and failed to recognize Him as the Messiah (and even killed Him) lost their title as the Chosen People to Christianity. Even worst, the Jews are viewed "as a people who never accepted or responded to their prophetic leaders and teachers,"[19] and according to early Christian writings God had already rejected the Jewish people when Moses broke the tablets following the golden calf episode.[20]

Paul preached the gospel of Christ throughout the second part of his life and brought multitudes to the new faith. But along with his spiritual message, he conveyed a deep hatred for the Jews. It was mainly Paul who shifted the guilt for the crucifixion of Jesus from the Romans to the Jews, leaving behind him violent anti-Semitic texts. For Paul, the Jews were responsible not just for the death of Jesus, but also for murdering their own prophets, for hating humanity, and for violating God's will: "the Jews, who killed both the Lord Jesus and the prophets and drove us out, and displease God and oppose all men, by hindering us from speaking to the Gentiles that they may be saved. But God's wrath has come upon them at last!"[21]

It is easy to read the deep personal animus in these words, but Paul's vitriol had an evangelical purpose as well. Christianity could not merely claim to have super-seded Judaism, it needed to delegitimize its predecessor, to dispose of the older religion as a valid alternate, that is, competing, path to God. Christian hatred of Judaism was necessary as part of the process of supersession—the transfer of the mantle of the Chosen from Judaism to Christianity. Professor David Flusser explains that "Christian anti-Judaism was not a coincidental lapse" but a neces-sary development serving as "godfather to the formation of Christianity."[22]

In pursuing this approach St. John far surpasses even Paul's vehemence. In John's gospel Jews are not only responsible for killing Christ, they become iden-tified with the devil. Writing in about 100 CE, John purportedly reports on what Jesus himself said about the Jews (he clearly speaks about *all* Jews, using the word "Jews" sixty times in the text): "Why do you not understand what I say. . . . You are of your father, the Devil, and your will is to do your father's desires. . . . The reason why you do not hear them [the message of God brought by Jesus] is because you are not of God."[23] Both Paul and John speak about "the Jews," all of them, now and for generations to come, as the devil and the killers of Jesus. Later, in the third and fourth centuries, Greek Church fathers such as St. John Chrysostom (the "golden-mouthed" so-named for his eloquence) were especially violent in their attacks against the Jews, accusing them of ridiculing the cross, blaspheming God, and insulting His son.[24]

As the Catholic Church had done before them, some leaders of the Protestant Reformation, Martin Luther (1483–1546) in particular, began with friendly overtures to the Jews in the expectation that they would convert. In 1523, Luther published an article favorable to the Jews: "Jesus Christ was Born a Jew." The arti-cle proposed achieving the redemption of the Jews through conversion. Luther attacked Catholics for treating the Jews "as if they were dogs and not human beings. They have nothing to say about them but to curse them and seize their wealth. . . . I would advise and beg everybody to deal kindly with the Jews and to instruct them in the scriptures; in such a case we could expect them to join us. . . . We must receive them kindly and allow them to compete with us in earning a livelihood . . . and if some remain obstinate, what of it? Not everyone is a good Christian."[25]

But the Jews did not respond as Luther expected, and he turned on them savagely, leading an unprecedented campaign of anti-Jewish hatred, principles of which would later be incorporated in the National-Socialist doctrines of the 1930s. Luther's manifesto "On the Jews and their Lies" (1543) is one of the most virulent anti-Semitic tracts ever penned. The Jews are "our plague, our pestilence, our misfortune." Christians "are at fault in not avenging the innocent blood of our Lord. We are at fault in not slaying them. Rather we allow them to live freely in our midst despite all their murdering, cursing, blaspheming, lying, defaming."[26] At the end of his manifesto, he provided a prescription of what can be considered a forerunner of the "Final Solution" of the Jewish question:

> Firstly, their synagogues should be set on fire. Secondly, their homes should likewise be broken down and destroyed. Thirdly, they should be deprived of their prayer-books and Talmuds. Fourthly, their rabbis must be forbidden under threat of death to teach any more. Fifthly, passport and travelling privileges should be absolutely forbidden to the Jews. Sixthly, they ought to be stopped from usury. Seventhly, let the young and strong Jews and Jewesses be given the flail, the axe, the hoe, the spade, the distaff, and spindle, and let them earn their bread by the sweat of their noses. We ought to drive the rascally lazy bones out of our system. Therefore away with them . . . may all be free of this insufferable devilish burden— the Jews.[27]

Luther, in many ways the father of German nationalism, had a great influence on German attitudes toward the Jews and his writings were widely quoted by the Nazis.

The power of Luther's denunciations and those of his Catholic predecessors is such that they continue to haunt the collective consciousness two thousand years after Christ's death. The release of Mel Gibson's movie *The Passion of the Christ* in February 2004 was perceived by Christians and Jews alike not merely as just another piece of entertainment for filmgoers but as a major religious experience in itself. Christians were enthusiastic that the roots of their religion were being recreated by the most powerful communication organ of this contemporary age—the cinema. Jews, for a similar reason, feared that the brutal depiction of Christ's death, evidently at the hands of the Jewish authorities in first-century Jerusalem, would cause a chain-reaction, rekindling the worst anti-Jewish prejudices and hatred. Jews perceived the film as blaming the Jews for killing Jesus, which historically was seen as the "blood guilt" by many anti-Semites, and was, therefore, the justification for attacks on Jews. Christian defenders of the movie said that it followed a literal interpretation of the Gospels, and as we have seen— according to the original text of the New Testament, all Jews bear the blame for the crucifixion.

In *The Passion of The Christ* Gibson depicts ugly and repulsive Jews manipulating the mighty Roman Empire into agreeing to crucify Jesus. Pontius Pilate, who in reality crucified thousands of people (it was the routine punishment of the time), is portrayed as an almost sympathetic character, and it is only Jewish pressure that determines the fate of Jesus. The movie disregards not only the historic fact that the Romans executed Jesus as a Jewish troublemaker whose claims they regarded as a capital offense, but also ignores the changes in Church doctrine on this subject made by Vatican II's Nostra Aetate of 1965 (see later in this chapter), which rejected the blood libel against the Jews.

Gibson himself, as is now well known, is an adherent of a group of ultraconservative traditional Catholics, who refuse to accept the Vatican II declarations and the new references to the Jews as the Chosen People. Adding fuel to the fire is the fact that Gibson's father, Hutton Gibson, is a notorious Holocaust denier, which inevitably raised speculation about anti-Semitic influences in Gibson's background. Hutton Gibson, who is also a traditional Catholic, told the *New York Times* that the Second Vatican Council, which approved the changes in doctrine toward the Jews, was a "Masonic plot backed by the Jews."[28] In August 2006 when the police arrested Mel Gibson in California for suspected drunk driving he made amazing statements to the arresting officer about "f—ing Jews," adding that "the Jews are responsible for all the wars in the world."[29] The true point, though, has nothing to do with the Gibsons personally. It is, rather, the continuing effect of the hatred propagated first by Paul of Tarsus two millennia ago as part of a campaign to validate Christianity's claim to the mantle of the Chosen.

In revivifying the blood guilt myth, *The Passion of The Christ* both played to Christianity's deep-seated anti-Semitism and distorted the historical reality. An Anglican priest, Dr. Giles Fraser of Oxford University, took issue with many of his colleagues when he published a stern warning reminding people that the blood libel that "the Jews killed Jesus," which the movie reiterates, was responsible for sending millions of Jews to their death. The movie, he says, like the conventional interpretation of the Gospels, is torn from its historic context. The denunciations in the New Testament, writes Fraser, were part of the conflict between the synagogue and the new Christian communities that were in the process of establishing themselves. The "vitriol leveled against the Jews," Fraser writes, "was generated by a small and insecure community" of those Christians who had left the Jewish community, diatribes in an "intra-Jewish sectarian polemic."[30]

## The Doctrinal Conflict

New Testament scholars agree that the final text of the Gospels was edited long after the events described, and in so doing, the editors wanted to vilify the Jews and vindicate the Romans whose goodwill they sought. In the Vatican "Document on the Teaching of Judaism," issued in 1985, there is even an unusual admission of responsibility: "It cannot be ruled out that some references, hostile or less than favorable to the Jews, have their historical context in conflicts between the nascent Church and the Jewish community. Certain controversies reflect Christian-Jewish relations long after the time of Jesus. To establish this is of capital importance if we wish to bring out the meaning of certain Gospel texts for the Christians of today."[31]

An examination of the attitudes of Christianity to the Jews shows how the complex issue of the Chosen and its Gentile replacement creates both confusion and hatred. On one hand, there is the hate preached by Paul and subsequently reiterated over the centuries. Based on the gospels, this hatred lay at the core of some of the cruelest atrocities perpetrated against the Jews. It lay behind the massacres of the Crusades in the Middle Ages, the pogroms of czarist Russia, and the extermination program of the Nazis. It is appearing once again in new forms at the onset of the twenty-first century. Yet Saint Paul himself, after spreading the message of hate, still speaks of the Jews as the Chosen People: "I say then, Hath God cast away His people? God forbid. For I also am an Israelite, of the seed of Abraham, of the tribe of Benjamin. God hath not cast away His people. . . . Even so then at this present time also there is a remnant according to the election of grace. . . . As regards the Gospel they are enemies of God . . . but as regards election they are beloved for the sake of their forefathers."[32] Even in their degradation and infamy, it seems, the Jews still enjoy a special, that is, Chosen status. "Salvation," so John relates Jesus' words, "is of the Jews."[33]

Christianity's birth from Judaism created a doctrinal conflict that has played itself out over the centuries in both theological debates and genocidal outbreaks and has yet to be fully resolved. Jews are the superseded and vilified remnants of a community that should have disappeared with the advent of the Messiah. But Judaism is also the very root of Christian spirituality upon which Christianity has an intrinsic theological dependence. To justify their own election, Christians must preach about the sins of the Jews and their rejection, but at the same time they need to acknowledge the source of their own revelations, the Covenants, and the Jewish Bible (the Old Testament). The Jews had their own interpretations regarding God's Covenants that were codified through their oral Torah— the Talmud—and viewed as part of their Sinai tradition. This is why for centuries (and still by anti-Semites today) the Talmud was an object of censorship, persecution, and burning by medieval Christianity. For Christianity the Talmud was the veil over Jewish eyes that didn't let them realize the new and "true Israel," but for the Jews, who rejected the idea of theological supersession, the Talmud was the shield and barrier that has maintained their chosenness over the ages. In Christian art, in paintings and sculpture from the Middle ages, there are thousands of works showing the sharp contrast between the Synagoga and the Ecclesia (the Church). The Synagoga, the Jews, is depicted as blinded, turned away from God on her way out being replaced by the Ecclesia, Christianity, which symbolizes vitality, confident with its way to the future, as the Chosen, the "New Israel".[34] Similarly in the infamous production of the passion in the German village of Oberammrgau, which was for many centuries a center for anti-Jewish incitement, including during the Nazi era, there is still today in the revised version clear references to the replacement of the Jews by Christianity as the Chosen People of Israel.[35]

This Christian ambivalence toward the chosenness of the Jewish people is the key to an understanding of the relations between Jews and Gentiles and the causes of anti-Semitism. Christian displacement of the Jews as the Chosen People requires acknowledgment of those who have been displaced. But at the same time, the claim of supersession demands for its full validation the absorption, that is, the conversion, of the Jews into the new, universal congregation of believers.

It is this doctrine of displacement that has, more than anything else, fixed the image of the Jew in the eyes of Christians for most of Christianity's two-thousand-year history. On the one hand the Jewish patriarchs and prophets laid down the basic tenets of faith and prefigured the coming of Christ. On the other, the Jews of Jesus' time perfidiously refused to acknowledge His Messiahship and were collectively guilty of His crucifixion, damning all their succeeding generations with blood guilt. At the same time the universal claims of Christianity demanded that the Jews must be converted as part of the salvation of mankind. Both the blood libel against the Jews and the need to convert are direct corollaries of the struggle against the original Chosen People. Since the killing of Jesus subsequently gave rise to Christianity as the "New Israel—the new Chosen," this process can only be finally fulfilled by the conversion of the remaining Jews, the adherents of the "Old Israel." Christian theologians might argue that there are variations among the churches and denominations about this process, but they all share it to a lesser or greater extent in their doctrines.

A Christian historian, Roy Eckhardt, in his study of the attitude of the Church toward the Jews, has explained that neither the Catholic nor the Protestant churches were prepared to accept a people who were not ready to embrace the true faith. They regarded the Church and truth as identical and their anti-Semitism was a reflection of the doctrine, which required them "to discriminate against those who refused to recognize that the Church possesses the Truth."[36] In Christian theology, in other words, it is inevitable that Jews should suffer and that their suffering should be documented, because this is the fundamental base of the evidence for the displacement: the transfer of the mantle of the Chosen to Christianity. Because of their sins, Christianity posits, Jews are an accursed people, their Temple was destroyed and they were condemned to dispersion and exile. The suffering of the Jewish people, according to the founders of Christianity, lies in their refusal to renounce Judaism and embrace the new faith. As shown in Chapter 7, the real divide in the attitudes of different Christian churches and theologians toward the State of Israel lie in their position on the chosenness of the Jews and their interpretation of the supercession theology.

For centuries, Christian activists developed the Jewish stereotypes, which entered religious teachings and popular consciousness. Saint Augustine, in the fourth century, created concepts that were to become a part of Church dogma for many centuries. The Augustine doctrine emphasized the condition of the Jews as a dispersed people, lacking both land and sovereignty, to illustrate why they were a rejected, accursed, and despised nation. The biblical heroes of the Jews were removed from the context of Jewish history leaving only the wicked ones, starting with Cain, to whom Augustine compares the Jews. The loss of Jewish sovereignty, according to Augustine, marked the transfer of divine favor from Judaism to Christianity.[37]

At the end of the fourth century, Christianity became the official religion of the Roman Empire and measures to humiliate the Jews were reinforced. The few privileges they had enjoyed were withdrawn; rabbinical jurisdiction over the Jewish community was abolished or seriously restricted. Jews were not allowed to proselytize and were forbidden to enter into sexual relationships with Christians. The Church officially declared that the Jews are a "wicked sect" and "abominable," while Christianity was the "venerable religion."

The Jews were allotted a special role by Christianity, to be eternal witnesses to their forefathers' crime of rejecting the divine message. This role sometimes protected the Jews against oppression, but at the same time it was the rationale for maintaining their status of humiliation because of their fundamental heresy. These two expressions of hatred were permanent features in the history of Jewish-Christian relations: a threat of annihilation for the Jews' crimes against Christ, and a need to maintain their inferior position so as to prove the transfer of election from the Jews to the Christians. The Christian imperative to obtain from the Jews confirmation that Jesus is the Messiah, and with that to affirm their displacement as the Chosen People, lies at the heart of the Church's two thousand years of anti-Semitism.

## Islam and the Chosen

As the early Christians had done before him, Mohammad started his campaign with a conscious effort to bring the Jews within the fold of Islam. Mohammad said at the outset that he had no intention of abrogating the Bible, neither the Old nor the New Testaments. The tenets of the new religion and the Quran were revealed to him by Allah (God) through the medium of the Angel Gabriel. At the same time, he traced his genealogy to Abraham through his son Ishmael, maintaining that Abraham belonged to neither Judaism nor Christianity, but was to be revered as the first expounder of monotheism. The Quran refers to the Jews numerous times as the "People of the Book" (together with the Christians). Mohammad tells the Jews (9:65–67), "Ye People of the Book, why dispute ye about Abraham. . . . Abraham was not a Jew nor yet a Christian; but he was upright, and bowed his will to that of Allah."[38]

According to Arab sources, some twenty Jewish tribes lived in and around the city of Medina. Their beliefs, contrasting sharply with the pagan idol worship of region's Arab tribes, were part of Mohammed's world and powerfully influenced him, especially their devotion to the concept of one God. Mohammed accepted the Jewish God and prophets and many Jewish practices, including initially the orientation of prayers toward Jerusalem. He adopted many of the Jewish dietary laws and based Islam on the uncompromisingly Jewish monotheistic belief.

Mohammed saw Abraham as the *progenitor* of Islam and himself as another Moses—who is mentioned in the Quran more than one hundred times.

But despite Mohammed's dramatic gesture toward the Jews, facing Jerusalem in prayer along with his followers for sixteen months, the Jewish tribes failed to convert. When he realized that the Jews were not going to join his new version of Judaism, he determined to establish a separate religion. From that point on relations with his Jewish neighbors deteriorated quickly, and after declaring that Mecca, not Jerusalem, was the holy city, in 628 CE Mohammed attacked the Jewish tribes, *dispossessing*, enslaving, exiling, and massacring them.[39]

Mohammad's initial attitude toward the Jews is of great interest, especially in our current period of such pervasive Muslim religious hatred. As described in the Quran, Mohammed praised the Jews. He referred to them as the "Chosen People" and to the Land of Israel as their "Promised Land." The Quran acknowledges the Jews' Covenant with God: "O Children of Israel! Remember my favor which I bestowed upon you and that I exalted you above all people"[40]; and "Allah made a covenant of old with the Children of Israel,"[41] and again: "Moses said unto his people: O my people! Remember Allah's favor unto you, how He placed among you prophets, and made you kings, and gave you that which He gave not to any other among the peoples. O my people! Go unto the holy land which Allah hath ordained for you."[42]

The Quran particularly exhorts the Children of Israel regarding the Land of Israel, telling them to "[d]well securely in the Promised Land."[43] God says, the Quran relates, that He has "settled the Israelites in a blessed land."[44] Needless to say, given the contemporary Arab campaign to deny any Jewish links to the Land of Israel, this and similar comments about the Jews and their land are nowhere to be found in the rhetoric of today's Muslim or Arab leaders. But the Quran goes further and recounts favors shown by God to Israel in delivering them "from the People of Pharaoh,"[45] and referring to events related in the Book of Exodus (the plagues and the miraculous parting the waters): "He divided the sea and saved you and has drawn Pharaoh's people within your very sight."[46] The Quran refers to Moses at Sinai where he stayed forty nights while the Children of Israel worshipped the golden calf. It emphasizes the Covenant between God and His Chosen People and relates the incidents in the desert: the provision of manna, the people's constant grumbling, the attempt by Moses to strike water from the rock, and other events on the Jews' journey toward the Land of Israel.

Though there are references to Jesus and Christianity in the Quran, it is clear that the major battlefield within the text itself, and probably the only one, is with the Jews. The Quran is very clear in reaffirming the Jewish narrative on the choosing in Sinai, including the legacy of the Promised Land: "And then Moses said to his people: 'O my people! Remember the favor of Allah bestowed upon you when He raised prophets among you and made you kings and gave you what He had not given to any other among the nations. O my people! Enter the holy land which Allah has prescribed for you and turn not on your backs for then you will turn back losers."[47]

As shown sura 5 of the Quran presents the Muslim doctrine of supersession, and the commentators explain that Islam is replacing "the backsliding of the Jews and Christians from their pure religions to which the coping stone was placed by Islam." What follows is referred to by traditional Islamic commentary as "the memorable declaration": "This day have I perfected your religion for you, completed my favor upon you, and have chosen for you Islam as your religion."[48] The verse puts it bluntly: the favor of Allah, which went initially to the Jews, has moved in its perfected form to Islam. The supersession of the Jews is also embodied in the text of the Quran, which reiterates how God bestowed the "special favor" to Israel and "preferred" them "to all others."[49] The Saudi edition, using traditional commentary, explains in its self-convincing tone that here "[t]he argument about the favors to Israel is thus beautifully rounded off, and we now proceed to the argument in favor of the Arabs as *succeeding* [my emphasis] to the spiritual inheritance of Abraham."[50] Ironically, in doing so, this commentary recognizes, unlike other interpretations, that the Jews were the first to follow Abraham as the spiritual founder of their religion.

All these details are recounted as a prelude for the transfer of the Covenant and the election of Islam in place of the Jews. The Jews did not deserve to be the Chosen People, and because of their sins they are condemned to "degradation in this world."[51] The Jews are accused in the Quran of falsehood, of distortion, and of being "corrupters of the scriptures."[52] For instance, the Jews of Eilath, as the Quran relates, not only broke the laws of the Sabbath but scornfully persisted in their wrongdoings; hence they were severed from society and "changed into detested apes."[53]

As a result, Allah removed the title from the Jews and bestowed it on Islam: "And remember, we took the covenant from the Children of Israel."[54] "Allah did aforetime take the covenant from the Children of Israel, and we appointed twelve chieftains among them . . . but because of their breach of their covenant we cursed them and made their hearts grow hard."[55]

Both Jews and Christians are referred to in the Quran as Peoples of the Book, sometimes together: "We gave Moses the Book and followed with a succession of messengers. We gave Jesus the son of Mary clear signs and strengthened him with the holy spirit."[56] But the Quran is unambiguous concerning the eventual fate of nonbelievers. Time and again, it calls for *jihad*, holy war, against the unbelievers and refers to both Jews and Christians, with epithets such as "infidels," "monkeys," and "pigs." The concept of the Chosen is also embodied in the role of the head of the Islamic community. For many centuries, an Islamic ruler referred to as *caliph*, a word that combines the meanings of "successor" and "deputy." As Professor Bernard Lewis explains Islam regarded Christianity as its rival for world domination early on because Christianity was also defined as both a religion and a civilization. The magnificent Dome of the Rock in Jerusalem, completed before the end of the seventh century, was meant to convey the clear message that Islam was the premier religion, just as the Dome so obviously overshadowed Jerusalem's Church of the Holy Sepulcher. Lewis points out that the message to the Jews and even more so to the Christians, was that their revelations, though once authentic, had been corrupted by unworthy custodians and were therefore superseded by the final and perfect revelation embodied in Islam. "Just as the Jews had been overcome and superseded by the Christians," Lewis writes, "so the Christian world order was now to be replaced by the Moslem faith and the Islamic caliphate." The message was again that "the Jews and later the Christians had gone astray and had followed false doctrines. Both religions were therefore superseded, and replaced by Islam, the final and perfect revelation in God's sequence." The verses on the coins and on the Dome of the Rock condemned the corruption of the true faith, and there was a direct message from the caliph to the Roman emperor: "Your faith is corrupted, your time has passed. I am now the ruler of God's empire on earth."[57]

Islam ambitions for world domination, which come as a natural corollary of their chosenness, are strongly rooted in the Quran and are amplified and elaborated in the Hadith. The world, in Muslim tradition, is divided into the House of Islam (Dar al-Islam), in which Muslim government rule and Muslim law prevails, and the rest is the House of War (Dar al-Harb), which is ruled and inhabited by the infidels who must submit to the Muslim rule and faith.[58] This kind of incendiary language is preached not only in the Middle East but also by Muslim leaders in America and Europe. Saudi-backed organizations in America speak of the "Islamic World Order" and issue the call to make Islam the dominant faith in America and to become "the only accepted religion on earth."[59] In Europe, Muslim militant leaders speak openly about *jihad* and the rule of Islam. In Britain they have spoken about "an Islamic flag hanging outside Number Ten Downing Street." In Geneva a local *imam* (the religious leader of the mosque) exhorted his followers to "impose the will of Islam on the godless society of the West," and another British Muslim preacher told his followers that "[o]ur Moslem brothers from abroad will come here one day and conquer and then we will all live under Islam in dignity."[60]

The treatment of both Jews and Christians under Islam was similar, meant to maintain their servile and humiliated status as underclasses lacking basic rights, to be treated with contempt and disdain. Since both religions were officially recognized, their adherents were considered to be *dhimmis* ("protected peoples"). While they were superior to the pagans and were free to practice their religious rites and organize their communities, they were required to pay a special poll tax for the privilege. Their inferior status also involved the wearing of a distinctive badge (the yellow badge originated in Baghdad before being adopted in Europe). Jews were not allowed to bear arms or ride horses; they were prohibited from constructing new synagogues.[61]

Under Islamic law, the attitude toward non-Muslims was based on arrangements that Mohammed had made with the Jewish tribes of the Hejaz, in the peninsula of Arabia. He had expected them to acknowledge his prophetic mission and join his faith. When they rejected his efforts "he waged *jihad* against the Jews of Medina, beat them, decapitated their men folk in the public square (save one, who converted), and divided their women, children, animals, and property up among his followers."[62] While the *dhimma* law protected Jews, the protection could be revoked at any moment, subjecting their lives and property to the will of their rulers.

There were periods of tolerance for Jews under Islam, and they were spared the consistent massacres and expulsions that characterized Christian Europe. However, even under Islam, Jews were attacked violently on many occasions. In Morocco and Muslim Spain in the eleventh century, thousands were massacred in riots—long before the horrors of the Crusades. "The so-called 'Golden Age,' when Jews played an active role in the cultural life of medieval Islamic Spain, was itself a myth invented by Jews in nineteenth-century Europe as a reproach to Christians, ironically taken up by Moslems in our own time as a reproach to the Jews."[63] Maimonides, considered the greatest Jewish thinker of the Middle Ages, was said to have enjoyed a close relationship with the Islamic authorities. But on the eve of the "Golden Age," he wrote about the suffering of the Jews under Islam in his famous "Epistle to the Jews of Yemen" (*Igeret Teiman*): "[T]he people of Ishmael, who persecute us severely, and who devise ways to harm us and debase us."[64] And further, "[i]t is on account of our many sins that God has hurled us amidst this nation of hostile Ishmael. . . . Never has a nation risen up that is more injurious to us than this people; nor one which has come to degrade us and decimate us and make hatred for us their chief intent."[65]

## Borrowing from the Chosen

While there is a wide recognition among scholars of Islam on the influence of Judaism on Islam, there is much less awareness to it among the general Muslim public. There is no comparable expression or sentiment of "Judeo-Christian" in Islamic-Jewish relations,[66] though the influence of Judaism on Islam is unquestionably more explicit and significant in theological terms than on Christianity. While Judaism plays a foundational, even parental, role in the development of Christianity, and consequentially contributed ideationally, morally, and materially to the evolution of Western society, the impact and rootedness of Judaism in Islam is profoundly more significant in terms of narrative, theology, and, most deeply, the notion of chosenness.

A reading of the Quran leaves a striking impression on how heavily the text refers to, and uses expressions and ideas derived from, the Jewish sources of his time. One finds many of the Old Testament stories, mainly concerning the children of Israel in the desert, reproduced in the Quran, sometimes in a precise fashion and in other cases expanded via folklore and fables extracted from the Talmud. As shown extensively in several academic studies (see later in this chapter), a significant number of the biblical accounts are reproduced in the Quran and sometimes garbed in their talmudic and midrash cloak.

In terms of the theological doctrine there is far more similarity between Islam and Judaism than between Christianity and Judaism. Judaism and Islam are closer and almost identical in their statement on the absolute unity of God, which Jews recite three times a day (twice in the morning) and Muslims in each of their five daily prayers. They have both a unique systems of religious law that is interpreted and refined by oral tradition, which can override the written laws. They both developed a logical system for deriving religious law from sacred texts, which allowed for the evolution of an extensive responsa literature (the rulings of rabbis under Jewish law in response to questions submitted to them in writing over the centuries). The Quran and the Hadith contain voluminous references, teachings, norms, ethics, and sayings that mirror, in style and structure, the development of Jewish religio-legal texts and traditions. Islam has also adopted the Jewish concept of God studying in heaven as a role model for how human beings should worship and behave.

Like Christianity, textual Islam does not hide the fact that several Jewish practices were adopted as part of its inception. Suras 2 and 3, which are considered by Islamic authorities to be at the heart of the Quran, drew mainly from Jewish sources, and there is a feeling of anti-Jewish polemics in many more verses. These polemics, mainly with the Jews of Medina, take a central place in the text highlighting how troubled was Mohammad by their attitudes. The historical conditions at the birth of Islam are definitive regarding both the presence of Jewish communities in and around Medina and that these Jews possessed biblical and rabbinic Jewish texts as well as a tradition of talmudic learning. The Quran makes no secret of Mohammad's attempts to win the adherence of the Jews; in fact, Islamic sources show that there was a great intimacy between him and the Jews. Muhammad ibn Ishaq ibn Yasar, who lived in the eighth century and collected the oral traditions that formed the basis of the first biography of Mohammad, wrote that "[i]t was the Jewish rabbis who used to annoy the apostle with questions and introduce confusion. The Quran would come down in reference to these questions of theirs."[67]

No wonder then that some of the founders of modern Islamic studies in Europe were Jewish scholars who had a strong background in Jewish religious texts and could therefore identify and appreciate the theological roots of Islam. Ignaz (Yitshaq Yehuda) Goldziher, who is often hailed as a founder of the academic scholarship of Islam, was born in 1850 into an Orthodox family, and as a brilliant student of the Talmud would later develop the distinction between the Koran and the Sunna (those religious actions that were instituted by the Islamic prophet Mohammad) just as he witnessed within Judaism between written and oral teachings. Similarly, as a learned Jew who knew the difference between halakah (Jewish law) and haggadah (the more legendary stories and ethics) he could more easily approach the layers of law, ethics and eschatological tenets within the Hadith. Goldziher regarded Judaism and Islam as kindred faiths and even viewed Islam as a "Judaized Meccan cult." He expressed as well his deep admiration to the philosophical aspects of Islam.[68]

Less known in the field of Islamic studies is the contribution of Rabbi Abraham Geiger who preceded Goldziher by more than a half of a century and published his dissertation on Islam in 1833. Abraham Geiger is better known as a German rabbi who laid the foundation of Reform Judaism, which claimed that in order to meet modernity Jews should adjust and sometimes reject outmoded Jewish laws and traditions. In Geiger's view, Judaism should be an evolving and changing religion that brings holiness into the modern world. As part of the reforms in Jewish law and worship, Geiger sought also to remove all nationalistic elements from Judaism, particularly the "Chosen People" doctrine.

However, before entering the enterprise of Reform Judaism, Geiger published a book on Islam under a title that strikes a dissonant chord in today's liberal circles and would be termed as insensitive and definitely not "politically correct." Geiger, who was born in a strictly Orthodox family, had a deep knowledge of the Bible and the Talmud; his handling of the sources and his careful analysis won him widespread praise among the handful of scholars then devoted to the academic study of Islam. The book gives a very clear and positive answer to the question raised in the title: *Did Muhammad Borrow from Judaism?*, but its modern English edition (1970), testifying to changes in sensitivities, was given the less provocative and rather neutral title, *Judaism and Islam.*[69]

Geiger's answer to the eponymous question is unequivocally positive, as he writes in the introduction, "It is assumed that Muhammad borrowed from Judaism, and this assumption, as will be shown later, is rightly based."[70] He concludes his work with an unambiguously straightforward claim: "Muhammad borrowed a great deal from Judaism"—most notably what he absorbed from the Jewish oral tradition—"he sometimes altered it to suit his purpose."[71]

Geiger's book was originally submitted as part of a contest at Bonn University asking for inquiry of the Jewish sources of the Quran. The young Geiger, twenty-two years old, won the prize and received his doctoral degree for it in 1834. A year later he published it "at the expense of the author," but it took more than sixty years for Geiger's contribution to appear in English translation, and with an astonishing impetus. The English translation (in 1896) by F. M. Young (from the Ladies' League in Aid of the Delhi Mission) was commissioned in India to help Christian missionaries in their "dealings with Muchammadans."[72] This is an interesting twist of the chosenness replacement approach. Perhaps, Christian missionaries did not think that Judaism in poor condition and dispersed at the end of the nineteenth century, would attract Muslims in India but rather thought that since Islam is theologically closer to Judaism than to Christianity it would be fitting to proselytize them to Christianity via Judaism.

Geiger's concept of borrowing is alien and even dangerous in today's clash with Islamists. Muslims would reject any concept of "borrowing" from Judaism, and any suggestion of "borrowing" would be considered a blasphemous absurdity. For a devoted Muslim, Islam cannot "borrow" because the Quran is "the repository of God's verbal communications to the Prophet."[73] The prophet is not a borrower but rather an innovator who simply presented a new revelation by God who gave up on His former unworthy custodians, those Chosen ones who had betrayed their Covenant with Him.

In comments made in an Islamic Web site the authors M. S. M. Saifullah and Imtiaz Damiel reject Geiger's assertion and other writers who are serving the aims of evangelical Christian missionaries who want to show "that the Qur'ân is a worthless book copied from the Bible and Mohammad being an imposter." The self-declared statement of the Web site called "Islamic Awareness" aims "to educate

Muslims about questions and issues frequently raised by Christian Missionaries and Orientalists [scholars of Islam]."[74]

Leaving semantics aside (borrowed versus revealed), the Quran still contains hundreds of references to the Jewish Bible. There are about a hundred direct references in the Quran to the Jews by name: either as "Jews" or as "children of Israel" or even as "those who followed the right path." About one-third of the verses revealed in Medina (the other part of the Quran was revealed in Mecca) deal with the Jews. The Quran includes stories on at least fifty different figures from the Jewish Bible.

Geiger shows how so many basic terms in Islam were borrowed from Judaism such as ark, Eden, hell, divine presence, rabbinic scholars, Sabbath, and so on, and he emphasizes that the basic concept of Islam, the unity of God, "must have been of Jewish rather than of Christian origin." [75]Also adopted is the notion of the end of the days and the Messiah. In comparison, there are very few ideas that were borrowed from Christianity and their religious impact is marginal. On many occasions Geiger shows why the Quran not only borrowed from the Hebrew Bible but also adopted the Mishnaic interpretation of Jewish law. Since Mohammad borrowed much by means of oral communication, he was not necessarily aware, according to Geiger, to differences between sacred texts and the later postbiblical sources that contain layers of midrash and exegesis.

Another more recent scholar and, Abraham I. Katsh from New York University, published a book in 1957 on Judaism in Islam that shows the heavy impact of biblical and talmudic sources on the Quran, covering most of the narratives that deal with the history of theology and monotheism. More even than Geiger, Katsh adopts a verse-by-verse approach, and the results are astonishing in showing the impact of rabbinical Judaism and the Hebrew Bible on Islam.[76]

At the conclusion of his thesis on the Jewish roots of Islam, Geiger dedicated a special appendix to explain what he viewed as a contradiction: if Mohammad has borrowed so much from Judaism why does the Quran contains so many anti-Jewish statements?[77]

Geiger in his soft style explains what is basically the most obvious explanations of Christian anti-Semitism: "Muhammad's aim was to bring about a union of all creeds, and no religious community stood more in the way of the attainment of this end that the Jews with their many cumbersome laws." However, he borrowed so much because "he loved the old Abraham customs and kept to them." Since the Jews annoyed and ridiculed him "he wished therefore to make a final separation from these hateful Jews, and to this end he established entirely different customs." And Geiger refers to those Arab sources (among the followers of Mohammad) who admitted that these changes were made in order "of abolishing resemblances to the Jews."[78] It is clear to conclude from Geiger's analysis that we have here the same "supersession complex" that we had witnessed in Christianity. It seems that the similarity to Judaism and more so the inherent dependence on it would make the Jews the worst enemies of Islam and the target of incitement and hatred.

Geiger claims, and this sounds logical, that several religious practices of Islam were made deliberately in direct opposition of the Jews in order to widen the gulf between the religions and to please the Arabs with some compromises. That is why, unlike Judaism, supper precedes prayer and why cohabitation with the wife on the night of the fast is permitted, as well as other changes removing Jewish dietary laws (besides the prohibition of swine).

In today's intellectual environment, a scholarly work such as this written by Abraham Geiger can hardly survive, though ironically Geiger was a liberal Jew and a reformer of the Jewish religion. Jewish critics such as Norman A. Stillman argue that Geiger tends to give exaggerated view of the Jewish contribution to the Quran, but he misses the point and fails to reject the premise that Judaism is the major source of inspiration on the philosophy and practices of Islam.[79] Even worse is the apologetic criticism against Geiger that imposes hypocritical postmodern values on the early nineteenth-century liberal and reform-minded Geiger. Typically William M. Brinner defines Geiger's title as "provocative" and calls instead for "extreme caution through the minefields of suspicion, misunderstanding, and hubris on both sides," and instead he suggests to adopt the contemporary academic fashion of "sophisticated realization of the complexity of historical development," which prefers to speak on interaction between the religions."[80]

When scholars change their role into diplomats and the academy follows the diplomatic golden rule of "constructive ambiguity," it is quite doubtful how can one maintain academic standards. The diplomatic and scholarly orientation is the self-declared motto in the book sponsored by the Institute of Islamic/Judaic Studies at the University of Denver with the aim to provide "a nonpolitical, neutral scholarly ground" to look for mutual influences. Diplomacy is a desired and well-intentioned goal for political purposes, but it can be a major impediment for a sincere and scholarly attempt to comprehend the religious background of conflicts and disputes. Brinner may be right in looking for expressions of Islamic influences on Jewish culture and even Jewish thought in the Middle Ages, but he is completely wrong in applying this principle on Geiger's research. Geiger deals with the origins of Islam where it is clear that there is no reciprocal influence but simply a borrowing process, some would say appropriation, with adjustments and distortions.[81]

Geiger cannot be blamed for belittling the originality of the other as Brinner suggested because the Quran himself is based on Judaic tenets, legacy and legendary, and not vice versa. Islam can claim to be a new and even the final revelation, but it cannot hide its own assertions on the chosenness of Judaism. Geiger's basic premises, and his unsophisticated walk "through the minefields of suspicion," are indeed missing today in the ongoing debate on the relations between Islam, Western civilization, Christianity, and Judaism. Geiger's thoughts on Islam from 1833 are more relevant and critical than many volumes of contemporary Middle East studies for our understanding of the most sensitive agenda the world faces today in the "clash of civilizations" (see last chapter) or in the Arab-Israeli conflict.

## Between Islam and Christianity

It is clear that throughout most of history Christianity was the most active and prolific force in spreading hatred of the Jews. This was part of the rivalry for the title of Chosen, because the Jews were an immediate threat since they were pre-sent *throughout the Hellenic world* and the Jewish origins of Christianity were undisputed. The challenge of Judaism was especially pointed because the new religion was created by a Jew, belonging to a Jewish family, and its apostles and central figures were practicing Jews. This may explain why the Christian obses-sion with the Jews is consistent, intensive, and comprehensive. Moreover, it is why Christianity devoted so much effort to developing a doctrine that would include accusations, a machinery of humiliation, and attempts to impose con-version.

There is also a theological difference between Christianity and Islam concern-ing God's revelations. Christianity, although it became a separate entity, refrained from declaring itself a new religion, but rather maintained that it was the "true Israel," basing itself on the previous revelations to the Jews. In brief, Christianity does not have a Covenant of its own with God. The Christians were chosen only to replace the former Chosen People, who had sinned and were therefore removed from their position. Unlike Islam, Christianity finds its legitimacy as well as its historic roots in Judaism and the Old Testament. For Christianity then, the challenge was how to prove the Jews guilty of crimes that would be serious enough to be condemned in the eyes of God. This is why the crucifixion of Jesus, in its most negative and horrific versions vis-à-vis the Jews, has been so central for the legitimacy of Christianity.

Islam, on the other hand, up until the twentieth century, felt less compulsion to justify its chosenness and to develop argumentation justifying its displacement of the Jews. Mohammad was an Arab, not a Jew, and he created the new religion of Islam in an Arab land. Consequently, although he borrowed a great deal from Judaism, the origins of Islam were less intertwined with and less troubled by asso-ciations with the older faith. Still, in the Quran hatred of the Jews is more pro-found than hatred of Christians. Generally, the Quran rejects both Peoples of the Book, whether Jew or Christian, and states clearly that believers should beware of both: "O ye who believe! Take not the Jews and the Christians for your friends and protectors . . . those in whose hearts is a disease."[82] But the Quran is unequivocal as to which is worse: "Strongest among men in enmity to the Believers wilt thou find the Jews and pagans; and nearest among them in love to the Believers wilt thou find those who say, 'We are Christians': because amongst these are men devoted to learning . . . and men who have renounced the world, and are not arrogant."[83]

It is clear from the Quran that Mohammad was deeply disappointed with the attitude of the Jews, whom he had so assiduously tried to attract to the new faith. They were for him the children of Abraham (the father of Arabs too), the people of Moses (his own predecessor), as well as the original Chosen of God. And the Jews had rejected Mohammad; that is, they had rejected the word of Allah that he had brought, an unforgivable offense.

There is a clear contradiction between the assertion in the Quran that God is not changing His word and the claim that the Jews are no longer His people. How can a devout Muslim accept changes or denial regarding the Jewish chosenness or their Promised Land when the Quran says, "Never think that Allah would fail His messengers in His promise."[84] The Quran, which tells at length the story of the Children of Israel in the desert, never denies God's promise of the Land of Israel to the Jews and their descendants and yet there is no hint even in the Quran that this land was to be given to the Arabs.

But in addition to such intimate issues between Mohammed and the Jews, early Muslims also acted from practical considerations. At the time of Islam's birth, Christianity was shaping its doctrines throughout Europe and the Eastern Roman Empire in conjunction with those who ruled a large part of the contemporary world. Jews, on the contrary, were a weak people who had been deprived both of their lands and their sovereignty. "Behold!" says the Quran. "Allah said; 'O Jesus! I will take thee and raise thee to myself and clear thee (of the falsehoods) of those who blaspheme. I will make those who follow thee superior to those who reject faith, to the Day of Resurrection."[85] The same message is emphasized in the commentaries on the Quran; the Christians are a preferred people, in contrast to the Jews who rejected both Jesus and Mohammed. The political and economic realities of the time reinforced a preference for the Christians and the condemnation of the Jews. This was not only a doctrinal issue, but a clear matter of expediency.

Traditional Islam found ways to accommodate the continued existence of the Jews, denigrating them, damning them, claiming to have taken the Chosen mantle from them, but at the same time acknowledging and protecting them. The twentieth and twenty-first centuries, though, have witnessed an abrupt change in Islam's approach. Islamic anti-Semitism has grown far more sophisticated and lethal. Increasingly, Islamic spokesmen have adopted Christian stereotypes such as blood libels, poisoning of wells by Jews, and racist theories. In its new manifestations of anti-Semitism, Islam has combined the *Protocols of the Elders of Zion* with Nazi theories and developed its own genocidal variety of hatred, in a concentrated and intensive effort that is all too reminiscent of Hitler's Germany.

In this the Chosen factor has become more dominant than it was previously. During the twentieth century, the Arabs confronted two critical challenges. On the one hand, they were humiliated by European colonialism. On the other, they faced a new adversary: the Jews and Zionism, which challenged the ancient and confirmed Muslim Arab belief in their own chosenness. The Arabs lost their sovereignty and faced the truly daunting prospect of modernity. In addition, they had now been defeated on the battlefield, not once but several times, by a small Jewish nation—which brought to the fore old rivalries for the title of the Chosen People, an issue long settled and ingrained in Muslim psychology.

Thus, the Jewish defeat of Arab armies in 1948, 1956, and in particular 1967 were far more than simply a blow to national honor and pride. Jewish successes opened a theological Pandora's box, sealed shut over thirteen hundred years ago with Islam's putative assumption of the Chosen designation. Many Arab and Muslim religious leaders perceived the reemergence of a strong Jewish state in the Holy Land as a blunt theological challenge. Islam had long treated the Jews as servile infidels who, according to the Quran, were "afflicted with humiliation and poverty" feeling "the wrath of God."[86] The renewal of this disgraced and down-trodden nation in their old Promised Land and Chosen City is thus an event fraught with deeply unsettling theological implications.

Under Muslim rule Jews were not allowed to bear arms or even ride horses; they were considered the epitome of cowardice.[87] The idea of this very people, whom Allah has humiliated, returning to the Holy Land by means of its own armed might is not something that can be easily accepted, or perhaps not accepted at all. To make matters worse, the great Enlightenment ideas of eman-cipation and human rights never reached the Arab world. So while the West has had time to adjust itself to the idea of competent and resourceful modern Jews, for the Arab world the sight came as a profound shock. This was a great deal more than just a cultural clash. It seemed and still seems to many a direct refutation of Quranic teachings (98:6): "The unbelievers among the People of the Book . . . shall burn forever in the fire of hell. They are the vilest of all creatures."[88]

In the 1968 Al-Azhar conference in Cairo, held at the most prestigious mosque and university of the dominant Sunni branch of Islam (often compared to the Harvard of the Islamic world), Islamic religious leaders and scholars from twenty-four countries produced a quasi-official position of Islam on the Jews. This document includes a direct attack on the alleged Jewish distortion of God's initial revelation to Islam and on the Jewish opposition to Mohammad. The con-ference reinterpreted and indeed misrepresented the historical sources, trans-forming them into proofs of the Jews' essential evil. Several religious leaders there spoke about the Jews in the most extreme language with special references to the terrible sins and crimes of the forefathers of today's Jews who told lies about Allah. The Jews were defined as "the worst enemies of Islam," "the best friends of the Satan, . . . hostile to all human values in this world, a curse that spread among the nations standing "behind all conspiracies and corruption in the world"[89] This Al-Azhar document made the Jews not just the humiliated *dhimmis* of the past, but rather a challenge to the primacy of Islam.

In his book *Our Battle With the Jews* published posthumously in 1970, Sayyid Qutb, the founding ideologue of radical Islam blames the Jews for all types of perversions threatening the religious values of Islam: "Behind the athe-ist, materialist conception is a Jew [Marx]; behind the bestial sexual conception, a Jew [Freud]; behind the destruction of the family and the disruption of the holy bonds of society, a Jew [Durkheim]," and his editor adds a fourth, Jean-Paul Sartre, making him a Jew for this purpose, as the inspirer of the literature of dis-integration and ruin."[90]

Today's Muslims, and not just the so-called Islamists, draw openly the simi-larities between the Jews in the Quran and contemporary Jews by using the most derogative and deadly anti-Jewish expressions cited in their holy book. For instance, just one of endless of quotes, the *imam* of the al-Haraam mosque, the most important mosque in Mecca, Sheikh Abd Al-Rahaman Al-Sudayyis called Allah to annihilate the Jews and referring to them as "the scum of the human race" speaking on the "current behavior of the *brothers of apes and pigs*, their treachery, violations of agreements, defiling of holy places . . . is connected with deeds of their forefathers during the early period of Islam."[91]

These attitudes are certainly not new, but they are more pervasive and wide-spread today. Since the establishment of the State of Israel, Islamists and jihadis have recycled the refrain, "*Khaibar, Khaibar ya yahood, jaish Mohammad sawfa ayud*" (Remember Khaibar, O Jews, the Army of Mohammad is coming back). This Quranic episode about the Jewish tribes in Khaibar, a town north to Mecca, was often used by militant Islam, and not only the extremists and terrorists. This episode defines the current war against Israel and the Jews in Quranic terms. Significantly, this historic clash of Mohammad with the Jews was entirely about the replacement of the Chosen: The Jews were accused for betraying agreements made with the Prophet and continued with their adamant refusal to convert to Islam. Many Jews were killed, many were forced to convert, and the rest fled.

### Post-Holocaust Doctrine on the Chosen:

In June 1943, while the Nazis were executing their "Final Solution" of the Jewsih question Pope Pius XII reaffirmed the doctrine of supersession in his encyclical Mystici Corporis Christi saying "the New Testament took the place of the Old Law which had been abolished . . . [this]effected a transfer . . . from the Synagogue to the Church."[92] Even after the Holocaust, the Church authorities were very tardy in daring to question its anti-Jewish doctrines and attitudes. In the view of many historians, the leading anti-Semitic institution in Europe in 1945, one in which anti-Jewish doctrines were deeply embedded on solid histor-ical foundations, was the Roman Catholic Church."[93]

It was only in 1965, that the Catholic Church, in the famous Nostra Aetate declaration of Vatican II, convened by Pope John XXIII, modified its doctrine removed the "blame" from "the Jews of today" and even from those who were alive at the time of the Crucifixion. However, the conservative bishops rejected a draft proposal that explicitly and unequivocally declared that "the Chosen People cannot without injustice be termed a deicidal race." They also objected to, and won, the elimination of references to past persecutions by the Church and Christianity's responsibility for them. The document was of historical impor-tance in changing the Church's attitudes toward the Jews, but it reiterated its position on the Chosen: "Although the Church is the new People of God, the Jews should not be presented as repudiated or cursed by God".[94]

Typically, Nostra Aetate starts by referring to both Abraham and Moses (the major agents of the Chosen), recalling "the spiritual bond linking the people of the New Covenant with Abraham's stock" and more directly stating that

> The Church of Christ, recognizes that according to the divine mystery of salvation, the origins of the Church's faith and her election are already found among the Patriarchs, Moses, and the Prophets. The Church professes that all who believe in Christ—Abraham's sons according to faith—are included in the same patriarch's call and likewise that the salvation of the Church was mystically foreshadowed by

the Chosen People's exodus from the land of bondage. The Church, therefore, cannot forget that she received the revelation of the Old Testament through the people with whom God in His inexpressible mercy designed to establish the ancient covenant.[95]

*Nostra Aetate* opened the door for a revitalized process of dialogue between Christianity and Judaism, and this time, despite many difficulties and crises, the terms of the debate were more equal and basically different from the medieval disputations. The Jewish side in the dialogue was composed of members of an international umbrella group of Jewish organizations, and their counterpart in the Vatican was the Commission for Relations with the Jews, which was established in 1970. Over time, the teachings of Vatican II have permeated the Catholic hierarchy, with the message that the Church no longer denies the validity of Judaism or claims that it is a "fossilized faith."[96]

Pope John XXIII went even further when composed a prayer prior to his death in which he departed from traditional Christian teaching and inaugurated a process of taking responsibility for a more positive reference to the Chosen People: "We realize now that many, many centuries of blindness have dimmed our eyes, so that we no longer see the beauty of Thy Chosen People and no longer recognize in their faces the features of our firstborn brother. We realize that our brows are branded with the Mark of Cain. . . . Forgive us the curse which we unjustly laid on the name of the Jews. Forgive us that, with our curse, we crucified Thee a second time."[97]

Pope John Paul II made more progress than any of his predecessors with regard to the Vatican's relations with the Jews, though he was more restrained on the doctrinal aspects. He will be remembered for his policy changes that led to a remarkable number of creative and path-finding declarations—on the Holocaust, on anti-Semitism, in restoring the historical recognition of the primacy of the Jewish religion, on recognition and relations with the State of Israel, and finally for his historic trip to Israel in March 2000, which gave clear recognition of Israel sovereignty, with his visits to the Jewish holy places and the Yad Vashem Holocaust Memorial in Jerusalem. However, as we will see later, the attitude of Pope John Paul II to the Holocaust and Judaism are still under the shadow of the Church's displacement doctrine.

Early on in his pontificate, which began in 1978, John Paul II indicated that he intended to embark on a change of church policy towards the Jews. He did this by dealing directly with the question of the Chosen by emphasizing that the Covenant between God and the Jewish people was neither broken nor superceded, because God does not renege on his promises. In a historic visit to the Travestere Synagogue of Rome in 1986, he referred to Judaism as "our elder brother in faith."[98]

Judaism was defined by John Paul as "the religion that is closest to our own—that of the people of God of the Old Testament" and "the New Covenant . . . is rooted in the vocation of Abraham, in God's Covenant with Israel at Sinai, and in the whole heritage of the inspired prophets."[99] In this new attitude, John Paul illustrated how a change of policy can lead to a more selective reading of the texts and how new interpretations of Christian history should determine contemporary relations with the Jews. As a result of the new thinking that he proposed, Catholics today speak openly of the Jewishness of Jesus, and there is more emphasis on teaching the Old Testament and the Hebrew language.

The Pope has also explained how Jewish suffering is related to the Chosen concept: "This extraordinary people continues to bear signs of its divine election. I said this to an Israeli politician once and he readily agreed, but was quick to add, 'If only it could have cost less!'"[100]

But it seems that even a Pope who expresses such progressive views on Judaism could not or did not choose, to deny the replacement theory. After demonstrating the changes in policy and the recognition of historical mistakes, the Pope returns to the traditional Christian desire concerning the conversion of the Jews: "Perhaps because of this, Israel has become more similar to the Son of Man, who, according to the flesh, was also a son of Israel. . . . The New Covenant has its roots in the Old. The time when the people of the Old Covenant will be able to see themselves as part of the New is, naturally, a question to be left to the Holy Spirit. We, as human beings, try only not to put obstacles in the way (and continue) the dialogue between Christians and Jews."[101]

In September 2000, the Vatican issued another document, known as Dominus Iesus. This document was a reminder that the old dogmas still persisted, but under a new guise. The document recognized the "equal personal dignity" of every representative of a non-Catholic denomination in interreligious dialogue, but it stressed that the Roman Catholic Church is the "instrument for salvation of all humanity."[102] The author of the document, Cardinal Ratzinger, currently Pope Benedict XVI, explained that "Catholics do not want to impose Christ on the Jews, but they are waiting for the moment when Israel will also say yes to Christ."[103] Also, as shown by Dr. Sergio Minerbi, the Pope's letter, *Dominum et vivificantem* written on May 18, 1986, once more raises the question about who was responsible for the death of Jesus, and it again pins the blame on the Jews. However, in the Catechism of 1995 there is a return to the more enlightened language of 1965. So, overall, the record of the Vatican is mixed and confusing.[104]

Pope John Paul II also drew a clear division regarding the theological relations between Judaism and Islam. He said Judaism is "the religion which is closest to our own" while the theology of Islam "is very distant from Christianity."[105] God in Islam, as explained by the Pope, is ultimately beyond our world of comprehension and is therefore a religion without hope of redemption. The Quran has reduced the divine revelation, unlike the Old Testament where God speaks "about Himself . . . through the Prophets," and in the New Testament, "through His Son." In this context, it should be remembered that according to Jewish tradition, God spoke on Mount Sinai directly to His people without intermediaries. His successor, Benedict XVI, regards only Christianity and Judaism as a "faith" and his remarks linking Islam to violence in September 2006 ignited protest and riots around the world.[106]

Evidently Mel Gibson did not consult the American Catholic bishops' guide-lines, or perhaps he deliberately intended to show in *The Passion of Christ* that he takes the anti-Semitic text of the New Testament at face value. The American bishops referred to the accounts of Jesus' death and crucifixion in the gospels with clear doubts, implying that some of the facts might have been fabricated: "[I]t is necessary to remember that the Passion narratives do not offer eyewitness accounts or a modern transcript of historical events, but rather were twisted by the theological 'lenses' of each individual author of the Gospels who wrote his piece according to the perceived needs and emphases of his particular community at the end of the first century, after the split between Jews and Christians was well under way."[107]

How can the issue of chosenness be removed from the agenda so as to allow dialogue and a subsequent improvement in relations? This stumbling bloc is included in a statement published by a Jewish group by the name *Dabru Emet* ("Speak the Truth" a phrase taken from the Book of Zechariah), devoted to the cultivation of Jewish-Christian relations, which summarized "twenty one cen-turies of oppression" by Christianity. The statement was part of an ongoing dia-logue that led to a joint statement signed by a hundred and fifty rabbis and Jewish scholars from the United States, Canada, the United Kingdom, and Israel. This states, among other things, that "[r]eligious hatred of the Jews was based on two major theological beliefs: blaming all Jews, past and present, as responsible for the execution of Jesus Christ; the supersessionist or displacement theology, which relegates Judaism to an inferior position relative to Christianity.[108] It is evi-dent that any serious effort to improve relations and the dialogue between Jews and Christians must involve confronting the issue of the Chosen.

## Toynbee: "Bewildered by the Jews"

The eminent British historian, Arnold Toynbee, was a conspicuous example of another type of attitude toward the Jews: impressed by, but lacking in all sympa-thy for their achievements. Not openly anti-Semitic, he nevertheless warned against what he perceived to be Jewish double loyalty. Unable or unwilling to appraise Jewish existence in rational terms, Toynbee, in a celebrated public debate at McGill University in 1961 with Jacob Herzog, then Israeli ambassador to Canada, referred to the Jews as a "fossilized nation," demanding that if Western civilization wants to survive it must be emancipated from "Judaic self-centered-ness."[109] The Canadian debate was a replay of the disputations of the Middle Ages. At the same time, he spoke about the gifts of the Jews and their role in spreading their essential truth to the world.

As a historian who dealt with the broad sweep of civilizations, Toynbee failed to formulate a grand theory that would fit the Jewish case, therefore his argu-ments are full of contradictions. On one hand, he maintained that the Jews are turning themselves into Gentiles and, on the other, he suggested that the Jews have a role "to convert the world." Discussing Christianity and Islam, Toynbee posited that "it is an extraordinary thing that twice in history the Jews have allowed outsiders to run away with their religion and spread it over the world." And he asks rhetorically, "Does not the real future of the Jews and Judaism lie in spreading Judaism in its authentic form, rather than in its Christian or Moslem form, over the world? After all, the Jews must have a more authentic form of Jewish monotheism than that which the Christians or the Moslems have. Is not this the Jews' future gift to the world?"[110]

In the twelfth volume of his monumental *A Study of History*, entitled "Reconsiderations," we perceive how Toynbee attempted to present a sophisticated approach to the Jewish issue. But even his "grand theory" is full of inconsistencies and the "fossil" metaphor failed to address the historic saga of the Jews. In *A Study of History*, Toynbee retraces the stories of twenty-one civilizations that rose and fell during the course of history. He maintains that the fact that the Jews were able to maintain a national identity while lacking political independence or even a common language and dispersed in every corner of the world, is an irrational phenomenon that leaves every historian bewildered.[111]

However, it was Toynbee, more than any other non-Jewish historian (and even Jewish historians), who struggled in his secular, historical approach, with the concept of the Chosen People. A careful reading of *A Study of History* shows that behind his "fossil" metaphor there is a very simple concept that Toynbee utilizes more than his fellow historians—that of the Chosen. Time and time again, with all the criticism and cynicism that he can conjure up, the concept of the Chosen emerges in Toynbee's writings as the crucial key to an understanding of Jewish theology, history, nationality, and the survival of the Jews in the Diaspora. Moreover, he goes even further in using the Chosen concept as the driving force in the history of humankind. He argues convincingly, that half of humanity— the Christians and Muslims—are driven by their rivalry with the Chosen People—the Jews and by their claim of having replaced them. Toynbee, inadvertently, emerges as a latter-day Balaam (the Gentile prophet who, in the book of Numbers, was commissioned to curse Israel but ended up blessing it [see next chapter]), who provides us with one of the most cogent analyses of Jewish existence and its relations with the other monotheistic faiths. In his view, the case of the Jews illustrates the relativity of the interpretation of history, since the Jews "have told their own story from the standpoint of a self-proclaimed Chosen People in whose eyes all other human beings are Gentiles."[112] At the same time, Toynbee can hardly blame the Jews for what both Christianity and Islam accepted, namely that the Jews were elected by God as the Chosen People. Therefore, in the same breath he has to admit that "[i]n the Christian-Moslem half of the present day world, this Jewish standpoint has been accepted . . . in regard to Jewish history in the Pre-Christian, or, alternatively, the Pre-Moslem, age."[113]

Toynbee argues that both Christianity and Islam have accepted "uncritically," the Jewish version of history. The Muslims, like the Christians before them, accepted the thesis that the "Torah is the word of God," but when the Jews pointed out to Mohammad that he had misunderstood some of the biblical stories, he blamed them for "falsifying their own holy scriptures." Toynbee states that "[l]ike Christianity, Islam presupposes Judaism and could never have come about had Judaism not been in existence already."[114] Mohammad presented his people with the same type of God that the Jews already had: "Besides being the God of the Universe, he was to be the national God of the Arabs. Islam was to be a revival of the pure religion of Abraham, and this time 'the Chosen People' of Abraham's lineage were to be the Arab offspring of his son Ishmael instead of the Jewish offspring of his son Isaac." Both religions developed their own versions of replacement, and in the words of Toynbee both "accept, in principle, the Jews' belief in the divine inspiration of the Torah and the consequent belief in the Jews' special status as the recipients of this divine revelation. On the other hand, the tables have been turned on the Jews by the Christians and the Moslems in their appraisal of Jewish history since the beginning of the Christian or, alternatively, the Islamic era."[115]

Toynbee admits several times that his own Christian upbringing limits his objectivity in analyzing the nature of Jewish religion and its history. He also admits that perhaps the choice of the term "fossil" "may not have been a felicitous one for conveying the historical fact that I wanted to describe." At the same time, he says that one cannot ignore the impact of Jewish history after the advent of Christianity and Islam, because the Jews refused to disappear and survived as a persistent minority in both Christian and Muslim environments, making "a deep mark on both Christian and Islamic history as living Jews and not merely as dead Jewish forerunners of Christianity and Islam. Thus the Jews have not ceased to count, even in terms of Christian and Islamic history; and *a fortiori* they have not ceased to count in terms of their own history."

Toynbee rejects the perception that Judaism did not develop after the advent of Christianity, although he admits that his own Christian education in childhood made him less objective. On the contrary, he says, the completion of the Jerusalem Talmud by the end of the fourth century CE and the Babylonian Talmud a hundred years later, suggests the opposite. The fact is, he points out, Jews were able to survive many ordeals and disasters and successive pressures from Christianity and Islam. This was achieved only because of stubborn Jewish insistence on preserving their distinctive national identity so as to remain Jewish under all circumstances.[116]

Everything that Toynbee himself maintains demonstrates that his term "fossil" was misplaced, both in the Jews' desire to cling to their own identity and in maintaining their unique lifestyle in the Diaspora. This stubbornness also demonstrated the desire to return to their own land and to re-establish there a state that would embrace "the whole of Eretz Israel (The Land of Israel)." He refers to the "Post-exile Jewish Diaspora as one of the most successful examples of a community able to preserve its identity and vitality in spite of penalization, persecutions, and massacres—creating a model for mankind as a whole as a 'wave of the future.'"[117] Toynbee quotes the Israeli historian, Jacob Talmon, who explained how this "traumatic twist" in Judaism helped to sustain the belief in chosenness despite the constant onslaughts "of national disaster and exile."[118]

Even more explicitly, Toynbee says that the Jews succeeded in maintaining "their distinctive national identity" for more than twenty-five hundred years without the benefit of a political framework of a state with a territorial basis. By clinging to the concept of a "Chosen People," the Jews kept the sense of a national mission and maintained it even after losing their statehood

The real denunciation of Toynbee was actually written one hundred years earlier by a Jewish scholar on the history of religions, Nachman Krochmal (1785–1840) who wrote, leading on from Maimonides, *A Guide for the Perplexed of This Time*, showing the uniqueness of Jewish history, which, unlike that of other nations and civilizations, undergoes a cycle of rise and decline time and again. This cycle began with Abraham, rose to a zenith under Solomon and the First Temple, and reached a nadir with the destruction of the Temple and the subsequent exile five hundred years later. But despair in Jewish history does not imply fossilization, nor does it imply disappearance. At such low points, some Jews may think that the Jewish enterprise is over, and if God's will is defeated they should adopt assimilation. Others do not surrender but find solace in prayer while awaiting redemption. Unlike other civilizations, such as ancient Egypt, Greece, and Rome, which experienced only one cycle of birth, apogee, and decline, the Jewish people never dies; they just keep repeating the cycle and this is the best possible proof of God's guiding hand in Jewish history.[119]

## Other Observers

Conflicting attitudes to the Jewish people has characterized many Gentile observers in different places and throughout different periods. They are impressed by the uniqueness of the Jewish experience, but at the same time they regard it as a potential threat. Mark Twain (1835–1910), recorded his impressions of the Jews:

[The Jew] has made a marvelous fight in this world, in all the ages, and has done it with his hands tied behind him. He could be vain of himself, and be excused for it. The Egyptians, the Babylonian, and the Persian rose, filled the planet with sound and splendor, then faded to dream-stuff and passed away: the Greek and the Roman followed, and made a vast noise, and they are gone; other peoples have sprung up and held their torch high for a time, but it burned out, and they sit in twilight now, or have vanished. The Jew saw them all, beat them all, and is now what always was, exhibiting no decadence, no infirmities of age, no weakening of his parts, no slowing of his energies, no dulling of his alert and aggressive mind. All things are mortal but the Jew; all other forces pass but he remains. What is the secret of his immortality?[120]

When it comes to the wisdom of the Jews, Twain made some astonishing comments that, had they been made by a Jew, would have been considered as sheer racism: "The difference between the brain of the average Christian and that of the average Jew—certainly in Europe—is about the difference between a tadpole's and an archbishop's. It is a marvelous race—by long odds the most marvelous race that the world has produced."[121] But herein exactly lies the thin border between philo-Semitism and anti-Semitism. Mark Twain is full of admiration for the Jews for their brains, but does not want them to accumulate more power. This is why Twain, like many other Christians, would have preferred to maintain the Jews in a position of inferiority, lacking, for instance, instruments of power and sovereignty. He was very concerned about Jewish visions of the ingathering of exiles—namely Zionism, and he reacted to Herzl's plans in *Harper' Magazine*: "If that concentration of the cunningest brains in the world was going to be made in a free country. . . . I think it would be politic to stop it. It will not be well to let that race find out its strength. If the horse knew theirs, we should not ride any-more."[122]

Another interesting Christian thinker is Nicholas Berdyaev (1874–1948), a Russian philosopher who was influenced by the Catholic Leon Bloy, and who struggled to develop a coherent theory that would reconcile his admiration of the Jews with the deep-rooted Christian anti-Semitism that he had absorbed in his religious upbringing as a child. Since Berdyaev was opposed to Communism and Bolshevism, he was deported by the Soviet authorities in 1922 as one of a group of outstanding Russian scientists and philosophers. After three years in Berlin he moved to Paris, where he became one of the Russian philosophers best known in the West. An important dimension of his thinking is his writings on the Jews, which focused on the mystery of their existence (see following chapter) and the complexity of Christian attitudes toward them. In general, Berdyaev held a deep admiration for the Jews and the very fact of their existence that, in his view, defied all theories and explanations. But at the same time he reflects, particularly in his early writings, on the Christian resentment of the Jews because of Jewish treatment of Jesus as just another Jew. Nevertheless, Berdyaev makes a strong case against hatred and persecution of the Jews, warning against the rise of anti-Semitism.

Jews, Berdyaev explained in 1938, cannot be a normal nation: "Israel is a people with an exceptional religious destiny, and it is this which determines the tragic element in its historic destiny. How could it be otherwise? God's Chosen People, who at one and at the same time gave us the Messiah and rejected him, could not have an historic destiny like that of other people. . . . Christians are bound to acknowledge the election of the Jewish people, but they do so most often against their will and try as much as possible to forget it."[123]

Paul Johnson, the distinguished British writer and historian, is an outstanding exception because he combines what other Gentiles writers missed: an admiration of the Jews, deep compassion for their persecution by Christianity, and above all the ability to integrate the history of the Jews into a coherent structure and theory. In order to overcome the abnormal features and mysterious ingredients in Jewish history, he takes the concept of the Chosen and uses it as a part of the Jewish saga. Johnson who wrote a monumental history of the Jewish people argues that "no people has ever insisted more firmly than the Jews that history has a purpose and humanity a destiny." Unlike Toynbee, Johnson did not try to insert the history of the Jews into a straitjacket of some grand theory of civilization. However, he claims that by studying nearly four thousand years of Jewish history, one can touch upon many moral and philosophical questions concerning the meaning of history and the role of the human race in history. As a Christian, Johnson learned that the New Testament had replaced the Old, and therefore he decided to write about the "people who had given birth to my faith."[124]

According to Johnson, the history of Western civilization and mankind in general cannot be understood without studying the history of the Jews. In every experience, including in their suffering, the Jews have this role of "being a pilot-project for the entire human race." The State of Israel poses a dilemma to all mankind because it was "founded to realize a humanitarian ideal, discovering in practice that it must be ruthless simply to survive in a hostile world. . . . We all want to build Jerusalem. . . . It seems to be the role of the Jews to focus and dramatize these common experiences of mankind, and to turn their particular fate into a universal moral."[125]

Though Johnson's book is rich with the history and analysis of the three great religions, he deliberately avoids the religious debate about the identity of the Chosen People because if the perception is so powerful, the historian must relate to it as a fact. "The Jews believed they were a special people with such unanimity and passion, and over so long a span, that they became one. They did indeed have a role because they wrote it for themselves. Therein, perhaps, lies the key to their story."[126]

# CHAPTER 4

# Global but Apart

God made charity with the Children of Israel by dispersing them among the nations.

—Talmud, *Pesachim* 87)

Jewry exists in the world with a single purpose, that of proving to all peoples the existence of national, as well as religious mystery. . . . The Jews have a mission to fulfill in world history, and this mission goes beyond all national missions. It speaks of an existence broader than the national one.

—Nicholas Berdyaev)[1]

God made the Jews His "peculiar people . . . by many curious rites and customs [He] marked us out from all other nations, so that we cannot at the same time mingle with them and yet be Him . . . we must exist alone . . . [this is] the great and holy essence of our law.

—Benjamin Disraeli, on David Alroy,
the Jewish crusader of the twelfth century[2]

## The Mission of the Jews

The Talmud's statement on Jewish dispersion is an intellectual attempt to reconcile what can be seen as conflicting elements of the Chosen. On one hand, the "charity" that God gave to the Jews is basically a safety measure, so they will not be forced to live under a regime that may become hostile and persecute them. Since the Jews often faced physical threats, it was their dispersion that enabled them to survive. When one community is in distress, another that is stronger and safer, can provide succor. A more universal approach is posited in the commentary that the Jews have to be dispersed because they have a special mission to fulfill the prophecy of Isaiah and provide a "Light unto the Nations."[3] This is a clear assignment of the Chosen, as God tells Abraham, "All the nations of the earth shall bless themselves by your descendants, because you have obeyed my command,"[4] and later to Jacob, "[A]nd you shall spread out powerfully westward, eastward, northward and and southward; and all the families of the earth shall bless themselves by you and by your offspring."[5]

While Jews acknowledge in their prayers that they were exiled because of their sins, they also developed a sophisticated sense of "Diasporism" and made it part and parcel of their Chosen mission. This is another dimension of the Jewish paradox: the Chosen People has a Chosen land, yet at the same time, it has a special dual mission: to be the Chosen both in the Diaspora and in its own land at the same time. This is a condition with no precedent or parallel among the nations, and that is why it does not fit any existing theory concerning the human experience, as it says in the Bible, "[A]nd who is like you the people of Israel, one nation on earth."[6]

Christians and Western scholars recognize that the Jews are the remnant of a once great nation that had accepted the special mission given to them by God. But it is much more difficult for nonreligious rationalists, among them many Jews, to explain the underlying mystery—how did the Jewish people last so long? Many observers agree that there is more than a grain of mystery in the Jewish existence, which defies the rules of regular history. This mystery cannot be resolved by rational analysis, but clearly the unique condition of the Jews is intimately intertwined with the concept of the Chosen, or at least, with the perception of the Chosen.

Most rabbis did not expand much on the complexity of the universal mission of the Jews. In exile and under oppression, or at best under conditions of discrimination and prejudice, Jews in the Diaspora did not elaborate on the mission of a "Light unto the Nations." It seems from the context in Isaiah, that the "Light unto the Nations" is not necessarily an assignment for the end of the days but an active duty against idolatry and the oppression of human beings. It speaks about the Gentiles in the days of Cyrus. A "Light unto the Nations" is, therefore, part of the mission of the Chosen, maybe part of the imposed mission, the burden. As Isaiah speaks on behalf of God, "My Chosen People. I fashioned this people for myself that it might declare my praise."[7] It is also clear that Orthodox rabbis in general did not develop a coherent approach concerning the contribution of Jews to the general causes of mankind. There are, of course, some references in the Bible to the universal aspects of Judaism, but they are in fact virtually nonexistent in rabbinical literature. The secular contribution of Jews to society in general and their high profile and achievements in different fields of life, is not a subject of traditional Jewish writings. Many Orthodox rabbis regarded emancipation as a threat to their authority and a prelude for assimilation.

There are, however, a few rabbis who experienced themselves brutal expulsion or confronted the influence of foreign cultures who explained Jewish dispersion as part of the mission of the Chosen. Rabbeinu Bachya (1263–1340) from Spain explained that the dispersion of the Jews is essential for all mankind because it is the task of the Jews to disseminate among the nations the knowledge of the laws and teachings of God.[8] Similarly, five hundred years later, Rabbi Samson Raphael Hirsh in Frankfurt, explained that dispersion is part of the mission of the Jews because "God removed them from upon their soil . . . and He cast them to another land,"[9] with the clear goal that they should continue to serve God there.[10]

Maimonides said that Jews should be proactive in weaning non-Jews from their false gods, namely the pagans.[11] Another medieval sage, Ovadia Sforno, wrote that being a "kingdom of priests" means "to instruct all of mankind to call in unison on the name of the Lord and serve him with one accord."[12] In *The Kuzari*, Judah Halevi wrote,

> The dispersion of Israel was a divine arrangement in order to spread among the nations of the earth the light of his spiritual possessions. Israel is like unto a seed of grain that is imbedded in the ground, remains invisible for a time, seems changed into its constituting elements, and retains no trace of its original form; but after a time it begins to germinate and assumes again its original form, throws off the distorting integuments, refines its elements and changes them in accordance with its nature until it gradually reaches its highest point of development, to be recognized by Christianity and Islam.[13]

Within this framework Halevi referred to the Jewish mission of dispersion as part of its suffering, to be accepted with humility and patience. The Jews, Halevi said, are the only people left from the ancient world because they are servants of God the sufferings of whom atone for all the sins of the world. It is precisely the misery of the Jewish condition that testifies to its mission. Rabbi Kook, who wrote at the beginning of the twentieth century, also referred to the mission of spreading the truth about God to mankind in exile. This is why halakah was created to keep the Jews in a state of dispersion. The success of Christianity and Islam proves, in his view, the degree of spiritual influence of the Jewish people.

Isaac Ben Judah Abravanel (1437–1508) wrote about the two dimensions of dispersion: security and the spiritual mission. His view has special significance because of his background, which combined scholarship with statesmanship. Abravanel was a philosopher and leader of Spanish Jewry at the time of the Expulsion and wrote a comprehensive commentary on the Bible. In his comments to Isaiah 52:13, he explains that while exile and dispersion brought suffering to the Jews, it is part of their mission to uphold the Jewish religion with pride and to be prepared to debate it with the Gentiles without apology. He argued that with its spiritual powers the Jewish people will succeed "to bring nations under the divine . . . and will remove their false beliefs" and that the Jews will not be deterred even under great Gentile pressure. In Deuteronomy 32:26, it is written, "I had said, I will scatter them, I will cause their memory to cease from man." Abravanel maintained that the Jews were scattered because of the danger involved in concentrating them in one place. By way of example, he suggests that Troy was destroyed together with all its citizens by the Greek army, because they were gathered together, unlike the Jews who, thanks to God's charity, were dispersed. Abravanel concludes that when God did take care of this dispersion, the kings of Britain and France destroyed all trace of Jews in their lands.[14]

Secular Jewish writers like the British philosopher George Steiner, argue that the true mission of the Jews is to be found in their exile. The Jews are guests among the nations, as aliens, refugees—restless and dispossessed. Only then, outside their homeland, can the Jews fulfill their role as the moral conscience of the nations and their cultural vanguard, as prophets who deliver lofty human ideals.[15]

In the Jewish Reform movement, there was a clear attempt to move away from traditional Jewish distinctiveness and to concentrate on other aspects of the Chosen. In the Pittsburgh Platform, which was adopted in 1885, the Reform Jews indicated that they did not wish to be a nation apart, in fact they did not wish to be a nation at all. Nevertheless, the concept of chosenness is central to them too, but in a very universal fashion: "We recognize, in the modern era of universal culture of heart and intellect, the approaching of the realization of Israel's great messianic hope for the establishment of the kingdom of truth, justice and peace among all men. We consider ourselves no longer a nation, but a religious community. . . . We are convinced of the utmost necessity of preserving the historical identity with our great past. Christianity and Islam being the daughter religions of Judaism. . . . [W]e extend the hand of fellowship to all who co-operate with us in the establishment of the reign of truth and righteousness among men."[16]

Kaufman Kohler, who was the guiding spirit and convener of the Pittsburgh Platform, was a great believer in Israel's mission and election, which he regarded as "the central point of Jewish theology and the key to an understanding of the nature of Judaism."[17] In continuing the trend in Reform Judaism, which had originated in Germany, Kohler was notable for his ringing condemnation of "Ghetto Judaism." His condemnation included rejection of the dietary laws of *kashrut* and other outward marks of the Chosen, but at the same time developing the universal message of Judaism into the form of a "glorious mission" to be spread all over the world.[18] "Israel's mission is not to convert the world to Judaism" he said, but to "unfold and spread the light of the monotheistic truth, and also to die, if need be, as martyrs for the Only One and Holy God." Kohler had very strong convictions regarding the Chosen, emphasizing that both Christianity and Islam "owe their origin" to Judaism. In his view, the purpose of living in America and the Diaspora in general, lay in this special mission. This approach justifies a very strong chauvinistic approach to the Chosen: "Only a people that lives forever, passing from one stage of culture to another, as did and does the Jew, can claim to be God-chosen prophets and expounders of the world's highest truth. God and the Jew are inseparable. . . . The Jewish people is immortal, because it is ever linked with the God of life."[19] In another book by Kohler a special chapter was dedicated to "The Election of Israel" where he writes that "[t]he central point of Jewish theology, and the key to an understanding of the nature of Judaism is the doctrine 'God chose Israel as His people,'" and he immediately links this to the role of the Jews in the Diaspora, "to spread among mankind the lofty truths of religion."[20]

The Reconstructionist leader, Rabbi Mordecai Kaplan (as mentioned in Chapter 3) who desired to keep Judaism intact as a religion, had to invent a new approach. Since he was anxious that there be no segregation from the cultural life of the Gentile majority, and therefore, did not want to emphasize the separateness of Judaism, he "ruled out the most striking of all Jewish doctrines, the faith of Jews that they were the Chosen People."[21] In this sense, Kaplan was indeed a "reconstructionist," as implied by the name of his movement, because unlike the Reform movement, he was actually trying to change the perception of the uniqueness of the Jews. Kaplan's ideas on the Chosen did not receive much support in America. Most Jews maintained their traditional mixture of public ambiguity on the subject, while the Reform Jews and others of less Orthodox views emphasized the sense of the universal mission of the Chosen: the "Light unto the Nations." But Kaplan found his own way of keeping the uniqueness of his Judaism by focusing on another aspect of the Chosen. This was Zionism and the support for an independent Jewish state in the ancestral homeland. While the Reform movement and some other Jewish organizations rejected or vacillated on this particular aspect of the Chosen, Kaplan became a spokesperson and ideologist for American mainstream Zionism well before the establishment of the State of Israel.[22]

Following the catastrophe of the Holocaust, the Reform Movement reconsidered the concept of a "Light unto the Nations," and there was a shift toward universal rational ethical thinking. The concept of martyrdom was brought into question, and Jewish suffering as the price of chosenness seemed to make less sense. One Reform rabbi ruefully complained in his New Year sermon in 1944, that many Jews wished that God had chosen another people and asked that "He would grant us a little *menuhah*, a tiny rest. We do not consider ourselves the stuff of saints and martyrs."[23] Later, when the rate of intermarriage started to grow dramatically, the Reform Movement took the concept of the Chosen to the extreme, arguing in the late 1970s, that promoting conversions through mixed marriages is the fulfillment of God's injunction of the role of the Jews to be a "Light unto the Nations."

## Living Apart

The two key features of the Chosen are embodied in the terms "unique" and "apart" yet this does not make the Jews superior in any moral way. There are Jews who are corrupt, dishonest, violent, and criminal, just as in any other nation. The Jews, according to their own teachings, can make a difference to humanity if they keep the Covenant and the commandments, as God told Abraham, "And shall all the nations of the earth bless themselves because you have obeyed my voice."[24] The uniqueness of the Jews began with their intangible God, remote, invisible in the "heights of heaven," as put by the Greeks, a concept unheard of in ancient times. Other races, long before Christianity, felt that the Jews had drawn apart and were unwilling to share their God with others. The Greeks, Romans, and pagan peoples felt that the Jewish concept of God radiates an "aura of exclusiveness and arrogance."[25]

The Gentile prophet Balaam who referred to the Jews as "a People that dwells alone and is not reckoned among the nations"[26] was commissioned by King Balak of Moab, to curse the advancing nation of Israel, but God thwarted his plan, and he could do no less than to bless the Jews. The Russian Christian philosopher, Nicholas Aleksandrovich Berdyaev, ratified the words of Balaam, several thousands of years later:

How mystifying is the historic destiny of the Jews! The very preservation of this people is rationally inconceivable and inexplicable. . . . By a strange paradox, the Jewish people, a historic people par excellence who introduced the very concept of the historic into human thought, have seen history treat them mercilessly, for their annals present an almost uninterrupted series of persecutions and denials of the most elementary human rights. . . . No other nation would have resisted a dispersion lasting so long without in the end dissolving and disappearing. But according to God's impenetrable ways, this people must apparently be preserved until the end of time.[27]

Like Balaam, Berdyaev carried the envy and prejudice saying that the Jewish trait of "self-importance" is irritating, but he explains that it is understandable because they were "always oppressed by others" and that is why they "sought compensation in the idea of election and its high mission."[28]

Jewish chosenness was always a two way street: It came from within, embodied in the rules of Jewish law, and it was reinforced by anti-Jewish decrees that always emphasized the uniqueness of the Jews. Judaism is far less missionary than Christianity and Islam, and it emphasizes the kingship of holiness and separateness.

For the same reasons that Jews tend to be apologetic on their chosenness, Jewish historians have often been reluctant to examine, methodologically and comparatively, the connection between Jewish dispersal and the processes involved in the globalization of the world economy. No one wished to be in the position of providing additional material for the well-known anti-Semitic canard of Jews controlling the finances of the world. Cecil Roth wrote that the study of the financial history of the Jews was always deficient and presented a distorted picture of reality. This distortion occurred, according to Roth, because the historical analysis was always tainted by the prevailing atmosphere and attitude towards the Jews: when times were good for the Jews, the writers would try to emphasize the Jewish contribution to the economy, while in a period of anti-Semitic persecution, the claim was that the Jewish contribution was marginal.[29]

Economic historians like the controversial German Werner Sombart explained that the combination of separateness and dispersion made the Jews harbingers and promoters of globalization. Werner Sombart's unequivocal statement concerning the Jewish contribution to the economy of medieval Europe appeared in his book about Jews and modern capitalism. According to Sombart, the Jews played a key role in overturning the medieval economic system and replacing it with capitalism. The Jews, who were always treated as a foreign entity in their respective countries of settlement, confronted the guilds that controlled intercity trade. Jewish merchants and artisans, forbidden to join the guilds, battled against their primitive and inefficient system—a system that sought to maintain a closed-shop, noncompetitive economy. It was characterized by enforced unity of wages, prices, and marketing. Since most economic opportunities within the cities were closed to Jews, they tended to leave their hometowns and become pioneers of international trade, thereby establishing the infrastructure of modern capitalism, marked by unlimited competition and guided by a central principle:

satisfying the customer. In comparing the most notable movements of financial centers between the fifteenth and seventeenth centuries to Jewish migration trends of the same period, Sombart contends that the wide dispersion of the Jews provided them with an outstanding knowledge of shifting economic systems. Sombart concludes, "It is indeed surprising that the parallels between Jewish wanderings and settlement and the economic fate of the various nations and their cities has not before been observed. Israel passes over Europe like the sun: at its coming new life bursts forth; at its going all falls into decay."[30]

An articulate defense of the Jews against the accusations by the *vox populi* on their role as moneylenders was written in 1748 by the French writer and philosopher Charles Louis Montesquieu. Montesquieu described how the Jews had reached their special position in the economic field, stating that commerce was developed in a process motivated by persecution directed against the Jews:

> Enriched by their abuses, the Jews were fleeced by the princes with the same tyranny: this consoled the people, . . . What happened in England will give an idea of what was done in other countries. King John had the Jews thrown in jail in order to get his hands on their property . . . there were few of them who had not had at least one eye gouged out, since this was how the king administrated his courts of justice. One of them, who had had seven teeth pulled out, one every day, on the eight day gave ten thousand silver marks. Henry III managed to extract from Aaron the Jew of York fourteen thousand marks, and another ten thousand for the Queen. In those times, violence was used to do what today is done in Poland with some moderation. . . . We can see how commerce emerged from the midst of harassment and despondency. Banished from one country after the other, the Jews found ways of saving their property. In this way they for ever gave up their fixed retreats; for any prince who was tempted to get rid of them would nevertheless not feel like parting with their money. . . . They invented bills of exchange; and, in this fashion, commerce was able to evade violence and continue to operate everywhere, whereby the richest merchant had only invisible assets which could be sent far and wide, leaving no traces anywhere. . . . The theologians were compelled to curb their principles; and commerce, which had been cruelly attributed to bad faith, was able to be received into the midst of probity.[31]

There are three religious principles that are often quoted by Jews and non-Jews alike as the prototypical indications of separateness: circumcision, the observance of the Sabbath day, and the dietary laws of *kashrut*. Each of these three are dealt with specifically in the Bible, emphasizing them as a central element of the Chosen and the unique nature of the Jewish people. Although most secular Jews do not keep the Sabbath and the dietary laws today, they are still a prominent feature in their Jewish awareness. When Antiochus IV Epiphanes issued his famous decree against the Jewish religion in 167 BCE, he specifically targeted these three: prohibiting the rite of circumcision, requiring that the Sabbath be violated, and ordering daily sacrifices of swine.[32] Jewish discontent at these edicts grew into rebellion that began in the small town of Modi'in, northwest of Jerusalem, led by Judas Maccabeus the Hasmonean and his sons, the Maccabees. The subsequent

Jewish victory in the battlefield restored Jewish hegemony to the Holy Temple, an event that is commemorated in the annual festival of Hanukkah.

The three precepts are often regarded as the primary Jewish identification with their God. In the first century CE, a Roman satirist described what he saw as the most significant features of the Jews:

> The Jew may worship his pig-god
> and clamor in the ears of the heights of heaven,
> but unless he also cuts back with a knife his foreskin
> and unless he unlooses by art the knotted head
> cast forth from the people
> he shall emigrate to Greek cities,
> and shall not tremble at the fasts of Sabbath imposed by the law.[33]

It is interesting to note that these three features that have kept the Jews distinct are issues of political contention for several Jewish communities in Western democracies today. In Sweden, there have been motions brought to parliament (also in 2003–4) attempting to impose restrictions on the Jewish practice of circumcision, and in several European countries, Jewish ritual slaughter (*shechita*) for the purposes of *kashrut* is prohibited by law, and there have been attempts by animal rights groups to restrict it even further. In Switzerland the law has prohibited *shechita* since 1893 and in 2003, there was even an attempt to restrict the import of kosher meat from other countries. In Britain, a report by the Farm Animal Welfare Council in 2003 called for a total ban on *shechita* and *halal* (Muslim slaughtering). In several Western countries, Jews who observe the Sabbath face problems at work, as do some university students regarding their attendance in classes and taking examinations that are scheduled for Saturdays. Sometimes the debate about Jewish religious practices contains overt anti-Semitic innuendos.

## Circumcision Starts with Abraham

The rite of circumcision is an inseparable part of the Covenant and became the most conspicuous physical evidence of identity for Jewish males. *Brit mila*, the Hebrew term for circumcision, contains the word *brit*—Covenant. From the sequence of the account in Genesis, it is clear that the pledges that God made to His Chosen People concerning the Promised Land, are dependent on the act of circumcision. God tells Abraham, "As for you, you shall keep my covenant—you and your descendants after you throughout their generations. . . . Every male among you shall be circumcised. You shall be circumcised in the flesh of your foreskins, and it shall be a sign of the covenant between me and you. He that is eight days old among you shall be circumcised: every male, throughout your generations . . . So shall my covenant be in your flesh an everlasting covenant."[34]

In Jewish tradition, the rite of circumcision is a law for which no reason is given in the Bible and is beyond human understanding. Nevertheless, many commentators have attempted to provide a philosophical insight to circumcision regarding it as an act chosen by God to distinguish His people, symbolizing the need for spiritual perfection and creating a physical mark, particularly on the reproductive organ, thus representing the eternal continuity of the people.[35]

The Hebrew word for foreskin is *orlah*, which in the scriptures, means a barrier or hindrance standing in the way of a beneficial result. Interestingly, the same word also appears later in the Bible in a metaphorical context: "Circumcise therefore the foreskin of your heart and be no longer stubborn."[36]

As noted by scholars, circumcision was one of the first markers of Jewish identity, and the emerging Christian Church took a deliberate decision to make circumcision a ritual that would draw a clear boundary between the Jews and the new religion. Although Jesus himself took circumcision for granted,[37] Paul made it into a significant symbol of otherness by emphasizing the outdated nature of the ritual. The issue was significant in the efforts to attract large numbers of Gentiles by changing dramatically the composition of the nascent Christian movement.[38]

Initially Paul only rejected the covenantal significance of circumcision, but increasingly he began to use it to illustrate the irrelevance of Judaism and condemned circumcision as a sign of the "slavery" from which Christ had come to release mankind. Already by the first century of the Christian era, circumcision had become a clear marker between Israel and those who joined "*Verus Israel.*"[39] Paul adapted the meaning of the Jewish interpretation of *orlah*, in its physical and spiritual sense, for his own purposes: "For he is not a real Jew who is one outwardly, nor is true circumcision something external and physical. He is a Jew who is one inwardly, and real circumcision is a matter of the heart; spiritual and not literal."[40]

### The Sabbath

The Friday meal, on the eve of the Sabbath, is a central element of Jewish family life, starting with *kiddush*, the blessing over the wine that contains a testimony to the Chosen. The kiddush begins with testimony to the fact that God completed the labor of creation in six days and rested on the seventh. The Hebrew meaning of Sabbath is "rest" or "cessation of work: "And on the seventh day God finished His work that He had done and He rested on the seventh day."[41] The second part of the *kiddush* is a reminder of the Exodus of the Children of Israel from Egypt. Maimonides explained that the Sabbath and Exodus are closely interwoven: The Sabbath is a symbol of God's creation, and the Exodus demonstrates His ability to control and manipulate nature. It is within this context that in the *kiddush* the Jews remember their status of having being Chosen: "Remember the holy Sabbath . . . a remembrance of the act of creation, and a memorial to the Exodus from Egypt. For you did choose us and sanctify us from all the nations."[42]

Jews were clearly recognizable by their observation of the Sabbath. The New Testament recounts, "And on the Sabbath day they went into the synagogue and sat down. After the reading of the law and the prophets, the rulers of the synagogue sent to them, saying, 'Brethren, if you have any word of exhortation for the people, say it.'"[43]

Why did Christians change the Sabbath day and replace it with Sunday observance? For several centuries, Christians kept both the seventh and the first day— Saturday and Sunday. The early Christians did not feel that by observing Sunday they were obeying the fourth commandment: "Remember the Sabbath day to keep it holy." According to *Chambers Encyclopedia* (on the article "Sabbath"), "By none of the Fathers before the fourth century is it (Sunday) identified with the Sabbath, nor is the duty of observing it grounded by them, either on the fourth commandment, or on the percept by Christ or His apostles."[44]

Observation of the Sabbath held a very strong attraction for pagans and later for the Christians: "The Church had to fight against the translation of the Jewish Sabbath into the Christian Sunday for nearly the whole of the first millennium of its existence."[45] Many Christians explain that they observe the first day of the week instead of the seventh day because Jesus rose from the dead on that day and authorized them to keep Sunday to mark His resurrection. Was the change because of a growing antagonism toward the Jews? Was it part of an attempt to establish a separate entity and to distance itself from anything that could be identified as Jewish?

It is clear that the leaders of Christianity regarded the observance of the Shabbat as a danger to their religion. Ignatius of Antioch, who died in the second century, demanded, "Let us, therefore, no longer keep the Sabbath after the Jewish manner and rejoice in days of idleness, for 'he that does not work let him not eat.'"[46] He was referring to Jewish Sabbath practices such as eating food that had been prepared on the previous day and walking only within a prescribed distance. Another warning told Christians that those who observe the Sabbath lose a seventh of their life in idleness. These examples and many more show "the bitter concern over those Christians who waver between their Jewish practices— particularly the Sabbath" and the effort "at all costs to separate Christianity from the synagogue by keeping a different day of the week as the Sabbath."[47]

In Russia, in some parts of the United States and elsewhere, there are Christian sects who continue to observe the Sabbath on the traditional seventh day—Saturday. The Seventh-day Adventist Church in America had in 2006 more than fourteen million baptized members whose doctrine states that the Ten Commandments continue to be binding upon Christians. These Adventists observe the Sabbath like the Jews from Friday sunset to Saturday sunset, and they claim that the change of the Sabbath day to Sunday lacks biblical authorization. Popular anti-czarist movements in Russia embraced Jewish symbols such as keeping the seventh day, even though they did not have any actual contacts with Jews. Since they knew that the czars were anti-Semitic, they chose to express their anti-establishment convictions through expressing sympathy to Judaism.[48]

What is clear, however, is that the Sabbath was a central identifying characteristic of the Jews and their chosenness, as is evident in the Sabbath prayers: "They shall rejoice in your kingship—those who observe the Sabbath and call it a delight. The people that sanctifies the seventh day—they will be satisfied and delight in your goodness."[49]

## The Dietary Laws—Kashrut

In Shakespear e's *The Merchant of Venice* the rich Jewish merchant Shylock, who is invited for dinner by Bassanio, answers him, "Yes, to smell pork, to eat of the habitation which your prophet the Nazarite conjured the devil into. I will buy with you, sell with you, talk with you, walk with you, and so following; but I will not eat with you, drink with you, nor pray with you."[50]

Kashrut is a very perplexing issue for the non-Jew. Judaism itself does not provide a clear-cut rationale for it except as a goal for separating the Jews from the rest of the nations as part of their universal mission. The term "kosher-style," which one occasionally sees, especially in American-Jewish restaurants, is misleading, because the laws of *kashrut* have nothing to do with the style or taste of the food served nor does it indicate any ethnic way of cooking. There are strictly kosher products of a Moroccan, Polish, or Indian character that reflect their geographic origins, but no specific "Jewish" taste. Similarly there are innumerable French, Chinese, Japanese, Mexican, or Italian restaurants that are impeccably kosher. What identifies kosher cuisine are several very specific religious criteria, not all of which have a rational explanation.

Throughout the ages there have been attempts to delineate a clear rationale for the Jewish dietary laws. Some of these call on motives of health, and even the psychological effect on the soul. The Pentateuch very clearly classifies the dietary laws as divine statutes (*hukim*) for which there are no logical explanations. However, it states clearly that the dietary laws are a device to maintain the uniqueness of the Jewish people. They are yet another example of the process of separation: "You shall therefore make a distinction between the clean beast and the unclean"; and then in the next verse this links to "You shall be holy to me, for I the Lord am holy; and have separated you from the peoples, that you should be mine."[51]

Rashi emphasizes the separateness of the Jews: "If you keep yourselves apart from the nations and their ways, you will be mine; otherwise you will belong to Nebuchadnezzar and his cohorts. Rabbi Elazar Ben Azaria taught: Do not say, 'I cannot stand pig meat! Rather you should say, 'I would like to savor pig meat, but what can I do? God forbade it and commanded me to separate myself from the nations in order to be His, and to accept His sovereignty upon myself.'"[52] So there is no logical explanation, but only the clear intent of separation and uniqueness.

The terms "clean" and "unclean" are used in the Bible, not in the physical sense, but as an illustration of spirituality and behavior. They are coupled with the Hebrew terms *tahor* and *tameh*, which mean purity and defilement, respectively. The aim is to reach a degree of holiness and separation, as the biblical text has it: "For I am the Lord your God: consecrate yourselves therefore and be holy, for I am holy."[53] When it refers to the injunction against mixing meat and milk, it says, "[F]or you are a people holy to the Lord your God"[54]; or "You shall be men consecrated to me; therefore you shall not eat any flesh that is torn by beasts in the field."[55]

Manetho, a Greco-Egyptian priest in the third century BCE, assailed the Jews for insisting on remaining apart from the rest of society. He complained that "the Jews do not drink or eat with us; do not participate in our civic life; they marry only other Jews; and they believe their God is superior to ours."[56] But there were other observers like the Emperor Julian who, while lamenting the decline of religion among the Greeks and Romans, praised the Jews for their belief in a "most powerful and most good god." He mentioned the laws of *kashrut*:

> For I saw that those whose minds were turned to the doctrines of the Jewish religion are so ardent in their belief that they would choose to die for it, and to endure utter want and starvation rather than taste pork or any animal that has not the life-blood squeezed out of it immediately; whereas we are in such a state of apathy about religious matters that we have forgotten the customs of our forefathers, and therefore we actually do not know whether any such rule was ever prescribed.[57]

We can see in the New Testament why the abolishment of *kashrut* laws is so central in the superssesion of the Chosen. Saint Peter tells about his vision when he "became hungry . . . fell into a trance" and saw "heaven opened and . . . a large sheet" containing all kinds of animals and a voice telling him, "Get up, Peter, kill and eat!" But Peter who was a Jewish Christian replies that "I have never ate anything impure or unclean" presumably nothing not kosher. But when the scene repeats three times and the sheet was gone Peter realizes that the Jews who killed Jesus Christ "by hanging Him on a tree" are no longer favored by God who now "accepts men from every nation who fear Him and do what is right." Instead Christ "is the one whom God appointed as Judge of the living and the dead." With the end of the *kashrut* laws, which separated the Jews from the rest of mankind, the transfer of the Chosen mantle is completed: "The circumcised believers who had come with Peter were astonished that the gift of the Holy Spirit had been poured out even on the Gentiles."[58]

Shakespeare, in *The Merchant of Venice* uses the Jewish dietary laws as an illustration of Jewish separateness, and perhaps as a perception of a primitive religion. It can even be argued that the primary theme of the play is, once again, rivalry over the title of Chosen. According to the critic, Barbara Lewalski, the theme of the play is the "victory of the New Law over the Old, and the triumph of Christian ethics over Hebraic legalism."[59] Antonio embodies the ideals of Christian selflessness, generosity, and love, while the Jew Shylock, who observes the dietary laws and is an ancestral descendant of the Old Testament, represents the antithesis to Christian benevolence. Professor Murray Roston goes further and suggests that the hatred shown toward Shylock, which seems so un-Christian-like is, in fact, very much in accordance with the New Testament where Paul treats the Jews like the devil, justifying his behavior because of their rejection of Jesus. And worse yet: the play contains "a re-enactment of the Crucifixion story set within the contemporary setting of Venice, where a Jew attempts to shed the blood of an innocent Christ-figure." The play contains many allusions, says Roston, to the "basic conflict between the Christians and the Pharisees, namely the claim that God 'has qualified us to be ministers of a new covenant, not in a written code, but in the spirit, for the written code kills, but the spirit gives life."[60] This is reminiscent of the same argument that Paul used with regard to circumcision (inward, of the heart, and not outward, in the flesh). Shakespeare wrote his play at a time when there were no Jews living in England, nor had been since their expulsion in 1290.[61] The Jews would return to England only after 1650, but the images were strong, and their unique and distinctive characters, including the laws of kashrut, were undoubtedly embedded in the minds of the contemporary theatergoers.

## Benjamin Disraeli: The Outspoken Voice of the Chosen

The mantle of the Chosen exists among the most assimilated and even converted Jews. Benjamin Disraeli (1804–81), among the most famous prime ministers of Great Britain, was also, in his own way, probably one of the most outspoken public figure ever on the concept of the Jews as the Chosen People. Outside the closed and arcane circle of Jewish religious writings, which are often restrained and selective on the issue of the Chosen, there has never been such an articulate promoter of the Chosen as Disraeli. His opinions about the Chosen People, were often a source of embarrassment and even irritation for the Jewish community of that time in Britain, which was struggling hard against prejudice and anti-Semitism. Disraeli was prime minister in 1868 and again in 1874–80 and was a favorite of Queen Victoria who was charmed by him. Disraeli was baptized in 1817—just before his Bar Mitzvah—following a long and insignificant quarrel that his father, Isaac D'Israeli, had with the Jewish Sephardic community of London. His childhood conversion was, however, enormously significant for British history because until 1858, Jews were not admitted to parliament, and Disraeli could never have become prime minister had he not been baptized.

Disraeli was brought up and educated as a Christian but maintained his Jewish identity and pride in many ways. As he developed a parallel literary career to that of his political one, he began to read many books on Jewish history and literature. He was always to remain something of an outsider in British society because of his character and his aura of Jewishness "which he could not escape even if he tried." But unlike many assimilated Jews, he did not fall into the trap of self-hatred and throughout his career, he knew how to reinvent his Jewish roots to further his personal political campaigns, without shame or frustration.[62]

The Jews were looked upon as a peculiar people, and Disraeli could not ignore statements coming from within his own party, such as a remark by Sir Robert Inglis, a Conservative member of parliament for Oxford University, who told the House of Commons in 1833 that "the Jews are strangers among us. And strangers they must continue to be. They must ever remain a distinct and separate nation."[63]

Disraeli's strong and consistent statements on the Jewish people were frequently incorporated in his public statements, including parliamentary debates, but also, in his many novels and essays. His books teem with Jewish characters who express strong views on the Chosen People. A close study of his books and his political career reveal an interesting consistency between his heroes and his own views and personality. His novels present a strong Zionist conviction, emphasizing the affinity between the Jews and Palestine. In May 1830, he embarked upon a seventeen-month visit to the Middle East, including a trip to Jerusalem, which had a tremendous effect on him.[64] His decision to take the trip and his subsequent writings on Zion and Palestine, testify to his views on the Jewish connection to the Land of Israel as an integral part of the Jews' uniqueness and otherness. On the way to the Middle East, he visited Italy to see the home of his ancestors and then he went to Jerusalem to see for himself the Jewish roots of Christian civilization. He was most impressed by Jerusalem as he writes in *Lothair*: "There are few things finer than the morning view of Jerusalem from the Mount of Olives."[65]

In his novel *Alroy* (1833), there is a Jewish hero who launches a campaign to reconquer the Holy Land from the Babylonian occupiers. David Alroy is defeated, and he fails to create a Jewish empire in Asia because he lacks the inspiration of Zion, but he refuses to commit apostasy (this is written by Disraeli the convert!) and by so doing receives personal redemption. On many occasions Disraeli would remind his readers about his own Jewish origins and the debt that Great Britain and Europe in general owed to the Jewish people.

Did Disraeli have dreams of becoming a Jewish leader, a liberator of the Holy Land? There is no doubt that his hero David Alroy is a Jewish response to the Christian Crusaders, reasserting Jewish rights to the Holy Land. *Alroy* is about Jewish messianism in the twelfth century, a work of fiction that emphasizes the centrality of Zion in Judaism, with reference to a time when Christians and Muslims were fighting over their rights in the Promised Land in the context of being the perceived successors of the Chosen. In this book Disraeli present his own psychodrama to compose an "allegory of the tension he felt between the lofty attraction of the pure messianic and national vision of his recently discovered people and the less spiritual temptations of worldly conquest and dominion." Disraeli had visions of a Hebrew state under the pure rule of Mosaic law and centered on a rebuilt Third Temple in Jerusalem. For Alroy, the twelfth-century dilemma is "submitting to martyrdom rather than denying his mission and renouncing his faith."[66] Alroy, as shown at the beginning of this chapter, explains that God made the curious laws in order to make the Jews His "peculiar people," but when he wants to lead the Jews back to their position as "the Chosen People" the ex-Jew, Lord Honain, tells him about the suffering that comes with it: "Chosen for scoffs, and scorns, and contumelies. Command me such a choice."[67] Disraeli makes Alroy a forerunner of Zionism who explains his ultimate desires: "You ask me what I wish? my answer is: the Land of Promise. You ask me what I wish? my answer is: Jerusalem—all we have forfeited, all we have yearned after, all for which we have fought—our beauteous country, our holy creed, our simple manners. . . . Yet again I will built thee, and thou shalt be built, O . . . Israel!"[68]

In Disraeli's novel, *Tancred* (1847), Zion is waiting for the Jews to return: "The vineyards of Israel have ceased to exist, but the eternal Law enjoins the

Children of Israel to celebrate the vintage. A race that persists in celebrating their vintage although they have no fruits to gather, will regain their vineyards."[69] The British historian Cecil Roth observed that Disraeli's Zionism sounds like "any Hassidic rabbi or sixteen-century Kabbalist."[70]

In *Tancred* there is a young aristocrat who goes to Palestine to return to Christianity its Jewish roots and foundations, which are at the base of Western civilization. He wants to experience again the revelation in Mount Sinai and the Land of Israel. He wants to "penetrate the great Asian mystery . . . what ought I to do and what ought I to believe."[71] Disraeli tells his readers that in order to solve the problems of modern Europe, one must return to the eternal principles that were uttered on Mount Sinai. These were the principles that were transmitted to humanity by the Jews, he says in *Tancred*, "[v]ast as the obligations of the whole human family are to the Hebrew race, there is no portion of the modern populations so much indebted to them as the British people." In *Tancred* Disraeli touches on the Chosen and the replacement theory of Christianity in asking why is it that the Saxon and Celtic races persecute the Jews "from whom they adopted laws of sublime benevolence, and in the pages of whose literature they have found perpetual delight, instruction, and consolation? That is a great question, which in an enlightened age, may be fairly asked." Jews, argues Disraeli, are basically very conservative with a clear bias toward religion, property, and natural aristocracy, but they became revolutionaries only because they were persecuted. They would naturally be close allies of the Conservatives.[72]

To express such opinions in Britain in the early nineteenth century was extremely unusual, particularly in light of the fact that Disraeli continued to write and exhibit his attachment to the Jewish people and to their uniqueness, while continuing to campaign for a seat in parliament and to become prime minister in a generally anti-Semitic environment. Two hundred years earlier, the Protector Oliver Cromwell, stated that the British are the Chosen People as a "people that have a stamp upon them from God."[73] In the seventeenth century, the so-called "British Israelites" developed a theory that the British people were descendants of the Ten Lost Tribes of Israel and that they are the real Chosen People, having replaced the Jews.[74] However, there were people in the parliament like Lord Ashley who led the "restoration" movement aimed to plant God's "Chosen People" in their ancient land (see Chapter 7).

Disraeli did not hesitate to include among his heroes, individuals whom anti-Semites love to hate. In *Tancred* and again in *Coningsby* (1844), he introduces Sidonia, a rich Jewish banker and an idealized version of Rothschild, who presents the outlook of the Jewish people and describes in a nutshell the link between anti-Semitism and the concept of the Chosen: "Favored by nature and by nature's God, we produced the lyre of David; we gave you Isaiah and Ezekiel. . . . Favored by nature we still remain, but in exact proportion as we have been favored by nature, so we have been persecuted by Man. . . . We have endured fifteen hundred years of supranational slavery. . . . [T]he Hebrew child has entered adolescence only to learn that he was the pariah of that ungrateful Europe that owes to him the best part of its laws, a fine portion of its literature, all its religion."[75] Sidonia, who is both an intellectual and wealthy, is in touch with all the outcasts of the world,[76] and critics argue convincingly that Sidonia is what Disraeli wanted people to think about himself: "[T]he most passionate statement of Disraeli's fantasy of Jewish chosenness . . . Disraeli's affirmation of the myth of the super-Jew, superior because a Jew."[77] Through Sidonia, Disraeli employs anti-Semitic images, but he explains that it is only because of their special qualities as a "first and superior class," that the Jews have the ability to survive persecution. This is the vicious circle that leads to the accusation that the Jews are too powerful and exert too much influence in politics, warfare, and the arts.[78]

In *Tancred* Disraeli wonders why the Jews are persecuted by those who owe them their cultural and spiritual heritage, and his answer is that it is precisely because of that. It is again the Chosen People that is hated and resented even in a time of enlightenment. As he wrote in a letter in 1860, this hatred against the Jews is a matter of jealousy, which was "influenced mainly by mortified vanity in never having been the medium of direct communication with the Almighty."[79]

In the same book, Disraeli writes that the Hebrews "are a miracle; alone of the ancient races they remain a memorial of the mysterious and mighty past. . . . Is it a miracle that Jehovah should guard His people? And can He guard them better than by endowing them with facilities superior to those among those whom they dwell?"[80]

Disraeli takes pride in the sense of chosenness, which he felt "both as a romantic and as a Jew," and he sees the Jewish hand in all significant strands of European history and all the creative flights of Western civilizations.[81] In the words of Cecil Roth, Disraeli remained, to the end of his life, "Jewish in sentiment."[82] In *Tancred* he brings forward the historic dilemma of the assimilated Jew in words he puts in the mouth of Mlle. de Laurella, who

> felt persuaded that the Jews would not be so much disliked if they were better known; that all they had to do was to imitate as closely as possible the habits and customs of the nation among whom they chanced to live; and . . . that a respectable Hebrew, particularly if well-dressed and well-mannered, might be able to pass through society without being discovered, or at least noticed. Consummation of the destiny of the favorable people of the Creator of the universe![83]

Disraeli was so convinced about the qualities of the Jews that he referred openly to the Jewish/Hebrew/Semitic race and although his conception of race was far different from theories later adopted by the Nazis, he has been accused of being "a spiritual ancestor of this Nazi brand of anti-Semitism."[84] This accusation has no foundation in fact because Disraeli was very clear about the positive affinity between Christianity and Judaism. He said that the Jews have racial primacy by virtue of their separateness, and that basically Christianity is a slightly modified form of Judaism. He spoke about race, which he regarded as "a key to history."[85] But this was an observation of historical fact and not an ideological differentiation between peoples. In his biography of Lord George Bentinck (1852), Disraeli explained that the Jews are an elite within the Semitic races because of their spirituality. They succeeded in surviving from ancient times because of their purity of blood and their natural conservative attitude toward religion, privilege, and property.[86] He was equally abrasive in referring to different Jewish races, viewing the Sephardim (Jews originating from the Middle and Near East to which he belonged, as opposed to the Ashkenazim of Europe) as the superior Jewish race.[87]

Disraeli dismisses the arguments of Christian anti-Semitism based on the doctrine of Jewish guilt for the crucifixion of Jesus. Eva, the beautiful Jewess, tells Tancred, who has fallen in love with her, "We have saved the human race, and you persecuted us for doing so." Similarly in *Sybil*, "Christianity is completed Judaism, the New Testament is only a supplement." Again in the words of Eva, "Half Christendom worships a Jewess, and the other half a Jew."[88] After having made these kinds of statements it would be inevitable that people would wonder whether Disraeli regarded himself as a Jew or a Christian. Disraeli himself, in his scintillating and witty style, once commented to Queen Victoria about his own identity, explaining that "I am the missing page between the Old Testament and the New." [89]

His most famous statement was made when in the House of Commons, a prominent Irish member, Daniel O'Connell, referred to Disraeli's Jewish ancestry in disparaging terms. Disraeli responded, "Yes, I am a Jew and when the ancestors of the right honorable gentleman were brutal savages in an unknown island, mine were priests in the Temple of Solomon."[90]

The Jewish community in Britain was embarrassed by Disraeli when he stressed the unique characteristics of the Jewish people. The *Jewish Chronicle* of August 9, 1850, published a clear criticism of Disraeli: "Jews are looking for justice, not as a peculiar race, or on account of a peculiar religion, but as citizens of the same state. We claim it not upon the ground of the eccentric fiction of one who praises the Jews to the skies—and he himself a descendant of Jews, but not a Jew."[91]

This reflects the typical tension between an outspoken outsider and the more inward-looking community that was struggling to maintain the delicate balance of being different (but not "peculiar") and at the same time equal to all other citizens. In such an environment the concept of the Chosen People was considered by the embarrassed Jews as being better left to the intimacies of the synagogue (and sometimes not even to be mentioned there), so that the outspoken Disraeli was perceived as an incipient threat to Jewish-Gentile relations. Disraeli was also prone to exchange arguments with the assimilated Jews themselves. In his books, when he calls to restore Jewish sovereignty, he criticizes Jews who are so eager to assimilate: "[A]shamed of their race and not fanatically devoted to their religion."[92]

In 1847–48, Disraeli supported Baron Lionel de Rothschild in his fight against the law regarding parliament to which he had been elected, but as a Jew was not permitted to join. In this struggle, Disraeli did not just engage in defending the liberal principle of religious tolerance, but rather emphasized the debt that Christianity and Europe, and especially Britain, owed to the Jews. The Jews should be permitted to sit in parliament because of this close affinity, the faith out of which Christianity was born. "Where is your Christianity?" he asked rhetorically, "[i]f you do not believe in their Judaism."[93]

In his last novel, *Lothair*, Disraeli returned to the basic Zionist principle of the link between Jews and the Holy Land. Disraeli's views were firm and in essence, he became a harbinger of political Zionism. He opened his heart to his young intimate Lord Stanley, the twenty-four-year-old son of his party chief, and shared with him the vision of restoring the Jews to Palestine. What Stanley wrote in his diary, straight from the mouth of Disraeli, can be read as an early draft of the Zionist program. The country, he wrote, had ample natural capabilities: all it required was labor and protection for the laborer. The ownership of the soil could be bought from Turkey; money would be forthcoming; the Rothschilds and other leading Hebrew financiers would help; the Ottoman Empire was falling into ruin and the Sublime Porte would do anything for money—all that was necessary was to establish colonies with rights over the soil and security from oppression. The question of nationality could wait until everything else had been solved. He added that these ideas were extensively believed by the Jews. The man who would carry them out would be the next Messiah, the true savior of his people. Stanley saw only one obstacle arising from the existence of two Hebrew races who had settled along the shores of the Mediterranean, who look down on each other, refusing even to associate with each other: "'Sephardim' I think [Disraeli] called the superior race."[94] It is no wonder that Herzl, in his newspaper *Die Welt*, listed Disraeli as the first name in a proposed series of literary profiles of "representative exponents of the Zionist Idea."[95]

During Disraeli's term as prime minister, the writer George Eliot published in 1876 her *Daniel Deronda* whose main heroes are Jews with a strong national awareness who despite being regular British citizens, are striving for a Jewish national renaissance. In her book Eliot praised the Jewish people for its great contribution to world civilization particularly in its cultural and moral aspects. She regards the Jews as a special people that was able to maintain its integrity despite persecution and suffering during two thousand years of wandering. Eliot was disillusioned with Christianity while deeply impressed with the Jewish vision of redemption. In *Daniel Deronda* she shows a powerful ability to penetrate the conflicting trends among the Jews: those who are loyal and proud in their uniqueness and those assimilated Jews who are mainly concerned with their pockets, food, lifestyle, and social status. Eliot explains why for both groups the real solution lies in the national renaissance of Israel.

A century later Dr. Jacob Herzog, then director-general of the Israel Prime Minister's Office under Golda Meir, related an interesting discussion that he had had with the first Israeli prime minister, David Ben Gurion, regarding Disraeli. Ben Gurion was surprised to learn that Winston Churchill had once written about Disraeli that "[d]espite everything, Disraeli never fully assimilated with the British people." Ben Gurion asked how it was possible that Churchill, himself a prime minister, could bring himself to write such a thing about one of the most distinguished of his predecessors. After all, Disraeli was one of the key builders of the British Empire who had brought the Suez Canal and India to the crown, a man of broad culture who had contributed so much to the philosophy of conservatism and was still enormously admired. Herzog, an observant Jew, told Ben Gurion in the words of the Jewish sages that "a Jew can be cut off from his own people, but this does not mean that he has necessarily become an integral part of another people." With regard to assimilated Jews, Herzog suggested that still in their heart, in their innermost feelings, they remain "suspended in limbo."[96]

Disraeli was perhaps more global than any other prime minister in Britain's history, but he would always remain apart in his own words and in the eyes of others. Churchill's statement about Disraeli was typical of his complex approach to the Jewish phenomenon. On another occasion, Churchill had said, "Some people like Jews and some do not, but no thoughtful man can deny the fact that they are beyond question the most formidable and the most remarkable race which has ever appeared in the world."[97] His wife, Clementine Churchill, was considered to be rather anti-Semitic, and it was said that she would not allow any Jew to cross her doorstep, not even Chaim Weizmann who was on close terms with her husband.[98]

There is even a myth concerning Disraeli's embrace of Judaism in his final hours. A biographer, Stanley Weintraub, mentions the rumor that on his deathbed, Disraeli uttered the words of the *Shema Yisrael* prayer.[99] However, there is no need to cling to rumors about a possible return to Judaism in his last hours because as we have seen, Disraeli never abandoned his Jewish identity and racial pride. Unlike many other Jews and often to their embarrassment, Disraeli spoke openly, on the question of Jewish chosenness and the critical contribution of the Jews to mankind. Though he was often provocative and outspoken, he had the courage to place on the agenda an issue that so many others had avoided. Disraeli should properly be regarded as one of the main proponents of Jewish chosenness and one of the forerunners of modern Zionism.

# CHAPTER 5

# Hating the Chosen
## Anti-Semitism

There is a midrash that tells a story about a Jew who walks by the Roman Emperor Hadrian and greets him. The Emperor calls out to him and asks him: "who are you?" "A Jew" comes the answer. The Emperor is angered and says to his councilors; "How dare a Jew pass the Emperor and greet him! Take him away and hang him!" A second Jew, who is following behind and sees the scene but cannot avoid passing, refrains from greeting. The Emperor calls out to him and asks him: "who are you?" "A Jew" comes the answer. The Emperor is angered again and rails at him; "you pass in the front of the Emperor and yet you do not greet him?" And he orders his counselors; "Take him away and hang him!" One of the counselors is puzzled by the scene and asks the Emperor; "I wish to understand what you are doing. One man greets you and you have him killed, and the other who does not greet you, you also have him killed. Why is this?" And the Emperor replies: "are you attempting to teach me how to get rid of my enemies?"

—Eicha Raba, 3:41

You made us as filth and rejected among the nations. All our enemies jeered at us.
—Eicha/Lamentations 3:45–46

God has granted to us, His Chosen People, the gift of the dispersion, and in this which appears in all eyes to be our weakness, has come forth all our strength, which has now brought us to the threshold of sovereignty over the whole world.
—*The Protocols of the Learned Elders of Zion*, 11D[1]

The midrash about the anti-Jewish Emperor Hadrian is basically a story of the irrationality of anti-Semitism, but it comes in a context where the dark side of the Chosen is exposed. It appears in the tractate that deals with the destruction of Jerusalem and is read on *Tisha B'Av* (the ninth day of the Hebrew month of *Av*—July/August), which is a day of fast and mourning marking the destruction of both the First and the Second Temples and the accompanying ravage and dispersion. The commentary relates to the verses where the Prophet

Jeremiah says, "We have transgressed and rebelled—you have not forgiven. You have enveloped yourself in anger and pursued us; you have slain mercilessly. You wrapped yourself in a cloud that no prayer can pierce."[2] Here the Chosen by God becomes the refused among the nations: "You made us as filth and rejected among the nations. All our enemies jeered at us."[3] And then comes the appeal: "You always championed my cause, O Lord, you redeemed my life. You have seen, O God, the injustices I suffer; judge my cause." The midrash ends with the saying that the Holy Spirit reiterated: "You have seen, O God, the injustices, you have seen all their vengeance, all their designs against me."[4]

Anti-Semitism is generally beyond reason. Jews are hated when they are successful and wealthy, and also when they fail and are poverty stricken—when they are too religious, when they assimilate and even when they convert; when they are capitalist or when they are communist; when they engage in finance and money lending but also when they are academics and scientists. A pious Jew will say that anti-Judaism is part of the Jewish trial as the Chosen People. Therefore, following a pogrom or an anti-Semitic incident, he would say, "Let us search and examine our ways and return to God."[5] But also, together with the divine spirit that inspires him, he continues to wonder how is it that God who sees "the injustices I suffer" does not come to "judge my cause." He continues to wonder why was it that God made Israel "as filth and rejected among the nations."[6]

\* \* \*

Jews are often rejected because of the will of others to become the Chosen. Spain can serve as another model for the effects of the Chosen factor on Christian-Jewish relations and as a root cause for anti-Semitism. The Spanish expulsion of the Jews in 1492, an example of ethnic cleansing, was the climax of anti-Jewish policies that had lasted for some two centuries. The declared goal was to force the Jews to convert to Christianity, but behind it there was another supersession act: to transfer the mantle of the Chosen to Spain. Christian Spanish literature of this period is marked by self-aggrandizement in praise of its world mission and its election by God, thus transforming Spain into the new "Promised Land" or "God's Land" and its rulers to a new House of David. In the latter half of the fifteenth century, the Spanish rulers were obsessed with the goal of completing the *Reconquista* (the recapture of Spain by the Christians from the grasp of the Muslims). As the goal was gradually reached, the Spaniards felt that "their generation had been divinely selected to see its fulfillment with its own eyes." They regarded the generation of 1492 as "composed of Chosen People" who had witnessed in the course of a few months, three momentous events: conquering the last Muslim enclave in Spain—that of Granada, the expulsion of the Jews, and Christopher Columbus' arrival in the New World as if to export the miracle of the *Reconquista* to the world. Columbus himself referred to this in apocalyptic terms, declaring that "God made me the messenger of the new heaven and the new earth" and writing to the king and queen that "the future ruler who would recover Mount Zion would come from Spain."[7]

When the Christian conquest of Spain was completed by the end of the fifteenth century, the claim of the Chosen was formally recognized by the Catholic rulers of Spain. As the Christian church had done before, Spain appropriated the Chosen concept for itself. This was formally declared by King Ferdinand and Queen Isabella, who referred to the messianic mission of spreading Christianity throughout the world, stating that Spain had inherited the title of the biblical Chosen People. During the reign of its Catholic kings, Spain was engulfed by messianic fervor and Ferdinand himself was seen as the messiah. The Spaniards regarded the expulsion of the Jews as a necessary part of the transfer of the title of Chosen to them.[8] Fray Juan de Salazar wrote in 1619, "We are His [C]hosen [P]eople in the New Dispensation . . . just as the Hebrews were in the time of the written law."[9] Salazar elaborated on the strong similarities between the two nations.[10] The real similarities, nonetheless, are reflected in the reasoning and practices of the hatred to the Jews as part of the Chosen struggle. The same attempt to get rid of the other Chosen People will cast the most deadly blow upon the Jewish people in the Holocaust of World War II (see Chapter 7).

Discussions about the suffering and the fate of the Chosen are not limited to the holy books of ancient times and even in our days accusations and hatred against the Chosen are not restricted to religious circles. The upsurge of anti-Semitism in the new century was coupled with the return of attacks against the Chosen. This new wave of anti-Semitism affected the Jews with surprise and a sense of shock and did not stem just from the usual quarters that disseminate the *Protocols of The Elders of Zion* or consistently preach hatred and genocide, but it became accepted in mainstream circles, in the guise of attacks on Israel or its supporters. The whole spectrum from extreme right to extreme left, as well as more respected circles of intellectuals resorted to the metaphor of the Chosen in one way or another. The following examples, taken from different parts of Europe in recent years, reveal what was both new and old in the so-called "New Anti-Semitism."

## The Greek

One statement came from the renowned Greek composer, Mikos Theodorakis, who at the end of 2003 exemplified the trinity of hatred: Israel, the Jews, and the Chosen. Theodorakis spoke about the Jews and their "arrogance" and even brought the Patriarchs Abraham and Jacob into the argument: "The Jews have the fanaticism, the self-awareness and the ability to assert themselves. . . . We the Greeks, did not turn aggressive like them because we have more history. Today it is possible to say that this small nation is the root of all evil; it is full of self-importance and evil stubbornness. . . . They have only Abraham and Jacob, who were shadows, while we have Pericles."[11]

Almost a year later in an interview with the Israeli newspaper *Ha'aretz* the genie came out of the bottle, and Theodorakis added more stereotypes of hatred and prejudice, including a specific reference to the Chosen People. Theodorakis tells how he was an admirer of Israel after the Holocaust, and he admits that his perceptions about Jews were planted in his childhood when Jews were his neighbors and classmates (most Greek Jews were sent to the death camps by the Nazis). Typically, he says that the Jews "were not different from the Greeks. . . . They were entirely Greek. They loved their work and loved their family. At school they were the best. Good friends, good neighbors. No problem." In the same breath he contradicts himself and explains that the Jews were always "the other," "different," and that "the Jews were the ones that crucified Christ!" His grandmother warned him not to go to the Jewish quarter during Easter because "the Jews put Christian boys in a barrel with knives inside. Afterward they drink their blood." He himself does not refute or condemn these blood libels. Like many other anti-Semites Theodorakis is also fascinated with the Jews: "To be a community that disregards all dangers and remains true to its origins—that's a mystery. . . . It is a metaphysical phenomenon. It cannot be explained." Theodorakis says that the Jews in France are successful and that they speak French perfectly, "but they are not French. They always think of going back to Jerusalem." The genie comes out again when the interviewer asks him, "In your opinion what is it that holds us Jews together?" Theodorakis answers, "It is the feeling that you are the children of God. That you are Chosen."

Theodorakis offers the usual mix of admiration, envy and hatred: "There are 200 Jews who won Nobel prizes. Christ, Marx and Einstein were Jewish. The Jews offered so much to science, art and music. They hold world finance in their hands. So it is only natural that they would see themselves as very strong. This gives them a feeling of superiority." In a moment of truth, Theodorakis adds his personal psychopathology for his prejudice and blames the Jews who in his words "control most of the big symphonic orchestras in the world;" for boycotting him for writing the Palestinian national anthem saying that since then he "cannot work with any great orchestra. They refuse me." Jews control much of the music world, he repeats, and in America they control much of the economy, certainly the mass media." And he continues to blame the Jews for controlling "the banks" and "Wall Street" and those who surround [President] Bush and control the policy of the United States."[12]

This hatred, including the comparison of Israelis to Nazis, comes from the most important Greek composer today, a national symbol who fought tyranny against the military regime in Greece. For such a person to repeat the old images and blood libels and to refer to the Jews as a secret society suggests that European anti-Semitism goes back to the roots of the rivalry with the Chosen, and the Jews rejection of Jesus' message of love. The Jews, in Theodorakis' words, cannot be accepted as regular members of the European community. They have different kinds of loyalties and they abuse their global power to incite and to cause evil. They are, in his words, "at the root of evil."

Theodorakis presented a Greek version of the Christian displacement theory of the Chosen. The Greeks are the Chosen, he postulates, because of their history and ancient heroes. This is a pre-Christian Hellenistic interpretation of the Chosen complex. The words of Theodorakis were not an outburst of venom but a reflection of the prevailing trend among Greek intellectuals. A few months earlier, in August 2003, a Greek cartoonist, Dimitri Kitsikis, drew a comparison between the Jews of the Warsaw Ghetto and the Palestinians in Ramallah and added, "It is a fact that the Jews are the Greeks' great rivals. . . . The Jews and the Greeks are competing as to who will reign over the planet. . . . I am sure we will beat the Jews."[13] As shown later, this motive of the rivalry over the title of the Chosen became critical in the worst catastrophes against the Jewish people. Previously, the Greek daily newspaper *Ethnos* published a caricature in which two Jewish soldiers dressed as Nazis with Stars of David on their helmets, drive knives into Arabs, while the accompanying text says, "Do not feel guilty, my brother. We were not in Auschwitz and Dachau to suffer, but rather to learn."[14]

## The Portuguese

Jose Saramago, the Portuguese Nobel laureate for literature, drew a shocking comparison between the Mukata—the headquarters of Yasser Arafat in the town of Ramallah, which he visited in 2002—and the death camp of Auschwitz. His attack made an intellectual switch: blaming the Jews for having been Chosen and accusing them for transforming the Holocaust into a banner of the Chosen People:

> Intoxicated mentally by the messianic dream of a Greater Israel which will finally achieve the expansionist dreams of the most radical Zionism; contaminated by the monstrous and rooted "certitude" that in this catastrophic and absurd world there exists a people chosen by God and that, consequently, all the actions of an obsessive, psychological and pathological exclusivist racism are justified; educated and trained in the idea that any suffering that has been inflicted, or is being inflicted, or will be inflicted on everyone else, especially the Palestinians, will always be inferior to that which they themselves suffered in the Holocaust, the Jews endlessly scratch their own wound to keep it bleeding, to make it incurable, and they show it to the world as if it were a banner.[15]

Here Saramago sums up in a nutshell the complex approach of hatred of the Jews, both for having been Chosen and, at the same time, monopolizing the suffering of the Chosen. According to Saramago, the Jews should not be permitted to tell the world that the Holocaust was the worst crime ever committed against a people. One can see his intellectual's anger for the special attention allocated to the Holocaust as a unique event, a different level of suffering. Saramago represents the vicious hatred of the new anti-Semitism, and in the same breath, he demonstrates the antiquity of this hatred. He starts with Israelis and Zionism, but in the same long sentence, he goes on to rail at the Jewish people, condemning everything: their religion, culture, race, policies, their monopoly on suffering, and of course, their chosenness. Saramago dealt already with this topic in another form in his controversial book *The Gospel According to Jesus Christ* (1991), which brought strong criticism from the Vatican for being blasphemous. In this book God becomes tired with His Chosen People—the Jews—and decides to take another Jew, Jesus, to die as a measure of a shock treatment for humanity in order to expand and deepen His reign as God.[16]

## The Italian

In Italy, two leading intellectuals and prominent in the media focused their attacks against Israel on the Jewish religion and its beliefs. They were using the similar Theodorakis' metaphors: attacking Israeli practices against the Palestinians and immediately switching to the general characteristics of the Jews, using strange a cocktail of old-type, liberal-Chistian, anti-Jewish accusations. Sergio Romano, Italy's ex-ambassador to Moscow and an editorial contributor to the most important Italian newspaper *Corriere della Sera* is a leading example of this mix of anti-Israeli attacks with virulent anti-Semitic texts. Romano wrote a distorted interpretation of Judaism, which he regards as "the dictatorship of the fastidious Jewish rules, a fossil catechism . . . of one of the most ancient, introverted, and backward religious faiths ever practiced in the West." This Judaism and its laws (the 613 laws of the Jewish religion: 248 positive rules and 365 negative ones), he says, is a reaction to the enlightenment and its is "angry, archaic, and psychologically impenetrable to any form of tolerance and coexistence."[17] (This accusation is baseless because Jewish laws preceded the enlightenment hundreds and even more than thousand years.) In another twist of facts Romano blames the victims—the Jews—for creating fascist anti-Semitism because of their own behavior: for the Jews' cosmopolitan in the eyes of the nationalists and for their separateness in the eyes of everybody. (As other anti-Semites he does not see the self-contraction in the accusation.) The reasons for the new anti-Semitism in his view are the privileged status of the State of Israel, which receives the backing of the powerful international Jewry. Also, he blames the paradox that made genocide so central in the history of the last century as a cause for the scrutiny of Israel policies (perhaps he tells the Jews stop alluding to the *Shoah*, the Holocaust, because it awakens anti-Semitism).

Barbara Spinelli, a leading journalist of the daily *La Stampa*, follows in Romano's steps in combining the attack against Israel with an assault against Judaism. She is using the same cocktail with a clear allusion to the "privileged" Chosen: "Israel constitutes a scandal . . . for the way it has been established, for the sacrifices its birth has inflicted on the Palestinian citizens who had not taken part in the annihilation of the Jews in Europe. Last, but not least, for the way in which Moses' religion inhabits our planet, validating rights that are often metahistorical rather than historical, linked to sacred texts more than to the regular becoming of the people and the time."[18]

## The Norwegian

A major public scandal erupted in Norway during the summer of 2006 following the publication of an article titled "God's Chosen People,"[19] which attacks Israel and the Jewish tradition. The article, which was compared by critics with Adolf Hitler's *Mein Kampf*, was written by Jostein Gaarder, an internationally renowned author who wrote the bestselling *Sophie's World*. Gaarder opens his article with the assertion that Israel is a matter of history and can no longer get recognition by the world and continues to argue that "we should call children's murderess by their name and we can never accept that those killers have a mandate from God and from history to justify their obscene acts."[20] Writing on the Jews Gaarder says that "we don't believe in the idea of a [C]hosen [P]eople and we laugh at this people's obsessions" and refers to the Ten Commandments as the "amusing stone tablets." The article was published in the leading newspaper of Norway *Aftenposten* and led to a series of exchanges with angry readers.

Like many other anti-Semitic intellectuals Gaarder starts with condemning Israel and denying its right to exist, but with open eyes he walks into his own trap when he goes from attacking Israel to attacking the Jewish people with the "crime" of claiming to be the Chosen (ignoring the fact that this claim is recognized both by Christianity and Islam). In his own words he rephrases the accusations raised by Mel Gibson in his movie *The Passion of Christ* and says that already in Jesus days there were Zionist terrorists adding that the Israelis celebrate today their victories as they celebrated the ten plagues against Egypt three thousand years ago. The Norwegian writer provides a very selective and prejudiced interpretation of the current war between Israel and the Hezbollah. While speaking on the Chosen God of the Jews he does not say a word about the very concept of Hezbollah, which literally means "The Party of God," another way of chosenness by divine. In his one-sided interpretation of history he does not say a word about the threat of radical Islam, the Jihadists, and in particular the centrality of the Chosen idea in the other religions then Judaism.

## Chosenness in Reverse

Anti-Semitism is an antithetical negative way to prove the uniqueness of the Jews. Singling out the Jews as the root of all evil and the primary source of the world's ills is a clear example of the doctrine of chosenness in reverse. Pinning the blame on the Jews for the faults of globalization, for the war against Iraq, for the attack against America at the World Trade Center in New York, and for the fluctuations of the financial markets were all recurring themes at the beginning of the present century. Still the "scapegoat" explanation is not sufficient; it is rather part of the attack against the Chosen, and sometimes it explains the timing of the attack when there is a specific political or social imperative to seek reasons for a disaster. The scapegoat, therefore, is the one that is rooted in the religion and culture of societies and even in the minds of some intellectual circles—that is, the Chosen. So it is not the scapegoat but rather the Chosen mantle that makes Jews the obvious target for prejudice.

Endless works have been written and theories developed concerning the causes of anti-Semitism. The topic is widely debated because a coherent and comprehensive theory is hard to develop. However, the problem is that many of the theories of the root causes of anti-Semitism focus on the historical conditions and circumstances at the time of specific events, so that the causes suggested come with religious, sociological, economic, political, and psychological explanations. These theories may help to understand the timing of a particular anti-Semitic wave or incident, but they do not provide a better understanding of the recurrence of hatred of the Jews as the most persistent hatred in the history of mankind.

Anti-Semitism should be viewed, therefore, not only as the most persistent hatred against any people, minority, religion or nation, but also as the oldest. This is because the Jews are the oldest civilization in existence, still carrying the same religious and cultural features of their origins when they introduced the world to monotheism and to God's Covenant with the Chosen. What appears to be a strictly religious belief has become from the beginning to today, a consistent source of both inspiration and irritation. This comes in waves; sometimes it brings admiration and sometimes hatred; sometimes Jews are praised for their contributions to mankind, and sometimes the same people are accused of evildoing. The common thread linking all this is the belief or disbelief that the Jews are the Chosen People or that they illegitimately claim to be such.

Nicholas Berdyaev provides an explanation for anti-Semitism. He rejects the conventional theories on the political and economic motives of anti-Semitism because in his view, anti-Semitism is part of the deep envy of the Jews. In his belief, the scapegoat theory is more serious because this is a human need that the Jews can provide: "When men feel unhappy and connect their personal misfortunes with historic ones, they try to make someone responsible for it . . . nothing is easier to exploit . . . than the culpability of the Jews. The emotional soil is always ready to receive the myth of the Jewish world conspiracy."[21] Why is the emotional soil so ready? Berdyaev's references to the Chosen Jews contain the complex attitude of Christianity: "A Christian must have the mystical feeling that every Jew bears upon himself the seal of the mysterious destiny of Israel, God's Chosen [P]eople, which gave Christ to the world but which also crucified him."[22] Berdyaev's inconsistencies are even more apparent when he says that religious anti-Semitism is obligatory for any Christian, while saying in the same breath, that "hatred of Jews—racial, domestic, political—is inadmissible for a Christian, but religious hatred of the anti-Christ aspect of Judaism is both possible and . . . inevitable."[23]

## What's New?

The "new" anti-Semitism of the third millennium is no different then the "old." It contains all the same components: the lies; the blood libels; the myths; the accusations of the Jews as a collective irrespective of where they live, using all the stereotypes from ancient and medieval times; corruption of the language of human rights; and finally by use of the concept of the Chosen. Hatred is preached by an unholy alliance of radical Islam, left-wing intellectuals, and right-wing politicians. It is a global phenomenon, which both focuses on Israel and the Jewish people as the source of all evil and, at the same time, consistently denies charges of anti-Semitism, rejecting claims that Jews are attacked and denying that Muslims are engaged in a worldwide concentrated effort of genocidal anti-Semitism.

Similar accusations even appear in America. James Moran, a Democratic congressman from Virginia, speaking, not by chance, to a church group, said in

March 2003, that President Bush went to war in Iraq only because of "the strong support of the Jewish community." [24]And the notorious right-wing Republican and conservative Pat Buchanan, spoke about a "cabal of polemicists and public officials" for initiating the [Iraqi] war for Israel's sake, referring to the Jews as people "who harbor a passionate attachment to a nation not our own." In so doing he raised again the old canard of double loyalty saying that the Jews "subordinate the interests of their own country claiming that 'what is good for Israel is good for America.'"[25] In 2007 two leading American professors, John J. Mearsheimer and Stephen M. Walt, published a book *The Israel Lobby and U.S. Foreign Policy*,[26] which accuses the lobby for perpetuating the myth of Israel as an isolated, beleaguered state surrounded by enemies and in need of America's unstinting financial and military support. Though the book is couched with thousands of "scholarly" footnotes, it arrives to the same description of the "Jewish cabal" myth in an academic fashion.[27]

The attacks on the Chosen and talk about the uniqueness of the Jews are not so new and the even preceded Christianity. The accusation that the Jews always unite together and that they are too influential was already made by Cicero in Rome. In Egypt in the third century when the Jewish community had been sharply reduced, a viciously anti-Jewish document was distributed, complaining about Jewish influence in high places, in a precursor of the *Protocols of the Elders of Zion*.[28]

The *Protocols of the Elders of Zion* have always accompanied new waves of anti-Semitism. This was the pattern at the beginning of the twentieth century, before the two world wars; in Eastern Europe and the Soviet Union during the anti-Semitic campaigns of the 1960s and 1970s; and in the Arab world in several waves in the twentieth century, including two film versions. In 1968, the *Protocols* were printed in a special edition for the Polish Military Academy and members of the Communist Party.

In Soviet anti-Jewish propaganda after the Six-Day War of 1967, Zionism was attacked because "it is based on the Judaic principle that the Jews are a "Chosen People." The Soviets brought quotations from the Bible and the Talmud to bolster their case. They alleged that the international conspiracy of the Jews is based on the claim that, as the Chosen People, they have the right "to enslave, oppress and exploit other peoples."[29]

### Anti-Semitism as a Divine Instrument

Among Jewish commentators, anti-Semitism is part of the burden of the Chosen or an instrument to strengthen Jewish identity. This was an important psychological aid to confront atrocities against God's Chosen. This approach appears in a variety of commentaries throughout the ages. The first incident of anti-Semitism, long before the Jewish era, appears in Genesis, when Isaac settles in Gerar and becomes successful and wealthy. The Philistines envied him and felt threatened by his success. As a result, the king asks Isaac to go: "And Abimelech said to Isaac 'Go away from us; for you are much mightier than we."[30] Rabbi

Samson Raphael Hirsch provides an interesting commentary to this verse on the suffering of the Chosen as an instrument to foster Jewish identity:

> The hate of the nations, who are jealous of the well-being of Israel in exile, is one of the supreme divine instruments to save Israel. If it were not for this Philistine hatred that forces Isaac into isolation against his will, he would easily indulge in his wealth and the prominence that it offers, and he would be deeply engaged in it far more than is fitting for the son of Abraham with his special spiritual mission. . . .
> We find out, therefore that this hatred is one of the greatest rescue instruments of the Jews. It goes together with their well-being and happiness in order to cancel its attractiveness and its effects of seduction and it provides a permanent warning and reminder on their mission as Jews.

So, in the view of Rabbi Hirsch, anti-Semitism is a divine instrument to save the Jews. This is part of their mission as the Chosen. Hirsch, in another commentary, treats the suffering of the Jews as part of their mission and writes, "Israel's sufferings in exile are the same as the sacrifices on the altar of the Temple."[31] When he wrote this passage, he could not have imagined what would befall coming generations of Jews in Nazi-occupied Europe.

Outside observers also make interesting comments on anti-Semitism as a tool for Jewish existence. The French philosopher, Jean-Paul Sartre, in trying to explain the mystery of the Jewish condition, wrote immediately following the Holocaust in 1946:

> The Jews who surround us today have only a ceremonial and polite contact with their religion. . . . [T]he Jewish community is the least historical of all, for it keeps a memory of nothing but a long martyrdom, that is, of a long passivity. What is it, then, that serves to keep a semblance of unity in the Jewish community? . . . It is neither their past, nor their religion, nor their soil that unites the sons of Israel . . . the Jew is perfectly assimilable by modern nations, but he is defined as one whom these nations do not wish to assimilate. . . . Thus it is no exaggeration to say that it is the Christians who have created the Jew by putting an abrupt stop to his assimilation. . . . The sole tie that binds them is the hostility and disdain of the societies which surround them. Thus the authentic Jew is the one who asserts his claim in face of the disdain shown toward him. . . . It is society, not the decree of God, that has made him a Jew and brought the Jewish problem into being. . . . It is us . . . our anti-Semitism, but equally our condescending liberalism—that have poisoned him. . . . [T]he anti-Semite makes him a Jew in spite of himself.[32]

Sartre, like Toynbee, regarded the Jews as a fossilized people, without a real rationale of existence, and he blamed the Gentiles, the anti-Semitic Christians for continuing to keep them as Jews by denying their assimilation. Sartre the existentialist cannot accept Jewish existence as a "decree of God"; therefore "the anti-Semite makes him a Jew in spite of himself." The history of anti-Semitism has shown time and again that, despite the claims of earlier Jew haters, and despite the naiveté of liberal Jews, for anti-Semites (and not just them) the Jew remains forever Jewish, and the Jew cannot escape his condition through social integration, complete assimilation, or even conversion.

Albert Einstein did not differ much from Sartre concerning the motives of Jewish existence: "Perhaps even more than on its own tradition, the Jewish group has thrived on oppression and on antagonism it has forever met in the world. Here undoubtedly lies one of the main reasons for its continued existence through so many thousands of years."[33] Elsewhere Einstein said, "It may be thanks to anti-Semitism that we are able to preserve our existence as a race."[34] Sigmund Meyer Kaufman said after the flare-up of anti-Semitism in Vienna in the 1880s, "I had forgotten that I was a Jew. Now anti-Semitism brought me to this unpleasant discovery."[35]

Baruch Spinoza wrote in the seventeenth century that "[e]xperience has shown that the hatred of the nations maintains the existence of the Jews."[36] As we see, different commentators each coming from their own perspective, reach the same conclusion on the role that anti-Semitism plays in preserving the Jewish people. It can be the hand of the divine; it can be the hostility and disdain of Christian society, but in the final analysis, all come to the same conclusion—that anti-Semitism is part of the burden of the Chosen, and anti-Semitism shapes the identity of the Chosen.

Anti-Semitism was a major driving force of political Zionism, which was led by assimilated Jews who felt that there was no future for meaningful Jewish emancipation through assimilation. Theodor Herzl, Max Nordau, and Leon Pinsker formulated their Zionist ideas as a result of anti-Semitism and the failure to achieve the integration that they so much desired. Herzl alone, even with some of his more assimilated friends, could not have stirred the masses without the adherents of *Hibat Zion* ("Love of Zion") a group of Zionists in Eastern Europe who came from religious backgrounds, without whom the movement could not have gathered momentum. But some of the leaders, including Herzl, arrived to Zionism because of anti-Semitism: "We are one people—our enemies have made us one in spite of us. . . . Distress binds us together. . . . [I]f our Christian hosts were to leave us in peace . . . for two generations . . . [the Jewish people would] merge entirely into the surrounding races."[37] After the First Zionist Congress, Herzl wrote in his diary, "The nation is a group of people in which their closeness is recognized and their unity is maintained by a common enemy."[38]

## International Order and the Chosen

Anti-Semitism is sometimes a mirror of the socioeconomic and political situation, fluctuating with the boom and bust of business cycles and in accordance with abrupt changes in the international system. When there is an economic crisis, demagogic politicians tend to look for scapegoats, and often these are the Jews. There is an intimate link between the international order and the eruption of anti-Semitism. At the beginning of the new century, the disillusionment with the "end of history," along with globalization, the crisis of European identity, and the fear of fundamentalist Islam, are all important sources for the attacks against the Chosen People and its sovereign state, Israel, just as there had been similar anti-Semitic eruptions in the past.

The historian Norman Cohn who wrote a comprehensive study of the *Protocols of the Elders of Zion* wrote that "a grossly delusional view of the world, based on infantile fears and hatreds, was able to find expression in murder and torture beyond all imagining. It is a case history in collective psychopathology and its deepest implications reach far beyond anti-Semitism and the fate of the Jews."[39] Despite the limits of social sciences, history can provide the laboratory for some social patterns and laws concerning anti-Semitism. There are similar patterns, linking the Crusades of the Middle Ages, the pogroms at the end of the nineteenth century, the Holocaust, and the beginning of the twenty-first century. In each case anti-Semitism was related to a major disruption in the international system, internal social tensions, and a need to delineate an enemy. In the nineteenth century, there was a reversal of the dominant trend after a period of Jewish emancipation that was coupled with prosperity, speedy development of capitalism and the market economy, and expansion of the middle classes. In the 1880s and 1890s, there was a clear reversal in the socioeconomic environment, and the Jews were immediately targeted as being responsible.

At that time, German scholars were involved in the famous Berlin anti-Semitism dispute that developed at the same time as the new German Reich was undergoing consolidation. Already then scholars identified the similarity between ancient and modern forms of anti-Semitism, and they agreed that the term was equally applicable to antiquity. German scholars made it clear that the chosenness of the Jews, the "God-given rights of the Jews" lies at the root of their behavior. In the late nineteenth and early twentieth centuries, the most favored theory was that the distinctiveness of the Jews, which is the result of the special nature of their religion, is the reason for anti-Semitism. Anti-Semitism was viewed then as "the simple result of the barrier which Jewry itself increasingly erected against the world in whose midst it lived."[40] Such a statement made at a time when most German Jews were becoming part of enlightened society at the expense of their religious observance is shocking. Even more extreme are other historians such as Eduard Meyer who blames Judaism for its "numerous bizarre attitudes and superstitious rites and customs . . . arrogant presumptuousness and . . . spiteful aloofness toward all those other creeds . . . energetic bustling in commercial life, which viewed the ruthless exploitation of the infidels as the good, God-given right of the Jews."[41]

This was the atmosphere that gave birth to the publication of the infamous *Protocols of the Learned Elders of Zion*, which relate to the so-called conspiracy and plotting by the Jews to take over the economy and government of the world. The *Protocols* are part of the Chosen myth, attributing to Jews unlimited powers.

Though the notorious forgery was probably written in Eastern Europe, possibly by members of the czarist secret police early in the twentieth century, the *Protocols* was inspired by the theories rooted in Christian thought and literature that came from Western Europe. It seems that the authors of the *Protocols* were impressed by wealthy Jewish individuals who were leaders of international trade, but also by the close ties between the Jewish communities and especially the efforts taken by American Jews to help poor communities in Eastern Europe. The large number of Jews in the Bolshevik revolutionary movement and later in high positions in Moscow, as well as the role of the Jewish communist Leon Trotsky in the victory of the Red Army over the Ukrainian nationalists, also helped to spread theories concerning the evil Jews.

In the year 1920 alone, the *Protocols* and other such stories on the "International Jew" were widely circulated in Britain, Germany, Italy, including in the Vatican daily newspaper, *L'Osservatore Romano*, and in the United States. In Germany alone, the book appeared in five editions. Later in the 1920s, the *Protocols* would affect prominent Americans such as Henry Ford, who published his own version. Norman Cohn regards the paranoiac fear of a worldwide Jewish plot and conspiracy as the heart of anti-Semitism. The *Protocols* still remain a central factor in modern anti-Semitism, but they are only one of the variations of the Chosen concept.

The *Protocols* are part of the same complex—the belief that the Jews who believe that they are the nation Chosen by God are running a conspiratorial body that aims to lead and rule the world, at the end of days. This myth played a decisive role in shaping world history since the end of the nineteen century by ushering in anti-Semitic campaigns at the end of the nineteen century and the beginning of the twentieth century. These campaigns took also the form of violent attacks and affected the huge Jewish emigration from Eastern Europe to the United States, inspiring the establishment of political Zionism, directly influencing the worst American Anti-Semitic outburst ever by Henry Ford and, without any doubt, reaching a record at the Holocaust inflicted by Nazi Germany. The *Protocols*, which are driven by a theory that seeks to undermine and refute the Chosen role given to the Jews in the Bible, continue at the twenty-first century to be the most widely distributed book in the world after the Bible (mainly, but not just, in the Arab-Muslim world).

The basic premise of the *Protocols* is that in order to create a favorable international order there is a need to get rid of the Jews and their perception of chosenness. The Jews, say the *Protocols*, have their sense of superiority over the Gentiles: "Have we not with complete success turned the brainless heads of the goyim (Gentiles). . . . [N]one may know it [the truth] except us, the Chosen of God, its guardians." The myth of the Jewish conspiracy, state the *Protocols*, is based on their belief that there cannot be "any other religion than ours of the one God with whom our destiny is bound up by our position as the Chosen People and through whom our same destiny is united with the destinies of the world." This destiny provides the Jew, as the Protocols argue, with huge economic power: "In our hands is the greatest power of our day—Gold. . . . Surely there is no need to seek further prove that our rule is predestined by God?. . . . This Chosen One of God is chosen from above to demolish the senseless forces moved by instinct and not reason."[42]

Anti-Semitism was on the rise in 1920 in both Europe and the United States. The combination of economic depression and the volatile atmosphere at the end of the decade again made victims of the Jews. They were no longer perceived as the harbingers of change: liberalism and capitalism. People were frustrated and angry and searched for a scapegoat. The scapegoat was always there, the eternal Chosen, and leaders and governments were happy that public resentment could be channeled to a convenient target. The Jews were again blamed for all the evils of the world. The Jews in the 1880s had been blamed for manipulating the financial market; now they were condemned for corruption, for controlling the media, and the decline of the political process.

The *Protocols* played a leading role in modern anti-Semitism because they focused on the triangle of the old/new hatred: the Chosen, the Jewish conspiracy, and the impact on the international order. The close relationship between the international order and anti-Semitism is reflected in the "educational campaign," as it was viciously dubbed by Henry Ford Jr., on the "Jewish evil"—"an attempt by the Jews to dominate the world." Henry Ford, the inventor of the automobile assembly line, posed the biggest threat ever to Jewish integration and existence in America in his virulent brand of Jewish hatred and a massive media campaign including the dissemination of the notorious czarist forgery of the *Protocols*. Henry Ford was influenced in his formative years during the latter half of the nineteenth century, by an atmosphere that dealt extensively with the new Chosen People—an American-Aryan race, in an era that was referred to as the "Great Century of Christian Expansion." Books written for young Protestant readers repeated the accusation that the Jews had killed Jesus and explained that sooner or later "the obsolete Jewish religion would give way entirely to the 'New Israel' of America."[43] Christian writers set an alarmist tone in light of the massive immigration of Jews from Eastern Europe that was taking place at the time and was, in their opinion, threatening the character of the country. The Reverend Josiah Strong whose book *Our Country: Its Possible Future and Its Present Crisis* had sold 175,000 copies, wrote enthusiastically about "the superiority of the Anglo-Saxon race, God's truly [C]hosen [P]eople."[44]

The editor of Ford's anti-Semitic magazine published in Detroit, *The Dearborn Independent*, was William J. Cameron was an adherent of the British-Israelites, a group who believed that the contemporary Anglo-Saxons were descended from the Ten Lost Tribes of Israel and that, therefore, Britain and the United States were the true Holy Land. According to Cameron's beliefs, "the Anglo-Saxons were the true 'Chosen People'—and not the 'Modern Hebrews' who were actually usurpers worshiping the subversive doctrines of the Talmud." They denied the Jewish origins of Jesus and claimed that Jesus was the forefather of the modern Germans, Scandinavians and British, and that the Anglo-Saxon and Celtic races were the "Ruling people, destined to master the world."[45] Henry Ford, whose Jewish hatred took the form of psychopathological madness, took upon himself to fight against what he regarded as the Jewish hoax of the Chosen People. A large part, and the main rationale, of Ford's own version of the *Protocols*, *The International Jew*, is dedicated to the denial Jewish chosenness, their Bible, and their history: "The Jews are NOT 'The Chosen People,' though practically the entire Church has succumbed to the propaganda which declares them to be so." With their Chosen theory the Jews were able, explains Ford, to convince Americans that it is wrong and "dangerous to oppose them in anything" and this is how they invaded American schools, their economy, their culture and their political system.[46] The problem, says Ford, lies in the "veil cast over the Christian mind as to the supposedly peculiar destiny of 'God's Chosen People'" and the Christian fallacy to read the Bible "through Jewish spectacles." In order to demolish the Jewish argument, Ford goes to dent the Jewish links to the Bible in creating an absurd argument that the role of the Chosen People was promised to the people of Israel and not the people of Judah that are the Jews nowadays. All the Bible big heroes such as Abraham, Isaac, Jacob, Moses, Joshua, Samuel, and "even Esther and Mordecai were not Jews," says Ford.[47]

In this respect it is interesting to see how outraged was Henry Ford with the Chosen pride of Benjamin Disraeli, and Ford dedicated special section in another volume of Jewish hatred for the convert prime minister who, in Ford's words, "was a Jew and gloried it." Ford directed his attack on Disraeli's Jewish hero Sidonia (based on Rotschild's character) "in whose personality and through whose utterances, Disraeli sought to present the Jew as he would like the world to see him."[48] Ford widely used Sidonia's quotes on the race of the Jews and their mission as the "Old Testament people" and his observations on the nature of power and finance. For Ford Sidonia is the ultimate myth: "Here is *The International Jew*, full dress; he is the Protocolist too, wrapped in mystery, a man whose fingers sweep all the strings of human motive, and who controls the chief of the brutal forces—Money. If a non-Jew had limned a Sidonia, so truthfully showing the racial history and characteristics of the Jews, he would have been subjected to that pressure that the Jews apply to every truth-teller about themselves. But Disraeli could do it." For Henry Ford, who is engaging in a public debate with American Jews there couldn't be a better argument to vindicate the *Protocols*: "American Jews say that the *Protocols* are inventions. Is Benjamin Disraeli an invention? Was this Jewish Prime Minister misrepresenting his people?"[49]

In February 1921 Ford explained why the *Protocols* were so central for his campaign: "They fit with what is going on. They are sixteen years old, and they have fitted the world situation up to this time. They fit it now." When people suggested that the *Protocols* had been forged by Russian government officials, a spokesman for Ford replied, "My only answer to this is what Mr. Ford said, 'Here we have the *Protocols*, and this is what happened.'"[50] In addition to the *Protocols*, Henry Ford was inspired by other anti-Jewish doctrines that originated in Germany in the nineteenth century and combined Aryan racism with "scientific" denial of the Jewish Bible.

## Rewriting Theology

Our historic inquiry of the Chosen shows how the nonreligious world subjects the Jews to the old religious dogmas. The world's obsession with the Jews found very strong expression in Germany at the end of the nineteenth century, and it was then that Gentile intellectuals created the strange and volatile cocktail of half-religious and half-scientific truths that led to the racist ideas and pathological hatred of the Jews adopted by Nazi Germany. Some of the anti-Semites concentrated on developing their own racist theory of the "Chosen Germans" or the "Aryan Nation." In addition, the Germans developed a few more anti-Semitic theories, including a clear attempt to deny the chosenness of the Jews and, in order to contradict the dilemma of the origins of Christianity, the very Jewish roots of Christianity. There were two disputations in Germany in the late nineteenth and early twentieth centuries that strongly challenged the narrative of Jewish history and the Chosen concept, denying the right of the Jews to exist as a separate community. The first was the *Antisemitismustreit* (1879–81), and the second was the *Babel-Bibel-Streit* (*Babylon-Bible Disputation* of 1902–3).

The campaign against the Chosen Jews started as a debate on biblical studies but ended up as a major anti-Semitic attack denying the Jewish Bible (the Old Testament) and accusing the Jews of fabricating the Bible stories and their election as the Chosen People. The leader of this attack was a German Orientalist, Friedrich Delitzsch (1850–1922), who was among the founders of modern Assyriology who delivered a series of lectures on the links between Babylon and the Bible. The first two lectures were attended by Kaiser Wilhelm II (January 1902 and April 1903) and several political and military leaders. Delitzsch reported on his trips to the archeological sites of the Near East and presented his radical theory that rejected the authenticity of the Old Testament and denied the Jewish origins of Christianity. His comparative studies of Babylonian culture and the world of the Bible were motivated by a blatantly anti-Semitic goal, and his views were welcomed by anti-Semites with joy and satisfaction. Delitzsch claimed the absolute superiority of "Babylon" over "Israel" claiming that the Bible is devoid of religious or moral value. His aims were revealed following World War I when he published his book about Judaism and the Jews: *The Great Deception*. The Kaiser, as a good Christian, found it difficult to reject the Old Testament, but he expressed satisfaction that Delizsch has "cut the Chosen People down to size."[51]

Delitzsch argued that the Bible was an imitation of Babylonian traditions, and he accused the Jewish prophecy in the Bible of spreading hatred to other nations. The God of the Jews should be condemned, said Delitzsch, since He is a warrior God, but particularly because He has selected "*only one Chosen nation*,"[52] and the rest of the nations are doomed for destruction that God will execute with His own sword. Delitzsch ridicules the Bible for the election of Israel: "This election is grotesque already in Old Testament grounds, since in hundred of passages that book shows that the Hebrew people did not even want to have Jehovah for a God or be loyal to Him. Who can believe that God could have chosen one people and conferred idolatry—a transgression punished in Israel with death on all the rest of mankind?"[53] Such remarks show how Delitzsch missed the point about the Bible, which never implies the glorification of the Chosen People. On the contrary, the Children of Israel are punished for their misbehavior, sins, and loss of faith.

Delitzsch, in his obsession, is ready under the guise of Orientalism and archeology, to contradict the Church Fathers on the Chosen Jews, and to deny the strong heritage of Judaism in Christianity. Delitzsch claims that the Old Testament is "unfit to be used as a normative scripture by the Christian Church." To argue that Christianity arose from Judaism, says Delitzsch, is a deception and to claim that "Jehovah has anything to do with our Christian God, is an unheard-of fraud perpetrated on all humanity."[54]

In attacking "chosenness," Delitzsch selects those passages that in his view express Jewish arrogance. He professes to be shocked by statements of exclusiveness such as Amos 3:2: "'You only have I known of all the families of the earth' which demonstrates that this God only concerned himself about the Hebrews and no others." Or Zechariah 8:23, which tells how non-Israelites will come to Jerusalem to worship the God of the Jews, or in the words of Delitzsch, "are only dragged along if they attach themselves to Jewish coat-tails." He concludes by expressing what is perhaps the central drive of anti-Semitism: "How incredible that the God in whom we Christians believe . . . would have elected one people as His own and condemned all others to perdition." Speaking to his Christian audience in Germany in 1920, he tells them why Jewish chosenness is a threat to Christianity, and even the Psalms are "full of the particularistic Jewish view of God" in which "the Gentiles are only called to praise Jehovah because He has blessed Israel, and must become Jews to share in any way in Israel's blessedness." He rejects the idea of Isaiah 56:7 that "Mine House shall be called a house of prayer for all peoples" (which he had been told is engraved above the door of many synagogues) and states, "This is not a liberal sentiment as people suggest" because according to the Jews, the Gentiles have to accept circumcision before joining the Jews in prayer.[55]

Being aware that in Christian Germany, he cannot attack the Chosen Jews without de-Judaising Jesus, and he therefore asserts, "Jesus was no Jew, but a Galilean, whose family was compelled to accept circumcision and Jewish law." This, of course, is a complete denial of the New Testament itself. In order to prove his thesis, Delitzsch introduces another classic anti-Semitic theory, saying that Jesus could not be a Jew simply because his personality and mentality cannot be Jewish, because of his "broad universalism and humanitarian outlook [which] are in sharpest possible contrast to the exclusive particularism of the Jews." Finally he proceeds to rewrite the all teachings of the Gospels and the Christian Church: "Christianity . . . is an absolutely independent, new religion—no mere higher stage in the development of Judaism . . . [and therefore] the study of the Old Testament as a theological subject should be abolished . . . and the New Testament must be freed from its embrace by the Old Testament. . . . [T]he teaching of Jesus must be worked out in their purity."[56]

The attack on the Old Testament shows how dependent Christian dogmas are on the complex of Jewish chosenness. Most anti-Semites are reluctant to elaborate on the sources of Jewish chosenness because this immediately requires questioning the very origins of Christianity and its dependence on the Old Testament, and to confront the complex issue of the supersession. Delitzsch is so much troubled by the Chosen factor, that he goes on to rewrite both history and theology. In his attempt to divorce Christianity from Judaism he in effect erases all origins of Christianity. Delitzsch is no different than many anti-Semites, he just replaces the evils of the supersession theory with a new evil theory about Judaism.

## The Clash: From the Crusades to 9/11

At the beginning of the third millennium it is clear that dreams of the end of history and of globalization are collapsing. As had happened in other phases of history, the Jews, both as individuals and collectively (the State of Israel) became the convenient scapegoat. Instead of the Cold War and nuclear deterrence that prevented war, in the place of globalization that encountered both economic and intellectual resistance, people started to speak about a "clash of civilizations."

During the Crusades of the eleventh to thirteenth centuries, Europe had witnessed a similar clash of civilizations. At that time too, it was between Christian Western Europe and Islam and the Jews then too were the scapegoats and victims of vicious anti-Semitism. True, any historical comparison is imperfect, but to ignore the history of anti-Semitism is irresponsible. The Crusaders' campaign was to restore the Chosen title to Christianity in the Holy Land, and later to the rest of the world. During the Crusades, Christianity developed the concept of a "just war," while on the other side, Islam revived in a new and brutal version, the concept of *jihad*—Holy War, including suicide missions by the Shi'ite *hashishin* ("assassins"). The First Crusade was declared on November 25, 1095, by Pope Urban II who called for a "Holy War" against Islam. The Pope used the concept of the Chosen, in a reference to the Franks (the Crusaders) as "a race chosen and beloved of God."[57]

The Crusader forces were already on their way to the Holy Land to fight the Muslims when some of their religious leaders told them to attack the Jews: "Look now, we are going to seek out our profanity and to take vengeance on the Ishmaelites for our Messiah, when here are the Jews who murdered and crucified Him. Let us first avenge ourselves on them and exterminate them among the nations so that the name of Israel will no longer be remembered, or let them adopt our faith."[58] The displacement of the Jews and the election of the new Chosen were the prime motive of the massacres. One of the Church leaders in the Second Crusade in 1146 who led the anti-Jewish incitement, Peter the Venerable, reminded his audience that the liberation of the Holy Sepulcher in the Holy Land reconfirms the rejection of the Jews and the election of the believers in Christ.[59] The massacres, the rapes, and the brutal attempts of conversion ("Accept baptism or die!") had a devastating effect on the Jewish psyche: it did not affect the Jewish belief in their chosenness, but it brought the Jews to focus more on the suffering dimension of their election and to sharpen their sense of separateness in their writings and liturgy. At this time, a specific paragraph against the Gentiles who fight God was incorporated in the text of the Passover Haggadah: "Pour our Thy wrath upon the nations that know Thee not and on the kingdoms that do not invoke Thy Name. For they have devoured Jacob and laid waste his homestead. Pour out Thy fury on them and let Thy blazing anger overtake them. Pursue them in anger and exterminate them from under God's skies."[60]

To their Sabbath prayers they added a passage called *Av harahamim* ("Father of Compassion"), which is a memorial prayer for the martyrs who died while sanctifying God's name. The prayer asks God:. . . . May He, before our eyes, exact retribution upon His foes; so that He will appease His land and His people." It continues with a dialogue with God, appealing to Him to defend the image and status of the Chosen: "And in the holy writings it is said; why should the nations say, 'Where is their God?' Let it be known among the nations . . . revenge for your servants' spilled blood."[61]

\* \* \*

The roots of Muslim rage and its hatred of the West, says Bernard Lewis, is its response to the West's assumption of superiority and to the perceived threat that Western culture is undermining the authority of Islam. Muslims attack secularism and the Jewish-Christian heritage and define the West as "God's enemy."[62] With the success of international terror attacks and the spread of Islam in the West, leaders of fundamentalist Islam use their own Chosen terminology and speak about the restoration of Islam so as to become the most dominant power in the world. Publications issued by al-Qaeda and others present a comprehensive concept of total extermination of Islam's enemies, and that category includes Jews, America, the democracies of the West, and the Christian infidels. The leader of *Hamas* refers to a *jihad* that will "bring Islam to a dominant global position and release it from the hegemony of America and its Zionist allies" and declares that the twenty-first century will be the "Islamic century, the century of liberation, victory, and the fulfillment of potential."[63] The spiritual leader of the worldwide Muslim Brotherhood, Sheikh Yusuf al-Qaradawi, promises that Islam will prevail and eventually become master of the entire world. Qaradawi declares that an Islamic victory will culminate in the conquest of Rome and the defeat of European Christianity and all other religions.[64]

Josef Joffe, the editor of the German magazine *Der Zeit*, explained why anti-Israelism has joined with anti-Americanism as part of the ugly European anti-Semitism. It is all interconnected, Joffe explains, the struggle against globalization, the use of anti-Semitic stereotypes of the "Elders of Zion" variety with their "control" of the media and the economic lobby in Washington. This, combined with European frustrations that stem from the breakdown in national identities and the blurring of the values that accompany the transition to a united Europe, have created the volatile mix.[65] In Britain, which is a close ally of the United States, the media spoke about the "Kosher Conspiracy" (a cover story in the *New Statesman* magazine) claiming that American policy is controlled by Jews. Similar statements were made by the French foreign minister and the German defense minister.[66] In France, observed Walter Russell Mead, one of the most durable components of anti-Americanism is the deep belief that the American financial system is controlled by the Jews. Many French people, he says, "grew up thinking of Uncle Sam as Uncle Shylock."[67] The mix of anti-Semitism with anti-Americanism has been a central element in political campaigns at the beginning of the new century. It reflects the changes in the international system, the still undefined balance of power, and the growing resentment against America, which brings in its wake, anti-Semitism. Those statements by intellectuals are translated by the masses of the radicals who are demonstrating against globalization blaming the Jews for the ills of the world economy. In Davos, Switzerland, at the World Economic Forum in 2003 the anti-globalization banner was accusing: "Nazis, Yankees, and Jews: No More Chosen Peoples!"[68]

# CHAPTER 6

# Shoah

## The Final Solution for the Chosen

The struggle for world domination will be fought entirely between us, between German and Jews. . . . There cannot be two Chosen People. We are God's People.[1]
—Adolf Hitler

Why do the Jews expect special treatment in Auschwitz only for themselves? . . . Do they still consider themselves the Chosen people?[2]
—Sister Teresa Magiera, the mother superior
of the Carmelite convent at Auschwitz, 1987

If there are ranks in suffering, Israel takes precedence of all the nations—if the duration of sorrows and the patience with which they are borne ennoble, the Jews are among the aristocracy of every land—if a literature is called rich in the possession of a few classic tragedies, what shall we say to a national tragedy lasting for fifteen hundred years, in which the poets and the actors were also the heroes?[3]
—Leopold Zunz (1794–1886) brought in George Eliot,
*Daniel Deronda*, 1876

It is true that there have been other instances of genocide in world history, and it is also true that many more non-Jews than Jews were killed in World War II, but there cannot be any doubt that the Holocaust remains a unique case that baffles human imagination. It may sound awesome and horrifying, but more than sixty years after the Holocaust one can argue that this was another act of revelation that the Jews contributed to the mythology of the suffering of mankind. Jews who are reluctant to discuss their role as the Chosen People would be terrified even to think of their contribution as the victims of the worst horrors in history. The Holocaust made Jewish suffering, even though the connotation seems terrible, into a "Light unto the Nations"—that is to say, a deadly warning about the vicious

---

*Shoah*: This Hebrew word for "Holocaust" is used more and more frequently to describe the uniqueness of the destruction of six million Jews during World War II. We have preferred to retain the word Holocaust in this book for the sake of clarity.

potential concealed in the human spirit. This is a role that even the most pious and religious Jew would find difficult and perhaps impossible to contemplate.

The world has recognized the incomprehensible nature and uniqueness of the Holocaust, despite the attempts by many to deny it or to lessen its proportions. This is not a foolproof guarantee for the prevention of another Holocaust or genocide, and it has clearly failed to contain the new and threatening waves of anti-Semitism. But in terms of its legacy in religious and cultural terms, in international law, and in human rights; in literature, the plastic arts, the cinema, and journalism, the Holocaust has become the unique yardstick of man-made horrors.

On January 27, 2004, a day that is marked in Europe as Holocaust Memorial Day (the day of the liberation of the Auschwitz death camp), the international media reported on two statements by major European leaders on this issue, both emphasizing its uniqueness in the annals of mankind. In Brussels, European Commission chief Romano Prodi declared that "the remembrance of the Holocaust, a tragedy that stands alone and unparalleled, has a universal value. . . . Out of the lessons of the Holocaust the new Europe was born, a united Europe, founded on respect for the human person, on the rule of law and on freedom."[4]

In Stockholm, the prime minister of Sweden, Göran Persson, told the Stockholm International Forum on the Prevention of Genocide that the "Holocaust was the greatest failure possible in the history of mankind."[5] Three years earlier, under the leadership of Persson, Sweden embarked upon an international drive on Holocaust education that featured international conferences with the participation of heads of states, special governmental task forces on education, and efforts to provide literature and curricula on the Holocaust to many countries in their native languages.

## The Theology of Suffering

The Holocaust is, perhaps, the biggest theological challenge for the Jewish people. Even those who were trained to regard Jewish suffering as part of the burden of the Chosen could not find the spiritual strength to comprehend this kind of horror. It raised serious questions for people of all faiths and ideologies, and there was a long process of comprehension before people were able to confront the realities of the Holocaust. There were two processes of reckoning: for the victims—the Jews and the non-Jews—and for the perpetrators, collaborators, and bystanders. It took time for people to grasp the facts and to slowly absorb the enormity in their collective consciousness. After many years of neglect and only limited moral confrontation, the Holocaust became a new and unprecedented yardstick for measuring suffering, genocide, and vicious hatred. Again, unwillingly, the Jews provided the world with another unparalleled concept and unthinkable expression of human behavior, with so many unanswered questions concerning God, man, and society. People searched for a frame of reference with which to compare the atrocities and human behavior but were unable to find one and were left with terrifying theological and moral questions.

Some religious people view the Holocaust as part of a divine plan, as a moral enactment in which the Nazis were God's agents to inflict suffering on the Jews.

Thousands of pious Jews went to the gas chambers chanting their credo of faith, believing that the punishment "was the work of God and itself proof that he had chosen them."[6] Not every Jew or survivor is ready to accept this radical approach to Jewish suffering. The Nobel Peace Laureate and Holocaust survivor, Elie Wiesel is straightforward when he speaks about the "terrifying theological implications" of the Holocaust, which amounted to, in his words, the breaking of the Covenant between God and the Jewish people "for the first time in our history."[7] Elsewhere Wiesel has written that "Auschwitz negates all systems, opposes all doctrines. . . . They cannot but diminish the experience which lies beyond our reach."[8] In a different fashion, secular Israelis were raising their criticism on the God of the Jews in essays and in poems. Nathan Alterman, the leading writer of the Labor Movement tied together the Holocaust with the fate of the Chosen in his "Among All Peoples." He wrote it in 1942 when the horrific reports where arriving to the Jews in Palestine but the magnitude of the "final solution" or even the term Holocaust was yet to be in use:

> When our children wept under gallows
> we were deaf to the world's anger
> for you have chosen us among all peoples
> loved us and favored us . . .
> Their eyes speak on:
> God of the fathers,
> we know
> you have chosen us among all the children,
> loved us and favored us.[9]

The issue of God's judgment has been always central in religious philosophy. How can one understand or justify God's goodness and omnipotence in view of the existence of evil? Why do righteous people suffer? Why do evil people avoid justice? How can a religious person explain evil? And why should the Chosen People suffer more than any other people?

In Jewish tradition, righteous people often pose such questions, as was done by the two pillars of the Chosen, Abraham and Moses. In the Talmud, Moses asks God to tell him the ways of the Holy One with regard to the dispensation of justice, and questions Him directly: "Master of the Universe, what is the reason that there are righteous people for whom things are bad . . . and wicked people for whom things are good?"[10] This exchange is made immediately after the Jews have sinned with the Golden Calf, and the Torah describes a major rupture between God and His people. The Talmud refers to Exodus (33:12–16) where Moses invokes the Chosen concept in order to save the Jews and implores God to "make Your ways known to me. . . . How, then, will it be known that I have found favor in Tour eyes—I and your people—unless you accompany us, and I and Your people will be made distinct from all other people on the face of earth." The Hatam Sofer (1799–1866) a leading ultra-Orthodox Hungarian rabbi, commented that the great fear after the sin of the Golden Calf, was that God might transfer the title of Chosen to some other people,[11] and that is why Moses wished to under-stand the ways of God and why he asked for a special intercession that would keep the Jews distinct.[12]

This is precisely why, in a prayer introduced to Jewish liturgy in the twelfth century after the Crusades, the Jews plead for both protection and revenge, telling God that at stake is the special relationship between the Chosen People and God: "Why should the nations say, 'where is their God?' Let there be known among the nations, before our eyes, revenge for your servants spilled blood."[13] The Jewish victims of the Crusades, like Moses in the Sinai Desert, appeal to God to try and convince Him that it is in His interest to keep intact His own rep-utation and the special status of the Chosen People.

In addition to their rational approach to suffering and catastrophe, Jews revert also to their mystic literature, including the Kabbalah. A common kabbalistic interpretation of evil has to do with the concept of "breaking the vessels," which according to the theosophic doctrine of Rabbi Isaac Luria from the kabbalistic school of Safed in the sixteenth century, means that sometimes there is a need to bring about destruction in order to prevent a catastrophe. This is a measure of *tikkun* ("repair"), a mystic safety valve that is used in the cosmos as part of the kabbalistic notion that you fix the world above in order to affect the physical world on earth.

Some Zionist rabbis would regard the restoration of Jewish sovereignty in the Land of Israel as a *tikkun* of the victims' souls, those whose death was required for the process of redemption. By this reasoning, the Holocaust was an act of divine intervention following the failure of the Jews to confront emancipation, and this failure would become the basis for a new history in the Holy Land. Other, more Orthodox rabbis, saw it as an *olah*—atonement sacrifice for past sins.[14] In Yossel Rakover's book, *Appeal to God*, which is a work of fiction about the Holocaust, the author recreates a figure resembling Rabbi Levi-Yitzchak from Berdichev who died in 1809 and was known as the "Defender of Israel." The rabbi frequently engaged in arguments with God in defense of the Jews. In Rakover's book, there is an attempt to try and take God to task in the ruins of the Warsaw Ghetto, and yet the Jews continue to believe in God, despite the suffering.[15]

Several Jewish thinkers, including religiously Orthodox ones, in their discus-sion about the role of God in the Holocaust use a rare concept: *hester panim* ("Hidden Countenance") of God at a time of severe disaster. The source is to be found in Deuteronomy 31:38: "Yet I will keep my countenance hidden on that day, because of all the evil they have done." God absents himself so as to express the punishment in very severe terms. There is no satisfactory answer. There is no clear answer with regard to the near-sacrifice of Isaac by his own father Abraham, and there cannot be an answer that will satisfy human comprehension.

In Hassidic literature, this is further developed in the concept of *hesed nistar* ("concealed kindness"), which is consistent with the teachings of the founder of Hassidism, Rabbi Israel Ben Eliezer Ba'al Shem Tov (ca. 1700–60), known by his initials as the *Besht*, who "viewed suffering as a hidden manifestation of the divine, purposely hidden in order to be sought." This is the kind of suffering, the

Besht says, that gives the opportunity to draw closer to God. The external fear that is created by the divine stimulates the inner fear that leads to the acceptance of suffering with love.[16] For many Orthodox Jews, the terrible experiences of the Holocaust were seen as a prelude to the arrival of the Messiah, a part and parcel of the unique status of the Chosen. The Talmud brings the concept of *hevlehi mashiah* (literally "birth pangs" [of the Messiah]) the stress of a woman in labor, namely, the trials and disaster that will prelude the coming of the Messiah.

Not all Jews could sustain their faith after the Holocaust. Many were unable to remain religious because they were neither able nor prepared to confront the idea of this unique suffering of the Jews. Others, who escaped the Nazi tentacles, could not wait to shed the burden of their Jewishness. There are estimates that a fifth of Holocaust survivors chose to leave Judaism after the Holocaust.[17] One example that received a great deal of publicity concerned Madeleine Albright, former United States Secretary of State, whose parents refrained from telling her about her Jewish origins and about the fate of her grandparents who perished in the Holocaust.[18] In another case in 2006 a Republican senator from Virginia, George Allen, denied on television his Jewish roots unaware that his Jewish mother, at the age of eighty-three, whose father was taken to a Nazi concentration camp, already admitted that she concealed her Jewishness for the sake and well being of her children.[19]

Christians find the suffering of the Jews as recounted in Isaiah as their source of redemption. This explains why the death camps of the Holocaust have became points of contention between Jews and Christians (such as at Auschwitz [see the discussion later in the chapter]), with the attempt of the Church to hold posthumous conversions of Jewish victims. The widely quoted verses in Isaiah have become a central theme for Christians who use them to tie together Jewish suffering with the supersessionist theory: "He was wounded for our transgressions, he was bruised by our iniquities, upon him was the chastisement that made us whole, and with his stripes we are healed. . . . And the Lord has laid on him the iniquity of us all."[20] Some Christian Zionist supporters of Israel, mainly Protestants, considered Hitler's persecution of the Jews as a divine plan in which God was acting through the enemies of the Jews in order to prepare them for Armageddon and the End of Days.[21]

## Final Solution of the Chosen: "There Cannot Be Two Chosen Peoples"

The scope of the Holocaust is too awesome and incomprehensible to be explained in terms of the rivalry for the Chosen title. However, there is no doubt that the issue was in the background of the thinking of many Nazis and German intellectuals. As shown earlier, the Chosen concept had been prominent in German intellectual thought since the early nineteenth century and was a part of German racist and anti-Semitic literature long before Hitler. This leads to the horrifying thought that the Germans eventually perpetrated the Final Solution because they believed that there was no room for two Chosen Peoples.

Nazi racism is by definition a Chosen People theory. Hitler and the National Socialists believed that the intellectual and physical differences between peoples could be defined and measured. It is true that in Nazi literature and later in the policies of National Socialism, racism was also directed against other nations and minorities. Germans rejected the French pretensions to cultural preeminence and emphasized German superiority over the Slavic peoples. When Nazis referred to the need to "purify the German race," they included gypsies, people of African descent, and Arabs. But they considered the Jews as the real challenge to German world domination. Hitler drew his racist ideas from many strands and sources in literature and elsewhere, but more than anything else he merged together, in an almost symbiotic process, his racism and his hatred of the Jews. The Jewish people were his overweening obsession and almost his exclusive target in his efforts to eliminate the "unfit" and to realize racial purity in a "victory of the better and the stronger." His pathological hatred of the Jews is evident in his writings, but what is less emphasized, and sometimes completely unrecognized, is the significance that he attached to the struggle with the concept of the Chosen.

Hitler's attitude to other races pales into insignificance beside his hatred of the Jews. The Jew in Hitler's view is "a force of almost cosmic malevolence, the chief obstruction to racial redemption."[22] Like previous (and later) anti-Semites, Hitler combines the contrasting images of the inferior and weak Jew with the superhuman and powerful Jew who is able to control world politics and economy. The Jew was responsible for the German capitulation in World War I and the ensuing socioeconomic miseries, but also for the damage done to the purity of the German race through the activities of prostitution and the importing of black servicemen into the occupied Rhineland.

*Mein Kampf* is the primary source for understanding Hitler's ideas about Jews and their fate. It was written when Hitler was in prison following the abortive putsch of November 1923, whose result was to declare the Nazi party illegal. The word "Jews" appears on almost every page of *Mein Kampf*; it even contains a chilling reference to the killing of thousands of Hebrews "under poison gas,"[23] indicating that this idea had been germinating in Hitler's mind for almost two decades before its first implementation. Basically *Mein Kampf* is about an apocalyptic conflict between the Aryans and the Jews, struggling for world dominion. It is a badly written book with brutal language including the worst kind of prejudices, but it appealed to the emotions of the masses. In it, Hitler appears to regard himself as the Messiah who fights against the Jew on behalf of God, the almighty creator. Hitler is fighting so that the Aryans will be seen as the Chosen race claiming that "We are God's people."[24]

We are unused to thinking of Hitler in any kind of relation to God. But this relationship was, in fact, integral to his conception. Hitler writes as if he were the savior of humanity chosen by God for the task; "Hence today I believe that I am acting in accordance with the will of the Almighty Creator: by defending myself against the Jew, I am fighting for the work of the Lord."[25] Hitler's racist theory claimed that the Aryans, by their very nature and by their blood, had been chosen to rule the world. Therefore the continued existence of the world depended on the successful effort of the Aryan race to maintain the purity of its blood and to reproduce itself "so that our people may mature for the fulfillment of the mission allotted it by the creator of the universe." The Jews are the prime obstacle of this mission, because "[i]t is the inexorable Jew who struggles for his domination over the nations." Marxism, in Hitler's view, is a leading element in the Jewish conspiracy—the goal of Marxism is to "destroy all non-Jewish national states" and then "to hand the world over to the Jews." By using "the organized mass of Marxism," Hitler explains, "he [the Jew] has found the weapon which lets him dispense with democracy."[26]

The Jews, according to Hitler, planned to take over the world through a conspiracy of international capital and Marxism. In a memorandum written in 1936, Hitler continued to link the threat of Marxism with Jewish power, which he claimed can bring about the final destruction of the German people: "Since the beginning of the French Revolution the world has been drifting with increasing speed towards a new conflict, whose extreme solution is named Bolshevism, but whose content and aim is only the removal of those strata of society which gave leadership to humanity up to the present, and replacing them by international Jewry. . . . For a victory of Bolshevism over Germany would not lead to a Versailles Treaty, but to the final destruction, even the extermination of the German people."[27]

Hitler wrote in *Mein Kampf* that he fights "[t]he Jewish doctrine of Marxism," which has made the Jews "victorious over other peoples of the world."[28] The war against the Jews is explained as the rivalry between the Jews and the Aryan "pure race" for world domination. The Jews are threatening the Aryan race because it stands in the way of Jewish world rule. Marxism is the Jewish "weapon . . . to subjugate and govern the peoples with a dictatorial and brutal fist." Zionism is the attempt of the Jews to make the rest of the world believe that they will be satisfied with a state in Palestine, while the real goal is to use Zionism as "a central organization for their international world swindle." In addition, the Jews are contaminating the Aryan race by means of sexual relations and by bringing people of African descent to the Rhineland with the same aim of "bastardization" of the Aryan race: "by contaminating and poisoning individuals through sex and by contaminating the arts, literature and the theater, ridiculing religion and making a mockery of national feelings," the Jew will throw the white race down "from its cultural and political height" and will become its master.[29]

The Jews provided Hitler with the necessary scapegoat that was a critical element in building up the Third Reich, on its way to becoming the Chosen nation. In this sense the Jews met this requirement because their satanic image was strongly implanted in the European mind through centuries of Christian teachings. Nazism was a religion because it had the three necessary characteristics of a religion: the perception of high power, the submission to that power, and the establishment of relations with that power. Hitler wanted to eradicate Christianity and replace it with a new cult: "a strong and heroic faith . . . in a God indistinguishable from blood and destiny." Hatred of the Jews was therefore an important element, which fell on the fertile ground of the anti-Semitic masses. The existence of a devil, explains the historian Leon Poliakov, "assured a better understanding of God; hatred of the unclean stimulated adoration of the divinity. The religion of the Master Race was perfectly suited for inspiring complete fear and submission in the faithful. . . . In the eyes of Hitler and the Nazis, the concept of a Chosen People symbolized the dishonored morality of the Gospels and the Judeo-Christian tradition."[30] This is the meaning of Hitler's assertion that "We [the Aryans] are God's people," and his plan to place the Aryans as the Chosen required the displacement, by any means possible including annihilation, of the Jews and their own claim to be the Chosen.

The Germans carefully watched the world reaction, or rather inaction, to their anti-Jewish policies and legislation. The world indifference to the fate of the Jews was highlighted in the Evian Conference in July 1938, which was organized under the initiative of President Franklin D. Roosevelt who was unanble to find countries willing to accept Jewish refugees and failed to condemn Germany's treatment of the Jews. The conference was received in Nazi Germany as another encouragement for embarking upon a series of anti-Jewish measures: the regulation in August 1938, requiring Jews to change their names—all males to "Israel" and all females to "Sarah"—the quotas for Jewish emigration from Vienna in August 1938, and the first attempt to expel them in October, 1938. All this culminated in the great *Kristallnacht* pogrom of November 9–10, 1938. In a memorandum issued by the German Foreign Ministry on January 25, 1939, it was clear that the Nazis were encouraged by the lack of world reaction saying, "[B]y now almost all the countries in the world have sealed their borders hermetically against the burdensome Jewish intruders" especially noting that the British government "has limited Jewish immigration into Palestine."[31]

Encouraged by the world's evident indifference to the fate of the Jews, Hitler himself, in a speech made five days after the foreign ministry memorandum quoted above, spelled out more of his plans, making it clear that his fight was aimed at those perceived to be God's Chosen, and while referring to the Bible, he made his most far-reaching statement concerning the Final Solution:

> The world has sufficient space for settlements, but we must once and for all rid ourselves of the opinion that the Jewish race was only created by God for the purpose of being a parasite living on the body and productive work of other nations. . . . During my struggle for power it was, in the first instance, the Jewish race that received my prophecies with laughter when I said that I would one day take over the leadership of the state . . . and that I would then settle the Jewish problem. Their laughter was uproarious, but I think that for some time now they have been laughing on the other side of their face. Today I will once more be a prophet: If the international Jewish financiers in and outside Europe should succeed in plunging the nations once more into a world war, then the result will not be the Bolshevization of the earth, and thus the victory of Jewry, but the annihilation of the Jewish race in Europe! The nations are no longer willing to die on the battlefield so that this unstable international race may profiteer from a war or satisfy its Old Testament vengeance. The Jewish catchphrase, "Workers of the world unite," will be conquered by a higher realization, namely "Workers of all classes and of all nations, recognize your common enemy![32]

Hitler's views fell on fertile intellectual ground. The concept of Germany-the-Chosen had already been popular in the nineteenth century. During that period

German scholars such as Otto Jahn, Ernst Mortiz Arndt, Heinrich von Treitschke, and Friedrich von Bernhardi preached the superiority of the German race and laid the framework for Hitler's theories. Romantic philosopher Johann Fichte spoke of the Germans as "the primal people," who only needed a "Zwingherr," a compelling leader, to mold them into what they essentially were, while Friedrich Lange, the early Austrian film director, wrote, "The German people are the elect of God and its enemies are the enemies of the Lord."[33]

Friedrich Nietzsche provides us with a typical mixture of admiration and hatred in his portrayal of the Jews:

> Every people and person has his unpleasant, yes, even dangerous traits; it is cruel to demand that the Jews be an exception. Perhaps their traits are particularly unpleasant and dangerous; and perhaps the young Jewish petty speculator is the most repellent invention of humanity. But I should like to know what the final balance sheet would be for this people that, not without the guilt of all of us, has the most unhappy history of all peoples, and to whom we owe the most noble of men (Christ), the purest sage (Spinoza), the most powerful book and the most effective moral law in the world.[34]

But Nietzsche's complex message was distorted by Germans-at-large who, in the racist and anti-Semitic atmosphere created by National Socialism, selectively singled out what they wanted most to hear.

To a large extent, German anti-Semitism was driven by this struggle with the Jews in the nineteenth century, reaching its heights in the notorious Berlin anti-Semitism disputes (Jews were accused of fabricating the Old Testament in order to portray themselves as the Chosen People) and continuing to evolve into the disasters of the following century. In the nineteenth century, some anti-Semites had spoken of a possible German-Jewish symbiosis. The concept of symbiosis, a particular and reciprocal relationship between Germans and Jews, even entered the Nazi era and Hitler himself. In a book published in 1939 entitled *Conversations with Hitler*, Herman Rauschning, a Nazi politician who broke with the Fuehrer and fled to Switzerland, reports Hitler's observation that "the Jew is evil incarnate. He has made a myth out of the Jew, and has made capital out of it." Israel, which according to Hitler is the historic people of the spiritual God, "cannot but be [the] irreconcilable enemy of the new, German, Chosen People." One of Hitler's comments quoted in the book reads, "The Jew is always within us. Yet it is easier to battle him as flesh and blood rather than an invisible demon. . . . Has it not struck you how the Jew is the exact opposite of the German in every single respect, and yet is as closely akin to him as a blood brother." After testifying how impressed he is with *The Protocols of the Elders of Zion* and that the Germans "must copy it—in our own way, of course," Hitler throws the doomsday bomb: "There cannot be two [C]hosen [P]eople. We are God's choice."[35] The passages from *Mein Kampf* and other quotes from Hitler provide the most explosive and awesome reflection on the Holocaust as part of the struggle with the Chosen. In history's long view, the Final Solution of the

Jewish Question can be seen as the climactic event of a conflict the Nazi Fuehrer summed up so succinctly *"There cannot be two chosen peoples."*

As shown in the previous chapter Henry Ford, who preached the worst kind of anti-Semitism in America, preceded Hitler in promoting the concept of the superiority of his race (the Anglo-Saxon race together with the Aryan race) as "God's truly [C]hosen [P]eople." Hitler's affinity with Ford was recognized very early in the history of Nazism. In the Nazi party headquarters in Munich in 1922, one could find copies of the German edition of *The International Jew* by Henry Ford and a framed photograph of the industrialist-author hung on the wall of Adolf Hitler's office.[36] Less known is the fact that that Ford, like Hitler, was convinced that there cannot be two Chosen Peoples. In some of the issues of *The Dearborn Independent*, we can detect the same ideas that later influenced Hitler, although in Detroit, and the hatred to the Jews is accompanied by biblical verses and theories. In several articles, which appeared between 1920–27, the theme of the Ten Lost Tribes was central in the process of the replacement of the Jews. There is clear hostility to the Jews, an emphasis on the rivalry between Christianity and Judaism with references to the Gentile "Chosen" and the "True Israelites" as opposed to the Jewish pretenders who take the name of Israel in vain. In an article on May 1923, the magazine predates Hitler in the treatment of the Chosen in an article: "Are the Jews the Chosen People?" The article quotes the Reverend William Pascoe Goard, the chief minister of the British-Israel World Federation, who issued a warning: *"[T]here is not room enough for both Israel and Anglo-Saxondom, if these are two separate conceptions. . . . It must be one or the other . . . the international banking ring outlined in the Protocols of the Elders of Zion or the Banner of the Lord."*[37]

Professor Hans J. Morgenthau, who is known as the leading proponent of the realist school in international relations, offered a similar analysis about the deadly tension between the Jewish concept of the Chosen and the Nazi ambitions to become a master nation. Without quoting Rauschning, Morgenthau provides a rational analysis of Hitler's grand design about the Jews. In a lecture in 1962, Morgenthau, who was not a religious or an active Jew, said that Jewish existence should be explained "in religious terms . . . through the concept of the Chosen People." The Chosen concept, Morgenthau said, "shows the competitive aspect of the relationship between the remnants of the Jewish People, on one hand, and the master nations on the other. Between them an inevitable, existential conflict exists; for the claim of a master nation to supremacy is incompatible with the Jewish claim to special relationship to God." For Hitler and for Nazi Germany the Chosen Jews was a threat since *"Jews by their very existence, deny the validity of the master nation's claim."*[38]

The infamous Nuremberg Laws, adopted in several stages from September 15, 1935, were the direct outcome of the doctrine aimed to preserve the Germans as the only Chosen People. The title of the law that forbade sexual relations between Germans and Jews is a sickening perversion of Hitler's mania on the Chosen: "The Law for the Protection of German Blood and German Honor."

It is interesting that one of the most distinguished leaders of German Jewry, Rabbi Leo Baeck tried to answer the racial anti-Semitism of Nazi Germany with references to the "Light unto the Nations" as the positive message of the Chosen. In a prayer he composed for the Reform Jewish communities to recite on the eve of the Day of Atonement, on October 10, 1935, he said,

> We will pray "Lord forgive us!" . . . and with the same courage with which we have acknowledged our sins. . . . [W]e express our abhorrence of the lie directed against us, and the slander of our faith. . . . Who brought to the world the secret of the Lord Everlasting, of the Lord Who is One? . . . Who brought to the world respect for man made in the image of God? Who brought to the world the commandments of justice, of social thought? In all these, the spirit of the prophets of Israel, the revelation of God to the Jewish people had a part. It sprang from our Judaism. . . . We stand before our God . . . the source of our survival. . . . "Behold, he that guarded Israel shall neither slumber nor sleep."[39]

The recital of this prayer was banned by order of the Germans, and Rabbi Baeck was arrested by the Gestapo.

There is a direct link between the religious hatred of the church, which included clear racial elements, starting with the Catholic Church and up to Martin Luther. German society was well prepared for the task as shown by Daniel Goldhagen in his book *Hitler's Willing Executioners*. Hitler had only to inject his diabolical theories into the traditional images of the Chosen doctrine, which was at the center of the Nazi theory of the "Master Race," adding the Final Solution element as its operational trigger. A German historian Hans Mommsen has said, "All Hitler had to do was to nod his head for the genocide to take place."[40]

A similar observation was made in Japan, focusing on Christian responsibility for the Holocaust. A Japanese Catholic, Michio Takeyama, was not satisfied with the explanation that Nazism was a different form of Jewish hatred with no connection to the Christian roots of German society. In 1963, in an essay entitled "The Bible and the Gas Chamber," he identified sources of hatred and Nazi policies in the New Testament. The passages that refer to the Jews as children of the devil, conspirators, evildoers, and beasts in human form, have become, in his view, an attitude fixed in the Christian "collective unconscious." What the Nazi leaders and the rank and file heard from Adolf Hitler and Heinrich Himmler was in conformity with Christian teachings.[41]

## The Appropriation of Suffering

Auschwitz has become the preeminent symbol of Jewish suffering in the Holocaust and the most extreme expression of the machine of the Final Solution. If we speak about the suffering aspects of the Chosen, Auschwitz is the place where more than one million Jews perished between 1942–45. The twin parts of the extermination camp, Auschwitz and Birkenau, became the ultimate symbol of the bureaucratic machinery of mass murder and genocide. Jews killed in Auschwitz outnumber by far all other national or ethnic victims.

For more than forty years Jewish suffering in the camp was not specifically acknowledged. Communist Poland exploited the site for propaganda purposes to manipulate and falsify the historical record in order to claim that the Poles suffered more than any other nation during the war. On this subject there was an unholy alliance between the Catholic Church and the communists, both of whom wanted to play down specifically Jewish suffering. The official guides and the literature published by the museum now standing at the site failed to indicate that it was the Jews who were overwhelmingly the principal victims. The Jewish victims were counted as Greek, Dutch, French, and Hungarian as well as Polish. Each of these groups had their own pavilion counting the Jews among their national victims.[42]

The Poles denied Jewish martyrdom as part of what Henryk Grynberg calls the "appropriation of the Holocaust."[43] This appropriation of Jewish suffering is a typical element in a pattern of historic revisionism and cynicism. Only later, and in several stages did the Poles agree to add a Jewish dimension to the exhibition following American-Jewish pressure. Today there is a pavilion in Auschwitz devoted to the Jews.

The Catholic Church also had its own agenda and regarded the camp as the "epitome of the suffering which lies at the heart of the Christian faith," and it had no qualms about capitalizing on the memory of the Jews murdered in Auschwitz."[44] In 1979, Pope John Paul II celebrated a mass at Birkenau before tens of thousands of Catholic worshippers who stood between two crematoria situated on the grounds of what might well be regarded as the largest Jewish cemetery in the world. This was part of the process of usurpation of memory, in accordance with church theology that persistently quotes Isaiah 53, as shown earlier, in order to appropriate the suffering of the Jews as part of the church's Chosen doctrine.

The crisis in Polish Catholic-Jewish relations became progressively worse in the late 1980s over a convent and crosses in Auschwitz, which had become another manifestation of the replacement theory, this time over Jewish suffering in the death camps. In 1984, a group of Carmelite nuns moved into a building abutting the walls of Birkenau and raised a twenty-foot-high cross in front of it. This action was in violation of a United Nations resolution declaring the Auschwitz-Birkenau complex to be an international historic site that should not be altered in any way. The convent was part of a nationwide proliferation of sites honoring Polish martyrdom during World War II. It was built with the support of Belgian Catholics in a building called the "Theater," which had been used for the storage of Zyklon-B canisters, the deadly poison gas used in the camp. In its fundraising campaign for the project, the Belgian group revealed their theological aim, explaining that the convent "will become a spiritual fortress and a guarantee of the conversion of strayed brothers from our countries as well as proof of our desire to erase the outrages so often done to the Vicar of Christ."[45]

In similar vein was the nuns' message explaining that they are there so as to pray for "mankind's true conversion of mind and heart to the mentality of Christ and the plan for God in Christ; for man's salvation and eternal life in his kingdom."[46] The concept of posthumous conversion was a clear affront to the Jewish victims and to the collective memory of millions who identify Auschwitz as the industrial center for the Final Solution. This was accompanied by a cynical and even vicious attempt to challenge the unique suffering of the Jews as part of a religious conversion process, by the same church that was historically responsible for spreading anti-Semitism.

The idea of the posthumous baptizing of Jews and members of other religions, is practiced by the Church of Jesus Christ of Latter-Day Saints—the Mormons, whose headquarters is in Salt Lake City, Utah. The Mormons concentrated on the baptism of Holocaust victims and later added to their database for posthumous conversion, famous Israelis and Jews such as David Ben Gurion, Theodor Herzl, Anne Frank, Moshe Dayan, and Albert Einstein. In 1995, the Mormons reached an agreement with American Jewish groups to remove the Jewish names from their database of four hundred million names, but by 2003 they still had not implemented this.[47]

In Poland, the appropriation of the Holocaust memory deteriorated into a major international crisis. The world's media was filled with stories about Jewish protests at the site and bitter exchanges that took place with the Catholic nuns and authorities. Cardinal Józef Glemp accused the Jews "who control the international media."[48] Another look at the anti-Semitic campaign of Cardinal Glemp shows how closely it was related to his war against the Chosen. In an earlier speech, he had accused the Jews of "plying Polish peasants with alcohol" and of "spreading communism" and accused Jewish businessmen for having "anti-Polish attitudes." The Jews, he said, are a nation who "speaks to us from the position of the Chosen People and who control the mass media in many countries"[49].

Elie Wiesel called these attempts an effort to "de-Judaize" the Holocaust,[50] while the former Catholic priest James Carroll is very clear about the ultimate goal: "the cross at Auschwitz evokes . . . everything that has separated Jew and Christian during the two thousand year-old conflict between the two religions. The technical term for that conflict is supersessionism. . . . The idea is that the Jesus movement, as it evolved into the church, effectively replaced the Jews as the Chosen [P]eople of God."[51]

After many protests and long drawn-out diplomatic activity, an agreement was signed in Geneva in February 1987, between representatives of the Catholic Church and Jewish groups, providing for the removal of the Auschwitz convent and the nuns and proposing instead a center for education and prayer situated five hundred meters from the original site. The agreed date was February 22, 1989, but the spirit of the agreement was ruptured when the nuns brought a seven-meter cross (the same one the had been used by the Pope during the 1979 mass) to a corner of the camp where it is visible to all visitors). After several years of bitter exchanges and clashes between Jewish protestors and the nuns, the convent was finally removed in July 1993, but the papal cross remained. Despite repeated Jewish protests and some Catholic promises, by 1998 another three hundred crosses had been planted around the papal cross. The crosses in Auschwitz testify how deep is the Church commitment to appropriate Jewish suffering and how critical it is for supercesssionist Chosen doctrine.

## The Divine Justice of Holocaust Suffering

As we have seen, only after fifty years did the Holocaust receive clear recognition from the Vatican for being a singular event in the annals of mankind. The process of seeing it as a unique event had to overcome many political and psychological barriers. In this process it is remarkable to see the role that Jewish victimhood and suffering played in affecting the perceptions that led to the new organ of human- itarian international law, the Convention on Genocide, leading later to sociocul- tural developments on a universal scale.

The Nuremberg war crimes trials, which started in November 1945, created a precedent in international law. However, they did not focus on the Holocaust, and for many survivors the trials were extremely disappointing because they vir- tually ignored Jewish suffering.[52]

The task of educating the world about the Holocaust was not easy for the Jews. The effort to transmit the message of unique suffering, the responsibility and the guilt, took almost two generations. The suffering of the Chosen was rec- ognized little by little and belatedly. The most difficult questions about German guilt, collaborators in other countries, the limited efforts of rescue and the silence of the outside world, were not discussed at all during the first years. The conspir- acy of silence was broken in 1961 by the capture in Argentina and the subsequent trial in Jerusalem of the Nazi war criminal, Adolf Eichmann, and the months of publicity that followed.[53]

Despite the publicity, the Eichmann trial did not inspire a movement of seri- ous confrontation. The trial was an *ad hoc* wake-up call that would have to wait for many more years before it developed into a real political process. The more serious soul-searching and interest in the Holocaust would only come later fol- lowing the writings of survivors such as Elie Wiesel and Primo Levi in the 1970s. Serious international consciousness was spurred by the American television miniseries, *Holocaust*, and other events commemorating forty years of the Holocaust during the 1980s, culminating in the end of the Cold War in the 1990s.

In the drama of the Holocaust, the story of Jewish suffering unfolded slowly, and there were a few individuals who played a role. One of them was Rafael Lemkin, the creator of the Genocide Convention. Lemkin, who actually coined the word "Genocide" (he always insisted on the capital G), was a Polish Jewish lawyer who had fled to Sweden during the Holocaust and served as a prosecution lawyer at the Nuremberg war trials. He himself had lost forty-nine members of his family in the Holocaust. Lemkin struggled to introduce into international law a legal mechanism against the systematic destruction of national, ethnic, racial, or religious groups.[54] By having genocide recognized as an international crime, he succeeded in the efforts that brought the United Nations to pass the Genocide Convention in 1948, manifesting the ideal set out in the preamble: to cooperate in freeing humanity of the "odious scourge" of genocide. Lemkin held a naïve belief in the power of words, and he thought that the right term could be a powerful tool that would create a universal sense of moral indignation. The secretary-general of the United Nations, Kofi Annan, regarded Lemkin as "one of the unsung heroes of the international human rights movement [who] infused the battle against genocide with new insight and passion, and almost single-handedly drafted an international multilateral treaty declaring genocide an international crime, and then turned to the United Nations in its earliest days and implored the member states to adopt it."[55]

This again, is an awesome exercise in measuring the effects of human suffering. Is it part of the Jewish mission to experience the systematic "destruction of a nation," so that a righteous person like Lemkin will be able to formulate in precise legal terms the terrible human consequences of the Nazi plan for the Final Solution? Is this part of the Chosen's burden and responsibility? Elie Wiesel, Primo Levi, and Rafael Lamkin, and other survivors, as well as the State of Israel in the trial of Eichmann, were the human instruments to address the universal "Light unto the Nations" message of the Chosen suffering.

In the case of the Eichmann trial the State of Israel performed a similar universal mission of the Chosen and despite the controversial abduction of the Nazi leader from Argentina the so called "divine Justice" was recognized in different places. In June 1960, immediately following Eichmann's capture and transfer to Israel, the *New York Herald Tribune* published a leader saying, "In judging the rights and wrongs of his [Eichmann's] removal from Argentina, one comes squarely against an unpleasant dilemma of having to make a choice between rules of legality and the demands of justice. The most important thing is that Eichmann should be tried. Justice, like God Himself, sometimes moves in a mysterious way."[56]

The case of Eichmann was unprecedented on many accounts. It was unique because of the magnitude of the crimes, because of the capture and the abduction, which were a clear violation of Argentinean sovereignty, and because of staging the subsequent trial in an Israeli court of justice. In other words, a felon was captured in country X and was brought to trial in country Y for crimes committed in country Z, and all that at a time that country Y did not in fact exist. Israel was putting to a trial a person who committed crimes before the establishment of the state, an unprecedented case of belated justice.

The *Estado De São Paulo*, regarded the trial of Adolf Eichmann in Israel as a measure that "helps to confirm the mighty force of divine justice which operates beyond time and beyond frontiers and which cannot be arrested by any means whatsoever, neither by protests from foreign ministries nor by the machinations of international jurists." And the newspaper added that "[i]t will be a tremendous religious act from the biblical aspect, an act to be carried out in an atmosphere of the awe of the Old Testament not only to recognize the justice of man that has been re-asserted."[57]

Along similar lines, the *Manchester Guardian* wrote on May 26, "There is a touch of Old Testament justice about the fact that Adolf Eichmann will now be tried in an Israeli court." In legal terms, the act of a kidnapping without authority in no way disables the criminal courts from proceeding against the accused. But in this particular case, it is hard to avoid terms such as the "Mighty force of divine justice" and the "awe of the Old Testament."[58]

Replying to the reservations raised by Eichmann's lawyer the Israeli court emphasized the uniqueness of the case. On the question of the abduction of Eichmann, the court coined a new concept: "[a] criminal escaping the family of nations." Such a person, who had committed crimes against humanity, could be brought to justice in any place, and any country was entitled to try him. Thus, the means by which Eichmann was brought to Israel were irrelevant. Nor did the judges consider the case to be extraterritorial, since the Final Solution also included Jews who lived in Palestine at the time of the World War II. Furthermore, the State of Israel came into being in order to ensure that people who committed crimes against the Jewish nation be called to account for their actions.[59]

The *Washington Post* treated the matter in the light of its historical significance transcending the issue of sovereignty rights: "Probably some international laws and conventions were bruised . . . but no one is disapproving so far. . . . Thousands of survivors . . . must feel deeply grateful to . . . [those] who on a dedicated mission of high adventure tracked down this gas-chamber degenerate through the years and brought him to book. . . . The Jews of the world have a rightful and powerful incentive to track down this brutal mass murderer. Had there been no Israeli state, Eichmann would still be at large, mocking the process of justice."[60]

David Ben Gurion, the Prime Minister of Israel who ordered the abduction of Eichmann, did not hide his vision of a "Light unto the Nations":

> The trial is the important thing, not the penalty. . . . [T]he trial is to show . . . people here and . . . throughout the world the danger of authoritarian society. . . . We want to establish before the nations of the world how millions of people, because they happened to be Jews . . . were murdered by the Nazis. We ask the nations not to forget it. . . . [T]hey should know that anti-Semitism is dangerous and they should be ashamed of it. . . . Those who undertook to search for him were morally right, although not perhaps formally, but sometimes there are moral obligations that are higher than . . . formal law. . . . Israel is the only inheritor of those (murdered) Jews.[61]

An interesting reaction came from Japan combining all the elements: the Chosen Jews, the unimaginable crimes, and the unprecedented trial. The attitude in Japan was of sympathy for the suffering of the Jews, but they objected to Eichmann's trial and the bypassing of the United Nations, which they thought would be a more appropriate tribunal. The Japanese wanted to link the Holocaust with their suffering by the atomic bombs at Hiroshima and Nagasaki, and they opposed the focus on retribution to Eichmann the individual. They criticized the eventual sentence of death as a form of terrorism disguised as justice: "Is this all there is to the wisdom of the Chosen Hebrews? . . . [T]hey simply yielded to the common behavior any nation could exercise. . . . Eichmann should have been spared and set free to choose his own destiny. They should have banished him after branding him with a swastika on his forehead."[62]

A clear vindication by another Japanese scholar Takeshi Muramatsu, cited the uniqueness of the case: "It is an unprecedented, unheard-of event that one nation planned and implemented the extermination of another. Where there is no precedent, there is no law, therefore procedures had to be primitive. A trial of a victimizer at the hands of the victims and their bereaved is similar in appearance to, but different in essence from, a trial of defeated power at the hands of the victorious. Why not understand this point?"[63]

The uniqueness of the Holocaust was recognized in the various reparations and restitution agreements that were signed between governments and the Jewish victims. There was no precedent for restitution for the unique collective crime of the mass murder of European Jewry who were citizens of many countries. The Germans themselves recognized at an early stage in the immediate postwar period that German crimes against the Jewish people called for substantial reparations. Germany was not bound by any clause of international law to pay compensation to Israel and the Jewish people, nor did the major powers exert pressure on her to do so. This was done by German free will, largely as a result of the personal realization of its chancellor, Konrad Adenauer, that this was a moral obligation. There was also no precedent for the unique structure of the negotiations that were carried by representatives of the newly born State of Israel together with representatives of Jewish organizations under the umbrella of the Conference on Jewish Material Claims against Germany. After the signing of the agreement in 1951, the prime minister of Israel, David Ben Gurion wrote to Nahum Goldmann, president of the World Zionist Organization and the Claims Conference, a letter of appreciation in which Ben Gurion commented:

> There is a great moral and political significance to be found in the Agreement itself. For the first time in the history of relations between peoples, a precedent has been created by which a great state, as a result of moral pressure alone, takes it upon itself to pay compensation to the victims of the government that preceded it. For the first time in the history of a people that has been persecuted, oppressed, plundered, and despoiled for hundreds of years in the countries of Europe, a persecutor and despoiler has been obliged to return part of his spoils and has even undertaken to make collective reparations as partial compensation for material losses. This is beyond question the outcome of the re-birth of the State of Israel. There has arisen a protector and a defender of its rights.[64]

Fifty years after the end of the world war, the moral questions re-emerged and occupied the public agenda as if it was a matter of urgent day-to-day business. Reviewing the phenomenon the magazine *Newsweek* published on February 24, 1997, a cover story about Jewish survivors and refugees after the war, under the headline, "War Without End—Why World War II Still Haunts Us All." The subtitle on the cover gave an unusual personal angle to the vicissitudes of human memory, in writing about the family story of the American secretary of state: "Madeleine Albright Talks about Her Hidden Past."[65]

During the course of 1995–98 and basically up until 2000, the Western media was flooded with information concerning plundered Jewish property. The phenomenon was amazing: material on the confiscation of property, bank deposits, and gold transactions, which would usually find a place only in specialist historical journals, found its way onto the front pages of national newspapers, capturing international media interest with extraordinary intensity.[66] For many observers this was a major surprise. In 1995, throughout Europe, ceremonies were held to commemorate the fiftieth anniversary of the end of World War II, and the general expectation was that this would be the final descent of the curtain on the horrors of the war. Some European leaders issued public declarations denouncing anti-Semitism and the crimes of the Nazis, and many delivered historic admissions of guilt on behalf of their countrymen and took responsibility for their nation's collaboration with the Nazis. In Germany itself, many intellectuals and politicians suffered from evident "Holocaust fatigue" and expressed the belief that the time had come for "normalization" of the national memory and an end to the interminable confrontation with the past.[67]

In other European countries discussion of monetary issues accentuated the moral dimension in the conduct of European countries during the Holocaust. Up to then it had been convenient for the Europeans to claim that it was Nazi Germany that had concocted, orchestrated, and carried out the Holocaust, while the rest of Europe was an innocent victim. But the issue of plundered property brought the subject of the Holocaust down to the level of private citizens, families, and communities—people whose property had been confiscated by local police, sometimes with the help of collaborators who provided lists of real estate and bank accounts (sometimes even before they were asked to do so by the Nazis) as well as greedy anti-Semites who, biding their time, waited for the opportunity to seize Jewish property.

Reports of various investigative committees reveal a share of responsibility that was to a large extent concealed through the years by silencing any public debate. Each nation created for itself a collective national memory, in which the facts became interwoven with myths, half-truths, and self-denial. The Austrians, for example, cultivated the myth of the *Anschluss*, portraying themselves as being the first victims of Nazi Germany's expansionism while conveniently forgetting that most Austrians had welcomed the Germans with wild enthusiasm. The French invented an artificial distinction between Vichy—the French regime that collaborated with Nazi Germany—and the "authentic" French people of the Republic (former President François Mitterand himself was a member of a pro-Vichy group in his youth, and he consistently refused to address their past), while the

Swiss were even more successful in convincing themselves and others of their model of "neutrality."

The clash between Swiss national myth and collective memory led to a major political crisis between the United States and Switzerland. What started as a clash between the World Jewish Congress and the Swiss evolved into a confrontation with the United States Congress when Senator Alfonse D'Amato of New York, chaired the Senate Banking Committee hearings on dormant Swiss accounts, while similar hearings took place in the House of Representatives. An international committee chaired by Paul Volcker, former chairman of the U.S. Federal Reserve initiated, in a joint effort with Jewish representatives, the overseeing and auditing of dormant Holocaust accounts, and the Swiss government and banks established a humanitarian fund for Holocaust survivors. Facing continuing criticism, the Swiss foreign minister, Flavio Cotti, issued an unusually introspective statement in January 1997:

> In Switzerland we were in fact rather proud of the overall balance-sheet of our conduct during the Second World War. Some of us were even blinded by the myth of a Switzerland imbued with zeal and uprightness. There were many among us who, looking back, thought that the protective hand of our patron St. Nichols de Flue, had been, as it were, the supreme guarantee against the extension of the war to our country. . . . [It was] a combination of truth, half truth and also myth, together with insufficient depth of historical knowledge. . . . Today we have to admit that we were wrong. . . . We are now determined to recognize this omission in its entirety.[68]

Norway was the first European country to appoint a commission to deal with the broader context of collaboration with the Nazis during the war, which had taken place in Norway under the puppet regime of Vidkun Quisling. When the majority of members of the commission did not want to take moral responsibility for the treatment of the Norwegian Jews during the war, the government and parliament sided with the minority report, which called for a "historical and moral perspective." In the words of the Minister of Justice Gerd-Liv Valla, "The losses of the Jews cannot be limited to economic calculation only. The organized deportation and the liquidation was mass murder, murder of a people. We cannot change what happened, but we can set a moral standard to remind everyone of this dark chapter in the history of Europe."[69]

In Sweden, another country that had remained neutral during the war, the Swedish media in 1996 began to report on the close commercial links including the transfer of strategic military items—between Sweden and Nazi Germany. In late 1996 and early 1997, the government appointed a commission of inquiry to examine the transfer of Nazi gold to Sweden and the fate of art works belonging to Jews that had also ended up in Sweden. In sharp contrast to the behavior of Switzerland, the prime minister of Sweden succeeded in turning his country's confrontation with the past into an international project on Holocaust education.

Two million copies of a book on the Holocaust, *Tell Ye Your Children*, were circulated to schools to fill the knowledge gap, and Prime Minister Goran Persson established the International Task Force for Holocaust Education. The climax of the process was the Stockholm Conference in January 2000, which brought together heads of state from forty-three countries, who drafted a commitment that the Holocaust should become an indivisible part of the study of human history and that its lessons of morality and human rights should become part of international law.[70]

An interesting part of the reports in the media was on the plunder of Jewish-owned art. This great culture robbery was described by art expert Hector Feliciano: "The Germans wanted, whenever possible, to destroy their enemies' souls, personalities and memories" that was reflected in their art collections.[71] Stuart Eizenstadt explained, "[L]ike the Holocaust itself, the efficiency, brutality, and scale of the Nazi art theft was unprecedented in history." This, says Eizenstadt, was part of Hitler's grand design to build his own Chosen race: "One of the Holocaust's greatest ironies is that its most malevolent perpetrators fancied themselves a new cultural elite. Hitler, an indifferent painter during his early years in Vienna, viewed the amassing of art as a necessary project in his creation of an Aryan master race."[72]

More than fifty historical commissions have been established to deal with various aspects of their country's behavior during the Holocaust. As a result, entire chapters of history have been revised and rewritten—often revealing a dark side of the past that has sometimes brought shame and embarrassment in its wake. Another revolutionary aspect was the establishment of commissions in major industrial companies and financial institutions such as Daimler-Chrysler, Degussa, Deutsche Bank, General Motors, Ford, and different insurance companies.

The work of these commissions compelled governments, intellectuals, academia, the media, and the general public to reflect on their own collective memory, national myths and to open suppressed chapters for additional scrutiny. The growing interest in Holocaust literature, exhibitions, and movies was a part of this process. In some places there was a direct effect on historical research and curricula in school and universities. A process of the globalization of Holocaust awareness had set in, transforming it as part of an expended agenda of universal moral values. Needless to say, this is no solace for the loss and ruination. befell the Jewish people. However, it is an important tool in the fight against human evil and Holocaust denial, and it reaffirms again, though without resolving the mystery, the role of the Jews as messengers of moral values, even if reluctantly, to the rest of mankind.

The Holocaust left the world mesmerized with its immensity, to such a degree that it has come to symbolize human evil and the suffering evil can inflict. Because of its uniqueness and far-reaching effect on mankind's conscience, Christianity has sought in various ways to appropriate the suffering of the annihilated Jews. In Auschwitz and Treblinka and Belzec, so the doctrine runs, it was all of humanity that suffered, not merely some particular people. And for the Jewish people themselves, the Holocaust has given rise to its own theology of suffering, intimately bound to the Chosen idea, reflecting in its morality the historical Jewish experience of persecution and massacre, and posing for all of mankind the ultimate question of God's justice. It seems "to be the role of the Jews," Paul Johnson writes, "to focus and dramatize these common experiences of mankind, and to turn their particular fate into a universal moral."[73]

# CHAPTER 7

# Israel

## A Chosen Nation in Their Chosen Land

In the beginning God created the heavens and the earth.

—Genesis 1:1

He created it and He granted it [The Land of Israel] to those He deemed fit.

—Commentary by Rashi to Genesis 1:1

Why not give Palestine back to them [the Jews] again? According to God's distribution of nations, it is their home, an inalienable possession, from which they were expelled by force. . . . [It is] a privilege opportunity to further the purposes of God concerning His ancient people.

—William E. Blackstone, a Gentile Zionist[1]

Racism and Zionism are racist creeds. The Zionists have come forward with the theory of the Chosen People, an absurd ideology. That is religious racism.

—Yakov Malik, ambassador of the Soviet Union to the United Nations, October 1973[2]

On the first words of the first verse of the first book in the Bible, Rashi, the most prominent commentator on the Bible and the Talmud, quotes the sages who posed the question; why did the Torah start with the story of creation? They argued that since the Torah is primarily a book of laws, it should have begun with the commandment of the new moon, which was the first Jewish law describing how the Jewish calendar is determined.[3] Why, nevertheless, did it begin with the story of the creation? The midrash provides the answer that this was done in order to establish that God is the sovereign of the universe: "He has shown the people the power of his works, in giving them the heritage of the nations."[4] If the nations accuse Israel of banditry, says Rashi, for seizing the lands of the seven nations of Canaan, Israel can respond, "The entire universe belongs to God. He created it and He granted it to whomever He deemed fit. It was His desire to give it to them and then it was His desire to take it from them and give it to us."[5]

Written in Europe at the end of the eleventh or the beginning of the twelfth century, this strong nationalist and religious-Zionist statement is effectively the biblical charter of the Jewish people over Zion, the Holy Land. Rashi's commentary is not exactly a convincing argument to present to the United Nations General Assembly, or for an op-ed piece in a Western newspaper, but to disregard it shows a basic lack of understanding of the origins of Zionism and its links with the concept of the Chosen. To ignore it is to miss the essence of the continuing struggle in the Middle East and the encounter between the Jewish state and the rest of the world. Moreover, a thorough study of comparative religious texts will show just how deep is the Arab-Israeli conflict and its coverage in the international media, enmeshed as it is in this source from Genesis and chosenness by God. Even the United Nations records show that the attacks against Israel and the Jews are frequently couched in the terminology of the Chosen People, by other peoples whose religion and culture developed from the same ideas and myths. In this complexity lies the hidden agenda of anti-Semitism and its manifestations in the Arab-Israeli conflict.

This chapter deals with several illustrations to the Chosen yet pariah position of Israel in international forums and its complicated posture under normative international law. In the words of the prophet Balaam, Israel is a state that cannot be reckoned among the nations, precisely because of its role as a Chosen People, subject to different standards and exposed to existential threats that are faced by no other country. The trial of the Nazi criminal Adolf Eichmann in Jerusalem (1961), Israel's pariah status in the United Nations, its unprecedented acts against terrorism, and its unique posture of nuclear ambiguity, or its campaign for Soviet Jews are all expressions of chosenness in international relations. In all cases we see once again why Israeli Jewish behavior and reactions cannot be judged by conventional international norms, simply because it needs to be treated both morally and legally, as a unique case without parallel or precedent.

\* \* \*

The fact that the struggle over the Holy Land is related to the ancient struggle over the Chosen concept lends Rashi's commentary critical importance as an insight into the conflicting images regarding Israel. While international power politics may determine the future "road map" of a settlement in the Middle East, there is no doubt that all these layers of religious beliefs, myths, and visions are critical to understanding why the world is constantly preoccupied with this drama.

What Rashi attempts to explain is that the Torah is not a history book, nor is it a code of laws in the established sense. In addition to specifically Jewish laws, it contains teachings about the relations between God and men and women and explores human values and morality and the role of humanity in the universe. It is in this context that we are told about the special relationship between God and His Chosen People and their Promised Land. This is admittedly a theological interpretation, but as we have already seen these ideas still preoccupy Jews and Gentiles, religious and nonreligious alike.

It is important to understand the historical context of Rashi's intellectual development. As we have seen earlier, Rashi experienced the massacres of the First Crusade. He himself heard the impact of the declaration of Pope Urban II in November 1095, at the Second Council of Clermont in Clermont-Ferrand, about the call to liberate the Holy Land from the hands of the Muslim infidels. The Pope called upon Christianity to wrest the Church of the Holy Sepulcher in Jerusalem from the "wicked race" promising remission of sins and eternal life to all who would take up the sword and join in the crusade. The Church referred to the second coming of Jesus, and the Jews in Europe were aware, particularly after the mass murder of their coreligionists, that Pope Urban's pronunciation also concerned them. Rashi saw this impending clash between Christianity and Islam as yet another chapter on Jewish suffering in exile, and he could only hold out the hopes and comforts recorded in the Jewish holy books.

Rashi was no ivory tower scholar, because at some point in his career, he also became a merchant running his family's vineyards and wine production, and he maintained business contacts with non-Jews. He was a practical visionary who, instead of declaring war, which was beyond his powers, selected the most powerful passage in the midrash to open his commentary on the Bible. His message, addressed to future Jewish generations and to the rest of the world was: let others fight over the Holy Land if they so choose, but the truth has already been stated in the first verse of Genesis. The message of God, the creator of the world, is that the Holy Land is the Promised Land of the Jews. This was Rashi's reaction to the other two contenders, Christianity and Islam, who were clashing over their conflicting claims to be the inheritors of the mantle of the Chosen. The Jews in the days of Rashi had no army, no military might, their only weapon, their faith, and their dream, lay in the power of the Bible.

Rashi, in his Bible commentary is very selective in his choice of talmudic midrashim. He emphasizes that Israel is the Chosen of God since it was the only nation that accepted the terms of the Torah while all the others refused. Rashi repeats this talmudic version of the election several times in his commentaries in order to show how close are the Jews to God, who followed them in their exile. The world was created, according to Rashi, just in order to give the Torah to Israel (Genesis 26:31) because they were Chosen and singled out of the rest of nations (Genesis 15:10; Exodus 15:16, 19:5) since they were the only one's to accept it (Deuteronomy 33:2) and since they are God's fiancée (Exodus 19:17, 34:1; Leviticus 20:3). All these, and many more commentaries, are also aimed to strengthen the validity of the Jewish claim over the land of Israel, which Rashi repeats time and again: (Genesis 14:19, 15:6; Exodus 6:4, 13:5) while emphasizing that Esau, namely Christianity, gave up its rights over the land.

## Normalization and the Chosen

Most of the early Zionists had studied the Bible and the Talmud together with the commentaries of Rashi. But their choosing of Zionism was an act of revolt against normative Diaspora Judaism and against the religious practices based on

Jewish law. The early Zionists did not explain their longing for a return to the Land of Israel in religious terms. The First *Aliya* (wave of immigration [in Hebrew, literally "to go up"]) took place during the 1880s, and it retained some traditional and religious beliefs; however, the religious element in the Zionist movement was only a small minority. Most of the members of what is referred to in Zionist terminology as the "Founding Fathers" were the secular socialist elements who arrived in Ottoman Palestine in the early twentieth century, and particularly the members of the first collective settlements (*kibbutzim*) who wished to escape the Jewish condition in the Diaspora. They spoke strongly about the "negation of the Diaspora," and they eagerly anticipated the "normalization" of Jewish life, without its religious aspects.

Normalization of the Jewish condition was always a dream to be aspired to: whether in the Diaspora or for the Zionists in Palestine. For the Diaspora, it was in the form of emancipation, and for the Zionists, it was the return to *Eretz Yisrael* ("the Land of Israel") and to sovereignty. For each it was in the hope of improving the Jewish condition and escaping from its fate, including the burden of the Chosen. The Zionists wanted to change the conditions of persecution and discrimination following the trends of emancipation: freedom, equality, and the right to self-determination. This, at least, was the external agenda. The internal Zionist agenda was to "cure" the mentality of exile and the spiritual condition of the Jews, which had become rooted following centuries of life without sovereignty. The norm of a healthy nation in the nineteenth century was one in which its inhabitants lived on their own national soil. The view was that Zionism had not come about just to solve the problem of assimilation and persecution. Zionism meant ending the "abnormal" condition of the Jewish people.[6] Zionists spoke about "the new Jew," and later there were those who even wished to disassociate themselves from what they perceived to be the "exilic" term *yehudi* ("Jewish") and replace it with the adjective *ivri* ("Hebrew") so redolent of the heroic past of the Children of Israel and the early Hebrews.[7]

The writer Arthur Koestler, who was born in Budapest and moved to Vienna, was caught between the wars in the two opposing movements of Communism and Zionism, and he explained the psychology behind his dilemma: "I became a Communist because I hated the poor and a Zionist because I hated the *Yid* [The Jew]."[8] For him, Zionism offered an escape from traditional Judaism.

The fact is that the desire for normalization was virtually unanimous within the Zionist movement; it was expressed by the political center of the more assimilated leaders of the movement such as Theodor Herzl and Max Nordau; it was strongly expressed as the ideal by socialists such as A. D. Gordon, David Ben Gurion, Dov Ber Borochov, Yosef Haim Brenner, and Micha Berdyczewski, as well as Chaim Weizmann and even people from the right of the movement like Vladimir Ze'ev Jabotinsky. Berdyczewski and Brenner were very critical of traditional Judaism and its exilic mentality. Brenner labeled Diaspora Jews as "Gypsies, filthy dogs, inhuman" and A. D. Gordon, the archtypical secular socialist prophet of manual and especially agricultural labor, labeled Diaspora Jews as "parasites."[9] Brenner who called to delete all references to the Chosen

People from the prayer books was the most admired writer in Israeli public schools, particularly those that were close to the Labor movement, and his collective works were given to their students as the graduation gift until the 1980s.

Despite their strong desires for normalization, outside observers such as Conor Cruise O'Brien are convinced that even secular Zionists were driven by the mysterious Chosen factor: "The central mystery of Zionism, it seems to me, is the relation within it of religion to nationalism, with the suspicion, within the mystery, that religion and nationalism may ultimately be two words for the same thing. The early Zionists were mostly avowed secularists, but their enterprise derived most of its power, and all its territorial orientation, from a religious book, and the ancient longing it inspired."[10]

O'Brien points out that people like Weizmann, Ben Gurion, and other Zionist leaders, though not religiously observant "in the wider sense . . . could not be anything else but very religious Jews indeed." Their "imaginations were saturated in the Bible," and they maintained a "burning faith in the restoration of the Chosen People to the Promised Land."[11] The secular socialists of the Second *Aliya* (1904–14) behaved as if they were following messianic signals concerning Jewish sovereignty and the redemption of the nation in its land.[12]

Rabbi Abraham Isaac Kook, the first chief rabbi of Palestine (1921–33), was known for his close attachment to the founders of the kibbutzim, the first collective-socialist agriculture settlements, viewing them as proof of the coming redemption. Being aware that many religious leaders found the attitude of these settlers to be antireligious, Rabbi Kook's rejoinder was, "It is pointless to wage a bitter and ill-conceived war against those who are loyal to one aspect of the Jewish character. . . . No matter what they may think, the particular element of the Jewish spirit that they may make their own, being rooted in the total life of our people, must inevitably contain every aspect of its ethos."[13] This was part and parcel of what Rabbi Kook regarded as the healing of the world by the emergent modern State of Israel.

When the secular but messianic Zionist David Ben Gurion testified in 1937 to the British Royal Commission headed by Lord Peel, he stated, "I say on behalf of the Jews that the Bible is our mandate—the Bible, which was written by us, in our own language, Hebrew, in this very country. This is our mandate. It was the recognition of this right that was expressed in the Balfour Declaration."[14] The nonobservant Ben Gurion stated that the Bible "was written by us" and demanded that the Jews be treated as the Chosen and that the rights and promises granted by God in the Bible should be honored.

Chaim Weizmann, in his appearance before the Peel Commission, referred to the racist laws and the anti-Semitism facing the Jews of Europe, and he spoke on the unique history of the Jews: "I believe the main cause which has produced the particular state of Jewry in the world is its attachment to Palestine. We are a stiff-necked people. We never forget. . . . This steadfastness which has preserved the Jews through the ages and through a career which is almost one long chain of human suffering is primarily due to some physical or pathological attachment to

Palestine. . . . In the East End of London, the Jew prays for dew in the summer, and rain in the winter."[15]

The Israeli writer, Amos Oz, a contemporary nonreligious Zionist, was reluctant to use terms such as "the Promised Land" and explained that in his eyes, Zionism is the redemption of a people but not of a land. However, he too could not deny the fact that Zionism centered on Israel "because here was the focus of their prayers and their longings . . . organically linked to the belief in the promise and the promiser." Oz had to accept this contradiction, adding that "we the nonreligious are condemned to live with inconsistencies and faults." Zionism is inconsistent, he stated, because it is a secular endeavor which is deeply based on a religious idea, the Jewish connection and yearnings for the Land of Israel.[16]

The confusion over the religious significance of the return of the Jews to the Promised Land is not just a problem for secular Jews; it also created strong opposition among the ultra-Orthodox who believe that the fulfillment of the Chosen is solely in the hands of God, the Messiah, and divine forces. The more that secular people like David Ben Gurion employed messianic language such as the Chosen or the "Light unto the Nations," the more angry religious anti-Zionists became.

Many people, Jews and non-Jews alike, refer to some of the strategic changes that have taken place in the region, as divine intervention. Jean-Paul Sartre, an agnostic, once pronounced what may sound as an almost theological approach to Israel: "I cannot judge the Jewish people by the accepted rules of history; the Jewish people is something beyond time, and we cannot pass judgment on this dilemma of Israel-Arab relations without taking this into account."[17] Some years later, in May 2004, the president of the Sorbonne, Professor Jean-Robert Pitte, would say that what is needed in the Arab-Israeli conflict is "divine intervention which comes rarely but is necessary in unique cases."[18]

As we have seen earlier, David Ben Gurion was an outstanding example of Jewish secular-messianism, yet at the same time, imbued with biblical language and the vision of the prophets, with a consistent focus on the destiny of the Chosen and the mission of a "Light unto the Nations." This brand of secular-messianism represented a central motif in the development of modern Zionism.[19] In a lecture to senior officers of the Israel Defence Forces (IDF) in April 1950, Ben Gurion told them that, similar to any other army in the world, the IDF also has an educational mission. However, unlike other armies, the IDF has a special educational mission because of the historical uniqueness of Israel. This uniqueness, he explained, is because of the "moral-intellectual struggle that our people has faced with our neighbors since its inception, and the vision of the end of days that our nation carried in its heart through all generations. Our current mission is the ingathering of exiles, which is the central fact of our day which has no parallel in the annals of other nations and not even in the annals of our nation. From this there are implications for the future of our nation, our security and our position nationally and internationally, and perhaps, to a large extent, for the future of mankind."[20]

In Ben Gurion's words, there are undoubtedly themes that can be considered messianic in the language of the Chosen. He refers to the Jewish belief in the supremacy of the spirit that helped to win the war against the Arabs. He says that this is the belief that accompanied the Jews from Sinai until these very days. Similarly, this spiritual supremacy gave the Jews "messianic belief and the desire for national and universal redemption." Unlike other nations who look back to their golden ages that had disappeared, the Jews, Ben Gurion suggested, look towards the future according to the vision of Isaiah, and explained, "This kind of spirit and belief helped our people in our suffering and brought us to the beginning of our national redemption, which contains also the first sparks of the redemption of mankind." In his words the Jews always "regarded themselves as the Chosen People and this was justified in light of its unique religious-moral awareness."[21] The Jewish nation, he said, differs from all other nations in principle, in substance, and in its fate, with different rules of existence.[22] Israel was not, in his eyes, just another destination for Jewish immigrants or refugees, but the Promised Land with a special destiny and universal mission.[23]

## United Nations Disputation with the Chosen

The attitude towards Israel, Zionism, and the Jews in the United Nations is yet another arena of the struggle against the Chosen. Even critics of the policies of the State of Israel cannot deny that the UN obsession with Israel led the organization to moral bankruptcy in 1975 with the vote equating Zionism with racism, a vote that was only revoked sixteen years later in an unprecedented move in the history of the organization. The 1975 vote cannot be viewed as an isolated outburst of a corrupt majority. It was rather a reflection of the consistent attacks and later the denial of Israel's very right to exist as a state, which are, in themselves, at odds with the fundamental principles and practices of the United Nations Charter.

The struggle against Zionism and the expressions of anti-Semitism in the United Nations can be seen as a modern variation of the historic disputations and polemics between the Jews and the rest of the world in ancient and medieval times. The United Nations provides a forum, adjusted to the political realities of the twentieth century, for raising some of the same considerations that were the subject of the infamous disputations of the Middle Ages. Historical comparisons are not always accurate but are still another proof of the old adage that history tends to repeat itself. The literature concerning the disputation and polemics between Jews, Christians, and Muslims provides interesting food for thought. According to the American historian Judah Eisenstein, who gathered together documents of many of the disputations of the Middle Ages into a single volume published in 1929, the disputations were held against the wishes of the Jews, forced on them "under compulsion, and imposed by their enemies, where they were forced to be apologetic and to defend their faith." In those days the disputations were primarily of a theological nature, and the Jews were accused of being "inferior and terrible, either because of their race and their ignorance of worldly wisdom . . . or because of their faith and laws." In each generation, continues

Eisenstein, "there were scholars among the other nations that would chastise the Jews for stealing Canaan from its inhabitants."[24]

The 1975 disputation in the United Nations indeed centered on the rights of the Jews over "Canaan" (the Land of Israel), but they also embodied other attacks against Israel and the Jews. Even before the establishment of the state, the United Nations had engaged in a highly polemical process that questioned Israel's right to exist. After the November 1947 resolution on the partition of Palestine, it was still unclear what would be the decision of the General Assembly. The process involved uncertainty, major surprises, and a sudden shift in the pattern of voting. There was a clear sense of history in the making when the United Nations voted on the right of the Chosen People to re-establish a sovereign state in their own Promised Land. The bestselling book *O Jerusalem* by Larry Collins and Dominique Lapierre, reflected the popular view about the vote: "No debate in the brief history of the United Nations had stirred passions comparable to those aroused by the controversy over the land to which each of its members might in some way trace a part of its spiritual heritage."[25]

Moshe Sharett, the foreign minister and later the prime minister of Israel, wrote about the historic vote in the United Nations on November 29, 1947: "That sleepless night, multitudes of Jews in Palestine and in the Diaspora sat glued to their radios and counted each of the votes of the different nations that were going to decide the fate of their nation, either for freedom or for continued slavery. A wave of exhilaration swept Palestine as the vote ended. The defects of the partition plan and the harm implicit in it were forgotten. The nation heard the sound of the *shofar*—the ritual ram's horn—which brought tidings of redemption with the approval of the organized world."[26] It was not just a feeling of redemption but once again a sense of divine intervention, just two years after the Holocaust, when God was hidden. The American President, Harry S. Truman, acted on the partition resolution and on recognizing Israel on May 14, 1948, against the advice of most of his officials including a very hostile attitude and warnings by his Secretary of State George Marshall. No doubt that Truman's Baptist upbringing and his faith in God and the Bible played a role in his thoughts, and he would boast after leaving office that he was a modern Cyrus, the Persian King who repatriated Jewish exiles and authorized the rebuilding of the Second Temple and the Judean state.[27]

The nadir of the UN campaign against the Chosen, which amounted to a full-fledged rejection of Israel's right to exist, took place twenty-eight years later. In November 1975, the United Nations passed the infamous Resolution 3379, which equated Zionism with racism, a resolution that was received with shock and disbelief throughout the democratic world. As explained by the American representative at the Third Committee of the General Assembly, where the resolution was first introduced, the logic was simple: racism is of course illegal, and if Zionism equals racism, and since the State of Israel is a Zionist state, it is therefore also illegal. That this was seen to be the implicit meaning of the resolution was already evident in a broadcast by Radio Damascus on November 20, 1975, calling on the terrorist organizations to exploit the resolution and to use it as dynamite in order to blow up Zion Square in Jerusalem.[28]

This had been part of the Palestinian strategy immediately after the establishment of the Palestine Liberation Organization (PLO) and the adoption of its covenant in 1964 (long before Israel occupied the territories in 1967) when the PLO published a work by Hassan Sa'ab on *Zionism and Racism* using expressions such as "the final solution" as a Zionist goal and "the Chosen Race." The goal of the resolution was the delegitimization of Israel, but it also gave a degree of political justification for anti-Semitic activities within the Soviet Union.[29] At the same 1975 General Assembly, another anti-Israeli resolution was passed that was overshadowed by the impact of the Zionism-racism resolution. This resolution on Palestinian rights completely ignored the rights of Jews and the State of Israel. In Yasser Arafat's words at the time, "This resolution infers the liquidation of the existence of Israel, since the Palestine homeland is Palestine, and Palestine at present is Israel."[30]

The vocabulary at the United Nations is different from that of the disputations of the Middle Ages, but there is no real difference in the level of hate and in the final goal. William F. Buckley, while acting as a member of the American delegation to the United Nations General Assembly for three months in 1973, expressed his astonishment when he found out that the UN was actually running an anti-Semitic campaign without disturbance and described the organization as "[t]he most concentrated gathering of anti-Semitism since the days of Hitler's Germany."[31]

The Soviet ambassador Yakov Malik was clear in October 1973 when he blamed Israel and Zionism for their "theory of the Chosen People, [which is] an absurd ideology."[32] The ambassador of Jordan, Nassem Nuseibeh transferred the Chosen accusation to the Security Council chambers in March 1979, when he blamed the Jews and Israel for seeing themselves as the "master race" and referred to Jewish philanthropy as "the Gestapo of the Zionist movement."[33] In December 1980 Nuseibeh stated that there is a Jewish "cabal which controls, manipulates and exploits the rest of humanity by controlling the money and wealth of the world." He continued to vent his hatred in calculated accusations:

People like Rothschild every day, in ironclad secrecy, decide and flash round the world how high the price of gold should be on each particular day. . . . [T]here is Mr. Oppenheimer[34] of South Africa, who holds 15 million blacks in bondage in order to exploit and monopolize the diamonds, uranium and the other precious resources which rightfully belong to the struggling African people of South Africa and Namibia. It is a well-known fact that the Zionists are the richest people in the world and control much of its destiny. Indeed, in the United States itself, which has a national income of upwards of $2,000 billion per annum, while millions of hard-working God-fearing Americans are unemployed, the Zionists own a lion's share of that great abundance. Official figures have shown that they have the highest per capita accumulation of all segments of American society, including the descendants of the immigrants who came 300 or 400 years ago.[35]

## Through the Eyes of Zionist Gentiles

Jews, and especially Israelis, often fail to appreciate the full historic significance of the re-establishment of the State of Israel. Sometimes, as shown in the case of the Prophet Balaam, a Gentile may understand better the uniqueness of the Jewish condition. When Jews were loosing their sovereignty in their land, Gentiles could interpret this as a vindication of the denial of their Promised Land. Not just Christians but even Greeks like the philosopher Celsus of the second century CE would allude sarcastically to the "Promised Land" by remarking, "We see what sort of land it was of which they [the Jews] were thought worthy."[36] The return to Zion created different reactions as can be seen in Psalm 126, which is included in the prayers for the Sabbath and festivals and in the grace before meals: "When the Lord restored the fortunes of Zion, we were like those who dream. . . . [T]hen they said among the nations, the Lord has done great things for them." The Gentiles, the psalmist suggests, can sometimes detect the drama of Jewish history before the Jews themselves.

In the sixteenth century there was a clear resurgence of what can be termed as proto-Christian Zionism influenced by the Protestant Reformation and its emphasis on the Bible. On one hand the British Christians regarded themselves as God's Chosen People "the new Israel," but at the same time they preached (as for instance the Anglican clergyman Thomas Brightman in 1585 or Member of Parliament Henry Finch in 1621) to support the Jewish return to Palestine in order to hasten a series of prophetic events that would culminate in the return of Jesus. From the very beginning of the nineteenth century this trend was transformed into a religious-political movement that preceded and affected Jewish Zionism. The contribution of Christian Zionism to the origins of Jewish Zionism has been overlooked in the literature, and it deserves a special research and studies. This form of Christian Zionism, mainly in its Anglican and American versions, was older than the modern and more secular version of Jewish Zionism. While early Christian Zionists believe that Christians represent the new and true children of Israel who inherited God's promises to the ancient Hebrews, they also believe that the Jews have a unique and a "Chosen" role in modern history and that they would return to the Holy Land before the return of Christ. These unique doctrines were founded among fringe movements in Christianity throughout the ages and were regarded as marginal and extreme, if not heretical, among the mainstream churches but nevertheless they had a major impact on politics, religion, and history.

The eternal Jewish link to the Land of Israel was especially strongly rooted in Britain and the United States, where it was part and parcel of the view that regarded the Jews as the Chosen People, and even among some circles in Catholic France. On April 20, 1799, Emperor Napoleon Bonaparte issued a proclamation to the Jewish people seeking their assistance in his efforts to conquer Ottoman-ruled Palestine. The proclamation is addressed to "the Rightful Heirs of Palestine," and it opens by declaring, "Israelites, the unique nation, whom, during thousand of years, lust for conquest and tyranny were able to deprive only of its ancestral lands, but not of name and national existence! . . . Isaiah and Joel foretold . . . that the ransomed of the Lord shall return, and come with singing unto Zion. . . . Rightful Heirs of Palestine! . . . Arise! . . . Hasten! . . . Now is the moment . . . to claim the restoration of your rights among the population of the universe which has been shamefully withheld from you for thousands of years."[37]

Evangelical backers of Israel are mostly influenced by theological dispensationalism, a doctrine which regards God as dispensing or administrating history into several periods in accordance with specific revelations before the era of Christ return. In England people like John Darby founded in 1830 the Plymouth Brethren whose dispensationalist doctrine coupled with millenarianism (the belief that Jesus would rule from Jerusalem for one thousand years) argued that all the biblical prophecies relate to the return of the Jewish people to its homeland prior to the second coming of Christ. In this respect they broke with the age-old Christian tradition that refused to recognize the viable existence of the Jewish people and particularly, its Chosen status. Lord Shaftesbury, a conservative evangelical Christian who adopted premillennial theology, had a strong influence on members of the Parliament and presented his pro-Zionist views to a still prejudiced and anti-Semitic elite of Britain (see Chapter 4 on Benjamin Disraeli). Lord Shaftesbury wrote in 1839 an essay in the prestigious literary journal the *Quarterly Review* under the title, "The State Restoration of the Jews" and pointed out, "the Jews must be encouraged to return [to Palestine] in yet greater numbers and become once more the husbandman of Judea and Galilee." When the British foreign secretary, Lord Palmerston, was involved with the so-called Eastern Question and concerned about the likely instability that would be created by the demise of the Ottoman Empire and its implications for Europe, he received a letter from Lord Ashley, a young member of Parliament, dealing with the issue of the Chosen People. Ashley, who was the stepson-in-law of Palmerston, was convinced that foreign policy in the East should be part of the fulfillment of the holy scriptures and that conditions were ripe "for the return of the Jews to their inheritance in the Land of Promise." Ashley told Palmerston that he had "been chosen by God, to be an instrument of good to his [C]hosen [P]eople." A leading article in *The Times*, also inspired by Ashley, proposed "to plant the Jewish people in the land of their fathers" under the protection of a European power, presumably Great Britain.[38]

Later, in *Daniel Deronda* (1876), the famous British author George Eliot would speak about the restoration of the Jews to Palestine where Mordecai the Jew proclaims, "[L]et there be another great migration, another choosing of Israel. . . . The sons of Judah have to choose that God may again choose them. The messianic time is the time when Israel shall will the planting of the national ensign."[39] Elliot's *Daniel Deronda* would make a lasting impression on several early and pre-Herzlian Zionists: on Eliezer Ben Yehudah, the father of modern Hebrew; on Israel Belkind and the "Bilu" movement that immigrated and settled in Palestine in the 1880s; and on the young Jewish-American poet Emma Lazarus (the author of the "The New Colossus," which appears on the base of the Statue of Liberty in New York) who would become an active proponent for a

Jewish homeland in Palestine.[40] Another British Gentile Zionist, Sir Laurence Oliphant, made an extensive journey to Palestine in 1879 to promote a settlement of large numbers of Jews there (before the first Zionist wave of Jewish settlement in 1882). Naftali Herz Imber, who served as the secretary of Sir Oliphant and maintained his correspondence with other Jews, would become (perhaps under Oliphant's inspiration), the author of *Hatikvah* (The Hope)—the national anthem of the State of Israel.

The Crimean War of 1855 between the Ottoman Empire and Russia over control of the holy places in Palestine stirred up religious feelings among the English.[41] The different statements issued then sometimes show confusion as to God's message, as well as a clear attempt to adjust the facts to Christian beliefs. One Christian scholar, writing in 1860, spoke about "God's public token of *Reconciliation* [italics in the original] to his ancient, and now penitent and believing people." Although he was not sure that they were going to be converted in the countries of their dispersion, he claimed that after their restoration in Palestine, they would get the "new heart" that was promised to them. Some Christians had been observing the colonizing activities of the Rothschilds and Sir Moses Montefiore in the Holy Land, and they regarded the decline of Turkey as "a step in Providence" toward fulfilling the divine purpose of restoring the Jews to their land.[42]

The fascination of Protestant Christians in England and America toward the Jews was not necessarily marking a new era of relations with their local Jews. However, in theological terms this was a revolutionary change and a break away from the age-old Christian tradition that refused to recognize the viable existence of the Jewish people. This new trend, sometimes called "restorationasim," regarded the Jews as critical agents of future redemption in a sharp contrast to the Catholic and Lutheranian doctrine, which portrayed the loss of Jewish sovereignty and their dispersion as punishment for their rejection, and even "killing," of Christ's first coming. The idea of Jewish revival in their Promised Land and the fulfillment of God's biblical promises to repatriate the Jews meant also the restoration of their Chosen status. This epochal shift received its best expression by the biblical and Hebrew Professor from New York University George Bush who wrote in 1844 that it was time to condemn "the thralldom and oppression which has so long ground them to dust" and instead the Jews should be elevated "to a rank of honorable repute among the nations of the earth" in their rebuilt state in Palestine.[43]

The return of the Jews to Zion was the fulfillment of a dream, and for many Gentiles it was regarded as a clear miracle by the Almighty. This of course does not contradict the fact that the idea of Zion, the strong desire of returning to their ancestral land, is a central pillar of Judaism and was a powerful factor that helped to hold the Jewish people together in the Diaspora. Also, Jewish presence in Palestine preceded Christian Zionism and was a permanent factor throughout the ages with periodic small waves of Jewish immigration from Europe and Islamic lands. Nevertheless, the so-called Christian Zionism preceded the Jewish forerunners of Zionism in political vision and action, and their political impact on decision making and public opinion cannot be exaggerated.

In the United States, Elias Boudinot (1740–1821), president of the Continental Congress and a close associate of George Washington predicted that the Jews "however scattered . . . are to be recovered by the mighty power of God, and restored to their beloved . . . Palestine." John Adams, the second president of the United States, imagined "a hundred thousand Israelites" marching triumphantly into Palestine and wrote, "I really wish the Jews in Judea an independent nation." And it was Mark Twain who complained about the empty lands in Palestine after his visit there in 1867: "There is not a solitary village throughout [the Jezreel valley,] its whole extent—not for thirty miles in either direction. . . . Come to Galilee for that . . . these unpeopled deserts, these rusty mounds of bareness."[44]

It was in a similar atmosphere that an influential Jew, Mordecai Manuel Noah, envisaged a settlement in 1825 on Grand Island in the Niagara River near Buffalo, New York, and named it "Ararat." He visualized the site as becoming an autonomous latter-day ark of refuge for Jews from all over the world under the auspices and protection of America. The idea met with ridicule, so Noah became a strong supporter of Palestine as a national home for Jews, and he was persistent in his efforts to collect funds and enlist Christian support for the project despite Jewish critics in America and Europe. In a speech in New York, Noah used the Chosen concept to convince his audience by suggesting that it was the mission of the United States, which had "been selected and pointedly distinguished in prophecy as *the* nation, which at the proper time, shall present to the Lord his chosen and trodden-down people and pave the way for their restoration to Zion." As did American Zionists after him, Noah did not regard Palestine as a destination for American Jews but for Jews from the rest of the world who were "bowed to the earth by oppression."[45]

The most famous of the Zionist millenarians in the United States was William Blackstone (1841–1933) who expounded his belief about the return of the Jews to the Land of Israel in his book *Jesus Is Coming*. Blackstone, who was a priest, added political and secular dimensions to his preaching and was active in organizing petitions (see the quote at the beginning of this chapter) on behalf of Jewish national aspirations. His initiatives were reported in the general and Jewish press, and he participated in several Zionist conventions.[46] The much criticized phrase attributed to the founders of the Zionist movement that Palestine was "a land without people, for a people without a land," which supposedly ignored the Arab presence in the area, was coined by Lord Shaftesbury and reiterated by William Blackstone.[47] Typically, before promoting the political restoration of the Jews in their Promised Land, Blackstone had to recognize their Chosen role and reject the prejudices of traditional Christianity toward the Jews and absolve them from the need to convert, as he did in most popular earlier book *Jesus Is Coming*.[48]

Along with the founder of political Zionism, Theodor Herzl, an Anglican chaplain from Vienna, William Hechler regarded Herzl and his Zionist enterprise as ordained by God in order to fulfill the prophetic scriptures. Hechler met Herzl before the convening of the first Zionist Congress and was very instrumental in arranging meetings for Herzl with several world leaders and officials, and his indirect contacts with the British elite would help later to secure the Balfour declaration on the Jewish homeland in 1917.[49] British Foreign Secretary Arthur Balfour himself was religiously well prepared for the Zionist enterprise by his Sunday school faith, and his prime minister, David Lloyd George, was even more receptive to the Zionist vision due to his training by fundamentalist Christian parents and churches on the geography of ancient Israel. Lloyd George admitted that he was far more familiar with cities and regions of biblical Israel than with the geography of his native Wales or of England itself. In the British war cabinet of 1917, there were several Zionist sympathizers that were driven by their Christian education, and some of those continued to act for Jewish national restoration even when Britain, acting under the League of Nations mandate in Palestine, began to distance itself from their commitment to the Jews. During the 1920s and 1930s when the British government was more hostile to the Jews there were several occasions that the "Gentile Zionists often outpaced the Zionist leadership," and unlike the Jewish Zionist they opposed the partition plans between Jews and Arabs in Palestine.[50] One of these Gentile Zionist, J. C. Wedgwood, explained how the Protestant, nonconformist tradition, prompted his group to champion the Zionist creed: "The Anglo-Saxons, more than any other race, wants to sympathize with the Jews, and would like to settle up for these last two thousand years. . . . We, too, find in the Old Testament, or Torah, convenient justification for all that needs justification in our relations with mankind. We, too, can laugh at ourselves, so sure are we of being in reality the Chosen People . . . Moses led out from Egypt, the first non-conformist, the first free thinkers to break away from idolatry and priestly rule. . . . Towards such a people one has a feeling almost of awe, they are so known, and yet so old and eternal."[51]

Both trends of Zionist Christians in Britain and in the United States based themselves on the words of God to Abraham in Genesis: "And I will make of thee a great nation . . . and I will bless them that bless thee, and curse him that curseth thee."[52] This and other similar passages are quoted also today by American evangelists who lobby for the State of Israel. For millions of fundamentalist and evangelical Christians the modern State of Israel is a fulfillment of biblical prophecy, and they regard God's Covenant with Israel as eternal and exclusive based on the same biblical texts that deal with the election of Israel as the Chosen and the treasured people. These Protestant evangelists support the maximalist claims of Jewish political Zionism, including Israel's sovereignty over all of historic Palestine including Jerusalem.

Among Christian Zionists in Europe are those who are driven also by guilty feelings about the Holocaust. In 1963, Dr. Basilea Schlink, a German Protestant and mother superior of a religious order for women, wrote a booklet that expressed a cry of Christian conscience for the "terrible history of persecution and extermination" together with an impassioned plea for support for the State of Israel as a fulfillment of prophecy for God's people. Israel, says Mother Schlink "is the people of God's choice," and theirs "is a gift of God, consistent with His plan." That is why Herzl's idea to establish a state in Uganda in 1901 was rejected by "pious Jews . . . [who] refused to go there [because] Jerusalem alone was in their heart, the Promised Land, promised to them by God."[53]

Unlike Catholics, at least before the Nostra Aetate of 1965, many evangelists believe that until the return of Christ the Jews will continue to reject him, and, unlike Martin Luther or traditional Catholics, they do not expect the Jews to convert in large numbers. They regard the attacks against Israel as an expression of the hatred by "fallen man" to God and His "Chosen People." A new book even argues that more and more evangelists who support Israel reject, at the same time, the replacement or supersession theology.[54]

There are those among the Protestant evangelists who view the re-establishment of Israel as an apocalyptic event, a prelude to eventual redemption and they are enthusiastic supporters of Israel. They are fascinated by the perceived "miracle" of modern Israel, the redemption of the Jewish people after centuries of suffering and their return to their own land that had been starved by centuries of neglect. Tens of thousands of them visit and pray for the well-being of Israel and participate in fund-raising for the country. Evangelist Zionists stress that "God's Covenants are still applicable to the Jewish people, that the Holy Land rightfully belongs to the Jews, and that God would punish those who sought to harm his Chosen People." One of the most renowned leaders of the evangelical movement, Reverend Billy Graham, remarked in his film "His Land," "Do you know what impresses me about Israel? It is that God really has a long memory . . . God promised it [to restore the Jewish people] and He is delivering on that promise in His Land."[55]

American evangelists support the immigration of Jews to Israel from Russia, Ethiopia, and even groups from the United States, as part of the prophets' visions of the ingathering of the exiles. For them the Jews and in particular the State of Israel still maintains some of the dimensions of the Chosen. They support right-wing groups in Israel and put pressure on the American administration on behalf of Israel. Some evangelical groups were engaged in missionary work as part of their belief that the Jews will repent for their refusal to recognize Jesus and that the Jews will ultimately accept Christianity in the process of their redemption.[56] However, those who were active in support of Israel and Zionism in the past and today avoid any kind of missionary activity.

One of the prominent leaders of these groups is the Reverend Jerry Falwell, a media star who preaches to millions on religious television programs. He speaks out very forcefully on the American religious commitment to Israel, on the Jewishness of Jesus, and on the eventual construction by Israel of the Third Temple on the site of the Dome of the Rock in Jerusalem. He refers to the Jews as the "Chosen People of God," and he established the "Christian Embassy" in Jerusalem when nearly all foreign governments moved their embassies to Tel-Aviv after Israel passed the Jerusalem Law in the Knesset.[57]

Some Christians among the evangelical Christians, regard the return of the Jews to Holy Land as part of the "end-of-the-days" scenario that will lead to the second coming of Jesus. Christians who supported the Zionist movement from its beginning attached great theological significance to this. At the beginning of the twentieth century they declared that "the rise of the Jewish people in world leadership" is the only genuinely positive sign of the times. The Balfour Declaration and the capture of Jerusalem by General Allenby in 1917 were viewed as a sign of the imminent coming of the Messiah. Christian groups in America discussed "The Regathering of Israel in Unbelief," and a bestselling book claimed that "the times of the Gentiles . . . have run their course . . . [and] God will again resume His dealings with the Hebrew people." After the establishment of the state these views were reaffirmed, and there was an expectation that God was making good on the "Old Testament predictions."[58] But some Zionist Christians were worried that the Jews were too secular and that they would return to the Holy Land as unbelievers.

Jewish liberal groups in America often express concern about the strengthening of the Christian right, but this is part of a larger debate on the role of religion in a democratic society and the meaning of the church and state separation in the Constitution. However, in recent years it is clear that the more liberal Protestant churches who deny the Chosen role of the Jews are engaged in anti-Israel activities and strongly promote measures of boycott against Israel. Some Jewish leaders have called the boycott initiatives an anti-Semitic campaign aimed at choking Israel via economic means while, at the same time, the same churches facilitate money transfers to charitable institutions accused of financing terror against Israeli and Jewish civilians.[59] In sharp contrast to the liberal Protestants the pro-Israel groups of evangelist in America have created an unprecedented mechanism of fundraising on behalf of Israel, which has brought in recent years hundreds of millions dollars for welfare and immigrant absorption through local councils in Israel. The money is channeled through the International Fellowship of Christian and Jews, led by Rabbi Yechiel Eckstein, an Orthodox Jew, and there are no signs of attempts for missionary activities among the Jewish population. This Christian foundation is based on a steady flow of millions of small donations from ordinary citizens who are stirred by sermons full of religious fervor about the Chosen Jewish People and the coming of the Messiah.[60]

Walter Russell Mead explains in *Foreign Affairs* that religion shapes the American character and "influences the ways Americans respond to events beyond their borders." The shift toward conservative Protestantism, he explains, "has already changed U.S. foreign policy in profound ways," and in regard to Israel "the increased influence of evangelicals has been evident." Russell quotes John Hagee, one of the leading evangelical pastors, treats God's Covenant with Abraham on the Chosen Jews as policy guidelines for the United States: "Will we believe and obey the Word of God concerning Israel, or will we continue to equivocate and sympathize with Israel enemies?"[61]

It is another paradox of Christian-Jewish relations that the Jews provided the Zionist Christians with their book—the Jewish Bible (the Old Testament)—which will ignite, almost two millennium later, the Christian movement for the historic return of the Jews to their Promised Land. These Gentiles, like those in the words of the psalmist, feel that they are eyewitnesses to miracles of which the Jews themselves are not yet fully aware.

## The Vatican and the Promised Land

Theodor Herzl's meeting with Pope Pius X in 1904 was a major disappointment and even a learning experience on the nature of Christian hostility towards Jews. In this meeting Herzl had tried to obtain the support of the Vatican for the Zionist efforts to bring about the return of the Jews to Palestine. The Pope gave him an uneqivocal double rejection: both denying Jewish claims for a state of its own and denying the religious legitimacy of Judaism. He did not attempt to conceal the fact that his strong opposition stemmed directly from the Chosen concept. In May 1896, Herzl had met with the papal nuncio in Vienna, Monsignor Antonio Agliardi, and he wrote in his diary, "I believe Rome will be against us, because she does not consider the solution of the Jewish question in a Jewish state, and perhaps even fears it."[62] The inability of the Vatican to comprehend the existence of a Jewish state with Jerusalem as its capital is central for the understanding of the many obstacles that are in the way even today for peace in the Middle East. In 1897, four months before the first Zionist Congress took place in Basel, the Jesuit journal *La Civiltà Cattolica*, known for its anti-Semitic tenor, published what can be seen as the theological position of the Vatican concerning the return of the Jewish people to its homeland: "1827 years have passed since the prediction of Jesus of Nazareth was fulfilled, namely that Jerusalem would be destroyed . . . that the Jews would be led away to be slaves among all the nations, and that they would remain in dispersion until the end of the world."[63]

The Vatican was deeply concerned after the first Zionist Congress, and it embarked upon an international campaign against the projected return of the Jews to the Holy Land. The secretary of state of the Vatican, Cardinal Merry del Val, cited the Church's "highest principles" on the Jewish religion: "I do not quite see how we can take any initiative in this matter. As long as the Jews deny the divinity of Christ, we certainly cannot make a declaration in their favor. Not that we bear any ill will towards them. . . . The history of Israel is our own heritage, it is our foundation. But in order for us to support the Jewish people in the way you desire, they would first have to be converted."[64]

Herzl wrote that his meeting with the Pope did not start well because he could not bring himself to kiss the Pope's ring as he had been advised. When Herzl raised his request for support for the creation of a Jewish state in Palestine, the Pope replied with the supersessionist theory, "We will not be able to stop the Jews from going to Jerusalem, but we could never favor it. . . . The Jews have not recognized our Lord, and so we cannot recognize the Jewish people. . . . The Jewish faith was superceded by the teachings of Christ, and we cannot admit that it still enjoys any validity. . . . And so, if you come to Palestine and settle your people there, we will be ready with churches and priests to baptize all of you."[65] The Pope even rejected Herzl's appeal to condemn anti-Semitism, and in fact appeared to justify persecution of the Jews: "The Jews . . . had time to acknowledge his [Jesus] divinity without any pressure. But they have not done so to this day."[66]

In the light of the Zionist efforts, the Catholic Church regarded the new political developments as impinging on its own standing as the "'New Israel,'" namely that of the Chosen. The Vatican desperately tried to obtain some sort of foothold in Palestine and to establish control over at least some of the holy places. Representatives of the Holy See lobbied intensively after the end of World War I because they wished to have a Catholic country appointed as the mandatory power instead of Protestant Great Britain. In 1947, when the partition plan for Palestine was finalized, the Vatican used its influence among certain Catholic countries, especially those of Latin America, to ensure the internationalization of Jerusalem under the aegis of the United Nations. However, this was opposed by both the Hashemite Kingdom of Jordan and Israel who controlled the two halves of the divided city between 1948 and 1967.

For the Christian Churches the establishment of the State of Israel in 1948 presented a major challenge, shattering years of theological belief based on the dispersion of the Jews who would not be able to exercise political sovereignty in a state of their own. A change in church policy towards Israel was not anticipated by the experts even as late as the early 1990s. Recognition of the State of Israel was a major theological obstacle for the Vatican since it would represent a historic shift in the status of the Chosen People. Even in the light of the Holocaust, the establishment of the state in 1948 was not welcomed by the Vatican. The official Vatican newspaper, *L'Osservatore Romano*, explained that "[m]odern Israel is not the true heir of biblical Israel, but is a secular state. . . . Therefore the Holy Land and its sacred sites belong to Christianity, the True Israel."[67] For many years Israel was treated as a pariah state by the Vatican; there were no diplomatic relations, and for years it could not bring itself to even refer to it by its name (including during the one-day visit by Pope Paul VI in 1964).

During all this time, the Vatican had no compunction in recognizing every other country on earth: tyrannical regimes, dictatorships, or atheist Communists—but not a sovereign Jewish state. The Church was unable to reconcile hundreds of years of anti-Semitism and its doctrines based on replacement of the humiliated nation that had been exiled and dispersed. In the eyes of the Church, the suffering of the Jews was the result of their unwillingness to accept the divinity of Jesus, and the Vatican was unable to confront its own inaction during the Holocaust or to attempt to change its theological policy toward the Jewish state.

Nevertheless, realities in the Holy Land imposed on the Vatican a practical agenda that forced it into more contacts with Israel. Following the Six-Day War the Vatican dropped its internationalization proposals in favor of a scheme for an internationally guaranteed statute for Jerusalem and the holy places. Realizing that Israel was in *de facto* control of the Christian holy places, the Vatican moved to upgrade its contacts with Israeli officials. But only after thirty years of the state's existence did Pope John Paul II, for the first time, refer openly to Israel's right to exist and the Jewish people's right to a safe haven. This brought about a palpable thaw in Vatican-Israel relations. Evidence of the cautious approach can be seen in the fact that in the Nostra Aetate of 1965 and the Vatican Guidelines of 1974, there was still no reference to the State of Israel. Only in 1985 did the Vatican affirm "the existence of the State of Israel" emphasizing that this recognition was being extended on the basis of "the common principles of international law."[68]

The early 1990s presented the Vatican with a major challenge making its policy toward Israel irrelevant and a potential source of embarrassment. The collapse of the Soviet Union and the Gulf War of 1991 had brought about far-reaching changes in the international system that directly affected the State of Israel. All the former Communist countries established diplomatic relations with Israel, as did China and India and even a few Islamic countries. The Vatican was left isolated with the members of the "Rejectionist Front" of extremist Arab and Muslim countries that adamantly refused to recognize Israel.

The recognition of Israel by the Catholic Church is also recognition of the rights of the Jewish people to have a state of its own. The Jews in the Diaspora understood that diplomatic relations with Israel would also imply an improvement in their own standing with relation to the Church. As Bernard Wasserstein said, "The establishment of diplomatic relations between Israel and the Vatican . . . marked a further advance in Catholic-Jewish relations—in some ways of greater symbolic importance for the Diaspora than for Israel itself."[69]

The 1993 agreement between Israel and the Holy See came as a surprise and nullified the predictions of many observers. However, in retrospect, it was a clear act of political realism by the Vatican, which was anxious not to be excluded from the peace process that was moving at a fast pace and creating strong expectations. The exchange of ambassadors was a deviation from almost two thousand years of theological doctrine and a clear departure from the Vatican's displacement doctrine of the Chosen. It had taken almost a hundred years for the Vatican to accept the reality of the new state. It had traversed a long way from the Pope's declaration at the end of the nineteenth century that "we cannot recognize the Jewish people" and his assertion that the idea of Jerusalem as the capital of a reconstituted State of Israel would be contrary to the prediction of Christ.

## The Arab Predicament

Israel is the central scapegoat for the Arab predicament and the crisis within Islam, and the Chosen factor is often used in the obsessive Arab campaign. By harnessing the power of Islam to the hatred of Israel, Arab regimes could inflame their populations by concentrating on a few basic aspects of the Chosen: religion, land, the holy places and *jihad*—Holy War, in order to counteract pressures for internal change. There is a tendency in Israel to belittle Arab anti-Semitism and to treat it as part of the political conflict in the Middle East, and Israeli governments are unwilling to demand a crackdown on Arab anti-Semitism as a precondition for peace talks.[70] This is a because of the Israeli desire for normalcy and to escape from the historic burden of the Chosen. Many Israelis fail to realize how the features of the Chosen have made Israel the main object of anti-Semitism in the twenty-first century.

Fundamentalist Islam is engaged in a struggle with Christianity, Judaism, and the West at large. America is defined as the "Great Satan," and Israel is the "Little Satan." The hatred of the Jews is overwhelming because it features in both the struggle against Israel and in the persistent claim that America is run by Jews. The correlation between America and Israel has a religious as well as a strategic political background. The popular concept of the Judeo-Christian heritage combines the roots of Christianity with other common values reflected in the political tradition of freedom, human rights and democracy. These basic tenants of Western civilization are sadly lacking in most of the Arab world.

More moderate Muslims and Arabs, who are themselves threatened by fundamentalist Islam, try at least to strengthen their alliance with the Christian world and to minimize the strong legacy in America of the Judeo-Christian roots. This was reflected in a debate following remarks by Secretary of State Colin Powell who said that Iraq was "an Islamic country by faith, just as we are Judeo-Christian." Powell had to correct himself out of deference to Americans of other faiths or of none and said, "[W]e are a country of many faiths now." But even this retraction did not satisfy American Muslims who maintained that they are closer to Christianity than the Jews because of Islamic reverence for Jesus and Mary, while ignoring the other religious-cultural values that are virtually non-existent in today's Muslim societies.[71] In Europe, politicians avoid speaking about "Judeo-Christianity," and now choose to refer to the traditions of Greco-Roman civilization rather than offend Muslim voters.[72]

Links between Islam and Christianity, harnessed to the cause of Muslim anti-Semitism, incorporated Christian anti-Jewish images and stereotypes in their propaganda. For instance, Palestinians propagate the old canard that the Jews murdered Jesus. When armed Palestinians took control of the Church of the Nativity in Bethlehem in March 2002, the Palestinian media throughout the Christian world rushed to spread images of the stand-off with Israeli troops. Yasser Arafat's advisor, Bassam Abu Sharif, in *Al-Sharq Al-Awsat*, a Saudi-owned newspaper published in London, in an orgy of pathos accused the Israelis of firing at a statue of the Virgin Mary statue during the siege, saying, "The sad smile of the Virgin Mary as she shields her son the Messiah did not prevent the soldiers of the Israeli occupation from taking up positions to shoot at the face of this Palestinian angel [Jesus] and murder the smile . . . so as to murder what they had not managed to murder in two thousand years. In Bethlehem, a new crime was committed. This, of course, was a failed attempt to murder peace, love, and tolerance, just as their forefathers tried to murder the prophetic message when they hammered their nails and iron stakes through the body of the Messiah into the wooden cross."[73]

The director-general of the Palestinian ministry of information spoke about the "Israeli colonialist occupation" and their "talmudic offensive which tears the pages of the Quran, and which offends the master of the prophets, Mohammad . . . and the blessed Virgin, mother of Christ."[74] The most common trend in Arab anti-Semitic writing today is the equation of Zionism with Nazism, adding that, just as the Nazis had believed in the superiority of the Aryan race, the Zionists believe in their doctrine of the "Chosen People."[75]

In their campaign against Israel, the Palestinians have developed two major falsehoods: denying the links of the Jews to the Land of Israel and creating a false history of Palestinians in the same land. In the same way as did Christianity before them, the Palestinians argue that they have been the historical owners of the land for thousands of years and that, therefore, they are the Chosen People who have superseded the Jews. The claim that the Palestinians are entitled to the Land as the seed of Ishmael, the first-born child of Abraham, cannot be supported by the text in Genesis, which states clearly that the Covenant of God with Abraham, including the Promised Land, will be established with Issac and with the Jewish people who are his descendants (and this promised was passed to Jacob and not to Esau).[76] Moreover the Quran states quite clearly (5:21) that Moses said to his people, "O my People! Enter the Holy Land which God has written for you."[77] "Written" in the Quran means the unchangeable law, the Torah, a decree by God to the people of Moses.

In order to reconcile the Quran narrative Muslim clergymen begun to present the Jewish religion as part of Islam and make the Islamic rule in today's Palestine as a prolongation of the Islamic rule of David and Solomon, as two Islamic Kings. In addition they developed a new ideology that makes the specific territory of Palestine Holy under Islam. This clear attempt to emulate the concept of the Jewish Promised Land contradicts the basic tenets of Islam, which disregard the concept of territory and is against the fundamentalists approach against making Palestine and Jerusalem central to Islam.[78] As part of their struggle against Israel, Islamic and Palestinian leaders have invented new religious myths transforming Palestine into a holy *waqf* (Islamic holy property) land, which is "rooted neither in Islamic legal texts nor in historical practice."[79]

The Palestinians have the clear goal of recruiting Christians to their struggle, and despite the hijacking of Christian history there has been no outcry from Christian quarters. At a press conference at the United Nations in Geneva on September 2, 1983, Yasser Arafat declared, "We were under Roman imperialism. We sent a Palestinian fisherman called Saint Peter to Rome: he not only occupied Rome, but he also won the hearts of the people. We know how to resist imperialism and occupation. . . . Jesus Christ was the first Palestinian fedayeen [fighter] who carried his sword along the road on which today the Palestinians carry their cross."[80] When Pope John Paul II visited Syria in May 2001, the Syrian President Hafez al-Assad took the opportunity to deliver anti-Jewish remarks live on television including the accusations of blood libels, while the Pope was seated by his side. Al-Assad was clearly trying to agitate Muslims and recruit Christians to his *jihad* against Israel and the Jews, by adopting the vocabulary of the Chosen struggle. He spoke about the Israelis and Jews as ontological enemies of God, who are attempting "to kill all the principles of divine faiths." He invoked the accusation of the Jews as Christ-killers, and he fabricated an Islamic analogy that, in the same way as the Jews had betrayed and tortured Jesus, the Jews had also tried to commit treachery against the prophet Mohammad. Neither the Pope nor any members of his entourage made any attempt to repudiate the gross manifestations of anti-Semitism, the false accusations, and the call for violence against the Jews.[81]

Fundamental Islam has adopted the images and prejudices of Christianity including the accusation against the Chosen and the most extreme expression of it in *The Protocols of the Elders of Zion*. Professor Yehuda Bauer says that the study of Islam is important for Holocaust scholars because the same patterns and threats are present and a second Holocaust is perfectly possible: "In radical Islam there are forces which are mentally prepared—given the power—to carry out genocide against others." Traditional Islamic sects like the Saudi Wahabists in the past did not make specific references to Jews. Now they speak explicitly about destroying the Jews: 'Their language is a mixture of that of the Nazis and the Quran."[82]

In December 2001, the Saudi newspaper *Al-Watan* published a two-part article based on *The Protocols of the Elders of Zion*. The article, entitled "The Jewish Sense of Superiority in the World," speaks about a plan by Jewish organizations "to take over the world by sparking revolutions or taking control of the keys in various countries, first and foremost the United States and Russia." [83]

Yasser Arafat's statements on Palestine and Jerusalem very often include religious references, appropriating the Promised Land for Islam. On April 24, 2004, he told Palestinian protesters in Ramallah that "the nation of the bold is not defending just itself but also the holy places in the promised land [*sic*]. Millions of *shaheeds* [Islamic martyrs] are marching to Jerusalem."[84] In addressing the United Nations General Assembly in November 1974, Arafat rewrote again the history of Palestine, displacing both Christianity and Judaism in the process: "The world must know that Palestine was the cradle of the most ancient cultures and civilization. Its Arab people were engaged in farming and building, spreading culture throughout the land for thousands of years, setting an example in the practice of religious tolerance and freedom of worship, acting as faithful guardians of the holy places of all religions."[85]

*El Hayat*, an officially supported newspaper of the Palestinian Authority, quoted the Muslim writer Safinaz Kallan who stated that "there is no people or land named Israel, only Zionist thieves unfit to establish a nation or have their own language and religion." He blames the Jews who are defamed as "Shylocks of the land, busy emptying Palestinian pockets."[86]

The augmentation and modernization of the Hezbollah rocket capability poses a significant threat to Israel. Opposition to Israel's right to exist lies at the heart of the Islamic Republic's ideology. On December 31, 1999, before tens of thousands people at a Jerusalem Day rally in Tehran, Iranian supreme leader 'Ali Khamene'i declared, "There is only one solution to the Middle East problem, namely the annihilation and destruction of the Zionist state."[87] Israel's ability to deter an attack depends upon the retaliatory threat Israel poses to Iran. Should Tehran acquire nuclear weapons, the Iranian government's fear of Israeli retaliations would dissipate. On December 14, 2001, then-Iranian president 'Ali Akbar Hashemi Rafsanjani said, "The use of an atomic bomb against Israel would totally destroy Israel, while [the same] against the Islamic world would only cause damage. Such a scenario is not inconceivable."[88]

## Nuclear Ambiguity and Fighting Terrorism

As the only country in the world that is facing continuous threats to its existence Israel found itself in a unique situation. In defending itself against terrorism it had to develop means of pre-emptive strikes, which extended the limits of the generally accepted terms of self-defense under international law and in the nuclear field. Israel's well-known posture of ambiguity provided the cynical screen for many nations and observers that treated this as another instance of "chosenness."

During the John Kennedy administration, which was committed to pursue the Nuclear Non-Proliferation Treaty (NPT), Israel met strong opposition in Washington for its nuclear ambitions, and there were many signs that the countries were on a collision course. Kennedy regarded the Israeli nuclear program as a project that would precipitate an uncontrolled nuclear race in the Middle East and would foil his global anti-proliferation policy.[89] The atmosphere has changed with the administration of President Lyndon Johnson who replaced Kennedy after his assassination in November 1963 and was elected for a full term in 1964. Of course, there were other strategic factors involved and a basic commitment for Israel's existence, with its seeds planted already by Kennedy, but it is hard to escape some comments of religious fate about the new president that were found in the documents and tapes in the Lyndon B. Johnson Presidential Library in Austin, Texas. Johnson, who replaced the first Catholic president of America, grew up in a family and community of Christadelphians who define themselves as "Bible Believing People." The Old Testament plays a central role in their beliefs and upbringing as well as the very act of chosenness: "[T]he covenant struck between God and the people of Israel at Mount Sinai—'You shall be to me a kingdom of priests and a holy nation.'" What can be interpreted as a policy guide appears in the family album inscribed by Lyndon Johnson's grandfather on his picture: "Take care of the Jews, God's [C]hosen [P]eople. Consider them your friends and help them any way you can." Jessie Johnson Hatcher, the grandfather's daughter and the president's aunt, would maintain close relations with him during his presidency, and she herself would recite, "If Israel is destroyed, that day the world will end."[90]

In 2002, Nicholas D. Kristof, writing in the *New York Times*, expressed a rare justification in a retroperspective of twenty years, for the June 1981 Israeli attack on Osirak, the Iraqi nuclear reactor. Kristof reminded his readers that after the attack Israel was condemned by virtually the whole world. The unprecedented pre-emptive strike on an as yet nonoperative reactor was perceived as an outrageous act of aggression. Even the sympathetic Reagan administration joined in the flood of condemnation. France declared it "unacceptable," and the British denounced it as "a grave breach of international law." An editorial in the *New York Times* said, "Israel's sneak attack on a French-built nuclear reactor near Baghdad was an act of inexcusable and short-sighted aggression." However, despite a policy of condemnation and temporary sanctions against Israel President Reagan explained why Israel should be treated differently: "It is difficult for me to envision Israel as being a threat to its neighbors. It is a nation that from the very beginning has lived under the threat from neighbors that did not recognize its right to exist as a nation.[91] In retrospect, said Kristof, "the condemnations were completely wrong. . . . Thank God that [Prime Minister] Menachem Begin overrode his own intelligence agency, which worried that the attack would affect the peace process with Egypt, and ordered the reactor destroyed. Otherwise Iraq would have gained nuclear weapons in the 1980s, it might now have a province called Kuwait and a chunk of Iran, and the region might have suffered nuclear devastation."[92]

On October 28, 1991, the American secretary of defense, Richard Cheney, thanked Israel publicly for the action it had taken against the Iraqi reactor, adding, "There were many times during the course of the buildup in the Gulf and the subsequent conflict that I gave thanks for the bold and dramatic action that had been taken some ten years before."[93]

The Israeli nuclear formula is another expression of the Chosen, in the defiance of the international regime of nonproliferation, but also the pariah, the only state that faces an open and consistent challenge to its existence. Israel's unique nuclear posture was an attempt to meet several conflicting demands. Israel could not join the nuclear club but wanted to project an aura of deterrence; it could not fully satisfy the Americans in their efforts against nonproliferation, but at the same time, it needed American guarantees to maintain its edge in the regional military balance. This brought about the innovation of nuclear ambiguity and gave birth to the often-repeated formula that "Israel will not be the first country to introduce nuclear weapons in the Middle East."[94]

Israel has been the major victim of terrorist attacks and has had to develop several techniques of reactions based on the concept of self-defense. It is interesting to see how after September 11, a debate was sparked among experts on international law on the adequacy of the current international law framework and how it will face the increasing challenge of the use of force by nonstate players.[95] "Global terrorism," says Alan Dershowitz, is "a phenomenon largely of our making. The international community—primarily the European governments and the United Nations, but also, at times, our own government [the United States]—made it all but inevitable that we would experience a horrendous day like September 11, 2001. We are reaping what we sowed. . . . Indeed there seemed to be almost a direct, one-to-one correlation between the targeting of innocent civilians by Palestinian terrorists and the legitimatization, even lionization, of the Palestinians and their leaders." [96]

Why was the world so dismissive of international terrorism? Was it possibly because the main victims of this terror were Jews, both in Israel and in the Diaspora? In the case of Palestinian terrorism, the international community responded by consistently rewarding and legitimizing it. Most of the literature and experience accumulated about international terrorism derives from the Middle East and the Palestinians. Palestinian and Arab terrorism against Israel started well before Israel entered the territories of the West Bank and Gaza after the Six-Day War of 1967, and even many years before the establishment of the state. Allowing the transformation of airplanes and airports into targets of terror was a watershed process in the appeasement of the terrorists and their sponsors.

Israel and the Jewish people have provided the battlefield for the most modern forms of international violence in the period following World War II. Deadly attacks against Israeli citizens at home and abroad and against Jewish targets almost everywhere, have become accepted as an unavoidable feature of international life, rather like anti-Semitism.

Terrorism can be regarded as the greatest catalyst of Palestinian legitimacy. After engaging in the hijacking of planes and killing hostages, murder at the Olympic Games, kidnapping and killing Western diplomats (all done by different sections of the PLO), Yasser Arafat was invited to speak at the United Nations General Assembly on November 13, 1974, where he received a hero's reception. The resolution that was adopted by the UN General Assembly by a large majority was not just a declaration of the "inalienable rights of the Palestinian people to sovereignty in Palestine"[97] but a clear challenge to Israel's right to exist. The resolution, which had nothing to say about the rights of the Jewish state, was a clear instrument intended to bring about annulment of the partition resolution of 1947. The resolution was a practical confirmation of the PLO Charter, which calls for the replacement of the State of Israel, through armed struggle by a Palestinian state. This resolution cleared the way for the 1975 resolution equating Zionism with racism.

In retrospect, one can recognize the "Light unto the Nations" effect of Israel's war against terrorism. International airports (and even domestic ones) have learned a great deal from the experience of Israel. Israeli counterattacks and rescue operations, such as that in the airport of Entebbe, Uganda, on July 4, 1976, when the government of Idi Amin provided safe haven to the terrorists who were holding their Jewish hostages (after a Nazi-like "selection" process,) would inspire several other governments to train special counterterrorism forces able to launch similar operations to release hostages if necessary.

The world's attitude to Palestinian terrorism brought about the collapse of any effort to build effective legal and political arrangements to fight terrorism. Since the 1970s, the United Nations continued to twist and turn through conflicting definitions of the various terrorist groups. The pariah status of Israel was reaffirmed in two different acts by United Nations organs that provided legitimacy to terrorist acts against Israel. On April 15, 2002, the UN Human Rights Commission in Geneva adopted a resolution that supported the use of any means in the struggle against the Israeli occupation—which basically means legitimizing terror in all its forms, including suicide bombings directed at civilians and children. The International Court of Justice in the Hague provided the legal cover for suicide bombings against Jewish civilians in its decision in July 2004 against the building of the separation fence between Israel and the Palestinian territories. The court refused to recognize Israel's right to defend itself against terrorist attacks including suicide bombers. The court took a radical interpretation of Article 51 of the UN Charter—which legitimizes the right of self-defense against armed attacks—by limiting it to attacks initiated by a sovereign state and not terrorist groups. Only the American judge on the tribunal, Thomas Burgenthal, a Jew and a Holocaust survivor, stated in his minority opinion that there was no basis for the attempt to restrict Article 51 in this way.[98]

Israel, as a victim of terrorism and under the declared Arab threat of annihilation by unconventional weapons, was the whistleblower and harbinger of the changes that have taken place since September 11, 2001. Western democracies have realized that security precautions might sometimes be at odds with established liberal practices of freedom in democracies. Despite much criticism and opposition from human rights groups, many countries around the world are now taking emergency steps to combat terrorism, under the clear knowledge that such "temporary" measures might compromise individual liberties. This is done in the full awareness that many of these measures might have to become permanent features of the new political and legal realities in world democracies and liberal societies. To argue that Israel is a "Light unto the Nations" concerning terrorism and nuclear threat may be seen as yet another example of Chosen hubris. However, it also shows the real nature of the double-edged sword of the Chosen: its mission and its responsibility together with the suffering and the threats to its existence. Israelis would be more than happy to surrender their role as forerunners in the war against terror and the nuclear threat.

Connor Cruise O'Brien explains that the so-called "siege complex" is not just a question of Israeli mentality, but rather a reality of the Middle East. This certainly cannot justify every political move of Israel, but in the words of O'Brien, "Israel cannot be other that what it is in terms of being a Jewish state in Palestine with its capital in Jerusalem." Although most of the founders of Zionism were secular, the return of the Jews to their own land and the creation of Israel must be explained, says O'Brien, in religious terms: "The Jewish state did not come into being as the European states did, through a long and gradual process, on the same territory, involving slow exclusions and accretions. The Jewish state was created through an unprecedented convergence of scattered people on a *former* national territory, and crystallized at an amazing speed; from a political dream to a state in less than seventy years. . . . The idea of the right of the Jews to return to Palestine, as transcending the will of the majority of the settled population of the area, is certainly basically a religious one (or a religious-national one), whatever secular forms it may from time to time assume."[99]

# CHAPTER 8

## Jerusalem
### The Chosen City

If I forget thee, O Jerusalem, let my right hand forget her cunning.
If I do not remember thee, Let my tongue cleave to the roof of my mouth;
If I do not prefer Jerusalem above my highest joy!

—Psalm 137

And all the nations shall flow to it, and many people shall come and say; "come let us go up to the mountain of the Lord, to the house of the God of Jacob; that he may teach us his ways and that we may walk in his paths," For out of Zion shall go forth the law and the word of the Lord from Jerusalem.

—Isaiah 2:3

Hep! Hep!
—An acronym for *Hierusolyma est perdita*, Latin for "Jerusalem is Lost"[1]

Glory to (Allah) Who did take His Servant for a Journey by night from the Sacred Mosque to the Farthest Mosque (*Masjid al-Aqsa*), whose precincts We did bless, in order that We might show him some of Our Signs: for He is the One Who heareth and seeth (all things).

—The only indirect reference to Jerusalem
(not by name) in the Quran: S. 17:1

For long expanses of time Jerusalem was a backwater, a remote, neglected place, the object of racial and religious memory and devotion but of no particular political concern to anyone. But in periods of conflict, as our own days attest, the city is transformed. It becomes the object of fierce, frequently bloodthirsty rivalry, the epicenter of hostility over the question of the Chosen.

Jerusalem is the Chosen City of the three great monotheistic religions, the site of passionately venerated holy places and equally passionate determination regarding who should control them. Conflict over the holy places is exacerbated by the fact that some of the same sites are claimed by both Jews and Muslims. Jerusalem is thus the political-religious problem of all problems, a prism that concentrates and magnifies the contention of Israelis and Palestinians. There is no single issue between the two peoples that arouses more emotion or seems less tractable.

In Jewish tradition, Jerusalem is the great physical link between the Chosen People and God. From David's time until the city's destruction by Titus in 70 CE, it was the Jewish religious center and the seat of government. At its heart were the First and then the Second Temples with their Holy of Holies, the dwelling place of the Divine Presence. In Diaspora, the Jews never ceased longing for Zion, synonymous since biblical times with the city itself, and more particularly with the Temple Mount. Jerusalem was (and is) embodied in their prayers, their holidays, and their hopes for redemption. It is to them their once-and-forever spiritual home. But not necessarily theirs alone. In another dimension of the tradition, Isaiah and other prophets say that Jerusalem will be transformed into a universal spiritual center for all peoples. "All nations," says Isaiah, "will flow to it."[2]

For Christians, Jerusalem is the primary setting of Jesus' life—the place of the Last Supper, the Crucifixion, and the Resurrection. It was in Jerusalem that Jesus took on Himself mankind's sins, paying for them with His life and in the process making His followers into the new Chosen People. The Church itself is the "New Jerusalem," a mystical image of the earthly city. In history the real Jerusalem has also served as a dramatic symbol of Jewish relegation and Christian ascendance. Left in ruins by Rome's armies, the demolished city was considered irrefutable evidence that God so hated the sinful Jews that He had abrogated His original Covenant and replaced it with a new, Christian dispensation.

Muslims, too, revere Jerusalem. For them the city is Al-Quds, Islam's third holiest site, surpassed only by Mecca and Medina. For Muslim believers the Temple Mount is where Mohammed prayed together with his predecessors in prophecy, Abraham, Moses, and Jesus. It was from there that he made his magical night journey to the foot of the heavenly throne where he was enveloped in the Divine Light, and it was to there that he returned through the seven heavens accompanied by the Archangel Gabriel.

So intense is the power of the Chosen City that followers of the three faiths have clung to Jerusalem both as a real place and as a transcendent spiritual symbol literally for ages. Jerusalem has riveted the attention and devotion of Jewish sages, Christian doctors, and Muslim saints. At times it has driven ordinary people insane. In an academic article in a professional journal of psychiatrists, Dr. Yair Bar El, director of the city's psychiatric hospital described what he called "Jerusalem syndrome,"[3] a form of hysteria that affects up to two hundred tourists every year. Many of these are previously healthy people, who suddenly conclude that they are in reality King David, the Virgin Mary, Jesus, the prophets or other biblical figures. Some of these people who come as normal tourists to Jerusalem end up in believing they are prophets, the Messiah, or even God. One such person was Michael William Rohan, a Christian sheep-shearer from Australia and a member of the "Church of God" who set fire to the Al-Aqsa Mosque in August 1969, creating a major political crisis.[4] The Arabs called the arson as a "Zionist crime," a Jewish plot to destroy the Muslim holy shrine. The Israelis arrested

Rohan, brought him to trial, and sentenced him to fifteen years imprisonment.

At the peace talks in Camp David in summer 2000, President Clinton came up with an unprecedented and innovative approach to the central problem of custodianship over the Temple Mount. Sovereignty would be divided into two vertical levels: the upper level for Muslims with the Dome of the Rock and the Al-Aqsa Mosque, and the lower level, underground, the site of the Temple foundations, for the Jews. But Yasser Arafat simply denied any Jewish connection at all to the Temple Mount (in the process effectively denying his own sources: the Quran, the Hadith, and other Islamic literature and tradition). His representative, Sa'ab Barekat, said that the very idea of the Temple is a Jewish invention lacking historical basis. Similarly Yasir Abed-Rabo, another senior official at Palestinian authority said to the *Le Monde* on September 25, 2000, that "there was never a Jewish Temple in Jerusalem." So said the Palestinian *mufti* of Jerusalem to the German *Die Welt* in January 2000: "There is not the smallest indication of the existence of a Jewish temple on this place in the past. In the whole city, there is not even a single stone indicating Jewish history." These statements contradict the Arab guidebook by the Supreme Muslim Council of Jerusalem issued in 1930, which declares, "This site is one of the oldest in the world. Its sanctity dates from the earliest times. Its identity with the site of Solomon's Temple is beyond dispute"[5]

At another point, Arafat told Clinton that the Temple had been located in Nablus rather than in Jerusalem.[6] President Clinton replied that "it is not just all the Jews around the world who believe that the Temple was there but the majority of Christians as well."[7] Clinton himself, even in this far-reaching concession on Jerusalem, could not deny his own upbringing in a Baptist church where as a child he got the warning of his pastor: "God will never forgive you if you don't stand by Israel."[8] It is clear that when there is such a loaded concept of religion and divinity, every claim becomes exclusive, eternal, and universal. If this is God's place, how can human beings possibly be expected to negotiate a compromise?

## Jerusalem in History and Legend

In Jewish tradition, the city of Jerusalem was Chosen by God: "The place which the Lord thy God shall choose to put His name"[9] It was King David's capital and the site of the Temple built by Solomon. The prophets castigated it for its sins, its hypocrisy, the superficiality of its worship, its social injustices, while virtually in the same breath they painted a vivid picture of a city cleansed of iniquity, the teacher of true religion to all peoples, the Chosen seat of the Almighty. In exile in Babylon, the Jews praised Zion in the immortal words of Psalm 137: "How shall we sing the Lord's song in a foreign land? If I forget thee, O Jerusalem, let my right hand forget her cunning, let my tongue cleave to the roof of my mouth if I do not remember thee; if I do not prefer Jerusalem above my highest joy!" Jews have referred to Jerusalem for three thousand years as the abode of the *Shekhina* (the divine presence of God) and as their only eternal capital.

Despite religious and economic sanctions, oppression, prohibitions, and expulsions, Jews have succeeded in maintaining at least a minimal presence in Jerusalem during the almost two thousand years since the fall of the Second Temple. At times the death penalty was invoked for entering the city; at other times the city's Jews were subjected to havoc and devastation. But always they kept a toehold, and they never stopped believing that one day they would regain what had been taken from them. In the earliest modern census records (from 1838), Jews constituted the largest ethnic group in the city, more than either Muslims or Christians, and before the end of the nineteenth century they were the majority of the city's population.[10]

The centrality of Jerusalem in Jewish life can hardly be exaggerated. In addition to mentioning Jerusalem several times in their daily prayers as well as in the grace after every meal, prayers for Jerusalem are included in the Jewish marriage ceremony. The bridegroom crushes a glass underfoot to symbolize his grief over the destruction of the Temple. In a house of mourning, visitors recite the traditional consolation: "May the Almighty comfort you and all the mourners of Jerusalem and Zion." The ninth day of the month of Av is a fast day to commemorate the destruction of both Temples. All synagogues throughout the world are constructed so that the Ark of the Law faces Jerusalem. During the Passover Seder and the prayers on Yom Kippur (the Day of Atonement), a highlight is the solemn pledge: "Next Year in Jerusalem." In the mystic literature of the Kabbalah, Jerusalem symbolizes the lowest level of the kingdom that rules the earth, and in the teachings of the Zohar, the angels of the *Shekhina* are the guardians of the city walls. According to Nachmanides, Jerusalem is especially suited for prophecy since "no curtain separates it from God. The prayers of all Israel rise to heaven in Jerusalem and its walls will eventually approach the Throne of Glory."[11]

According to Jewish tradition, Abraham (the first pillar of the Chosen) was the first Hebrew to go to Jerusalem. It was there that he was blessed by Melchizedek, King of Salem, and "priest of God Most High."[12] In Hebrew, Jerusalem is *Yerushalayim* from the words *Ir shalem* or *Ir shalom*, namely the "complete city" or the "city of peace." *Yerushalayim* is first called by that name in the Book of Joshua and in all is mentioned 657 times in the Old Testament and another 154 in the New Testament.

The Great Jewish Revolt of 66 CE and the resulting siege of Jerusalem constitutes one of the most important and horrifying events in Jewish history—commemorated each year with fasting and prayer on the Ninth of Av, the day when the Second Temple was set aflame. On that day in 70 CE the Jewish fighters who had defended the city for several years were put to the sword, and the survivors carried off into slavery. The city was razed, except for the three towers of Herod, which protected the camp of the Roman Tenth Legion. The destruction marked the end of Jewish sovereignty in the Holy Land and the beginning of almost two thousand years of exile.

Rabbi Yohanan Ben Zakkai, considered the architect of Judaism after the fall of the Temple, had opposed the Jewish revolt and as the deputy of the Sanhedrin (the council of seventy-one Jewish sages at the time of the holy temple) he was smuggled out of besieged Jerusalem in a coffin. He obtained from the Roman authorities permission to set up a center of Jewish learning in the town of Yavneh (Jabneh). The population of Yavneh had refused to join the revolt and concentrated on instituting new features of Judaism, such as organized communities, the Jewish calendar, the synagogue, and other elements to replace the lost Temple. Ben Zakkai realized that, with the loss of Jerusalem, Jewish spiritual efforts would need to be concentrated on what Heinrich Heine two millennia later would term "portable Judaism," whether in the Land of Israel or in dispersion. Ben Zakkai created the new and distinctive marks of the Chosen—a dispossessed people without land, without sovereignty, without the Temple, and without a capital. But the vigor of the new, decentralized faith was marked then and later by tears for the Chosen City's loss.

While Christianity was in its first formative stages, Jews also harbored beliefs about the coming of a Messiah who would redeem the Holy City. According to the Talmud, Rabbi Akiva, one of the great Jewish authorities, regarded Shimon Bar Kokhba, leader of the Second Jewish Revolt of 132–35 CE, as just such a leader and referred to him as the "anointed king." Other sages did not agree. Rabbi Johanan Ben Torta famously responded: 'Oh Akiva, grass will sprout between your jaws and the Son of David will still not have come."[13] Akiva himself was tortured to death by the Romans, who finally crushed Bar Kokhba and his fighters in Betar near Jerusalem in 135 CE.

After the Bar Kokhba revolt was put down the Emperor Hadrian decided to erect a Roman-style colony on the remains of the destroyed city. What was left of the ruins was leveled so as to erase any trace of previous Jewish existence. A new city arose, and Greek speakers were moved in to inhabit it. Jews were forbidden to enter on pain of death. The Romans called their new city "Aelia Capitolina" after the Emperor Aelius Hadrianus and the god Jupiter Capitolinus. In order to remove any remaining Jewish links to the land, the captured province of Judea was renamed *Palaestina*—after the long extinct Philistines of the Bible. These measures were part of a systematic program to separate the Jews from what was considered the core of their identity in order to pacify them permanently. It was Rome's campaign against the Chosen.

Despite the decrees, each year on the Ninth of Av Jews continued to visit the ruins, particularly the still-standing western supporting wall of the Temple plaza. An interesting commentary by Saint Jerome to the book of Zephaniah bears witness to this: "On the day of the Destruction of Jerusalem, you see people showing both in their bodies and their dress the wrath of the Lord. A crowd of pitiable creatures assembles and under the gleaming gibbet of the Lord and His sparkling resurrection and before a brilliant banner with a cross waving from the Mount of Olives, they weep over the ruins of the Temple. And yet they are not worthy of pity."[14]

From time to time the Jews benefited from a relaxation of the prohibition against pilgrimages, and at the end of the third century they were once more allowed to enter the city. Then, in 324 CE the Emperor Constantine the Great became the master of Palestine and Aelia Capitolina. Having accepted

Christianity for himself and much of the empire, Constantine established Jerusalem as a holy Christian city, creating facts on the ground to go along with Christianity's spiritual claims. New churches were built, marking sites associated with Jesus' life and death. In 335 the Church of the Holy Sepulcher was dedicated (on the ruins of a temple to Venus), at the place where, according to Christian tradition, the remains of the True Cross had been found. Jews were once again prohibited from entering the city, save on the Ninth of Av when they were allowed to lament on the Temple Mount amidst the ruins—mute testimony, in Christian eyes, to their displacement as the Chosen.

By this time evolved Christian doctrine maintained that the Jews would be left to mourn their destroyed holy places until they accepted the truth of Jesus' Messiahship and converted to Christianity. Christian writers argued that following the loss of Jerusalem and the Temple, the Jews no longer had an altar, priests, or sacrificial worship. Their religion was finished; the law of Moses a thing of the past, their holy Temple's destruction the clearest possible answer to their hopes for renewal and redemption. So central was Temple worship to the Jews, and so famous throughout the world had the Temple itself been, that Christian dogmatists failed to appreciate the Jews' ability to maintain their unique identity in the absence of its unifying power.

An interesting interruption in the Christianization of Jerusalem occurred in the year 363 when the Emperor Julian, who had reverted to Rome's pagan religious practices, ordered the reconstruction of the Temple.[15] Julian understood the significance of Jerusalem for Christian believers and the Temple ruins for Christian apologetics, and in his book *Contra Galilaios* (*Against the Galilean*), he presented a full-scale refutation of Christianity. By restoring Jerusalem to the Jews he planned to undermine Christian legitimacy and enlist the empire's Jews as allies in his religious endeavors. Work to rebuild the Temple started in the spring of 363 but was cut short by an earthquake. The premature death of Julian few weeks later in a battle on the Persian frontier brought an end to the idea, and after this brief interval Jerusalem again became Christian.

In 614, a Persian army lead by King Chosroes II besieged Jerusalem with Jewish assistance. The Persians captured the city, killed many of its inhabitants, and exiled the patriarch Zacharias and with him the True Cross. Subsequently the Persians handed the city over to the Jews, who ruled it under a leader known only by his symbolic name, Nehemia. The Persian incursion resulted in the destruction of most of Jerusalem's churches. But after a while the Persians, Zoroastrians with no religious investment in the place, handed the city back to the Christians, who rebuilt the holy sites under the patriarch Modestus. After bringing back the True Cross in triumphant procession in March 629, the Emperor Heraclius once again banished Jews from the city.[16]

Christians, however, did not have long to enjoy their renewed control of the Holy City. In 637 Omar I, the second Caliph, took Jerusalem after negotiating an agreement with the patriarch Sophronius, which assured Christian religious rights in the city. But Omar rejected Sophronius's demand that Jews would be prevented from living in the city and that Mount Moriah (the Temple Mount) would remain a waste area of ruins devoid of any new religious buildings.[17]

There were both religious and political reasons behind the Muslims' comparatively more benevolent attitude toward Jerusalem's Jews. Like Christians, they resented the Jews for not converting. But Muslims did not regard the ruins of Jerusalem as central to Islam, which had its origins not there but in Mecca and Medina. From a political point of view, Omar was concerned to diminish the Christian hold on the city. Against Sophronius' vehement opposition, he allowed seventy Jewish families from Tiberias to settle in the area southwest of the Temple Mount (which was to become the city's Jewish Quarter). There they were permitted to build a synagogue and a *beit midrash*, a study hall. Omar also decided to build a mosque on the Mount. According to some accounts, the Jews helped Omar identify the site of Mohammad's magical night journey, and the Al-Aqsa Mosque was constructed on the Mount's southern side so that Muslims praying there would direct their faces toward Mecca.[18]

In the period between the Arab conquest and the Crusades, Jerusalem became an increasing source of contention between Christianity and Islam. The Umayyad caliph Abd al-Malik attempted to make Jerusalem the chief holy city of Islam in place of Mecca, which at the time was controlled by his adversary, the counter-caliph Abdullah ibn al-Zubayar. As part of this effort, in 691 al-Malik completed the golden cupola over the *Qubbat al-Sakhra* (the Dome of the Rock). This magnificent edifice, meant not as a mosque but as a shrine to divert pilgrims from Mecca, is built over the site where, according to Muslim belief, the prophet Mohammad ascended to heaven on his mystical night journey. Although al-Malik's shrine was built in the context of an Islamic civil war, the structure was also intended as a statement of Islamic ascendance. Arab sources explain that the Umayyad caliph intended to show that the magnificent Dome of the Rock surpassed in its beauty all the churches of Jerusalem and, in particular, the Church of the Holy Sepulcher.[19]

The Dome of the Rock conveyed a clear message to the Jews, for whom the building site was sacred as the location of the Temple, and even more pointedly to the Christians, from whom Muslims had taken the city. The Quranic inscriptions on the Dome of the Rock explicitly denounce what Muslims regard as the principal error of Christianity: "Praise be to God, who begat no son, and has no partner" and "The one eternal God. He does not beget, He is not begotten, and He has no peer." The Dome announces, symbolically and literally, that Islam had now superseded both Judaism and Christianity in the struggle for the Chosen.

Although the Dome gave a monumental substantiality to Islam's claim on Jerusalem, historically, there is no question that Mohammed himself never set foot in the city. The prophet died in 632 while Jerusalem was still in Byzantine hands. Nor is there any question that as far as the Quran and Hadith are concerned Jerusalem was the Jews' holy city, playing the same role for them that Mecca played for Muslims. Jews have their *qiblah* (their direction of prayer—toward the Temple in Jerusalem), says the Quran, Muslims have theirs (toward the Ka'ba in Mecca) "nor would any of them accept the 'qiblah' of the other."[20]

The Quran together with Muslim commentaries is unequivocal regarding the site of the Temple and its Jewish heritage. The commentaries emphasize that the Jews were the first servants of Allah and that Israel was their land and it was the Jewish Temple that was destroyed first by the Babylonians, then by the Romans. The Quran itself puts it this way:

> We gave Moses the Book and made it a guide for the Israelites. . . . In the Book We solemnly declared to the Israelites: Twice you shall commit evil in the land. You shall become great transgressors. . . . And when the prophecy of your first transgression came to be fulfilled, We sent against you a formidable army, which ravaged your land and carried out the punishment. . . . And when the prophecy of your second transgression came to be fulfilled, We sent another army to afflict you and to enter the Temple as the former entered it before, utterly destroying all that they laid their hands on.[21]

The Quranic approach to Jerusalem is thus strictly in accordance with the city's Jewish history, even as it attempts to build the case for the supersession of the Jews by Islam.

The Islamic claim on Jerusalem is based on Mohammed's famous night flight on the back of the magical beast Buraq, first from Mecca to Jerusalem, where he prayed in the Temple with Abraham, Moses, Jesus, and other prophets, and then to the foot of the heavenly throne. The nature of the Islamic connection to the Chosen City thus differs qualitatively from that of Jews and Christians. Professor R. J. Zwi Werblowsky explains it this way:

> Islam provides us with perhaps the most impressive example of how a holy city can acquire a specific holiness on the basis of . . . [a] legend, superimposed no doubt on an earlier traditional sanctity of the place. Whereas in . . . Christianity the life and death of Jesus created religious facts (e.g. the Resurrection and the Ascension) and . . . the holy places, the Islamic case is the exact opposite. Beliefs and piety created religious facts and these, in turn, produced historical facts. . . . By . . . the fusion of the *isra* (journey) with the *al-Miraj* [the night flight], Islam linked itself to the holiness of Jerusalem traditional in Judaism and Christianity and integrated this legacy into its own religious system.[22]

But despite the construction of the al-Aqsa mosque and the Dome of the Rock, al-Malik's son and successor Suleiman decided not to pursue his father's efforts to make Jerusalem into Islam's chief city. Instead he moved his capital to Ramle, after which Jerusalem slowly disappeared as a focal point of Arab politics, religion, and historiography. Contemporary Christian writers, on the other hand, dwelled on the harassment and persecution of their coreligionists by the Muslims and sometimes blamed the Jews for the atrocities. And Christians in the city did suffer. In 966 the Church of the Holy Sepulcher and the Church of the Dormition on Mount Zion were burned down by Muslims.[23]

## The Crusaders' Holy War

Aroused by Pope Urban II's clarion call to liberate Jerusalem from the infidels, the knights and other followers of the First Crusade saw their quest as a holy mission. After massacring the Jews of the Rhineland, they marched to Asia Minor in 1097, firmly believing that they were the new Chosen People, taking up the vocation, which the Jews had forfeited. They were the army of God, while Muslims were God's enemies. Nor did the most extreme suffering or personal sacrifice deter them. Whenever they confronted hardships they would turn to the Bible, especially the Old Testament, and read about the sufferings of the Israelites in the desert. In this way they began to see their own suffering as a proof of their chosenness because if the original people of God had to suffer so much, surely this was an indication of their own unique relationship with God. They drew a parallel between their battles and the victories Israel achieved through divine intervention. The Battle of Dorylaeum Pass in Asia Minor they regarded as a miracle wrought by God, comparable to the crossing of the Red Sea by the Israelites. The nearer they got to Jerusalem, the more convinced they became about their new identity as the Chosen People. Throughout Christian Europe the reaction was overwhelming. People spoke not just about the mission of the Chosen, but in apocalyptic terms regarding the conquest of Jerusalem as a prelude to the "End of Days."[24]

In 1099 after a siege led by Godfrey of Bouillon, the Crusaders broke into the city, overwhelming the defense put up by Muslims and Jews together. The Jews sought refuge in the synagogues, which were set on fire by the attackers. Over the next two days most of the remaining Jews and perhaps forty thousand Muslims were slaughtered.[25] This frightful bloodbath destroyed Jerusalem's Muslim community and put an end to organized Jewish life in the city. Sixty-eight years later the famous Jewish traveler Benjamin of Tudela found only "[t]wo hundred . . . Jews [who] dwell in one corner of the city, under the Tower of David." [26]

Having conquered their Chosen City, the Crusaders reintroduced Christian religious life, and it was during the twelfth century that many traditions associated with Jerusalem and the life of Jesus were established, such as the route of the Via Dolorosa and the stations of the cross. Muslim shrines were turned into churches, and new churches were built. Jews and Muslims were not permitted to live in the city.

But with the defeat of the Crusader forces in the Battle of the Horns of Hittin in July 1187, Jerusalem was besieged and the Christian patriarch of Jerusalem surrendered to Saladin, the Kurdish commander of the Muslim army. Eight hundred years later, the Arab world was still looking for a second Saladin to defeat the infidels who now have possession of the Holy Land and Jerusalem. In his book about the Syrian president Hafez al-Assad, President Jimmy Carter wrote that Assad saw himself as a latter-day Saladin. On his office wall Assad kept a large painting depicting the battle of the Horns of Hittin.[27]

At the beginning of his struggle against the Crusaders, Saladin was motivated to fight the Franks because they were the enemies and oppressors of the Muslim people and was less inspired by a devotion to Jerusalem. This was to come later when Saladin and his armies arrived on the Mount of Olives opposite the city, from where he saw the Dome of the Rock and Al-Aqsa. In messages that he exchanged with the Crusader King Richard I (the "Lion Heart") each tried to explain why Jerusalem is his Chosen City. The English king wrote, "Jerusalem is for us an object of worship that we could not surrender even if there is only one of us left." Saladin replied, "Jerusalem is ours as much as yours: indeed it is even more sacred to us than it is to you, for it is the place from which our prophet set out on his nocturnal journey and the place where our community will gather on the Day of Judgment."[28]

Again, the historic pendulum moved to reassert the Muslim character of the Chosen City. This time Christians were forbidden to reside in Jerusalem (an exception was made for Eastern Orthodox Christians who retained the Church of the Holy Sepulcher). Saladin made a distinction between "good" and "bad" Christians; the bad were the Frankish Crusaders, whom he had expelled from the Holy City, but not the Greek and Eastern Christians, since they had not oppressed the Muslims. Most of the churches were converted or restored as Muslim shrines, and the mosques were purified: for example, the Church of St. Anne became a *madrassa* (Islamic religious college).

The Jews were invited by Saladin to live in Jerusalem once more, among them Jews from Yemen, North Africa, and Europe including a group of rabbis from France and England (1209–11).[29] Saladin was hailed throughout the Jewish world as the new Cyrus, and there was renewed enthusiasm for immigration to the Holy Land and talks about a forthcoming messianic age.[30] Saladin, the new possessor of Jerusalem, regarded the Jews as allies of Islam (albeit inferior infidels) because they were also enemies of the Crusaders.

The Christians again attempted to capture Jerusalem during the Third Crusade, and, in the negotiations that followed, the city was divided between the two faiths. Saladin and his successors "seem to have lost interest in the city, and in 1229 one of them even ceded Jerusalem to the Emperor Fredrick II as part of an overall settlement between the Moslem ruler and the Crusaders."[31] Ottoman forces attacked the city in 1244, massacred the Christians, and devastated the Church of the Holy Sepulcher. Jews were also victims of the killing, and in 1267 Nahmanides wrote that he had found only two Jewish cloth-dyers in Jerusalem. He persuaded more Jews to join the community, and he established a new synagogue. Muslim-Christian clashes continued through the fourteenth and fifteenth centuries, and the Muslims persecuted Christians, especially members of the Franciscan Order who had constructed a monastery on Mount Zion, as well as devastating churches including, once more, the Church of the Holy Sepulcher. During the same period, the small Jewish community was oppressed by both Christians and Muslims and suffered heavy taxation by the Mamluk administration.[32]

In the nineteenth century, the British consulate took upon itself the role of defending the Jewish population, and a Jewish agent of the Russian consul was protecting the forty Russian-Jewish immigrant families in the city. In 1840, the Sublime Porte (the Ottoman authorities) appointed a chief rabbi for Jerusalem, known as the *Haham Bashi*. With this more stable environment, the British philanthropist Sir Moses Montefiore began to finance buildings and a medical clinic in 1840 for the welfare of the Jews, and in 1854 the eighteen-bed Rothschild Hospital was inaugurated. In 1859, Dutch Jews opened sheltered housing for the indigent Jews of the city.

## The Modern Struggle over the Chosen City

The onset of modern political Zionism at the end of the nineteenth century again brought Jerusalem to the center of contention between the religions. The Christian reaction to the idea of a Jewish return varied. Pope Pius X, as we have seen (Chapter 7), rejected outright Theodor Herzl's requests for support. The official Catholic response to the idea of a Jewish homeland was perhaps most clearly summed up by Jesuit journal *La Civiltà Cattolica*, which stated that "[a]ccording to the Sacred Scriptures, the Jewish people must always live dispersed and wandering among the other nations, so that they may render witness to Christ not only by the scriptures . . . but by their very existence. As for a rebuilt Jerusalem, which could become the center of a reconstituted State of Israel, we must add that this is contrary to the prediction of Christ Himself."[33]

With its growing Jewish population, Jerusalem early in the twentieth century slowly began to change from a neglected, poverty-stricken provincial town into a city worthy of the name. The first major outbreak of violence occurred during Passover in 1920, when, despite the presence of a large number of British troops, Arab riots erupted, incited by rumors deliberately spread that the Jews intended to take control of the Muslim holy places. Amidst the widespread looting and destruction, 5 Jews were killed and 211 wounded. This atmosphere of hatred helped to consolidate the leadership of the Grand Mufti of Jerusalem, Haj Amin el-Husseini as the central figure in the anti-Zionist and anti-Jewish campaign.

On September 23, 1928, on the eve of Yom Kippur, the Grand Mufti declared that "the Jews are aiming to take possession of the Mosque of Al-Aqsa."[34] Following months of tension, the incitement burst into flame on August 23, 1929, in the form of attacks against Jews all over the country including in Jerusalem. One hundred thirty-three Jews were murdered. Jewish merchants fled from the Old City and moved to the new quarters outside the city walls. In the aftermath Muslim authorities rejected any agreement on arrangements for the Western Wall, and the situation continued to deteriorate.

Serving also as president of the Supreme Moslem Council, the Grand Mufti launched a fierce propaganda campaign in the Arab press. Realizing that the British authorities could not or would not restrain him, Haj Amin el-Husseini understood, in Conor Cruise O'Brien's words, that the British held a "marked sensitivity . . . to Moslem sensibilities, and a corresponding lack of sensitivity to Jewish religious sensibilities."[35] Believing that the British were seriously considering handing over the reins of power to the Arabs, the Mufti reasoned that by whipping up Arab feeling against the Jews he could contribute to the process.

By focusing on Jerusalem and attempting to deny Jewish rights to the city, the Mufti became the most prominent Palestinian leader and succeeded in enlarging a national conflict into a major religious conflagration, conveying to the Arab and larger Muslim world that Zionism presented a threat to the holy places of Islam.[36] In 1936, the Mufti accused the Jews of intending to rebuild the Temple in place of the Dome of the Rock, and in that year the "Arab Revolt" brought murder and sabotage to Jewish settlements throughout Palestine. Appearing before the British Peel Commission, sent to Palestine to examine "the roots of the problem," the Mufti maintained that Zionism was, in fact, a religious claim that was in fundamental conflict with Islam: "The Jews' ultimate aim is the reconstruction of the Temple of King Solomon on the ruins of the Haram al-Sharif, the Al-Aqsa Mosque and the Holy Dome of the Rock."[37]

The members of the Peel Commission understood that the situation of Jerusalem was so complicated that even the "surgical operation" that they had suggested for Palestine as a whole would be impossible in the Holy City. Their conclusion was that Jerusalem required a new and separate mandate. This recommendation in essence was incorporated into the United Nations partition resolution of November 29, 1947. Jerusalem was to become a *corpus separatum* under international rule, to be administrated by the United Nations. Jerusalem, the UN commission proclaimed, "is 'a sacred trust of civilization'—a trust on behalf not merely of the peoples of Palestine but of multitudes in other lands to whom those places, one or both, are Holy Places."[38]

By agreeing to the UN Partition Plan, the Executive of the Jewish Agency (the Jewish political authority in pre-state Palestine) gave their sanction to the proposal of the *corpus separatum*, which would have placed Jerusalem's one hundred thousand Jewish residents under international administration. David Ben Gurion explained many years later that this "was the price to be paid for statehood. We accepted the UN decision, everything. If the Arabs had accepted it fully, we would have carried it out fully." And Golda Meir added that "as painful as the idea was that Jerusalem would be internationalized. Had the Arabs gone along with the resolution, Jerusalem would not have been the capital."[39]

## The Forbidden City of the Chosen

At the time of Israel's War of Independence, Abd el Khader el-Husseini was the commander of the Arab military forces in Palestine. He, like his cousin the Grand Mufti, understood the battle for Jerusalem as part of the struggle for the historic and religious rights in the Holy Land. El-Husseini was a charismatic and effective leader who had been expelled from Palestine by the British in 1934 and returned to the country secretly in 1948. When he assumed command of the Arab forces, his major strategic objective was the Holy City and he vowed, "We will strangle Jerusalem."[40] He was killed on April 7, 1948, in a ferocious battle for the Castel, a hill that overlooked and controlled the city. The Jewish forces found a miniature Quran on his body, which they returned to his family. They also found a letter to his wife in Cairo into which he had slipped a poem intended for his son:

This land of brave men
Is our ancestors' land.
On this land
The Jews have no claim.

How can I sleep
When the enemy is upon it?
Something burns in my heart.
My country is calling.[41]

Husseini's poem portrays something of the depth of Arab feelings, which in part underlay the Arabs' flat rejection of the UN's Partition Plan, their declaration of war and their vows to annihilate Israel. In the war that followed, Jerusalem played a central role. With the city cut off by Arab forces, the Israeli army fought fiercely to defend it and keep it resupplied. Ben Gurion spoke emotionally of the "Chosen City" and its "redemption." "Until peace is proclaimed," he told the Provisional State Council, "and boundaries are decided upon by international authority, with the agreement of all sides, we speak of Jerusalem as within the boundaries of the Jewish State . . . as of now, to my regret, without the old city exactly as Tel Aviv."[42] He also declared later, "For the State of Israel . . . there has always been and will always be one capital, the eternal Jerusalem. Thus it was three thousand years ago and thus it will be, we believe, until the end of time."[43]

Eternal capital or not, when the War of Independence was over, the eastern part of Jerusalem, including the Old City, was in Arab hands. Jordan's King Hussein, the city's new ruler, strictly forbade any Jewish visits to the Jordanian sector, with its holy sites, including the Western Wall. The fact that the Chosen People could not enter its own Chosen City, even for a short prayer service at the Western Wall, was not seen as an act of injustice or violation of historic-religious rights. Under Jordanian rule, the authorities were responsible for the destruction of synagogues, *yeshivot* (religious seminaries), and cemeteries, all in violation of the International Convention for the Protection of Cultural Property in the Event of Armed Conflict.[44] The world's Christian communities, with their own sites protected and access guaranteed, acquiesced in all of it.

Israel's victory in the Six Day War of June 1967, however, brought a truly historic change to Jerusalem's holy places. With the city now unified under Israeli sovereignty, freedom of access was ensured for all religions. Israel's Supreme Court put this revolutionary change into perspective. "This [The Protection of Holy Places] law is the first time, following the many conquests and changes of government in the Land of Israel since the destruction of the Second Temple in 70 CE, that as a result of a military conquest, the civil administration has enacted a law which guarantees the rights of all religions to their holy places, without giving priority to one religion over another."[45]

This sensitivity to the devotional needs of Muslims was furthered in October 1970, when the Israel Supreme Court confirmed the government's right to prevent Jews from praying on the Temple Mount. There was no dispute among the five judges (including two religious judges) that the Mount is holy to the Jews, but considering the risks involved they all agreed that the government has the right to ensure law and order on the Mount. One religious judge, Moses Zilberg, while emphasizing the centrality of the Temple in Judaism, cited the Talmud, which says that the Temple was destroyed because the judges pronounced judgments strictly based on the Torah, implying that they did not consider other values that are sometimes supreme.[46] The other religious judge expressed his wish that one day there will also be Muslim religious leaders who will recognize Jewish rights on the Mount and will agree, as they did once, not just to let the Jews pray but to build a synagogue there.

## The Reunification of Jerusalem and Jewish Messianism

The return of the Jews to the Western Wall, the last remnant of the Jewish Temple, was a historic event, which was treated, in almost messianic terms by Jews as well as by many Christians. The Wall created an astonishing sense of religious-mystical feelings among Jews worldwide. In the words of Jacob Herzog, "Assimilated aristocrats and millionaires, children of mixed marriages, came to that stone wall and shed tears, without rhyme or reason." Even the pacifist Professor Martin Buber thought in biblical terms when he compared the victory with the Jewish exodus from Egypt.[47] Along with predictable messianic statements from the religious right, there were similar expressions from the labor movement. Moshe Dayan, the minister of defense, said in a speech delivered on the Mount of Olives, "We have returned to the [Temple] Mount, to the cradle of the nation's history, to the land of our forefathers, to the land of the Judges, and to the fortress of David's dynasty. We have returned to Hebron, Shechem [Nablus], Bethlehem, and Anatot; to Jericho and to the ford over the Jordan River. Our brothers, we bear your lessons with us. . . . [W]e know that to give life to Jerusalem we must station the soldiers . . . on the Shechem Mountains and on the bridges over the Jordan."[48]

Among religious Zionists there were highly emotional outbreaks of messianic enthusiasm. Their spiritual leader, Rabbi Zvi Yehuda Kook, had spoken three weeks before the war on Israel's Independence Day at the Merkaz Harav Yeshiva, the ideological center of right-wing religious Zionism. There he had delivered a prophetic message: "We have sinned!" he cried, and the audience began to weep. The speech was delivered in the still-divided Jerusalem, during the so-called "waiting period" when many Israelis anticipated the outbreak of war with a feeling that there could be a massacre. How, he asked, could "Israel, the Jewish state, leave the Temple Mount in the hands of Goyim? How could the Chosen People be content to settle in the Negev and the coastal plain while the true Holy Land was in enemy territory?"[49] Rabbi Kook was following in the footsteps of his eminent father who, in his writings, had emphasized the need to rebuild the Temple on Mount Moriah, because without the Temple, the Torah could not be observed in its entirety. The victory in the Six-Day War, just three weeks later, was viewed by many of his students as a God-given forerunner of the approaching messianic redemption.[50]

These deep religious passions animated a certain segment of the Israeli population. And in the usual "even-handed" Western approach to the Arab-Israeli conflict there was, and is, a tendency to compare Islamic extremists with Jewish extremists, suggesting that they are somehow equivalent and that they are the reason the cycle of violence persists. But such an argument rests on false premises. Unfortunately, extremists exist in every society, but the question is: to what extent are they tolerated by the majority and by the institutions of the state?

In the messianic excitement brought on by the Jewish victory and the return to the Old City, the Israeli government was crystal clear about limiting the extremes of religious fervor. According to some accounts, the Israeli commander of the Jerusalem area during the war, Major General Uzi Narkiss, warned the military's chief rabbi, Rabbi Shlomo Goren, that he would be thrown in jail if he continued to broach the idea of blowing up the Dome of the Rock and the Al-Aqsa Mosque on the Temple Mount. Rabbi Goren himself did not raise the issue again for the remaining twenty-three years of his life and denied that it had ever been a serious suggestion. Minister of Defense Moshe Dayan assured the *Waqf* (the Muslim religious authority) that it could continue its work of administering the holy sites. Dayan, himself a secular Israeli, would later invoke the ruling of the Orthodox rabbis that no Jew was permitted to set foot on the Temple area since he could inadvertently enter the site of the Holy of the Holies into which only the high priest could enter and that only on the holiest day of the year, Yom Kippur.[51]

Israeli extremists were never allowed to pursue their dreams regarding the Temple Mount. In his approach to the site, Dayan preferred pragmatism to the vision of the Chosen. While speaking on the "Godly scene" at the Temple Mount, and after saying in his speech that "we have returned to our holiest places and we will never leave them,"[52] he not only added that religious freedom and access to the holy sites for all would prevail, but he also made a historic decision to hand over the authority, and practical sovereignty on the Temple Mount to the *Waqf*, although he did insist that Jews should have free access. Later, he wrote in his autobiography that for the Muslims the Temple Mount is a mosque for prayers, but for the Jews it is merely a site of ancient historical memory. He attempted to draw a line between religious and political sovereignty (an idea that sounds eminently logical but is doomed to failure in the Middle East). On one hand he and his advisers felt the burden of Jewish history and identity, the symbol of Jewish sovereignty and spiritual life, which are buried under the buildings on the Temple Mount, but he decided on a rational approach and overrode his emotions. At one point he expressed his fears when he said, "[W]hy do we need this Vatican?"[53]

Religious extremism, though, was hardly extinguished by the government's policies. An American rabbi, Meyer Kahana, who had found the Jewish Defense League in America, established a small political party that succeeded in entering the Knesset in 1984. In fiery religious and nationalistic language, Kahana invoked the Bible, advocating that God's promises should be turned into actual policies regarding the occupied territories and Jerusalem: "God wants us to live in a country of our own, isolated, so that we live separately and have the least possible contact with what is foreign."[54] For Kahana, the doctrine of the Chosen was an absolute given and the promises to Abraham an incontrovertible fact, which made the Arabs into foreign usurpers. Kahana proposed that the Arabs should be offered financial inducements to leave the country of their own free will. If all else failed, though, they should be forced out. But in 1988 the Supreme Court cancelled his party's eligibility to stand for election on the grounds that it was promoting racism. Kahana was condemned by all the other political parties including those on the far right of the settlers' movement, and the president of Israel, Chaim Herzog, refused to meet him.[55] Two illegal groups of fanatics, motivated by Kabana's messianic talk of redemption, who in the 1970s and 1980s had planned to blow up the buildings on the Temple Mount, were caught by the security forces, tried, and sentenced to long prison terms.[56]

Since its establishment, Israel has had to come to terms with the unique status of Jerusalem, which it declared as its capital. Most of the world refrained from recognizing Jerusalem as the country's capital and virtually all the embassies are located in Tel-Aviv. Among the European nations, only the Netherlands and several Central American countries kept their embassies in Jerusalem. On July 30, 1980, the Knesset adopted the "Basic Law: Jerusalem the Capital of Israel." The almost universal condemnation that followed, demonstrated just how fragile is international legitimacy regarding Jerusalem as the capital of Israel. The passage of the law sharpened the criticism and highlighted the controversial status of the city so that the remaining embassies also transferred to Tel-Aviv. Costa Rica (in 1982), and later El Salvador (in 1984) with remarkable courage, have returned their embassies to Jerusalem but removed them again to Tel-Aviv during the Second Lebanon War in July 2006. Successive U.S. presidents have declared their intention to move the American embassy to Jerusalem, but all practical efforts so far have been thwarted by the State Department.

Another development was Egyptian President Anwar el-Sadat's historic speech to the Knesset in November 1977. In it he called for religious coexistence in Jerusalem. After visiting some of the sites sacred to the three religions, he told the Israeli parliament that Christianity and Islam look towards Jerusalem with reverence, "politically, spiritually and intellectually" as the "City of Peace." He issued a call to abandon the intolerance of the Crusades and to return to the spirit of Caliph Omar and Saladin who sought peaceful coexistence in the city.[57] But while both of these historic Muslim leaders had indeed favored the return of the Jews who had been evicted by the Christians, neither ever had any thoughts about sharing governance of religious sites or any sort of autonomy with the Jews who were, as we have seen, considered inferior infidels. In the peace treaty negotiations between Israel and Egypt, the issue of Jerusalem could not meet even with a preliminary agreement, and there was a need to arrange a hurried exchange of letters between the parties in order to avoid the collapse of the peace talks.

During the Oslo Talks in 1993, it was agreed that discussions on the future of Jerusalem would take place in the negotiations on the final settlement, but Chairman Arafat insisted on receiving specific assurances on Jerusalem in the interim agreement. Without informing the public, Foreign Minister Shimon Peres sent a letter in October 2003 to the Norwegian foreign minister under whose auspices the talks were held, providing assurances that the Muslim holy places would remain under Palestinian control. For the first time, he used the term "East Jerusalem" in an official letter, therefore legitimizing the *de facto* partition of the city. For nine months the Israeli government denied the existence of the letter. Arafat, however, exposed the letter during a trip to South Africa in May 1994 by alluding to it in a speech in a mosque, during which he declared the agreement with the Israel government to Mohammad's Quraysh Agreement of 628, which all Muslims understand as a shrewd deception on the part of the prophet.[58] Arafat declared that the *jihad* for Jerusalem would continue since Jerusalem "belongs" to the Muslim world. He declared that the crucial battle is over Jerusalem and referred to the agreement between Omar and Sophronius, which, according to some commentators, only permitted Christians to live in the Holy City while Jews were forbidden access. He ended his speech with the words, "Until the victory; until Jerusalem."[59]

## Denial and Rewriting of History

Yasser Arafat's tactic of saying one thing for Western ears and another for Muslims was well known. Yet the advent of Jewish sovereignty over Jerusalem, for the first time in two thousand years, came as such a profound shock to Arab mentality that it created the impetus not just for covert doublespeak, but also for the explicit rewriting of history. Jerusalem concentrates all the core questions of politics, faith, and the great historical clash of the three Chosen Peoples. In this context it should not, perhaps, be that surprising that history itself becomes twisted beyond recognition.

At the Camp David talks, the Palestinian representatives took positions that seemed incomprehensible to those who heard them. A few days before the beginning of the intifada, a PLO leader, Abdel Rabbo, adamantly denied that the Temple had ever existed at all: "The Israelis say that beneath the Noble Sanctuary [The Temple Mount] lies their Temple. . . . Looking at the situation form the archeological standpoint, I am sure there is no Temple. They have dug tunnel after tunnel with no result."[60] When Yasser Arafat met the Pope at the Vatican in February 2000, Chairman Arafat saluted him as the successor of Saint Peter, "a Palestinian." Peter, of course, like Jesus himself and all of his disciples, was in fact, a Jew.[61]

Arab apologists often attempt to rewrite the history of Palestine and Jerusalem, but Camp David was the first time that such a thing had surfaced during the formal process of peace negotiations—to the astonishment of the participants. In denying Jewish historic and religious rights to Jerusalem, Arafat demanded full and exclusive Palestinian sovereignty and was deaf to any and all suggestions concerning the Temple Mount that fell short of that.

The denial of any Jewish links to Jerusalem is a fairly recent trend that has entered Arab and Muslim propaganda as part of a comprehensive effort to invent a new historic narrative concerning the Holy Land. It must be emphasized that this is something that goes completely beyond the historic confrontations among the three claimants to chosenness. Suppression, exclusion, and even massacre have riddled Jerusalem's history. But no party to these things has ever attempted to deny history; on the contrary, supersession or replacement has always built on a commonly accepted historical narrative. Mohammed never thought to deny the Jewish history of Jerusalem and the Promised Land, no more than did Paul. On the contrary, both affirmed it. Godfrey of Bouillon wiped out the Muslim inhabitants of the city along with the Jews, but he knew that Muslims had been in the place for four hundred years, just as he knew that Jewish history there went back to biblical times.

But the new revisionist history of Jerusalem as presented by contemporary Muslim writers simply discard what until now had been at least a mutual agreement about worldly (if not spiritual) reality and unreality. The revisionists maintain that the Arabs ruled Jerusalem for thousands of years before the Israelites arrived. Arab archeologists identify the Jebusites as an ancient Arab tribe that migrated from the Arabian peninsula, together with the Canaanites, some three thousand years ago. The Jewish version of the history of Jerusalem, including that in the Bible, which is accepted by the Quran, is completely rejected. A religious *fatwa* ("decree") issued by the *waqf*, the Palestinian religious authority, states that David, Solomon, and Herod did not build the Temple, but rather they repaired something that had been standing there since the time of Adam. The new history even denies what has always been accepted by Muslims along with all other interested parties, along with all historians of these things—that the Al-Aqsa Mosque was constructed in the seventh century. According to the revised version, the mosque was actually built forty years after the construction of the mosque in Mecca by Adam, shortly after the seven days of creation. Other contemporary popular Islamic versions refer to Abraham and Solomon as the builders of the Al-Aqsa Mosque some four thousand years ago and treat both as Islamic figures with no Jewish connection.

*Waqf* officials in Jerusalem completely deny Jewish or Christian rights on the Temple Mount. According to Sheikh Akram Sabri, the mufti of Jerusalem and Sheikh Yusuf Kardawi, who resides in Qatar and is considered the most influential *mufti* in the Muslim world, the Al-Aqsa complex comprises all the surrounding areas as one unit, including all of the Western Wall. Their argument is that the Jews fabricated their links to the Western Wall as part of a grand conspiracy concerning the Temple and Jewish rights to Jerusalem. The northern branch of the Islamic Movement, an Israeli-Arab group, quotes an Egyptian archeologist, Abed al-Rahim Rihan Barakat, who wrote, "The myth of the fabricated Temple is the greatest crime of historical forgery."[62]

The changing Islamic attitude to Jerusalem is not just of revolutionary moment, it is profoundly disturbing. It means that at least some extremely significant Arab advocates are operating on a plane of reality that disregards the reality accepted as a matter of course by everyone else. More concretely for our purposes, it strikes a deathblow to the ability of the parties to reach any sort of compromise on the future of the Holy City. There is a clear tendency in today's Islam to imbue Jerusalem with the status of the Muslim Chosen City to the absolute exclusion of all other claims and, as a result, to make impossible a solution that would recognize Jewish historical rights and religious ties to the city. Jerusalem has taken its place at the center of the Arab cry for *jihad*, which often employs calls for genocide and other Nazi-like exhortations in the Muslim campaign against Israel and the Jews. Similar to Hitler's declaration in *Mein Kampf* (which is extensively quoted in the Arab world), the extremist Arab position maintains that there is no room for two Chosen People, most especially not in one Chosen City.

## Grounds for a Compromise?

Solving the conflict over Jerusalem is hardly simple, but it is obvious that it cannot be done without recognizing Jewish rights, and admitting that the concept of the Chosen Jerusalem started in Judaism. It often goes unrecognized, though, that within Judaism itself there is a strong universal dimension that can provide the basis for compromise on religious and political autonomy in the city. Different concepts that were raised in the peace negotiations such as "God's sovereignty" or "internationalization" of the religious sites can also be found in traditional Jewish sources.

The prophets emphasized the Jewish connection to Jerusalem, but they also envisaged the city as the universal goal for all mankind. While it is true that the prophet Joel voices extreme exclusionary views ("So you shall know that I am the Lord your God, who dwell in Zion, my holy mountain. And Jerusalem shall be holy and strangers shall never again pass through It."[63]), in fact the prophecy of Isaiah is more central in Jewish tradition. And Isaiah combines both the Chosen concept and the universal. First, the great prophet envisages the restoration of Jerusalem when God will forgive His own people:

"Comfort ye, comfort ye my people, says your God,
Speak tenderly to Jerusalem, and cry to her
That her warfare ended, that her iniquity is pardoned,
That she received from the Lord's hand double for all her sins.[64]

But at the same time, Isaiah emphasizes the powerful universal dimension of Jerusalem, which is part and parcel of a process of universal peace and disarmament: "And all the nations shall flow to it, and many peoples shall come and say: 'Come let us go up to the mountain of the Lord' to the house of the God of Jacob; that he may teach us his ways and that we may walk in his paths.' For out of Zion shall go forth the law and the word of the Lord from Jerusalem . . . and they shall beat their swords into plowshares and their spears into pruning hooks; nation shall not lift up sword against nation, neither shall they learn war anymore."[65]

In a similar vein the prophet Zechariah declared, "Many peoples and strong nations shall come to seek the Lord of Hosts in Jerusalem."[66] A later midrash, perhaps cognizant of the rivalry over Jerusalem, emphasizes the universal solution. "Zion," it says, "will be the Committee House for all the world . . . Jerusalem will be the lamp for the world's nations and they will walk under its light."[67]

Even Rashi, who has an unequivocal attitude toward Jewish chosenness, shares the universalistic vision about Jerusalem as the ideal for the "end of days." In his commentary to the Song of Songs he explains that the term "O daughters of Jerusalem" is a figurative reference to the nations of the world, all of whom will have a part in the Holy City. Jerusalem, says Rashi, will one day become the metropolis of all countries and draw people to her in streams to do her honor.[68]

# EPILOGUE

## Why Is the World
## Obsessed with the Jews?

God has distinguished us from the rest of mankind . . . God has made us unique by His laws and precepts . . . and our pre-eminence is manifested in His rules and statutes. . . . Therefore all the nations instigated by envy and impiety rose up against us, and all the kings of the earth motivated by injustice and enmity applied themselves to persecute us. They wanted to thwart God.

—Maimonides, 1172[1]

We have a tendency to drive the non-Jews crazy. There is something in our existence which leads whole civilizations to be obsessed with us. Earlier we drove the Europeans crazy and now we drive crazy also the Arabs. Something in our undefined existence causes this madness.

—A. B. Yehoshua, 2004[2]

Judaism is the oldest of the world's three major monotheistic religions and a forerunner of Christianity and Islam.

—*New York Times Almanac*, 2003[3]

[Jews are] Favored by nature and by nature God . . . but in exact proportion as we have been favored by nature, so we have been persecuted by Man . . . [becoming] the pariah of that ungrateful Europe that owed him the best part of its laws . . . all its religion.

—Sidonia, the Jewish banker
in *Coningsby* by Benjamin Disraeli, 1844[4]

The God of Jesus Christ, and therefore of the Church, is the God of Israel. The Jews remain the chosen people of God. The Jewish rejection of Jesus as the Son of God is an affirmation of faith that Christians must respect.

—James Carroll, a former Catholic priest, 2001[5]

Through Sidonia, the rich Jewish banker in *Tancred* and *Coningsby*, Benjamin Disraeli, the baptized Jew, conveys his very strong feelings on the fate of the Chosen People. Disraeli, the prime minister of Great

Britain, provides a clear answer to the frustration of the renowned Israeli author A. B. Yehoshua. The problem with Yehoshua as with most Jews (and non-Jews) lies in the undisputable reluctance, to deal with the Chosen concept as the central factor in Jewish relations with the rest of the world. Yehoshua says only that "there is something in our existence," but besides unclear references to the ambiguous Jewish identity, he is not ready to elaborate on why the world is obsessed with the Jews. In his book *On Behalf of Normalcy*, Yehoshua tries again to escape from the Jewish condition by ignoring its history, its Chosen dimension and by calling Israel to forget its Jewish Diaspora. Yehoshua continuously struggles with the subject:

> I have a fear because of the partial identity of the Jews. With their ability to penetrate the life of others. To live without borders, without taking responsibility. To be here and also there, yet not here and not there, and to maintain such an evasive existence: such an unclear identity. I think it is dangerous. I think that by penetrating deeply into the identities of other nations we are a threat to them. Something in our existence ferments fear . . . our intrusive mentality scares them and creates these sick interactions between us and them. . . . I am not justifying any anti-Semite. I am not trying to understand the anti-Semites but rather the anti-Semitic machinery. . . . It is about time we should understand that our ambiguous identity is causing individuals and groups who suffer a chaos of identity to cast on us awesome implications. Our mixture of religion and nationalism confuses and drives our neighbors crazy.[6]

Yehoshua is perplexed because he is not ready to recognize, as put by Sigmund Freud, that "the deeper motives of anti-Semitism have their roots in times long past."[7] The jealously that the Jews evoke in other peoples is explained by Freud, as being closely related to the Chosen concept and to the religious dependency of millions of people on this root cause. Yehoshua blames the Jews for their dispersion and absorption into other societies and civilizations but, unlike Toynbee, he is not ready to state that the other "two Judaic world-religions could never have come into existence if Judaism had not been in existence already."[8] Islam and Christianity, stated Toynbee, presuppose Judaism and both are driven by their rivalry and their claim of replacing the Jews. Here lies the peculiar "something" in Jewish history that is defined by the *New York Times Almanac*, that Judaism is the "oldest," the first of the monotheistic religions, and the forerunner of Christianity and Islam. The Jews cannot be a "fossil civilization" if they continue to be the driving force of so many others. Toynbee, never a friend of the Jews, while reluctant to dismantle his lifetime grand theory of history, explained far better than Yehoshua why the world is obsessed with the Jews: "The Jews' present-day importance, celebrity, and discomfort all derive from the historic fact that they have involuntarily begotten two Judaic world-religions whose millions of adherents make the preposterous but redoubtable claim to have superseded the Jews, by the Jewish God . . . dispensation, in the role of being this One True God's 'Chosen People.'"[9]

A different approach to the puzzle of Jewish identity comes from Dennis Ross, the former special envoy to the Middle East of the first Bush and Clinton administrations, and who chairs the Jewish People Policy Planning Institute, who said that Israel need not be a "normal" state. In sharp contrast to Yehoshua, Ross says that Israel has to be "abnormal" in order to maintain its Jewish identity and values and to continue together with world Jewry as a whole to offer the world a sublime moral model, as befits the "People of the Prophets."[10]

Chosenness is part of the Jewish psyche and not always can be explained in strictly religious terms. For instance the Oscar-winning actor Richard Dreyfuss, who grew up in an assimilated Jewish family in Los Angeles and was married to a non-Jew, gave his own striking definition for his Jewish identity in a public speech: "I am a passionately secular Jewish agnostic who sincerely believes that Jews are the Chosen People, so go figure! . . . I believe we are chosen to illuminate the Jewish condition. Our ethics are mankind's greatest victories."[11] Once more and a decade later, when he tells author Abigail Pogrebin about his complex identity, Richard Dreyfuss makes a confession: "I was one of those secret progressive Jews who believes that—Dreyfuss lowers his voice to a whisper—*We are the Chosen People. We are*. And even when that became not politically correct to say, I still do believe that."[12]

## The Centrality of the Chosen Concept

You do not have to be an observant Jew to accept the centrality of the Chosen concept in Judaism. You certainly do not have to be a Jew to recognize it. The Chosen is a central concept in the Bible, and its references to Israel and the Covenant that God made with the Jews lie at the foundations of the two other religions, and the very foundations of Western civilization. These commandments gave rise among the Jews to the sense of being a separate people in their relationship with God, and their observance of these commandments strengthened their identity and particularity. The historian Salo Baron, unlike Yehoshua, was clear about this peculiar "something": "[T]he Jewish religion without the 'Chosen People' is unthinkable, neither could it, like the other religions, be transplanted from the Jews to another people."[13]

The Canadian political scientist, Michael Brecher, who devoted many years to the study of the foreign policy of Israel says that the "sense of messianic mission" in terms such as a "Light unto the nations" the "bond with the Bible" and the "belief in the concept of Chosen People" was widely shared even by nonobservant Jews including the founding fathers of the State of Israel "though often concealed or denied."[14] The Jews are a Pariah People just because they are a Chosen People. The mantle of the Chosen was the gift to the Jews, but also their suffering, which made them the object of the world's obsession.

A young girl like Anne Frank writing her famous diary was in a pivotal position to grasp the most extreme expressions of the suffering of the Chosen. For many years there was a tendency to minimize the Jewishness of Anne Frank, and she became, indeed, a universal and supranational symbol of suffering from human evil. In the first editions of her diary some of the Jewish passages were excised. This was done by her father, Otto Frank, an assimilated Jew, who survived the war and who always emphasized the universal dimension of the book, which is also reflected in the Anne Frank House in Amsterdam. In the stage production of the diary, the portions that describe the celebration of Jewish holidays and the observance of Jewish customs even in the conditions of their hiding place, or the Zionist ambitions of the sister Margot to become a nurse in Palestine, and other deep and surprising expressions of Jewish feelings are missing.[15]

Missing also in the first edition of the diary but restored in the second edition, are her trenchant observations on the fate of the Chosen People and its suffering:

> Who has inflicted this on us? Who has set us apart from all the rest? . . . It's God who made us the way we are but it is also God who will lift us up again. In the eyes of the world, we are doomed. But if, after all this suffering, there are still Jews left, the Jewish people will be held up as an example. Who knows, maybe our religion will teach the world and all the people in it about goodness, and that's the reason, the only reason, we have to suffer. We can never be just Dutch, or just English or whatever, we will always be Jews as well, and we'll have to keep on being Jews. But then, we'll want to be.[16]

The perplexity over the conditions of Jewish existence call up different reactions. There are clear admirers such as Thomas Khill and Paul Johnson, and there is the "impressed hostile" such as Toynbee and the "bewildered observer" such as Nicholas Berdyaev and Mark Twain, all focusing in their own way, on the Chosen. Since Berdyaev was a devoted Christian who also expected the Jews to convert as part of human salvation, his analysis is full of contradictions. He admits that he is a victim of his religious upbringing, and therefore he presents confusing statements; on the one hand, maintaining that anti-Semitism is a sin while, on the other, explaining that religious hatred of the Jews is an important Christian principle. He concludes that the Jewish question will not be resolved "until the end of history" and declares that "[a] Christian must admit that the Jewish question is irresolvable to the end of the time . . . and anti-Semitism will never be overcome completely."[17] He was very clear about the mission of the Jews in their dispersion and their need to be apart in order to fulfill their mission. They are the Chosen People, and they brought to the world the idea of a personal God, which created "a dramatic relationship between man, people, and the transcended God, a meeting between the people and God by way of history."[18] The same double-edged sword and contradictory attitude can be found in former American President Jimmy Carter's statements in January 2007 after being accused of anti-Semitic tendencies and falsifying facts in his controversial book *Palestine: Peace Not Apartheid*. Carter expressed regrets about his "improper and stupid" sentence that justified Palestinian suicide bombings and terrorism but defended the rest of his criticism against Israel and resorted to the ultimate cause: "[A] lot of support for Israel comes from Christians like me who have been taught since they were 3 years old to honor and protect God's [C]hosen [P]eople from whom came people like our Christian Savior, Jesus Christ."[19] Critics of the former president like Jeffrey Goldberg have used the same frame of reference: "Carter, not unlike God, has long been disproportionately interested in the sins of the Chosen People. . . . This is a cynical book. . . . Carter [tries] to convince American evangelicals to reconsider their support for Israel . . . to scare them out of their position."[20]

Professor Hans Morgenthau, considered by many as the founder of international relations as an academic field of study, used the Chosen concept in order to explain the abnormal condition of the Jews. He argued that sometimes Gentiles perceive the condition better than the Jews themselves: "[T]he Jews . . . somehow have ties, however defined, which transcend the boundaries of the nations of which they are members. And whether you define these ties in terms of religion or any other term, if not obvious to Jews, it is obvious to the Gentiles that somehow the Jews owe allegiance to a God which transcends national boundaries. . . . This Jewish situation can be interpreted in religious terms and explained through the concept of the Chosen People."[21]

## Christianity and the Chosen

By no stretch of imagination can the Jews be accused collectively for Jesus' death. Millions of Jews were dispersed all over the ancient world (far more Jews were in the Diaspora than in the Land of Israel at the time of Jesus' death). It is not by accident that the New Testament accused Jews of all generations for killing Christ because the rival for the Chosen mantle continues forever. It confronts Christianity, Islam, or others at every turn when the Jews achieve prominence economically, politically, or when they become renowned scientists or academics. The world was bewildered when the Jews returned to their Promised Land and their Chosen City or when it finally comprehended the horrors of the Holocaust.

One way to begin is to focus on the common heritage by emphasizing the incontrovertible fact that Jesus was a Jew. After the Holocaust and perhaps because of it, many Christians tried to analyze their responsibility for anti-Jewish prejudice, and even more interesting, developed a clear need to examine their own faith's Jewish roots.[22]

It seems obvious, but neither Christians nor Jews are always ready for this kind of approach. Susannah Heschel writes that "the more Jewish Jesus could be shown to have been, the more Christians would respect Judaism." But are the Christians ready? In the nineteenth century Jews tried to do this, but the Christians preferred to demonstrate the difference: "For them, the more Jewish Jesus was shown to be, the less original and unique he was. If Jesus had simply preached the ordinary Judaism of his day, the foundation of Christianity as a distinctive and unparalleled religion would have been shattered."[23]

A British Catholic priest, Father Yves Dubois, has clearly pinpointed the problem between Judaism and Christianity in the supersessionist doctrine: "The whole supersessionist approach must be questioned and eliminated from the life of the Orthodox Church. . . . The urgency of a breakaway from anti-Judaism in the liturgical texts of the Orthodox Church is increased by the presence of anti-Semitism in our Church."[24]

In Germany, some Protestant theologians are questioning and in some cases even rejecting, the supersession theory. It is called "theology after Auschwitz," and its pioneer, the German philosopher Jurgen Moltmann says that the Jewish rejection and the Christian acceptance of Jesus as the Messiah—the promised Savior—are at some level compatible. Moltmann also maintains that Christians cannot really understand the Jewish situation because they never experienced anything comparable to the Holocaust.[25] It makes sense that without the supersession doctrine, the explosive concept of the Chosen would be treated differently. From this angle it is easier to understand why recent expressions of hate against Israel and the Jews resort to comparisons with the Nazis and the Holocaust, while denying the Jews claim to the Chosen title (Saramago and Theodorakis are clear examples—as illustrated in Chapter 5).

Some German Christians, such as Mother Dr. Basilea Schlink, accuse Hitler and the Nazis for waging war against God because of their obsessive envy with Jewish chosenness: "It was hatred against God because it was to the Jews that God had revealed Himself through His Yen holy Commandments." As a result, says Mother Basilea that because of it crimes during the Holocaust Christianity might lose its own election: "Woe to us when the hour of reckoning comes! Then it may be revealed that Jesus finds His likeness in Israel and not in us . . . we . . . are in danger of being rejected." German hatred against the Jews, explains Mother Baseila, was fed by the accusation that the Jews killed Jesus: "Yet in the background there often lurked very human fears of competition."[26]

The Vatican document on the Holocaust from March 1998, following some previous changes, marks a historic departure from many centuries of complete avoidance of references to the Jewish roots of Christianity. Referring to the "common future" the document says, "[I]n the first place we appeal to our Catholic brothers to renew the awareness of the Hebrew roots of their faith. We ask them to keep in mind that Jesus was a descendant of David; that the Virgin Mary and the Apostles belonged to the Jewish people; that the Church draws sustenance from the root of that good olive tree on to which have been grafted the wild olive branches of the Gentiles (Cf. Rom 11:17–24); that the Jews are our dearly beloved brothers, indeed in a certain sense they are 'our elder brothers.'"[27]

This approach, which stands at the root of the Judeo-Christian heritage, can reduce the confusion, envy, and hatred by offering a different interpretation on the links between Judaism and Christianity. Christianity should not be viewed as the replacement of Judaism because this would amount to a claim that God had reneged on his own promises to the Jewish people. There can be two and more Chosen Peoples or religions, and there need not be any interference with the beliefs and perceptions on the chosenness of either one.

## The Jew as the Pariah Among the Nations

Are attacks against the State of Israel attacks against the Chosen? Can Israel be immune from criticism because of being both the gift and the burden of the Chosen? While by no means perfect, Israel is in fact still the sole outpost of liberty and democracy in the Middle East. As its own citizens have demonstrated time and again, Israel is ready to pay a heavy price for peace and to expose itself to a major existential risk in probably the most dangerous region in the globe, confronting the hostility and denial of its legitimacy by its neighbors. Israel does not behave as an arrogant Chosen People, and its army and political institutions are under constant scrutiny unparalleled for a nation at war. Israel cannot and should not deny its Chosen heritage because as David Ben Gurion told the Peel Commission in 1937, "the Bible is our mandate."[28] Nevertheless despite this mandate from the divine, Ben Gurion together with the other leaders of the pre-state Jewish institutions accepted the United Nations partition resolution in 1947, which called for a two-state solution in Palestine. The Arab states rejected it outright and declared a war of annihilation against Israel. History repeated itself yet again, when the Palestinian leadership under Yasser Arafat rejected the two-state solution at Camp David in 2000.

As we have tried to show in this book, the demonization and denial of legitimacy to Israel is part and parcel of the old anti-Semitic attack against the Chosen. The envy, the hate and the double standard toward the Chosen very often overshadows the political debate with Israel. The attitude toward Israel in the international arena reflects the pendulum between the Chosen and the Pariah. The dividing line is very thin: one day Israel can be the darling for its David's fight against Goliath (the Six-Day War in 1967, after the Entebbe rescue operation in 1976, or in the early 1990s after the fall of the Soviet Union) and on another, it can be the object of contempt, censoring and de-legitimization (in the UN in 1975, during the Palestinian uprisings in the late 1980s or at the beginning of this century.) In the twenty-first century the UN General Assembly continues to approve every year about thirty resolutions condemning Israel as if there were no problems of poverty or genocide in the Sudan or international terrorism in Afghanistan, Iraq, Chechnya, or elsewhere. Even the hostile press has a strange record: on one hand Israel is admired for its pioneering spirit, for its intelligence, democratic institutions, its hi-tech aggressiveness against terrorism, and its tenacity, but at the same time it is condemned as racist, militant, xenophobic, uncompromising, and stiff-necked. The very act of singling out Israel for opprobrium and international sanctions—out of any proportion to any other party in the Middle East—is an act against the Chosen. Israel is so often the Jew among the nations, the Chosen Pariah that is not entitled to exercise its basic rights to self-defense.

The Jews in the Diaspora are closely connected to the fate of Israel and their condition continues to swing between the Chosen and the pariah. While many world leaders attended the ceremonies marking the sixtieth anniversary of the liberation of Auschwitz, in January 2005, the annual reports on anti-Semitism in several European countries revealed a continued increase in anti-Jewish incidents and publications. Today, while approaching the end of the first decade of the twenty-first century, the emancipation of the Jews still does not rest on solid ground. In most countries, Jews enjoy basic equality in terms of job opportunities and status, but basic security of Jewish life and the attitudes of the media and society at large is still reflective of the pariah condition. Some characteristics of the life of the Jews today can be regarded as modern expressions of some of the more egregious examples of discrimination against Jews in history. The distinctive marks of pre-emancipation such as the Ghetto walls, distinctive attire, or the yellow badge were replaced by the new features of the pariah of the international community. The fact that many Jewish community centers in Europe and Latin America are fortress-like and ringed by security guards, and that synagogues can be recognized, not by their distinctive architecture but by the police, soldiers, and policemen surrounding them, symbolizes the return of the pariah condition of the Chosen Jews. The world has succumbed to rules dictated by the terrorists and their supporters. The walls of the ghetto have been erected again at every El-Al boarding gate, or any other airline flying to Israel.

In addition to physical threats, the Jews and their sovereign state have had to confront the re-emergence of anti-Semitism, the worst of its kind since the Holocaust. Jews have been accused again by the media, by intellectuals, and by politicians, for their Chosen behavior, double loyalty, and their perceived efforts to manipulate world politics. Singling out the Jewish state as the whipping boy at the United Nations and challenging its right to exist is a consistent reminder of the medieval polemics between the Jews and Christianity and Islam.

## Islam and the Chosen

For many centuries Islam was less engaged than Christianity with the complex dilemma of its relations with the Chosen People, though as we have seen, the Quran is very clear in its own version of replacement and its claim of inheriting the mantle of the Chosen.

In a way similar to the New Testament, the Quran contains, together with anti-Jewish statements, clear recognition and respect for the Jews, the first Chosen People. The Quran declares that the Jews had been the recipients of an earlier revelation; that of the Chosen People of God with their Promised Land, and Jerusalem, their Chosen City. Contrary to Christianity, there was no tradition in Islam of deicide, and Muslims had no grounds for holding the Jews responsible for the disappearance of their prophet Mohammad who died from natural causes. However, whenever Muslims looked for pretexts for the hatred of Jews they looked back and cited accounts from the Hadith concerning supposed Jewish attempts on the prophet's life.[29]

The Muslim displacement theory did not base itself on being the "New Israel," but instead it appropriated the Jewish prophets and created a direct link with Ishmael, the son of Abraham. Unlike the Christians who blamed the Jews for an act (the crucifixion), which is central to their supersessionist doctrine, the

Muslims took a different route by declaring that Abraham, the father of the Jews was the "first Muslim." As a result, in the development of Muslim theology, there was less dependency on the history of the Jewish religion. But when Islam was threatened from within or without, the reaction of its leaders became harsher toward the other religions, frequently taking the form of discrimination and violent persecution.[30]

In Islam, as in Christianity, there is an important emphasis on the humiliated condition of the Jews as a result of their sins toward God and his prophets and because of their opposition to Mohammad. The Jews of Medina were defeated and were supposed to stay in a state of humiliation as long as they continued to deny the indications of God.[31] This state of humility became a prototypical condition of the Jews and is reflected in the Quran, in Islamic tradition, and in Arabic poetry and folklore.[32] The penetration of Western-Christian anti-Semitism in the nineteenth century and more forcefully in the twentieth century, therefore fell on fertile ground in the Arab world. The Zionist settlement in Palestine, the successive Arab-Israeli wars, and their repeated inability to defeat the Israelis on the battlefield were obvious incentives for the growing Arab anti-Semitism. What is overlooked, however, is how significant and threatening is the religious element that makes Arab Muslim hatred similar to the old Christian religious hatred: the envy and fear of the other "original" Chosen. The Jewish return to the Promised Land and its military victory against Arab armies that brought the Holy city under its control has transformed the Arab-Israeli conflict into a full-fledged struggle over the Chosen title.

Bernard Lewis shows how the worst manifestations of European anti-Semitism, in its theological and racist versions with the crudest inventions of the Nazis and their predecessors, have "been internalized and Islamized, [with] . . . even a Quranic twist." Lewis, writing in 1997, explains that "the classical Islamic accusations, that the Old and New Testaments are superseded because the Jews and Christians had falsified the revelations that had been vouchsafed to them, is given a new slant—that the Bible in its extant form is not authentic but is a version distorted and corrupted by the Jews in order to show that they are God's [C]hosen [P]eople and Palestine belongs to them."[33]

The roots of the envy toward Judaism are reflected in the Quran, and they clearly fall within the Freudian Chosen complex of the "deepest motives of anti-Semitism [which have their root in the past; they come from the unconscious." The obsession with the Jews and with Israel is strongly rooted in the Muslim holy texts, which say clearly that the rivalry with the Jews will continue till the end of the days: "The Last Hour will not come until the Muslims fight against the Jews, until a Jew will hide himself behind a stone or a tree, and the stone or the tree will say: 'O Muslim, there is a Jew behind me. Come and kill him.'"[34] This statement the second most famous Hadith collection among Sunni Muslims makes the war against the Jews a necessary condition and a prelude for the "Last Hour" supersession of the Chosen Islam ("there is no room for two Chosen Peoples"). The hatred is reflected again in a shocking Quranic verse:

Say 'o ye of Jewry! If ye think that ye are friends to Allah to the exclusion of
(other) men, then express your desire for Death, if you are truthful![35]

The commentary of King Fahd's Holy Quran (a traditional commentary) says
clearly that this verse is directed toward the Jews who do not follow the will of
Allah while they share "an arrogant claim to be a [C]hosen [P]eople, to be the
exclusive possessors of divine teachings . . . [and] if they claimed to be a special
friends of Allah, why do they not eagerly desire death, which would bring them
nearer to Allah?"[36] This elegant English edition of the Quran, which is widely distributed in Western Europe to guests and dignitaries including Jews, contains this
and numerous references to the arrogant Jews and their feeling of superiority.[37]

The campaign to deny the Jewish narrative on the Chosen People, Land, and
City was intensified by the Arab political establishment following the terror
attacks of September 11, 2001. For instance, in August 2004, the Saudi Armed
Forces Journal *published* an article, "The Jews in the Modern Era," which
claimed that "the majority of revolutions, coups d'etat, and wars . . . are almost
entirely the handiwork of the Jews." The author, Ma'ashu Muhammad, demonstrates how critical is the Bible and the denial of the Chosen in current Muslim
anti-Semitism: "They [the Jews] turned to [these methods] in order to imple-
ment the injunctions of the fabricated Torah, the Talmud, and the *Protocols* [of
the Elders of Zion], all of which call for the destruction of all non-Jews in order
to achieve their goal—namely that of world dominion. . . . [T]hey aspire to dominate the world in material, cultural, and spiritual terms in order to annihilate it."
The Saudi military is informed that the Jews already "control the economies of
the powerful countries" and this is why they succeed "to entangle their countries
in wars that result in benefits only for the Jews." According to the Saudi article,
the Chosen concept is the key to the Jewish conspiracy: "The Jews managed to
receive the support of groups of individuals in the world through the means of
religious distortions, whereby they deceived their victims [into believing] that
they are the [C]hosen [P]eople and that God wants them to once more take possession of Palestine, the [P]romised [L]and." The article continues to "quote"
Jewish leaders who claim that "[w]e are the ones who invented the story of a
[C]hosen [P]eople' and we established ourselves as saviors of the world."[38]

The Arab Muslim campaign against the Chosen Jews is moving in recent years
toward a similar ominous cocktail that characterized Christianity and Europe in
the twentieth century. On one hand the doctrine of contempt toward the Jews,
selecting from the Quran those preaching of humiliation and hate on the Jews (as
Christians could find in the New Testament) and on the other hand the denial of
the same passages that recognize the Jewish Chosen title, which in the Quran and
the Hadith deals directly with the Promised Jewish State and the Chosen City of
Jerusalem. This denial is not without precedents in Islam. At times that Islam was
in power there were some Muslim thinkers who did not accept the social mobil-
ity of the Jews and regarded their success as threatening. In order to deny the Jews
their new status they looked for similar methods of denial and rewriting. This
was the case of Ibn Hazm, the famous Andalusian-Arab philosopher from the

eleventh century, a period in which Jews, though still second-class citizens, were closer to elite circles in Muslim Spain. Ibn Hazm tried to discredit the Jewish chosenness by rejecting the biblical versions about people like Abraham, Moses, or David as preposterous and insulting, arguing that the Jewish Bible was written by an heretic (Kofer).[39]

People like Ibn Hazm had long complained about the growing Jewish influence on Islam in politics and religion. In addition to his attack on the Jewish vizier of Granada, Andalusia, Ibn Hazm was also concerned about Jewish influence in the religious sphere, mainly in dietary laws.[40] The Arab Muslim campaign is today focused on denying Jewish rights for a state, including continuing calls for the destruction of Israel. Political and military warfare is amplified with the flat denial of the Chosen features of the Jews even if it is done in full contradiction with their own Holy Book. As we have shown, Arab leaders deny the Jewish connection to Jerusalem, and what started as propaganda for internal consumption ended up with a full-fledged denial at the peace negotiations in Camp David in the summer of 2000. Arab television rejects the Old Testament claiming that there is no archeological evidence to support the biblical stories (despite the Quran's teachings on the People of the Book). A Syrian television series, *The Collapse of Legends*, claims that the Torah that the Jews hold to be holy, is nothing more than a forgery concocted by rabbis and that it has no connection with the Ten Commandments. The Torah, according to Syrian television is a fabrication of history designed to give the Jews a claim to the Land of Israel. Palestinian television follows the late Yasser Arafat's lead in Camp David by broadcasting documentaries disproving the "myth" that a Jewish Temple ever stood in Jerusalem. All this in addition to the consistent broadcasts of hate and incitement featuring anti-Semitic material and accusations of blood libel regurgitating the *Protocols of the Elders of Zion* and other Nazi-like material.[41] It is clear that it any sincere effort to reach a peace settlement in the Middle East, it will be incumbent upon Islam to change its approach to the Chosen role of the Jews and to redefine its dogma on the Promised Land.

Terrorist Islam must be dealt with for what it is: another global campaign for the Chosen title. Osama bin Laden was very clear when he announced in February 1998, the creation of the World Islamic Front for Jihad Against Crusaders and Jews, an umbrella organization for Islamic groups from Morocco to China with branches and supporters in Western Europe and North America. The massacres in Dharan, Nairobi, Dar es-Salaam, Aden, New York, Washington, Djerba, Karachi, Bali, Mombasa, Riyadh, Casablanca, Chechnya, Jakarta, Istanbul, and Madrid were all committed in the name of *jihad* and brought about the death of thousands. In the videotape that was found in the ruins of the attack in Madrid on March 11, 2004, the terrorist leader Sarhane Ben Abdel-Majid Fakhet referred back to 1492 when King Ferdinand and Queen Isabella completed the reconquest of Spain forcing Jews and Muslims to convert to Catholicism or leave the Iberian peninsula. The Spanish monarchs were convinced that they had replaced the Chosen Jews. In 2004 Fakhet, harking back to the Middle Ages struggle for the Chosen declared, "Blood for Blood, Destruction for Destruction." The leader of the international Muslim Brotherhood, Mahdi 'Akef said in December 2005 that his movement is global and dedicated to spreading Islam until it takes over the whole world, meaning in his words that "Islam will invade Europe and America."[42]

The writing on the wall became abundantly clear following the Twin Towers of September 11, when Osama bin Laden and his chief lieutenent, Dr. Ayman al-Zawahiri, appeared on the Al-Jazeera television station and said, "We will not accept that the tragedy of Al Andalus (Moslem Spain) will be repeated in Palestine."[43] Those who tried to seize upon this statement and take comfort that it was solely a war against Israel and the Jews, and maybe against America, failed to read the overwhelming material attacking the Crusaders, Christianity, Europe, democracy, and all the free world. The president of the Great Mosque in Granada, which was constructed with money donated by the governments of Morocco and the United Arab Emirates, refers to himself as the Emir of Spain and has declared that Granada will return to its "natural origins" of Islam after a five-hundred-year interruption. Spain's militant Muslims swear loyalty to Osama bin Laden and the ultimate goal to continue "jihad until martyrdom in the Land of Tarik ben Ziyyad" the original conqueror of the Iberian peninsula."[44] Experts explain that targeting Turkey and Spain was a clear jihadist strategy to cut the two bridges between the Islamic world and the West, which these two countries symbolize both geographically and politically. The goal is "to polarize people, Moslems and infidels. . . . Jihadists are the most fervent defenders of the notion of clash of civilizations."[45]

The Chosen concept in Islam appears as an exclusive domain of the *ummah* (the international Muslim community), the *khalifah* (the single world-state that fuses together religion and politics and is governed by Islamic law) that will rule all Islamic lands and peoples and subjugate the rest of the world to Allah. All these are preached widely today in the Muslim world with plenty of references to the Quran. When these aims are juxtaposed with claims by the "divinely inspired" Mahmoud Ahmadinejad, the president of Iran, the religious concepts become a matter of contemporary politics. Similarly, Mohammad Hassan Rahmani, the representative of the Iranian supreme leader, who stands even higher than Ahmadinejad in the Iranian hierarchy, explained on November 2006 in an article entitled "Why the Jews": "[T]he Jew is the most stubborn enemy of the believers. And the decisive war will decide the fate of humanity. . . . The reappearance of the twelfth Imam will usher in a war between Israel and the Shia."[46] Islamists, like Hitler, want to "liberate" the world of the Jews by exterminating them and Ahmadinejad, who received legitimacy by world leaders and by the United Nations, has put it in divine terms (October 2005): "Israel must be wiped off the map, as the Imam says."[47] When Ahmadinejad writes to President George Bush (May 8, 2006) that he is the leader of the world's struggle against a supposedly "Zionist-dominated" world,[48] the message sounded very similar to Hitler's awesome words: "There cannot be two Chosen People. We are God's People" (see Chapter 6).

As shown in this book Christianity could not move toward reconciliation with Judaism before it went to shake up it Chosen doctrine. It cannot be more indicative, and horrifying, to see the directives of Pope Pius XII regarding the replacement theology in the midst of World War II, while Jews were deported by hundred of thousands to their deaths in the gas chambers. The Pope, in his encyclical Mystici Corporis Christi of 1943, as if "exploiting" the persecution of the Jews, went to explain that "the New Testament took the place of the Old Law which had been abolished" and reaffirmed the principle that "a transfer from the Law to the Gospel, from the Synagogue to the Church" has been taken place.[49] It took the Catholic Church more than twenty years to reconsider this position and to modify it in light of the horrors of the Holocaust. But it was clear that in order to condemn anti-Semitism and to start a process of confrontation with the Holocaust and express regret, repentance and admission of some shared guilt (as stated in the 1998 Vatican document that refers to the *Shoah* and *Tesuvah*-repentance) there was a need to modify the theological doctrine of the Chosen. As described in Chapters 3 and 6, before rejecting the charge of deicide and before condemning anti-Semitism, the Nostre Aetate of Vatican II of 1965 had to refer to the Jews as "[t]he Chosen People" without qualifications. In 1986 Pope John Paul II went from the Vatican to his historic visit in the Synagogue of Rome, as if to reverse the 1943 declaration of replacement, and declared that the Jews are Christianity "elder brother."[50] Later, there was another need for a conceptual breakthrough (of almost a century) on the dispersion and humiliation doctrine that was the background of the Pope's refusal to accept Herzl's appeal for a Jewish state at the beginning of the twentieth century. The recognition of the Chosen paved the way for this change and allowed the Vatican to establish diplomatic relations with Israel and to follow with historic acts of sovereignty recognition during the papal visit to Israel in 2000.

Islam in its current crisis and ideological stagnation is still comparable to the era of the pre-Vatican reforms on the Jews, as far as anti-Semitism and Jewish sovereignty in Israel are concerned. In order to accept Israel as a political and independent entity in the Middle East, the Arabs and the Muslims will have to modify their doctrines on the Jews. Jews cannot be perceived as "apes and pigs" who must remain in their dispersed and humiliated condition, and not even as second-class human beings (*dhimmis*). Before a real political settlement between the Arabs/Islam and Israel can take place, Islam must find the formula which will reconcile its doctrine of the "perfected" and "favored" religion with the return of the Jews as a sovereign entity to the Middle East. The Quran, with so many references to Judaism and the Chosen Jews, can allow a clear recognition that along with the favored and Chosen Islam there are others who consider themselves as Chosen People.

The liberal-minded media did not like Huntington's term "clash of civilizations," as it was seen to be too simplistic and sweeping. Huntington who argues that America would be the primary victim of Islam has used different wording to describe the Chosen struggle: in describing Islam as "a different civilization whose people are convinced of the superiority of their culture and are obsessed with the inferiority of their power."[51] However, as we have seen, the anti-Jewish pogroms during the Crusades in the Middle Ages, the previous "clash of civilizations" were also led by groups (particularly the peasants) who were the products of centuries of brainwashing, that the Jews are the enemies of Christianity, of society and the murderers of the messiah. Thousands of Jews in the small communities of Europe were slaughtered and burned alive. For many years the Catholic Church tried to disassociate itself from those first Crusaders, and churchmen and historians propagated the myth that this was a "Peasants' Crusade."[52] Today it is clear that the anti-Semitic and murderous pogroms were a fundamental part of the Crusaders' campaign to restore its Chosen title and control over the Land of the Chosen.

The attack against Israel, Jews, the United States, and the West in general, is waged along with the ultimate design which is preached by Islamist leaders: *jihad* aiming to bring Islam to a dominant global position and release it from the hegemony of America and its Zionist allies. Islamists speak openly on fighting a global war to restore or create the big Islamic nation without borders or nationalism. In Europe militants call openly for Jihad and imposing the rule of Islam "on the godless society of the West."[53] The prominent Muslim scholar from Qatar, Sheikh Yusuf al-Qaradawi, the spiritual authority for the worldwide Muslim Brotherhood, issued an Islamic ruling that Islam will prevail and eventually become master of the entire world. One of the signs of triumphant Islam, according to Qaradawi, will be the conquest of Rome, thus defeating the bastion of Christianity and then going on to occupy Europe: "[T]he signs of salvation are absolute, numerous, and as plain as day, indicating that the future belongs to Islam and that Allah's religion will defeat all other religions. . . . Islam will return once more to Europe as a conqueror and as a victorious power . . . the beginning of the return of the righteous Caliphates."[54] According to the *New York Times*, Sheik Qaradawi's program, *Islamic Law and Life*, on Al-Jazeera satellite television "makes him about the most influential cleric among mainstream Sunni Muslims, the majority sect."[55]

The concept of global *jihad* emphasizes the fallacy of much of the Western media who try to minimize Islamic and al-Qaeda terrorism as a result of flawed American policy toward the State of Israel. They ignore all the obvious signs of a deliberate clash by Muslim fundamentalists who refer to global *jihad*, as a war against the Christian crusaders or the "Judeo-Crusaders" or even references to the "non-Arab Pharaonic" ruling family in Saudi Arabia. The leaders of radical Islam in Britain overtly speak about the need to overthrow secular regimes around the world and replace them: "[T]he West needs to understand what is really an inevitable matter; that is that Islam is coming back, the Islamic caliphate is going to be restored in the world very soon."[56]

## The Jewish Paradigm

One might have thought that in our predominantly secular and scientifically thinking world, people would have lost interest in the roots of the ancient religious beliefs. Instead we are witness to a religious reawakening, serious discussion about a perceived clash of civilizations, and a growing interest among the general public on the origins of the three monotheistic religions. Through use of the prism of the Chosen, we have tried in this book to offer an alternative view of Jewish history that has been deliberately neglected or overlooked. By introducing the Chosen concept as the key to Jewish-Gentile relations we have attempted to offer a paradigm to the mystery of the world obsession with the Jews.

It is evident that the impact of the Chosen concept at several major turning points in Jewish history deserves further exploration. The Chosen rivalry stands behind the Crusaders' massacres of the Jews from the eleventh through thirteenth centuries, and it was of major impact in the traumatic expulsion of the Jews from Spain in 1492 when the rulers of Spain regarded their generation as "composed of Chosen People."[57] In the twentieth century, as the analysis of German sources shows, the Aryan race theories of Nazi Germany and Adolf Hitler were driven by Hitler's concept that "We are God's People." Hitler regarded the Jews as an obstacle to Aryan chosenness and therefore had to be liquidated because "there cannot be two Chosen People. We are God's Choice."[58] The Holocaust, the ultimate suffering of the Chosen People, has become the symbol of radical evil, and this is why people try to deny it, or perversely, to compare Israeli practices to those of the Nazis.

Also contemporary history of the Arab-Israeli conflict is very much affected by Christian and Muslims beliefs and their interpretations of the Chosen concept in their policies with regard to the "Promised Land" and the "Chosen City" of Jerusalem. In both Christianity and Islam, the brutal attacks against the Chosen Jews started with revisionist writers who rejected their own scriptures based on the Old Testament in order to deny the chosenness of the Jews. The crisis of Islam which reached its climax at the beginning of the twenty-first century brought to the fore many undercurrents which had been previously ignored. The dominance of the *jihad* concept, martyrdom, and the quest for world domination has become coupled with the worst kind of hatred manifested towards the Jews. Most of the Muslim and Arab countries are today the purveyors of some of the extreme and vicious anti-Semitic propaganda seen since the days of Nazi Germany. Arab literature and media is full today with the worst expressions of the classical European/Christian accusations: the blood libels, ritual murders, the fabricated Talmud quotations, the masonic and *Protocols* conspiracy theories about the Jewish plan to take over the world. While terrorism is recognized as a threat to Western civilization, the media and most governments are less cognizant of the inherent anti-Semitic genocidal potential.

The attack against the Chosen Jews and the denial of the biblical sources on the election of Israel were central elements in the development of Nazism in Germany. The crimes of Hitler and the Nazis against the Jews were motivated by Aryan claims to chosenness. The real genocidal threat in Arab anti-Semitism today, which is widely overlooked, lies in the similar effort of Muslim clerics, intellectuals and political leaders to follow in the footsteps of the German Orientalist, Friedrich Delitzsch, or Henry Ford, in denying the Jewish links to Palestine and the biblical record, even though they are recognized by their own Quran. This denial is part of the larger effort to claim their own, exclusive, chosenness and the claim to the title of master religion/nation. The juxtaposition of rejecting Jewish chosenness and claiming the Chosen title in its place is, perhaps, the most deadly lesson to be learned from contemporary Jewish history. A compromise of two states in Mandatory Palestine must be, therefore, preceded by a change in the approach of Islam to the idea of the Jews' chosenness, without prejudging Islamic chosenness, and to redefine its dogma on the Promised Land.

So what is this "something" in the Jewish existence that according to A. B. Yehoshua "leads whole civilizations to be obsessed" with the Jews?

Benjamin Disraeli was among the few prominent figures who described, in straightforward language what is this "something" behind the obsession. In a letter from 1860 he wrote that anti-Semitism is a matter of jealously "influenced mainly by mortified vanity in never having been the medium of direct communication with the Almighty."[59]

In his campaign to allow Jews to be elected to the British parliament, Disraeli emphasized the debt which Europe and Christianity owe to the Jews and he asked rhetorically, "Where is your Christianity, if you do not believe in its Judaism?"[60]

There are a plethora of books and theories about anti-Semitism. There is no scientific answer to the conundrum and for each theory there are challenges based on different historic experiences. The Chosen concept helps to tie together the mystery of Jewish existence with the perplexity of anti-Semitism. The Chosen doctrine is critical for both Christianity and Islam, and surprisingly it is also central for many nonobservant Jews. The Chosen concept, and the continued existence of the Jews in their dispersion, exile without sovereignty, assimilation, and so much violent hatred, underline the need to go beyond conventional theories. Economic, sociological, and political theories are insufficient and even the scapegoat theory cannot explain why the Jews are so often the scapegoats even in places where there are no Jews. The religious inquiry is critical, not because all men are religious, but because almost all anti-Semites employ myths and prejudices which have strong religious roots. The Jewish mystery goes to the very roots of Christian and Muslim belief and dogma. Still it is not so much the religious world as it is the Chosen concept which goes to the very heart of the human experience, morality and its mission to the world.

Chosenness brings with it both a blessing and a curse, and in the words of Benjamin Disraeli, there is an "exact proportion" between being favored by God and being a pariah—persecuted by man.[61]

# Notes

## Chapter 1

1. "Mahathir fires parting shots," *CNN.com*, October 30, 2003, http://www.cnn .com/2003/WORLD/asiapcf/southeast/10/30/mahathir.retire/index.html.
2. See more on each country in the next chapters. See also Conor Cruise O'Brien, *God Land—Reflections on Religion and Nationalism* (Cambridge, MA: Harvard University Press, 1988).
3. Sigmund Freud, *Moses and Monotheism*, trans. Katherine Jones (New York: Vintage Books, 1967), 116.
4. Several books and an endless number of articles were written on the new anti-Semitism in the twenty-first century. See Gabriel Schoenfeld, *The Return of Anti-Semitism* (New York: Encounter Books, 2004); Phyllis Chesler, *The New Anti-Semitism: The Current Crisis and What Can We Do About It* (New York: Jossey-Bass, 2003); Abraham Foxman, *Never Again? The Threat of the New Anti-Semitism* (New York: Harper San Francisco, 2003); Ron Rosenbaum, ed., *Those whom Forget the Past: The Question of Anti-Semitism* (New York: Random House, 2004); and Alain Finkielkraut, "In the Name of the Other: Reflections on the Coming Anti-Semitism," *Azure* 18 (2004): 21–33.
5. Finkielkraut, 21.
6. *Aftenposten*, February 5, 2004.
7. Kenneth R. Timmerman, *Preachers of Hate—Islam and the War on America* (New York: Crown Forum, 2003), 21.
8. Craig Horowitz, "The Return of Anti-Semitism," *New York Magazine*, December 15, 2003, 5–6.
9. "Mahathir fires parting shots," *CNN.com*, October 30, 2003, http://www.cnn .com/2003/WORLD/asiapcf/southeast/10/30/mahathir.retire/index.html.
10. Ibid.
11. Craig Horowitz, "The Return of Anti-Semitism," *New York Magazine*, December 15, 2003, 5–6.
12. Paul Harris, "Who killed Christ?" *Observer*, February 8, 2004. See also press releases by the Jewish Anti-Defamation League (ADL), http://www.adl.org/ presrele/ASUS_12/4291.htm.
13. Matthew 27:25.
14. Jane Perlez, "Mahathir, Malaysia's Autocratic Modernizer, Steps Down" *New York Times*, November 1, 2003.
15. Amos 3:2.

16. "Memorable quotes for *Fiddler on the Roof* (1971)," *IMBd*, http://www.imdb.com/title/tt0067093/quotes.

17. Daniel Bell, "A Parable of Alienation," *Jewish Frontier* 13, no. 11 (November 1946): 14.

18. Abigail Pogrebin, *Stars of David—Prominent Jews Talk About Being Jewish* (New York: Broadway Books, 2005), 22.

19. Emmanuel Sivan, *Radical Islam: Medieval Theology and Modern Politics* (New Haven, CT: Yale University Press, 1985), 32.

20. Quran 2:65–66.

21. See these three examples among many others on the Internet: *Age of Islam*, http://www.ageofislam.com/; *The True Religion*, http://www.islamworld.net/true.html; *Realm of The Chosen One*, "My Islam, My perfect Religion," http://realmofthechosenone.blogspot.com/2006/12/my-islam-my-perfect-religion.html.

22. See the official site of the Library of Congress, http://www.loc.gov/about/facilities/

23. See http://people-press.org/reports/print.php3?PageID=728

24. Polls taken in summer 2002, http://www.religioustolerance.org/jud_chrr.htm.

25. Genesis 12:3.

26. Charles Murray, "Jewish Genius," *Commentary*, April 2007, 29–35.

27. Numbers: 23:9; see Chapter 4.

## Chapter 2

1. The Thirteen Principles of Faith are part of the weekday reading after prayers, and they are based upon the Maimonides formulation in his commentary to the Mishna (*Sanhedrin* 10). These principles were added in an era when Judaism found it necessary to react to different and rival approaches to faith. However, the Jewish religion never separated belief from performance, and most of Maimonides monumental works are dedicated to the observance of Jewish laws—God's commandments. In the morning blessings the song "Exalted the Living God," which is based upon the "Thirteen Principles of Faith" of Maimonides, there is already a clear reference to the chosen concept: "He [God] granted His flow of prophecy to his *treasured people*. . . . God gave *His people* a Torah of truth" (*The Complete ArtScroll Prayerbook* [New York: Mesorah, 1999], 15, emphasis added). The term "Chosen People" was less used by Jews, but, as shown, the very act of chosenness and the other expressions of uniqueness, separateness, and a treasured people are plenty and numerous in the Jewish sources.

2. Exodus 19: 3–8.

3. Exodus 24:7.

4. This appears in a midrash from Sifrei, a collection of midrashim in the books of Numbers and Deuteronomy (Deuteronomy 33:2).

5. Abba Eban, *Heritage—Civilization and the Jews* (New York: Summit Books, 1984), 26.

6. Ephraim E. Urbach, *The World of the Sages* [In Hebrew] (Jerusalem: Magnes, 1988), 472–73.

7. Maimonides, "Epistle to the Jews of Yemen," in Norman A. Stillman, *The Jews of Arab Lands: A History and Source Book* (Philadelphia: Jewish Publication Society, 1979), 241.

8. Talmud, *Shabbat* 88a.
9. Talmud, *Avodah Zarah* 2b.
10. Talmud, *Shabbat* 88a–b.
11. Esther 9:27.
12. Talmud, *Shabbat* 88a–b.
13. R. Travers Herford, *Judaism in the New Testament Period* (London: Lindsey, 1928), 97.
14. Maurice Samuel, *The Professor and the Fossil* (New York: Knopf, 1956), 106.
15. *ArtScroll Prayerbook*, 17, 143.
16. Talmud, *Berachot* 11b.
17. Leviticus 20:21–26.
18. Mishna, *Ethics of the Fathers*, 3:14, http://www.chabad.org/library/article_cdo/aid/2019/jewish/ChapterThree.htm
19. Deuteronomy 9:5.
20. Micah 4:4–5.
21. Isaiah 56:6–8.
22. Maimonides (Rambam), Mishneh Torah-Hilchot Melachim, Halacha 11, based on Talmud Sanhedrin 57a.
23. Deuteronomy 29:13–14.
24. Talmud, *Shavuot* 39a.
25. Rambam (Maimonides), quoted in *Yad Hachazaka*, sections 548–50, Mamre Institute, http://www.mechon-mamre.org/index.htm
26. Talmud, *Yevamot* 47a.
27. John Vinocur, "A Most Special Cardinal," *New York Times Magazine*, March 20, 1983, 29.
28. Talmud, *Shabbat* 89a.
29. George Steiner, *Errata: An Examined Life* (London: Weidenfeld and Nicolson, 1977).
30. Charles Silberman, *A Certain People* (New York: Summit Books, 1985), 79–80.
31. Quoted in Arnold Eisen, *The Chosen People in America* (Bloomington: Indiana University Press, 1983), 4.
32. Ibid., 3–4.
33. Mordechai Kaplan, *The Future of the American Jew* (New York: Reconstructionist Press, 1948), 219–20.
34. Charles S. Liebman, "Reconstructionism in American Jewish Life," in *American Jewish Year Book* (New York: American Jewish Community, 1970), 71:21.
35. *Sabbath Prayerbook* (New York: Jewish Reconstructionist Foundation, 1945). See also "Chosen" in *Encyclopedia Judaica* (Jerusalem: Keter, 1972), 5:502.
36. Jack Wertheimer, *A People Divided* (New York: Basic Books, 1993), 65.
37. Shalom Spiegel, *Hebrew Reborn* (New York: Macmillan, 1930), 375–89.
38. Neil Baldwin, *The American Revelation: Ten Ideals that Shaped Our Country from the Puritans to the Cold War* (New York: St. Martins Griffin, 2006), 20.
39. Genesis 12:1–2.
40. *Ethics of the Fathers*, 5:4.
41. Brought in Genesis in *The Chumash*, ArtScroll/Stone ed. (New York: Mesorti, 2001), 54.
42. Genesis 23:4.
43. Genesis, Artscroll/Stone ed., 23:4.
44. Paul Johnson, *A History of the Jews* (New York: Harper and Row, 1987), 7.

45. Genesis 18.
46. Genesis *Rabbah* 49.
47. Genesis 17: 9–14.
48. Genesis, Artscroll/Stone ed., 17:9–14, 21:1–8.
49. Jimmy Carter, *The Blood of Abraham—Insights into the Middle East* (New York: Houghton Mifflin, 1985), 4–5, 8.
50. Exodus 6:2–8.
51. Exodus 19:5–6.
52. Deuteronomy 28:15.
53. *Rashi* Exodus 2:11, in *The Chumash*.
54. Ibn Ezra commentary in *Exodus* Mikraot Gdolot, 2:11, http://he.wikisource.org/wiki
55. Exodus 15:1–4.
56. Exodus 12:15–19.
57. *ArtScroll Prayerbook*, 665–66.
58. Exodus 16:23.
59. Deuteronomy 5:15.
60. Exodus 31:13.
61. Maimonides, *The Guide of the Perplexed*, trans. Shlomo Pines (Chicago: University of Chicago Press, 1963), III:32, 527–528.
62. Paraphrased from Numbers 12:7 and Exodus 22:15.
63. Peter Schaffer, *Judeophobia—Attitudes toward the Jews in the Ancient World* (Cambridge, MA: Harvard University Press, 1977), 35.
64. Talmud, *Baba Batra* 9b.
65. See in Israel Jacob Yuval, *Two Nations in Your Womb—Perceptions of Jews and Christians* [In Hebrew] (Tel-Aviv: Am Oved, 2000), 95.
66. The Haggadah, based on Exodus 12. Text in Hebrew found at http://www.chabad.org/holidays/passover/pesach_cdo/aid/1735/jewish/The-Haggadah.htm
67. Judah Halevi, *The Kuzari—An Argument for the Faith of Israel* (Jerusalem: Sefer Va Sefel, 2003).
68. Ibid., 3:19.
69. Author's translation from the original Hebrew, http://benyehuda.org/rihal/Rihal1_1.htm1
70. Halevi, *The Kuzari*, 2:36.
71. Ibid., 1:95.
72. Michael Walzer et al., eds., *The Jewish Political Tradition* (New Haven, CT: Yale University Press, 2003), 2:13.
73. Baruch Spinoza, *Theological-Political Treatise*, Chapter 3 trans. Samuel Shirley (Leiden: E. J. Brill, 1991), 90–91.
74. David Novak, *The Election of Israel: The Idea of the Chosen People* (Cambridge, MA: Cambridge University Press, 1995), ch. 1 and pp. 22–23.
75. Arthur Hertzberg, and Aron Hirt-Manheimer, *Jews—The Essence and Character of a People* (San Francisco: Harper and Row, 1998), 141.
76. Baruch Spinoza, *Theological-Political Treatise*, 100.
77. Rabbi Samson Raphael Hirsch, *Commentary to the Siddur—Prayer Book* [In Hebrew] (Jerusalem: Rabbi Kook Institute, 1992), 8. In the Shabbat prayers, Hirsch explains that the Jews were elected in order to deliver the message of the Sabbath and this is the meaning of the prayer: "For us did You choose and us did You sanctify from all the Nations. And Your holy Sabbath, with love and

favor did You give us as a heritage" (255), and in the *Havdalah* service at the termination of the Sabbath, "Who separates . . . between Israel and the nations," he states again that Israel's role is to teach and pass the teachings to the rest of humanity (449) and again on the choosing in the festival prayers, he emphasizes the special mission and fate of the Jews (466).

78. Rabbi Hillel Silver, *Where Judaism Differed* (New York: Macmillan, 1956).
79. David Ben Gurion, *Biblical Reflections* [In Hebrew] (Tel-Aviv: Am Oved, 1976), 223–24, 242.
80. *The Chumash*, ArtScroll/Stone ed. (New York: Mesorah, 1993), 1263; *Song of Songs*, Artscroll ed. (New York: Mesorah, 1977), xii. Both follow the orthodox approach and bring the allegorical translation.
81. *Song of Songs*, 68.
82. Ibid., 67.
83. David Biale, *Eros and the Jews* (New York: Basic Books, 1992), 31.
84. *Song of Songs*, 3:11.
85. Ibid., 67.
86. David Biale, *Eros and the Jews*, 31.
87. Ibid., 4:5.
88. Ibid., 2:2, 6:2.
89. *Song of Songs*, 1:5–6.
90. Ibid., 4:5.
91. Isaiah 1:18.
92. For the text and Rashi, see *Song of Songs*, and for the Jewish-Christian disputation on the Song of Songs, see Professor Ephraim Urbach, *The World of the Sages*, 525, and the entire essay on pp. 514–36.
93. Talmud, *Megillah* 29a.
94. Talmud, *Sanhedrin* 7a.

## Chapter 3

1. Arnold J. Toynbee, *A Study of History—Reconsiderations*, vol. 12 (New York: Oxford University Press, 1964), 478–79.
2. Robert Wistrich, *The Longest Hatred* (New York: Pantheon Books, 1991), 13.
3. Paul Johnson, *A History of the Jews* (New York: Harper and Row, 1987), 166.
4. Matthew 5:17–19.
5. Acts 2:46, 3:1, 10:14.
6. Arthur Hertzberg and Aron Hirt-Manheimer, *Jews—The Essence and Character of a People* (San Francisco: Harper and Row, 1998), 69.
7. Vatican, "Notes for Preaching and Teaching," June 1985; Geoffrey Wigoder, *Jewish-Christian Interfaith Relations*, Policy Forum no. 14 (Jerusalem: World Jewish Congress, 1988).
8. F. Watson, *Paul, Judaism and the Gentiles—A Sociological Approach* (Cambridge: Cambridge University Press, 1986), 23–48.
9. Galatians 3:10.
10. Romans 3:28.
11. Johnson, 131.
12. Jeremiah 31:31.
13. Chaim Potok, *Wanderings—History of the Jews* (New York: Fawcett Books, 1978), 370–71.

14. Ibid., 145.
15. Maimonides, *Iggeret Teiman*, trans. Boaz Cohen, with notes by Abraham S. Halkin. Retrieved from http://en.wikisource.org/wiki/Epistle_to_Yemen/II.
16. Romans 8:14–19.
17. 1 Peter 9.
18. Conor Cruise O'Brien, *God Land—Reflections on Religion and Nationalism* (Cambridge, MA: Harvard University Press, 1988), 4.
19. Rosemary Ruether, *Faith and Fratricide* (San Francisco: Seabury, 1974), 131.
20. Gospel of Barnabas 4:8; for background and texts see http://barnabas.net/lifebarn-abas.htm. This is a strongly anti-Jewish document though outside the New Testament canon. Saint Barnabas, a Jew who joined the Gospels was a close associate of Paul and is mentioned in the New Testament (Acts 11:23 and more).
21. 1 Thessalonians 2:15–16.
22. David Flusser, *Judaism and the Origins of Christianity* (Jerusalem: Magnes, 1988), 587.
23. John 8:43–44.
24. Wistrich, 16.
25. Paul Lawrence Rose, *Revolutionary Anti-Semitism in Germany from Kant to Wagner* (Princeton, NJ: Princeton University Press, 1990), 7.
26. Malcolm Hay, *Europe and the Jews* (Boston: Beacon, 1961), 286.
27. Martin Luther, *Concerning the Jews and Their Lies*, repr. Talmage, Disputation and Dialogue, pp.34–36, cited in Michael L. Brown, *Our Hands Are Stained with Blood: The Tragic Story of the "Church" and the Jewish People* (Shippensburg, PA: Destiny Image, 1992), 14–15.
28. Peter J. Boyer, "The Jesus War," *New Yorker*, September 15, 2003.
29. *CNN.com*, "Gibson charged with drunken driving," http://www.cnn.com/2006/LAW/08/02/gibson.charged/index.html
30. Giles Fraser, "Crucified by Empire," *Guardian*, February 7, 2004.
31. Geoffrey Wigoder, *Jewish-Christian Interfaith Relations*, Policy Forum no. 14 (Jerusalem: World Jewish Congress, 1988), 7.
32. Romans 11:1, 5, 28.
33. John 4:22.
34. See Heinz Schreckenberg, *The Jews in Christian Art* (New York: Continuum, 1996).
35. Jeremy Cohen, *Christ Killers: The Jews and the Passion from the Bible to the Big Screen* (New York: Oxford University Press, 2007), 218–19.
36. A. Roy Eckhardt, *Christianity and the Children of Israel* (New York: King's Crown Press, 1948), 153.
37. Aurelius Augustine, "Against the Jews" [Adversus Iudaeos], quoted in Eugene Fisher, "The Holy See and the State of Israel: The Evolution of Attitudes and Policies," *Journal of Ecumenical Studies* 24, no. 2 (Spring 1987): 191–97.
38. Quran 9:65–67.
39. See the following: Johnson, 167; and for further background, Norman A. Stillman, *The Jews of Arab Lands: A History and Source Book* (Philadelphia: Jewish Publication Society, 1979); Bernard Lewis, *The Jews of Islam* (Princeton, NJ: Princeton University Press, 1987); Mark R. Cohen, *Under Crescent and Cross—The Jews in the Middle Ages* (Princeton, NJ: Princeton University Press, 1994)
40. Quran 2:47 and 122.
41. Quran 5:12.

42. Quran 5:20–21.
43. Quran 17:104.
44. Quran 10:93.
45. Quran 14:6.
46. Quran 2:50.
47. Quran 5:20–21.
48. Introduction to sura 5 in the popular Saudi edition, The Quran, The King Fahd's Holy Koran (Saudi Arabia: The Royal Palace, 2000).
49. Quran, 2:122–23.
50. The commentary to Quran on 2:122–23 in the Saudi edition.
51. Quran 5:41–45.
52. Quran 3:71, 4:46, and 3:63.
53. Quran 7:167.
54. Quran 2:83.
55. Quran 2:13.
56. Quran 2:87.
57. Bernard Lewis, *The Crisis of Islam—Holy War and Unholy Terror* (New York: The Modern Library, 2003), 43–44.
58. Ibid., 31–32.
59. Kenneth R. Timmerman, *Preachers of Hate-Islam and the War on America* (New York: Crown Forum, 2003), 291–93.
60. Patrick E. Tyler and Don Van Natta Jr., "Militants in Europe Openly Call for Jihad and the Rule of Islam," *New York Times*, April 26, 2004.
61. Bat Ye'or, *Islam and Dhimmitude—Where Civilizations Collide* (Madison, NJ: Fairleigh Dickinson University Press, 2002), ch. 2–3.
62. Johnson, 175.
63. Bernard Lewis, *The Jews of Islam*, 4; and Mark R. Cohen, *Under Crescent and Cross—The Jews in the Middle Ages*, 6.
64. Stillman, *The Jews of Arab Lands*, 233.
65. Ibid., 246.
66. There were some allusions in Islamic sources to describe the material based on Jewish sources, such as *Isra'iliyyat* (of Jewish, Israeli origin), but they are marginal and are taken with much hostility by today's Islamists.
67. Zeev Maghen, *After Hardship Come Ease: The Jews As Backdrop for Muslim Moderation* (Berlin: Walter De Gruyter, 2006), 15.
68. See Raphel Patai, *Ignaz Goldziher and His Oriental Diary* (Detroit: Wayne State University Press, 1987), 20.
69. Abraham Geiger, *Judaism and Islam* (New York: Ktav, 1970).
70. Ibid., xxix.
71. Ibid., 156.
72. Ibid., viii.
73. See http://www.islamic-awareness.org/Quran/Sources/BBsources.html.
74. Ibid.
75. Geiger, 78.
76. Abraham I. Katsh, *Judaism and Islam—Biblical and Talmudic Background of the Koran and its Commentaries* (Jerusalem: Kiryat Sepher, 1957).
77. Geiger, 157.
78. Ibid., 158.

79. Norman A. Stillman, "The Story of Cain & Abel in the Qur'ân and the Muslim Commentators: Some Observations," *Journal of Semitic Studies* 19 (1974): 231.

80. William M. Brinner and Stephen D. Ricks, eds., *Studies in Islamic and Judaic Traditions* (Atlanta: Scholars, 1989), ix.

81. Evidently, Brinner himself says in the same book that "Abraham has been taken over-in a sense- by Islam" (67), a statement that many Muslims will view as hostile and heretic. And another scholar, a Moslem, Mahmoud Ayoub, who writes in the same volume, is candid enough to say that that the Jews in Yemen and Madina "continued to play an important role in forming the Islamic faith and world view" (3).

82. Quran 5:51–52.

83. Quran 5:82.

84. Quran 14:47.

85. Quran 3:55.

86. Quran 61:2.

87. Bernard Lewis, *Semites and Anti-Semites* (London: Phoenix Giant, 1997), 129.

88. Quran 98:6.

89. Yossef Bogdansky, *Islamic Anti-Semitism as a Political Instrument* (Houston: Freeman Center for Strategic Studies, 1999), 84, 76.

90. Lewis, 169n4.

91. See http://www.us-israel.org./jsource/anti-Semitism/arapress0501.html, and http://www.alminbar.cc/alkhutab/khutbaa.asp?mediaURL=4331.

92. Pope Pius XII, Encyclical Mystici Corporis, July 29, 1943, para. 25–33. See http://www.vatican.va/holy_father/pius_xii/encyclicals/documents/hf_p-xii_enc_29061943_mystici-corporis-christi_en.html.

93. Bernard Wasserstein, *Vanishing Diaspora—The Jews in Europe Since 1945* (London: Hamish Hamilton, 1996), 131.

94. Garry Wills, *Papal Sin: Structures of Deceit* (New York: Doubleday, 2000), 19–26.

95. "Declaration on the Relationship of the Church to Non-Christian Religions," *Nostra Aetate* 4, October 28, 1965, reprinted in International Catholic-Jewish Liaison Committee, *Fifteen Years of Catholic-Jewish Dialogue 1970–1985* (Rome: Libreria Editrice Vaticana, 1988), 291.

96. Introduction by the editors, *Studies in Christian-Jewish Relations* 1 (2005–6): i–ii.

97. Friedrich Heer, *God's First Love* (New York: Weybright and Talley, 1967), dedication page.

98. John Paul II, *Crossing the Threshold of Hope* (New York: Knopf, 1994), 99.

99. Ibid., 95, 100.

100. Ibid., 99.

101. Ibid., 99–100.

102. For the text, references, and analysis, see Christian and Jewish Relations, Boston College, www.bc.edu/research/cjl/cjrelations/news.html.

103. National Catholic Reporter, October 6, 2000.

104. Sergio Minerbi, "The Church: Friend or Foe?" *Jerusalem Post*, January 24, 2003.

105. John Paul II, 93.

106. "The Passion of the Pope," *Time*, November 27, 2006, 23.

107. Bishops' Committee on the Liturgy, National Conference of Catholic Bishops, *God's Mercy Endures Forever: Guidelines on the Presentation of Jews and Judaism in Catholic Preaching* (Washington, DC: United States Catholic Conference, 1989), 10–12.

108. See *Dabru Emet*, http://www.religioustolerance.org/jud_chrr.htm.

109. Yaacov Herzog, *A People That Dwells Alone* (London: Weidenfeld and Nicolson, 1975).

110. Arnold Toynbee, "Is There a Jewish Future in the Diaspora?" *World Jewry*, April 1959, and the response by Trude Weiss-Rosmarin, "Is Toynbee Penitent?" *World Jewry*, May 1959, 33.

111. Toynbee, *A Study of History*, 194.

112. See *Dabru Emet*, http://www.religioustolerance.org/jud_chrr.htm.

113. Ibid., 477.

114. Ibid., 471.

115. Ibid., 471, 478.

116. Ibid., 478–83, 622.

117. Ibid., 483.

118. Jacob L. Talmon, "Uniqueness and Universality in Jewish History," *Commentary*, July 1957, 3.

119. Nachman Krochmal, "Guide for the Perplexed of the Day," in *The Writings of Nachman Krochmal*, ed. Simon Rawidowicz (Waltham, MA: Ararat, 1961).

120. Mark Twain, "Concerning the Jews," in Janet Smith, *Mark Twain on the Damned Human Race* (New York: Hill and Wang, 1962), 176–77.

121. Ibid., 177.

122. Ibid., 174–75.

123. Nicholas Aleksandrovich Berdyaev, *Christianity and Antisemitism* (New York: Philosophical Library, 1954), 6–7.

124. Johnson, 2.

125. Ibid., 586.

126. Ibid., 587.

## Chapter 4

1. Naphtali Prat, "Nikolai Berdiaev and the Jews," *Shvut* 3, no. 19 (1996): 14.

2. Paul Smith, *Disraeli—A Brief Life* (Cambridge: Cambridge University Press, 1999), 95.

3. See the Hebrew-language Steinzalts Talmud, *Pesachim* 87a (Jerusalem: Institute for Talmud, 1975).

4. Genesis 22:18.

5. Genesis 28:14.

6. 2 Samuel 7:23.

7. Isaiah 43:31–32.

8. Rabbeinu Bacya, *Cad Hakemah* (Jerusalem: Mosad Harav Koock, 1970), 22.

9. Deuteronomy 29:27.

10. Samson Raphael Hirsch commentary on *Genesis*, Perush al Hatorah (Jerusalem, Mosad Harav Kook, 1980), Devarim 29:27.

11. Maimonides, *Mishne Torah—Hilchot Melachim*, 8:10, 9:1, Mamre Institute, http://www.mechon-mamre.org/index.htm.

12. Exodus 19:6.

13. Judah Halevi, *The Kuzari—An Argument for the Faith of Israel* (Jerusalem: Sefer Va Sefel, 2003).

14. Abravanel on the Torah [in Hebrew] (Jerusalem: Chorev, 1985), Devarim 32:26.

15. George Steiner, *Errata: An Examined Life* (London: Weidenfeld and Nicolson, 1997), 54–62.

16. For the all text and more see Elliot N. Dorff, *Conservative Judaism: Our Ancestors to Our Descendants* (New York: United Synagogue of America, 1985), 236–37.

17. Kaufman Kohler, *Jewish Theology, Systematically and Historically Considered* (New York: Macmillan, 1928), 323.

18. Kaufman Kohler, *Backwards or Forwards? A Series of Discourses on Reform Judaism* (New York: Congregation Beth El, 1885), 34–38.

19. Kaufman Kohler, "Israel's Mission in the World," in *Hebrew Union College and Other Addresses* (Cincinnati, OH: Ark, 1916), 161–67.

20. Kaufman Kohler, *Jewish Theology* (New York: Macmillan, 1928), 323–28.

21. Arthur Hertzberg, *The Jews in America* (New York: Simon and Schuster, 1989), 260.

22. Samuel Friedman, *Jew vs. Jew—The Struggle for the Soul of American Jewry* (New York: Simon and Schuster, 2000), 73.

23. Arnold Eisen, *The Chosen People in America* (Bloomington: Indiana University Press, 1983), p. 59 and ch. 3 ("Reform Judaism and the 'Mission unto the Nations'").

24. Genesis 22:18.

25. Peter Schaffer, *Attitudes toward the Jews in the Ancient World* (Cambridge, MA: Harvard University Press, 1997), 34.

26. Numbers 23:9.

27. Nicholas Aleksandrovich Berdyaev, *Christianity and Antisemitism* (New York: Philosophical Library, 1954), 3.

28. Ibid., 4–5.

29. Cecil Roth, "The Economic History of the Jews," *Economic History Review* 19, 2nd series (August 1961), 131–35.

30. Werner Sombart, *The Jews and Modern Capitalism* (Edison, NJ: Transaction, 1982), 13. The English text was originally published in London in 1913. The book was first published in Germany in 1911.

31. Charles Louis de Secondat Montesquieu, *De L'Esprit Des Lois* (1748), Livre XXI, chap. XX.

32. 1 Maccabees 1:45–47.

33. Schaffer, 77–78.

34. Genesis 17:9–13.

35. See Genesis, ArtScroll/Stone ed., 568–69.

36. Deuteronomy 10:16.

37. John 7:22–23.

38. See in Maren R. Niehoff, "Circumcision as a Marker of Identity," *Jewish Studies Quarterly* 10, no. 2 (2003): 102.

39. Ibid., 103.

40. Romans 2:28–29.

41. Genesis 2:2.

42. *The Complete ArtScroll Prayerbook* (New York: Mesorah, 1999), 361.

43. Acts 13:14–16.

44. Chambers Encyclopedia (New York: Collier, 1882), 8:401.

45. A. Marmorstein, *Studies in Jewish Theology* (1950), 224.

46. 2 Thessalonians 3:10.

47. Louis H. Feldman, *Jew and Gentile in the Ancient World* (Princeton, NJ: Princeton University Press, 1993), 401–2.

48. Shmuel Ettinger, "Moscovite Russia and Its Attitude to the Jews," [In Hebrew] *Zion* 18 (1953): 161–68.
49. ArtScroll prayer book, Shabatt prayers, 250.
50. William Shakespeare, *The Merchant of Venice* (Leipzig: Bernh Tauchnitz, 1943), 11.
51. Leviticus 20:25–26.
52. Rashi in *The Chumash-the StoneEdition* by ArtScroll (New York: Mesorti, 2001); Leviticus 20: 26
53. Leviticus 11:44.
54. Deuteronomy 14:21.
55. Exodus 22:30.
56. Arthur Hertzberg and Aron Hirt-Manheimer, *Jews—The Essence and Character of a People* (San Francisco: Harper and Row, 1998), 61.
57. Schaffer, 70–71.
58. Acts 10:9–45.
59. Barbara K. Lewalski, "Biblical Allusion and Allegory in *The Merchant of Venice*," *Shakespeare Quarterly* 13 (1962), 330; and also Douglas Anderson, "The Old Testament Presence in *The Merchant of Venice*," *Journal of English Literary History* 52 (1989), 119.
60. Murray Roston, "Sacred and Secular in *The Merchant of Venice*," in *Sacred and Secular in Medieval and Early Modern Cultures*, ed. Lawrence Besserman (New York: Palgrave, 2006), 88. This refers to 2 Cor. 3:6 in the New Testament.
61. See John Gross, *Shylock—A Legend and Its Legacy* (New York: Touchstone, 1992).
62. For the general biographic details see the sources below. The quotes in this paragraph are from Edgar Feuchtwanger, *Disraeli* (London: Arnold, 2000), ix, 3.
63. H. S. Ashton, *The Jew at Bay* (London: Phillip Allen, 1933), 155.
64. Paul Smith, *Disraeli—A Brief Life* (Cambridge: Cambridge University Press, 1999), 25.
65. Cecil Roth, *Benjamin Disareli—Earl of Beaconsfield* (New York: Philosophical Library, 1952), 75.
66. Smith, 95.
67. Alroy, http://www.ibiblio.org/disraeli/alroy.pdf, 4:45.
68. Ibid., 7:5, 23.
69. "Disraeli," *Encyclopedia Judaica* (Jerusalem: Keter, 1971), 6:107.
70. Roth, 74.
71. Smith, 88.
72. Smith, 90–91, and Feuchtwanger, 88.
73. Conor Cruise O'Brien, *God Land—Reflections on Religion and Nationalism* (Cambridge, MA: Harvard University Press, 1988), 26–27.
74. David S. Katz and Richard H. Popkin, *Messianic Revolution* (London: Penguin, 1999), 170–72.
75. Stanley Weintraub, *Disraeli: A Biography* (New York: Truman Talley, 1993), 216–17.
76. Smith, 65.
77. Philip Rieff, "Disraeli: The Chosen of History," *Commentary*, January 1952, 31.
78. Ibid., 68–69.
79. Ibid., 102.
80. John Vincent, *Disraeli* (New York: Oxford University Press, 1990), 35.
81. Smith, 93, 102.

82. Roth, 67.
83. Smith, 93.
84. Roth, 67.
85. Smith, 69, and Roth, 67.
86. "Disraeli," *Encyclopedia Judaica*, 107.
87. Feuchtwanger, 89.
88. Roth, 73; Smith, 88–90.
89. Paul Johnson, *A History of the Jews* (New York: Harper and Row, 1987), 324.
90. Clifton Fadiman, and André Bernard, *Bartlett's Book of Anecdotes* (Boston: Little, Brown, 2000), 168.
91. Smith, 100.
92. "Disraeli," *Judaica Encyclopedia*, 109.
93. Michael Flavin, *Benjamin Disraeli: The Novel as Political Discourse* (Eastbourne, UK: Sussex Academic Press, 2005), 125.
94. Smith, 96.
95. Ibid.
96. Yaacov Herzog, *A People that Dwells Alone* (London: Weidenfeld and Nicolson, 1975), 126–27.
97. N. Rose, "Churchill and Zionism," in *Churchill*, ed. R. Blake and W. R. Louis (Oxford: Oxford University, 1993), 147.
98. Yehuda Bauer, "In Search of Definition of Antisemitism," in *Approaches to Antisemitism-Context and Curriculum*, ed. Yehuda Bauer (New York and Jerusalem: American Jewish Committee and the International Center for University Teaching of Jewish Civilization, 1994), 12.
99. Weintraub, 658.

## Chapter 5

1. *The Protocols of the Learned Elders of Zion*, trans. Victor E. Marsden (London: Briton Publishing Society, 1923), Protocol 11D.
2. Eicha/Lamentations 3: 42–44.
3. Eicha/Lamentations 3:45–46.
4. Eicha Raba (Hebrew) 3: 40–60.
5. Lamentations 3:40.
6. Lamentations 3:45.
7. David S. Katz and Richard H. Popkin, *Messianic Revolution—Radical Religious Politics to the end of the Second Millenium* (London: Penguin, 1999), 17.
8. Yossef Kaplan, "Jews and Judaism in Political and Social Thought of Spain in the Sixteenth and Seventeenth Centuries," in *The Hatred of Israel Throughout the Ages*, ed. Shmuel Almog (Jerusalem: Shazar Center, 1980), 175.
9. Salazar, in M. J. Cohen and John Major, *History in Quotations* (London: Cassel, 2004), 334.
10. Juan de Salazar, *Politica Espanola* (Logrono, 1619), 79ff., quoted in Kaplan, 175.
11. Interview with Mikis Theodorakis, *Jerusalem Post*, November 11, 2003, and *Macedonian Press Agency*, November 13, 2003.
12. Interview with Mikis Theodorakis, *Ha'aretz*, August 27, 2004.
13. *Wall Street Journal Europe*, November 7, 2003.
14. *Ethnos*, April 7, 2002.

15. Quoted from the Spanish newspaper *El Pais*, in Paul Berman, "Bigotry in Prin," *Forward* (New York weekly), May 24, 2002.

16. Jose Saramago, *The Gospel According to Jesus Christ* (New York: Harcourt Brace, 1994).

17. Sergio I. Minerbi, "Neo Anti-Semitism in Today's Italy," *Jewish Political Studies Review* 15 (Fall 2003): 3–4.

18. Ibid.

19. Jostein Gaarder "God's Chosen People,"*Aftenposten*, August 5, 2006.

20. Ibid.

21. Nicholas Aleksandrovich Berdyaev, *Christianity and Antisemitism* (New York: Philosophical Library, 1954), 11.

22. Naphtali Prat, "Nikolai Berdiaev and the Jews," *Shvut* 3, no. 19 (1996): 6.

23. Ibid., 8–9.

24. http://www.cnn.com/2003/ALLPOLITICS/03/11/moran.jews/.

25. Pat Buchanan, "Whose War?," *American Conservative*, March 24, 2003, http://www.amconmag.com/03_24_03/cover.html.

26. John J. Mearsheimer and Stephen M. Walt, *The Israel Lobby and U.S. Foreign Policy* (New York: Farrar, Straus & Giroux, 2007).

27. There were endless articles that reacted to Mearsheimer and Walt's book. This sample speaks about the anti-Semitic tendencies and rejects the major premise of *The Israel Lobby* (or the "cabal" myth): Jeff Robbins, "Anti-Semitism and the Anti-Israel Lobby," *Wall Street Journal*, September 7, 2007, A15; Leslie H. Gelb, "Dual Loyalties," *New York Times*, September 23, 2007.

28. Louis H. Feldman, *Jew and Gentile in the Ancient World* (Princeton, NJ: Princeton University Press, 1993), 175.

29. Shmuel Ettinger, "Soviet Antisemitism after 1967," (Hebrew repr., Jerusalem: Hebrew University, 1985), 53.

30. Genesis 26:16. and Samson Raphael Hirsch commentary on *Genesis* (Hebrew) Perush al Hatorah, Jerusalem, Mosad Harav Kook, 1980.

31. Ignaz Maybaum, *The Jewish Mission* (London: James Clarke, 1949), 158.

32. Jean Paul Sartre, *Anti-Semite and Jew* (New York: Schocken Books, 1965), 65–69, 91, 134–37. Originally published in French in 1946.

33. Albert Einstein, "Why Do They Hate the Jews?" in *Ideas and Opinions*, ed. Carl Seelig (New York: Bonanza Books, 1954), 196.

34. Albert Einstein, *About Zionism: Speeches and Letters*, trans. Leo Simon (New York: Macmillan, 1931), 33.

35. George E. Berkley, *Vienna and Its Jews* (Cambridge, MA: Abt Books, 1988), 81.

36. Baruch Spinoza, *The Theological-Political Essay* (Jerusalem: Hebrew University, 1962), 42.

37. Paul Mendes-Flohr and Yehuda Reinharz, eds., *The Jew in the Modern World* (New York: Oxford University Press, 1995), 534–37.

38. Yehiel Alfred Gottschalk, *Ahad Ha-ham and the Jewish National Spirit* (Jerusalem: WZO, 1992), 40.

39. Norman Choen, *Warrant for Genocide: The Myth of the Jewish World-Conspiracy and the Protocols of the Elders of Zion* (London: Eyre & Spottiswoode, 1967), 268.

40. Peter Schaffer, *Attitudes toward the Jews in the Ancient World* (Cambridge, MA: Harvard University Press, 1997), 3.

41. Ibid.

42. *The Protocols*, 13C, 14A, 22, 25.

43. Neil Baldwin, *Henry Ford and the Jews—The Mass Production of Hate* (New York: Public Affairs, 2001), 28.

44. Ibid., 33.

45. Ibid., 98.

46. Henry Ford, *The International Jew—The World's Foremost Problem*, abridged ed. prepared by Gerald L. K. Smith (Los Angeles: Christian Nationalist Crusade, 1954), 26, 55.

47. Henry Ford, *Aspects of Jewish Power in the United States*, vol. IV of *The International Jew* (Dearborn, MI: Dearborn, 1922), 238–39.

48. Ibid., vol. II of *The International Jew*, 188, capitalization in original.

49. Ibid., 192, 196.

50. Baldwin, 160.

51. "Delizsch," *Hebrew Encyclopedia*, vol. 12, *Jerusalem, Masada, 1970*, and the *Judaica Encyclopedia*, vol. 4. (Jerusalem: Keter, 1990).

52. Emphasis added.

53. Emil G. Kraeling, *The Old Testament since the Reformation* (London: Luttewortt, 1955), 153.

54. Ibid., 149, 153.

55. Ibid., 153, 155–56.

56. Ibid., 159, 161.

57. Jonathan Riley-Smith, *The First Crusade and the Idea of Crusading* (London: Athlone, 1986), 25.

58. Quoted in *Chronicle of Rabbi Eliezer bar Nathan*, in Schlomo Eidelberg, ed. and trans., *The Hebrew Chronicles of the First and Second Crusades* (Hoboken, NJ: Ktav, 1996), 80.

59. Peter the Venerable, *Sermones tres*, ed. Giles Constable (Cambridge, MA: Harvard University Press, 1967), 232–54.

60. Israel Jacob Yuval, *Two Nations in Your Womb—Perceptions of Jews and Christians* [In Hebrew] (Tel-Aviv: Am Oved, 2000), 141.

61. *The Complete ArtScroll Prayerbook* (New York: Mesorah, 1999), Shabbat prayers 315.

62. Bernard Lewis, "The Roots of Islamic Rage," *New Yorker*, November 2001, 32.

63. Peter the Venerable, "Sermones tres," 232–54.

64. Jonathan D. Halevi, "Al-Qaeda's Intellectual Legacy: New Radical Islamic Thinking Justifying the Genocide of Infidels," *Jerusalem Viewpoint*, December 1, 2003, 5.

65. Josef Joffe, "The Axis of Envy—Why Israel and the United States Both Strike the Same European Nerve," *Foreign Policy* 132 (September–October 2002): 68.

66. *Daily Telegraph* (London), October 21, 2002; William Safire, "The German Problem," *New York Times*, September 19, 2002; and "French FM: US Jewry More 'Intransigent' than Israel," *Jerusalem Post*, April 25, 2002.

67. Walter Russell Mead, "Review Essay: Why Do They Hate Us?" *Foreign Affairs* 82, no. 2 (March/April 2003): 141.

68. Mark Strauss, "Antiglobalism's Jewish Problem," *Foreign Policy*, November–December 2003, 58.

## Chapter 6

1. Hermann Rauschning, *Hitler Speaks—A Series of Political Conversations with Adolf Hitler on His Real Aims* (London: Thornton Butterworth, 1940), 234, 238.

2. Michael C. Steinlauf, "Poland," in *The World Reacts to the Holocaust*, ed. David S. Wyman (Baltimore, MD: Johns Hopkins University Press, 1995), 151.

3. George Eliot, *Daniel Deronda* (1876; repr., New York: Barnes & Noble, 2005), 455.

4. *EU Business*, April 26, 2004.

5. *Ha'aretz*, January 27, 2004.

6. Paul Johnson, *A History of the Jews* (New York: Harper and Row, 1987), 519.

7. Elie Wiesel, "Jewish Values in the Post-Holocaust Future: A Symposium," *Judaism* 16, no. 3 (Summer 1967): 281–82.

8. Elie Wiesel, "Art and Culture after the Holocaust," in *Auschwitz: Beginning of a New Era?* ed. Eva Fleishner (New York: Ktav, 1977), 408.

9. Nathan Alterman, *Hatur Hashevi'I*, trans. Menachem Lorberbaum (Tel Aviv: Hakibbutz Hamehuchad, 1977), bk. 1, pp. 9–10, in Michael Walzer et al., eds., *The Jewish Political Tradition* (New Haven: Yale University Press, 2003), 81–82.

10. Talmud, *Berachot* 7a.

11. This was also an early Christian claim that appears in the Letter of Barnabas. See chapter 3, note 11 in this book.

12. Talmud, *Berachot* 7a.

13. Av Harahamim [Father of Compassion], a Sabbath prayer, *The Complete ArtScroll Prayerbook* (New York: Mesorah, 1999), 267.

14. "Orthodox Religious Thought," *The Holocaust Encyclopedia*, ed. Walter Laquer (New Haven, CT: Yale University Press, 2001), 459–61.

15. See Zvi Kolitz, "Yossel Rakover's Appeal to God," in *Out of the Whirl-Wind*, ed. Albert H. Friedlander (New York: Union of American Hebrew Congregations, 1968), 390–99.

16. Pesah Schindler, *Hasidic Responses to the Holocaust in the Light of Hasidic Thought* (Jersey City, NJ: Ktav, 1990), 34–35.

17. Arthur Hertzberg and Aron Hirt-Manheimer, *Jews—The Essence and Character of a People* (New York: Harper San Francisco, 1998), 52.

18. "Madeleine Albright Talks about Her Hidden Past," *Newsweek*, February 24, 1997.

19. Avi Beker, "Choosing to Remain a 'Forced Convert,'" *Ha'aretz*, October 9, 2006.

20. Isaiah 53:5.

21. Paul S. Boyer, *When Time Shall Be No More: Prophecy Belief in Modern American Culture* (Cambridge, MA: Harvard University Press, 1992), 192, 209, 404–5.

22. "Racism," in *The Holocaust Encyclopedia*, 508.

23. Lucy S. Dawidowicz, *The War Against The Jews 1933–1945* (New York: Bantam, 1975), 3.

24. Ibid., 27.

25. Adolf Hitler, *Mein Kampf* [My Struggle] (New York: Houghton Mifflin, 1969), 60.

26. Dawidowicz, 23–26.

27. "Hitler's memorandum 1936," in *Documents on the Holocaust* (Jerusalem: Yad Vashem, 1999), 89.

28. Hitler, 60.

29. Ibid., 293–96.

30. Leon Poliakov, *Harvest of Hate—The Nazi Program for the Destruction of the Jews of Europe* (Philadelphia: Jewish Publication Society, 1954), 5–6.

31. "German Memorandum on Immigration," *Documents on the Holocaust*, 98–131.

32. Ibid., 134–35.
33. Israel Zangwill, *Chosen Peoples: The Hebraic Ideal Versus the Teutonic* (New York: Macmillan, 1919), 23.
34. Friedrich Nietzsche, *Complete Works*, vol. 8 (Stanford, CA: Stanford University Press, 1995), 337.
35. Rauschning, 232, 235, 238.
36. Neil Baldwin, *Henry Ford and the Jews—The Mass Production of Hate* (New York: Public Affairs, 2001), 172.
37. Ibid., 266, 387n14.
38. Hans J. Morgenthau, *The Tragedy of German-Jewish Liberalism* (New York: Leo Baeck Institute, 1962), as reprinted in M. Benjamin Mollov, *Power and Transcendence—Hans Morgenthau and the Jewish Experience* (New York: Lexington Books, 2002), 108.
39. Leo Baeck, *Documents on the Holocaust*, 88–89.
40. Interview with Prof. Yehuda Bauer, quoted in *Post-Holocaust and Antisemitism*, 24.
41. Tetsu Kohno, "Japan after the Holocaust," in *The World Reacts to the Holocaust*, ed. David S. Wyman (Baltimore: Johns Hopkins University Press, 1996), 580.
42. See Alan M. Dershowitz, *Chutzpah* (Boston: Little, Brown, 1991), 140–42, and Laurence Weinbaum, *The Struggle for Memory in Poland—Auschwitz, Jedwabne and Beyond*, WJC Policy Study (Jerusalem: Institute of the World Jewish Congress, 2001), 200.
43. Henryk Grynberg, "Appropriation of the Holocaust," in *Commentary*, November 1982.
44. Robert Jan van Pelt and Deborah Dwork, *Auschwitz, 1270 to the Present* (New Haven, CT: Yale University Press, 1996), 369.
45. Steinlauf, 140.
46. Weinbaum, 27.
47. "Mormons' Lists," *Jewish Week*, December 19, 2003.
48. Steinlauf, 141.
49. Ibid., 151.
50. Dershowitz, 150.
51. James Carroll, *Constantines's Sword—The Church and the Jews* (New York: Houghton Mifflin, 2001), 58.
52. Dalia Offer, "Israel," in *The World Reacts to the Holocaust*, 873.
53. David Wyman, "Introduction," in *The World Reacts to the Holocaust*, xix.
54. Samantha Power, *A Problem From Hell: America and the Age of Genocide* (New York: Basic Books, 2002), chapter 2 deals at length with Raphael Lemkin's efforts to lobby for American action against Nazi atrocities in Europe.
55. Charity Wire, *American Jewish Committee*, June 19, 2001, www.charitywire.com/charity.
56. *Eichmann in the World Press* (Jerusalem: Israeli Ministry of Foreign Affairs, 1960), 3.
57. Ibid., 5.
58. Moshe Pearlman, *The Capture of Adolf Eichmann* (London: Wiedenfeld and Nicolson 1961), 166.
59. "Eichmann," in *The Holocaust Encyclopedia*, 163.
60. *Eichmann in the World Press*, 7.
61. *Saturday Review*, April 8, 1961, and David Ben Gurion, *New York Times Magazine*, December 18, 1960.

62. Ibid.
63. Tetsu Kohno, "Japan after the Holocaust," in *The World Reacts to the Holocaust*, 578–77.
64. Nachum Goldmann, *Autobiography: Sixty Years of Jewish Life* (New York: Holt, Rinehart, and Winston, 1969), 274.
65. *Newsweek*, February 24, 1997.
66. Avi Beker, "Unmasking National Myths—Europeans Challenge Their History," in *The Plunder of Jewish Property During the Holocaust—Confronting European History*, ed. Avi Beker (London: Palgrave, 2001), 10.
67. Ibid., 29–30, notes 1–2.
68. Address by Swiss Foreign Minister and Federal Councillor, Flavio Cotti, to the Swiss People Party, January 17, 1997, quoted in Beker, "Unmasking National Myths," 15.
69. Beker, "Unmasking National Myths," 18.
70. Sven Fredrik Hedin and Goran Elgemyr, "Quiet Collusion: Sweden's Financial Links to Nazi Germany," in *The Plunder of Jewish Property During the Holocaust*, ch. 11, and Eizenstat, 347–48.
71. Hector Feliciano, "The Great Culture Robbery: The Plunder of Jewish-Owned Art" in Avi Beker, *The Plunder of Jewish Property*, 165.
72. Eizenstat, 187.
73. Johnson, 586.

# Chapter 7

1. William Blackstone, "May the United States Intercede for the Jews," in *Christian Protagonists for Jewish Restoration*, ed. Joseph Celleni (New York: Arno, 1977), 13–14. Quote comes from a petition submitted to President Benjamin Harrison in March 1891, which was signed by 413 prominent Christans and Jews in reaction to a wave of pogroms in Russia in the 1880s.
2. Yakov Malik, *United Nations, General Assembly Official Records*, October 21, 1973.
3. Exodus 12:2.
4. Psalms 111:6.
5. See Rashi in *Genesis* 1:1. *The Chumash* (The Pentateuch), Stone ed., by ArtScroll (New York: Mesorti, 2001).
6. Menahem Brikner, "The End of Zionism? Thoughts on the Wages of Success," *Dissent* 32, no. 1 (Winter 1985): 77–82.
7. Yael Zrubavel, *Recovered Roots, Collective Memory and the Making of Israeli National Tradition* (Chicago: Chicago University Press, 1995), 25–26.
8. Geoffrey Wheatcroft, *The Controversy of Zion* (New York: Addison-Wesley, 1996), 184.
9. Howard M. Sachar, *Diaspora—An Inquiry into the Contemporary Jewish World* (New York: Harper & Row, 1985), 480.
10. Conor Cruise O'Brien, *The Siege* (London: Weidenfeld and Nicolson, 1986), 18.
11. Ibid., 50.
12. Anita Shapira, *Berl* [In Hebrew.] (Tel-Aviv: Am Oved, 1980), 166.
13. Quoted in Arthur Hertzberg, *The Zionist Idea* (Garden City, NY: Doubleday, 1959), 426.
14. O'Brien, 225.
15. Ibid.

16. Amos Oz, "The Meaning of Homeland," in *Zionism: The Sequence* (New York: Hadassah, 1998), 250–51.
17. Quoted in Yaacov Herzog, *A People that Dwells Alone* (London: Weidenfeld and Nicolson, 1975), 51.
18. *Ha'aretz*, May 23, 2004.
19. David Ohana, *Messianism and Mamlachtiut [sovereignty]—Ben Gurion and the Intellectuals: Between Political Vision and Political Theology* [In Hebrew] (Sdeh Boker, Israel: Ben Gurion University Press, 2003), 3.
20. David Ben Gurion, *Biblical Reflections* [In Hebrew] (Tel-Aviv: Am Oved, 1976), 7.
21. Ibid., 26–28.
22. Ibid., 71–72.
23. Ohana, 73, 203.
24. Eisenshtadt, Yehuda David, *Polemics and Disputations* [In Hebrew] (New York: Menorah, 1929), entry "Pulmus."
25. Larry Collins and Dominique Lapierre, *O Jerusalem* (London: Grafton Books, 1986), 3.
26. Moshe Sharett, *At the Nation's Gate, 1946–1949* [In Hebrew] (Tel-Aviv: Am Oved, 1966), 60–61.
27. Michael Oren, *Power, Faith, and Fantasy—America in the Middle East 1776 to the Present* (New York: W. W. Norton, 2007), 475–76, 488–501.
28. Ibid., 87. On the legal meanings of the UN campaign against Israel, see Julius Stone, *Israel and Palestine: Assault on the Law of Nations* (Baltimore, MD: Johns Hopkins University Press, 1981), 42–43.
29. Hassan Sa'ab, *Zionism and Racism*, Palestine Essays No. 2 (Beirut: Research Center, Palestine Liberation Organization, December 1965), 9.
30. *Al-Balagh*, Beirut, January 5, 1975. See in Martin Gilbert, *The Arab–Israeli Conflict—Its History in Maps* (London: Weidenfeld and Nicolson, 1976), 107.
31. William F. Buckley Jr., *United Nations Journal: A Delegate's Odyssey* (New York: Anchor, 1977), 55–57, and for Buckley's statement see "Anti-Semitism at the UN," *Congressional Record*, March 11, 1981, E993.
32. Malik.
33. *UN Security Council Official Records*, S/PV.2128, March 16, 1979, 27.
34. Even second-generation converts cannot escape the diatribes and persecution of anti-Semites. Harry Oppenheimer, the son of a Jew who converted to Christianity, was a member of a Christian Church, which was, incidentally, known for its criticism of the apartheid regime of South Africa.
35. *General Assembly Official Records*, A/35/PV.86, General Assembly meeting, December 8, 1980, 38–40.
36. Louis H. Feldman, *Jews and Gentiles in the Ancient World* (Princeton, NJ: Princeton University Press, 1993), 130.
37. Sharon R. Keller, ed. *The Jews—In Literature and Art* (New York: Konemann, 1992), 162–63. There are some doubts about the authenticity of this proclamation but, in any case, its very publication shows a trend in the society.
38. E. Hodder, *The Life and Times of the Seventh Earl of Shaftesbury*, vol. 1 (London: Kegan Paul, Trench, Trubner, 1886), 310–11, quoted in Geoffrey Wheatcroft, *The Controversy of Zion* (New York: Addison-Wesley, 1996), 1–2.
39. George Elliot, *Daniel Deronda* (New York: Barnes & Noble, 2005), 473–75.
40. Alexander Edward, "George Eliot's Rabbi," *Commentary* 92 (1991), 28–32, and Arthur Zeiger, "Emma Lazarus and Pre-Herzlian Zionism," in *American Jewish*

*Women and the Zionist Enterprise*, ed. Shulamit Reinharz and Mark A. Raider (Waltham, MA: Brandeis University Press, 2004), 13–17. In November 1895 Herzl himself would meet the pro-Zionist British Colonel Albert Goldsmith, who would introduce himself as the prototype of Daniel Deronda, the son of converted Jews who has return to Judaism and regards Herzl vision on the Jewish State as "the idea of my life" in Amos Elon, *Herzl* (New York: Schocken Books, 1986).

41. Israel Feinstein, "Early and Middle Ninteenth-Century British Opinion on the Restoration of the Jews: Contrasts with America," in *With Eyes Toward Zion-II*, ed. Moshe Davis (New York: Praeger, 1986), 81, 96.

42. Leonel E. Kochan, "Jewish Restoration to Zion" in Moshe Davis, *With Eyes Toward Zion-II*, 102, 104–5.

43. George Bush, *The Valley of Vision* (New York: New York University, 1857), 17.

44. Mark Twain, *The Innocents Abroad* (New York: Oxford University Press, 1966), 349, 366.

45. Hertzberg, 97. See also the entry on Noah in the *Encyclopedia Judaica* and the book by Jonathan D. Sarna, *Jacksonian Jews: The Two Worlds of Mordecai Noah* (New York: 1981).

46. Yona Malachy, *American Fundamentalism and Israel* (Jerusalem: Institute of Contemporary World Jewry, 1978), 136–41.

47. William Blackstone, *Jesus Is Coming* (Chicago: Revell, 1908), 17.

48. Ibid., 240–41.

49. Elon, 105.

50. N. A. Rose, *The Gentile Zionist—A Study in Anglo-Zionist Diplomacy, 1929–1939* (London: Frank Cass, 1973), 62, 139, 227.

51. J. C. Wedgewood, *The Seventh Dominion* (London: Labour, 1928), 119–21.

52. Genesis 12–3.

53. M. Basilea Schlink, *Israel My Chosen People—A German Confession Before God and the Jews* (London: Faith Press, 1963), 5, 15, 56.

54. David Brog, *Standing with Israel: Why Christians Support the Jewish State* (Lake Mary, FL: Front Line, 2006).

55. David A. Rausch, "Evangelical Protestant Americans," in *With Eyes Toward Zion-II*, edited by Moshe Davis (New York: Praeger, 1986), 324–26.

56. Nancy T. Ammerman, "North American Protestant Fundamentalism," in *Fundamentalism Observed*, ed. Martin E. Marty and R. Scott Appleby (Chicago: University of Chicago, 1991), 32.

57. M. Simon, *Jerry Falwell and the Jews* (New York: Middle Village, 1984); Jerry Falwell, *Nuclear War and the Second Coming of Jesus Christ* (Lynchburg, VA: Old time Gospel, 1983); and G. Greenberg, "Fundamentalists, Israel and Theological Openness," *Christian Jewish Relations* 19 (1986): 27–33.

58. David S. Katz and Richard H. Popkin, *Messianic Revolution* (London: Penguin, 1999), 152–53.

59. Avi Beker, "The Christmas/Hanukkah Story," *Ha'aretz*, December 23, 2004, and "Guardians of the Fence," *Ha'aretz* August 28, 2005.

60. Avi Beker, "Christian Donations Welcome Here," *Ha'aretz*, May 31, 2005.

61. Walter Russell Mead, "God's Country?" *Foreign Affairs* 85, no. 5 (September/ October 2006): 24.

62. Sergio I. Minerbi, *The Vatican and Zionism—Conflict in the Holy Land 1895–1925* (New York: Oxford University Press, 1990), 95–96.

63. Ibid., 96.
64. Raphael Patai, ed. *The Complete Diaries of Thedor Herzl*, vol. 4 (New York: Herzl, 1960), 593–94.
65. David I. Kertzer, *The Popes Against the Jews—The Vatican's Role in the Rise of Modern Anti-Semitism* (New York: Vintage Books, 2001), 225.
66. Patai, 1602–4.
67. Daniel Goldhagen, *A Moral Reckoning—The Role of the Catholic Church and its Unfulfilled Duty of Repair Holocaust* (New York: Knopf, 2002), 239.
68. *Notes on the Correct Way to Present the Jews and Judaism in the Preaching and Catechesis in the Roman Catholic Church*, VI, 25, 1985, http://www.vatican.va/roman_curia/pontifical_councils/chrstuni/relations-jews-docs/rc_pc_chrstuni_doc_19820306_jews-judaism_en.html.
69. Bernard Wasserstein, *Vanishing Diaspora—The Jews in Europe since 1945* (London: Hamish Hamilton, 1996), 158.
70. Abraham H. Foxman, *Never Again?—The Threat of the New Anti-Semitism* (New York: Harper San Francisco, 2003), 237–38.
71. "Special Report on Christian Jewish Relations," *Economist*, April 10, 2004.
72. Bat Ye'or, *Islam and Dhimmitude—Where Civilizations Collide* (Madison, NJ: Fairleigh Dickinson University Press, 2002), 382.
73. *Al-Sharq Al-Awsat*, March 20, 2002.
74. *Al Hayat Al-Jadeeda*, July 7, 1997.
75. Menahem Milson, *Countering Arab Antisemitism* (Jerusalem: Institute of the WJC, Policy Forum, 2003), 13.
76. Genesis 15:18–21.
77. Quran 5:21.
78. See Andrea Nusse, "The Ideology of Hamas: Palestinian Islamic Fundamentalist Thought on the Jews, Israel and Islam," in *Studies in Muslim-Jewish Relations*, vol. 1, ed. Ronald L. Nettler (Oxford: Harwood Academic, 1993), 106–9.
79. Yitzhak Reiter, "All of Palestine is Holy Muslim *Waqf* Land—A Myth and Its Roots," in *Law, Custom, and Statute in the Muslim World*, ed. Ron Shaham (Boston: Brill, 2007), 173–97.
80. Bat Ye'or, 319.
81. *Syrian News Agency*, May 5, 2001. See also Goldhagen, 243–44.
82. Yehuda Bauer, *Post-Holocaust and Anti-Semitism* 3 December 2002, Jerusalem Center for Public Affairs.
83. See the *Middle East Media Research Institute*, December 28, 2001, http://www.memri.org
84. *Ha'aretz*, April 25, 2004.
85. *United Nations General Assembly Official Records*, November 13, 1974.
86. *Al Hayat Al-Jadeeda*, November 5, 1997.
87. *Daily Telegraph* (London), January 1, 2000.
88. *Agence France-Presse*, December 14, 2001.
89. Avner Cohen, *Israel and the Bomb* (New York: Columbia University Press, 1998), 99–108, 155.
90. Michael Karpin, *The Bomb in the Basement—How Israel Went Nuclear and What That Means for the World* (New York: Simon and Schuster, 2006), 243.
91. Avi Beker, "Denuclearization Without Glasnost," in *Arms Control Without Glasnost: Building Confidence in the Middle East*, ed. Avi Beker (Jerusalem: Israel Council on Foreign Relations, 1993), 179.

92. Nicholas D. Kristof, "The Osirak Option," *New York Times*, November 15, 2002.

93. Avi Beker, "Denuclearization Without Glasnost," 161.

94. For the Israeli position, see Avi Beker "A Regional NPT for the Middle East," in *Security or Armageddon—Israel's Nuclear Strategy*, ed. Louis Rene Bered (Lexington, MA: Lexington Books, 1985), 128.

95. See Yutaka Arai-Takahashi and Nico J. Schriver, "Responding to International Terrorism: Moving the Frontiers of International Law for 'Enduring Freedom'?" *Netherlands International Law Review* no. 271 (2001).

96. Alan Dershowitz, *Why Terrorism Works—Understanding the Threat, Responding to the Challenge* (New Haven and London: Yale University Press, 2002), 2, 53.

97. Avi Beker, *The United Nations and Israel-From Recognition to Reprehension* (Lexington, MA: Lexington Books, 1988), 82–84 and the text of the resolution in Appendix K of the book, 167–69.

98. International Court of Justice, http://www.icj-cij/. See also Avi Beker, "We Saw the Signs Already in 1994," *Ha'aretz*, September 7, 2004, and Leanne Piggott, "Judge's Ruling Rewrites UN Charter on Self-Defence," *Australian*, September 7, 2004.

99. O'Brien, 653, 656.

## Chapter 8

1. "Hep!" is a famous anti-Semitic agitation used as incitement during attacks against the Jews in the Middle Ages, in the later pogroms, and also before the Holocaust in Europe. George Soros, the great financier and philanthropist, recalls as a child being taunted by cries of "Hep! Hep!" in pre–World War II Hungary. See Michael Kaufman, *Soros—The Life and Times of a Messianic Billionaire* (New York: Vintage Books, 2003), 7.

2. Isaiah 66:12.

3. Bar-el Y., Durst R., Katz G., Zislin J., Strauss Z., Knobler H. Y., "Jerusalem Syndrome," *British Journal of Psychiatry* 176 (2000): 86–90.

4. "The Burning of Al Aqsa" *Time*, August 29, 1969, http://www.time.com/time/magazine/article/0,9171,901289-2,00.html.

5. Abed-Rabbo and the guide book in *Jerusalem Post*, January 26, 2000.

6. "Camp David and After: An Exchange—An Interview with Ehud Barak," *New York Review of Books*, June 13, 2001. Dennis Ross says that Arafat was "challenging the core of the Jewish faith, and seeking to deny Israel any claim in the old city" (Dennis Ross, *The Missing Peace* [New York: Farrar, Straus, and Giroux, 2004], 694, and for President Clinton's reaction, 718).

7. Shlomo Ben Ami, *A Front Without a Rearguard—A Voyage to the Boundaries of the Peace Process* [In Hebrew] (Tel-Aviv: Yedioth Ahronoth Books, 2004), 219.

8. Bill Clinton, *My Life: The Presidential Years* (Westminster, MD: Knopf, 2005), 466.

9. Deuteronomy 12:20–21.

10. See the statistics from the *Encyclopedia Britannica*. See also Martin Gilbert, *Jerusalem—Rebirth of a City* (London: Chatto and Windus, 1985).

11. Entry on *Jerusalem Encyclopedia Judaica* (Jerusalem: Keter, 1973).

12. Genesis 14:18.

13. Eicha Raba, 2:4.

14. Paul Johnson, *A History of the Jews* (New York: Harper and Row, 1987), 143.

15. Michael Avi-Yonah, "The Roman Period and Byzantine Jerusalem," in *Jerusalem* (Jerusalem: Jerusalem Pocket Library, 1973), 42–43.
16. Ibid., 47.
17. Abdul Hadi Palazzi, *The Jewish–Moslem Dialogue and the Question of Jerusalem*, Policy Study No. 7 (Jerusalem: World Jewish Congress Institute, 1997), 9.
18. Eliyahu Ashtor and Haim Ze'w Hirschberg, "Arab Period in Jerusalem," in *Jerusalem—Rebirth of a City*, and Moshe Gil, *A History of Palestine, 634–1099* (New York: Cambridge University Press, 1992), 48–49, and Palazzi, 12.
19. Ashtor and Hirschberg, 51.
20. Quran 2:145.
21. Quran 17:7.
22. Eliyahu Tal, *Whose Jerusalem* (Jerusalem: International Forum, 1994), 66.
23. Ashtor and Hirschberg, 52–54, and Ori Standel, "The Arabs in Jerusalem," in *Jerusalem*, ed. John M. Oesterreicher and Anne Sinai (New York: John Day, 1974), 150.
24. Karen Armstrong, *Holy War—The Crusades and Their Impact on Today's World* (New York: Anchor Books, 2001), 175, and August Krey, *The First Crusade: The Accounts of Eye-Witness and Participants* (Princeton, NJ: Princeton University Press, 1921), 38.
25. Krey, 262.
26. Eliyahu Tal, *Whose Jerusalem*, 82.
27. Jimmy Carter, *The Blood of Abraham—Insights into the Middle East* (New York: Houghton Mifflin, 1985), 81.
28. Ron Geaves, *Islam and the West Post-9/11* (London: Ashgate, 2004), 200.
29. Ibid., 66–67.
30. Joshua Prawer, *The Latin Kingdom of Jerusalem: European Colonialism in the Middle Ages* (London: Oxford University Press, 1972).
31. Bernard Lewis, *The Crisis of Islam* (New York: Modern Library, 2003), 50, and James Parkes, *Prelude to Dialogue: Jewish-Christian Relationship* (London: Vallentine Mitchell, 1969), 116.
32. Lewis, *The Crisis of Islam*, 68–76.
33. Ibid., 96.
34. Philip Mattar, *The Mufti of Jerusalem: Al-Hajj Amin Al-Husayni and the Palestinian National Movement 1917–1949* (New York: Columbia University Press, 1988), 35.
35. Conor Cruise O'Brien, *The Siege* (London: Weidenfeld and Nicolson, 1986), 183.
36. Yehoshua Porath, *The Emergence of the Palestinian-Arab National Movement 1918–1929* (London: Frank Cass, 1974), 271–72.
37. O'Brien, *The Siege*, 226.
38. Ibid., 227.
39. Ibid., 228.
40. Larry Collins and Dominique Lapierre, *O Jerusalem* (London: Grafton Books, 1986), 81.
41. Ibid., 255.
42. Ibid., 81.
43. *Divrei HaKnesset* [Protocols of the Israeli Parliament], December 13, 1949.
44. Stephen Adler, "The Jerusalem Law: Origin and Effects," in *Jerusalem: Aspects of Law* (Jerusalem: Jerusalem Institute, 1983), xxxvi.

45. Ibid.
46. Talmud, *Baba Metziah* 30b.
47. Harold Fisch, *The Zionist Revolution: A New Perspective* (London: Weidenfeld and Nicolson, 1978), 87.
48. Bernard Avishai, *The Tragedy of Zionism: Revolution and Democracy in the Land of Israel* (New York: Farrar, Straus, and Giroux, 1985), 245.
49. Fisch, 87.
50. Kare Armstrong, *The Battle for God—A History of Fundamentalism* (New York: Ballantine, 2001), 290–92.
51. Nadav Shragai, *The Temple Mount Conflict* [In Hebrew] (Jerusalem: Keter, 1995), 29–30, and David Horovitz, *Still Life With Bombers—Israel in the Age of Terrorism* (New York: Knopf, 2004), 87.
52. Armstrong, *The Battle for God*, 290–92.
53. Uzi Narkiss, *One Jerusalem* [In Hebrew] (Tel-Aviv: Am Oved), 213–14; Moshe Dayan, *Avnei Derech* (Tel-Aviv: Yedioth Aharonot), 13, 52; and Shragai, *The Temple Mount Conflict*, 18–24.
54. Raphael Mergui and Philippe Simonnot, *Israel's Ayatollahs: Meir Kahane and the Far Right in Israel* (London: Saqi Publications, 1987), 45, and Ehud Sprinzak, *The Ascendance of Israel's Far Right* (Oxford: 1991), 223–25.
55. Armstrong, *The Battle for God*, 349.
56. Shragai, *The Temple Mount Conflict*, part 3.
57. Walter Lacquer and Barry Rubin, eds. *The Israel-Arab Reader: A Documentary History of the Middle East Conflict* (London: Weidenfeld and Nicolson, 1964), 598.
58. In the year 628, Mohammad signed a ten-year pact with the powerful Quraish tribe after having been pursued from Mecca to Medina. The pact was needed by Mohammad to gain time in order to consolidate his forces. Two years after signing the treaty, Mohammad attacked Mecca and slaughtered all the members of the Quraish tribe in direct violation of the treaty.
59. Shragai, *The Temple Mount Conflict*, 383–85.
60. *Le Monde*, September 22, 2000.
61. James Carroll, *Constantine's Sword—The Church and the Jews* (New York: Houghton Mifflin, 2001), 635n4.
62. Nadav Shragai, "A Campaign of Denial to Disinherit the Jews," *Ha'aretz*, May 11, 2004.
63. Joel 3:17.
64. Isaiah 40:1–2.
65. Isaiah 2:2–4.
66. Zechariah 8:22.
67. *Psikta rabatti* [Late book of Midrash-Hebrew], in "Jerusalem," Encyclopedoa Judaica.
68. Rashi, in *Song of Songs*, ArtScroll (New York: Mesorah, 1977), 5:8.

## Chapter 9

1. *Iggeret Teiman*, trans. Boaz Cohen, notes by Abraham S. Halkin, http://en.wikisource.org/wiki/Epistle_to_Yemen/II.
2. "Interview with A. B. Yehoshua," *Ha'aretz*, March 19, 2004, 28.
3. *New York Times Almanac* (New York: Penguin, 2003), 484.

4. Quoted in Stanley Weintraub, *Disraeli: A Biography* (New York: Truman Talley Books, 1993), 216–17.

5. James Carroll, *Constantine's Sword—The Church and the Jews* (New York: Houghton Mifflin, 2001), 566.

6. *Ha'aretz*, March 19, 2004, 28.

7. Sigmund Freud, *Moses and Monotheism*, trans. from the German by Katherine Jones (New York: Vintage Books, 1967), 116.

8. Arnold J. Toynbee, *A Study of History—Reconsiderations*, vol. 12 (New York: Oxford University Press, 1964), 477.

9. Ibid., 478–79.

10. Avi Beker, "Giving Up Normalcy," *Ha'aretz*, July 13, 2004.

11. J. J. Goldberg, *Jewish Power—Inside the American Jewish Establishment* (New York: Addison-Wesley, 1996), 69–70.

12. Abigail Pogrebin, *Stars of David—Prominent Jews Talk About Being Jewish* (New York: Broadway Books, 2005), 274.

13. S. W. Baron, *A Social and Religious History of the Jews*, 2nd ed., vol. 1 (New York: Columbia University Press, 2001), 3.

14. Michael Brecher, *The Foreign Policy System of Israel* (London: Oxford University Press, 1972), 242.

15. Dina Porat, "A Diary for All Mankind," *Ha'aretz*, September 3, 2004.

16. Anne Frank, *The Definitive Edition, Diary of a Young Girl*, ed. Otto H. Frank and Mirjam Pressler (New York: Bantam Books, 1997), April 11, 1944.

17. This and the following quotes are from Naphtali Prat, "Nikolai Berdiaev and the Jews," *Shvut* 3, no. 19 (1996): 6–7, 15–17.

18. Ibid., 17.

19. Pam Belluck, "At Brandeis, Carter Responds to Critics," *New York Times*, January 24, 2007.

20. Jeffery Goldberg, "What would Jimmy Do?" *Washington Post* (Book World), December 10, 2006. Goldberg refers to Carter's complains about the wide spread secularism in Israel and recalls telling Prime Minister Golda Meir during his first visit in Israel that "a common historical pattern was that Israel was punished whenever the leaders turned away from devout worship of God" (Review of Jimmy Carter, *Palestine: Peace Not Apartheid* [New York: Simon & Schuster, 2006]).

21. Hans Morgenthau, *The Tragedy of German-Jewish Liberalism* (New York: Leo Baeck Institute, 1962); appears also in Hans Morgenthau, *Politics in the Twentieth Century*, 1:247–56, and brought as part of Morgenthau's Jewish thought in M. Ben Mollow, *Power and Transcendence: Hans J. Morgenthau and the Jewish Experience* (New York: Lexington Books, 2002), 108.

22. "Special Report on Christians and Jews," *Economist*, April 10, 2004.

23. Susannah Heschel, *Abraham Geiger and the Jewish Jesus* (Chicago: University of Chicago Press, 1998), 11.

24. Yves Dubios, "Orthodox Liturgy and Judaism," *Common Ground*, no. 1 (1996).

25. "Special Report on Christians and Jews," *Economist*, April 10, 2004.

26. M. Basilea Schlink, *Israel My Chosen People—A German Confession Before God and the Jews* (London: Faith Press, 1963), 14, 27–28.

27. Commission for Religious Relations with the Jews, "We Remember: A Reflection on the Shoah," Vatican City, March 16, 1998, reprinted in Geoffrey Wigoder,

*Jewish–Christian Interfaith Relations—Agenda for Tomorrow*, Policy Forum no. 14 (Jerusalem: WJC Institute, 1998), 52.

28. Conor Cruise O'Brien, *The Siege* (London: Weidenfeld and Nicolson, 1986), 225.
29. Marc Cohen, *Under Crescent and Cross—The Jews in the Middle Ages* (Princeton, NJ: Princeton University Press, 1994), 24.
30. Bernard Lewis, *Semites and Anti-Semites* (London: Phoenix, 1997), 124.
31. Quran 2:61.
32. Lewis, *Semites and Anti-Semites*, 128.
33. Ibid.
34. Appears in different versions in the Hadith as, for instance, Sahih Muslim 41/6981.
35. Quran 62:6.
36. *The King Fahd's Holy Koran* (Saudi Arabia: The Royal Palace, 2000), commentary to 62:6.
37. This Quran edition, which is quite common and popular in the Islamic world, was given to the author in an official visit of world Jewish leaders at the Great Mosque of Paris by the Mufti of Paris Dalil Boubakeur, the leader of the French Council of *Musulman* Faith who is considered a moderate Islamic leader. For more anti-Jewish references in this edition see there the commentary on sura 2 verses 85, 92, 94.
38. Ma'ashu Muhammad, "The Jews in the Modern Era," *Al-Jundi Al-Muslim* [The Saudi Soldier], in *MEMRI* [Middle East Media Research Institute] 768, special dispatch, August 20, 2004.
39. See in Chava Lazaruz Yafe, *Olamot Shzurim* (Jerusalem: Bialik, 1998), 64–65.
40. Camilla Adang, "Ibn Hazm's Criticism of Some 'Judaizing' Tendencies among the Malikites," in *Medieval and Modern Perspectives of Muslim-Jewish Relations*, ed. Ronald L. Nettler (Oxford: Harwood Academic, 1995), 1–15.
41. Ehud Ya'ari, "Not Just Anti-Semitic Lies!" *Jerusalem Report*, June 12, 2002.
42. Moshe Yaalon et al., *Iran, Hizbullah, Hamas and the Global Jihad: A New Conflict Paradigm for the West* (Jerusalem: Jerusalem Center for Public Affairs, 2007), 78.
43. Lawrence Wright, "The Terror Web," *New Yorker*, August 2, 2004, 44, 47.
44. Tracy Wilkinson "Islam's Claim on Spain," *Los Angeles Times*, January 18, 2005.
45. Wright, 51.
46. Iranian State News Agency (Isna), November 16, 2006.
47. Ewen MacAskill and Chris McGreal, "Israel Should Be Wiped Off the Map," *Guardian*, October 27, 2005.
48. "From Khomeini to Ahmadinejad," Hoover Institute, policy review, January 2007, http://www.hoover.org/publications/policyreview/4884331.html.
49. Pope Pius XII, Mystici Corporis Christi, http://www.vatican.va/holy_father/pius_xii/encyclicals/documents/hf_p-xii_enc_29061943_mystici-corporischristi_en.html.
50. Gerald L. Zelizer, "Respect for Faith's 'Elder Brother,'" *USA Today*, April 5, 2005.
51. Samuel P. Huntington, *The Clash of Civilizations and the Remarking of World Order* (New York: Simon & Schuster, 1996), 218.
52. Jonathan Riley-Smith dissolves the legend of the "Peasants' Crusades" and proves that they were regular armies and not fanatical hordes of peasants. See Jonathan Riley-Smith, *The First Crusade and the Idea of Crusading* (London: Athlone, 1986), 51–58.

53. Patrick E. Tyler and Don Van Natta, "Militants in Europe Openly Call for Jihad and the Rule of Islam," *New York Times*, April 26, 2004.
54. Jonathan D. Halevi, "Al-Qaeda's Intellectual Legacy: New Radical Islamic Thinking Justifying the Genocide of Infidels," *Jerusalem Viewpoints* 508 (December 1, 2003).
55. Neil MacFarquhar, "Muslim Scholars Increasingly Debate Unholy War," *New York Times*, December 10, 2004.
56. Faisal al Yafai, "The West Needs to Understand It Is Inevitable: Islam is Coming Back," *The Guardian*, November 11, 2004.
57. David S. Katz and Richard H. Popkin, *Messianic Revolution—Radical Religious Politics to the end of the Second Millenium* (London: Penguin, 1999), 17.
58. Hermann Rauschning, *Hitler Speaks—A Series of Political Conversations with Adolf Hitler on His Real Aims* (London: Thornton Butterworth, 1940), 234, 238.
59. Paul Smith, *Disraeli—A Brief Life* (New York: Cambridge University Press, 1999), 102.
60. Michael Flavin, *Benjamin Disraeli: The Novel as Political Discourse* (Eastbourne, UK: Sussex Academic Press, 2005), 125.
61. Stanley Weintraub, *Disraeli: A Biography* (New York: Truman Talley, 1993), 216–17.

# Bibliography

## Books

Armstrong, Karen. *The Battle For God—A History of Fundamentalism*. New York: Ballantine Books, 2001.

———. *Holy War—The Crusades and Their Impact on Today's World*. New York: Anchor Books, 2001.

Ashton, H. S. *The Jew at Bay*. London: Phillip Allen, 1933.

Avishai, Bernard. *The Tragedy of Zionism: Revolution and Democracy in the Land of Israel*. New York: Farrar, Straus, and Giroux, 1985.

Baldwin, Neil. *The American Revelation: Ten Ideals that Shaped Our Country from the Puritans to the Cold War*. New York: St. Martins Griffin, 2006.

———. *Henry Ford and the Jews—The Mass Production of Hate*. New York: Public Affairs, 2001.

Baron, S. W. *A Social and Religious History of the Jews*. New York: Columbia University Press, 2001.

Bat Ye'or. *Islam and Dhimmitude—Where Civilizations Collide*. Madison, NJ: Fairleigh Dickinson University Press, 2002.

Beker, Avi, ed. *Arms Control Without Glasnost: Building Confidence in the Middle East*. Jerusalem: Israel Council on Foreign Relations, 1993.

———, ed. *The Plunder of Jewish Property During the Holocaust—Confronting European History*. London: Palgrave, 2001.

———. *The United Nations and Israel-From Recognition to Reprehension*. Lexington, MA: Lexington Books, 1988.

Ben Gurion, David. *Biblical Reflections* [In Hebrew]. Tel-Aviv: Am Oved, 1976.

Berdyaev, Nicholas Aleksandrovich. *Christianity and Anti-Semitism*. New York: Philosophical Library, 1954.

Berkley, George E. *Vienna and Its Jews*. Cambridge, MA: Abt Books, 1988.

Biale, David. *Eros and the Jews*. New York, Basic Books, 1992.

Bishops' Committee on the Liturgy, National Conference of Catholic Bishops. *God's Mercy Endures Forever: Guidelines on the Presentation of Jews and Judaism in Catholic Preaching*. Washington, DC: United States Catholic Conference, 1989.

Blackstone, William. *Jesus Is Coming*. Chicago: Revell, 1908.

Bodansky, Yossef. *Islamic Anti-Semitism as a Political Instrument*. Houston: Freeman Center for Strategic Studies, 1999.

Boyer, Paul S. *When Time Shall Be No More: Prophecy Belief in Modern American Culture*. Cambridge, MA: Harvard University Press, 1992.

Brecher, Michael. *The Foreign Policy System of Israel*. London: Oxford University Press, 1972.

Brinner, William M., and Stephen D. Ricks, eds., *Studies in Islamic and Judaic Traditions*. Atlanta: Scholars, 1989.

Brog, David. *Standing with Israel: Why Christians Support the Jewish State*. Lake Mary, FL: Front Line, 2006.

Brown, Michael L. *Our Hands Are Stained with Blood: The Tragic Story of the "Church" and the Jewish People*. Shippensburg, PA: Destiny Image, 1992.

Buckley, William F., Jr. *United Nations Journal: A Delegate's Odyssey*. New York: Anchor Books, 1977.

Bush, George. *The Valley of Vision*. New York: Saxton & Miles, 1847.

Carroll, James. *Constantine's Sword—The Church and the Jews*. New York: Houghton Mifflin, 2001.

Carter, Jimmy. *The Blood of Abraham—Insights into the Middle East*. New York: Houghton Mifflin, 1985.

———. *Palestine: Peace Not Apartheid*. New York: Simon and Schuster, 2006.

Chesler, Phyllis. *The New Anti-Semitism: The Current Crisis and What Can We Do About It*. New York: Jossey-Bass, 2003.

Clinton, Bill. *My Life: The Presidential Years*. Westminster, MD: Knopf, 2005.

Cohen, Avner. *Israel and the Bomb*. New York: Columbia University Press, 1998.

Cohen, Jeremy. *Christ Killers: The Jews and the Passion from the Bible to the Big Screen*. New York: Oxford University Press, 2007.

Cohen, M. J., and John Major. *History in Quotations*. London: Cassel, 2004.

Cohen, Mark R. *Under Crescent and Cross—The Jews in the Middle Ages*. Princeton, NJ: Princeton University Press, 1994.

Choen, Norman. *Warrant for Genocide: The Myth of the Jewish World-Conspiracy and the Protocols of the Elders of Zion*. London: Eyre & Spottiswoode, 1967.

Collins, Larry, and Dominique Lapierre. *O Jerusalem*. London: Grafton Books, 1986.

Dawidowicz, Lucy S. *The War Against the Jews 1933–1945*. New York: Bantan, 1975.

Dayan, Moshe. *Avnei Derech* [In Hebrew]. Tel-Aviv: Yedioth Aharonot, 1975.

Dershowitz, Alan M. *Chutzpah*. Boston: Little, Brown, 1991.

———. *Why Terrorism Works—Understanding the Threat, Responding to the Challenge*. New Haven, CT: Yale University Press, 2002.

Dorff, Elliot N. *Conservative Judaism: Our Ancestors to Our Descendants*. New York: United Synagogue of America, 1985.

Eban, Abba. *Heritage—Civilization and the Jews*. New York: Summit Books, 1984.

Eckhardt, A. Roy. *Christianity and the Children of Israel*. New York: King's Crown Press, 1948.

*Eichmann in the World Press*. Jerusalem: Israeli Ministry of Foreign Affairs, 1960.

Eidelberg, Schlomo, ed. *The Hebrew Chronicles of the First and Second Crusades*. Translated by Schlomo Eidelberg. Hoboken, NJ: Ktav, 1996.

Einstein, Albert. *About Zionism: Speeches and Letters*. New York: Macmillan, 1931.

Eisen, Arnold. *The Chosen People in America*. Bloomington: Indiana University Press, 1983.

Eisenshtadt, Yehuda David. *Polemics and Disputations* [In Hebrew]. New York: Menorah, 1929.

Eliot, George. *Daniel Deronda*. 1876. Reprint, New York: Barnes & Noble, 2005.

Elon, Amos. *Herzl*. New York: Schocken Books, 1986.

Fadiman, Clifton, and André Bernard. *Bartlett's Book of Anecdotes*. Boston: Little, Brown, 2000.

Falwell, Jerry. *Nuclear War and the Second Coming of Jesus Christ*. Lynchburg, VA: Old time Gospel, 1983.

Feldman, Louis H. *Jew and Gentile in the Ancient World*. Princeton, NJ: Princeton University Press, 1993.

Feuchtwanger, Edgar. *Disraeli*. London: Arnold, 2000.

Fisch, Harold. *The Zionist Revolution: A New Perspective*. London: Weidenfeld and Nicolson, 1978.

Flavin, Michael. *Benjamin Disraeli: The Novel as Political Discourse*. Eastbourne, UK: Sussex Academic Press, 2005.

Flusser, David. *Judaism and the Origins of Christianity*. Jerusalem: Magnes, 1988.

Ford, Henry. *Aspects of Jewish Power in the United States*. Vols. 2 and 4 of *The International Jew*. Dearborn, MI: Dearborn, 1922.

———. *The International Jew—The World's Foremost Problem*. Abridged and edited by Gerald L. K. Smith. Los Angeles: Christian Nationalist Crusade, 1954.

Foxman, Abraham. *Never Again? The Threat of the New Anti-Semitism*. New York: Harper San Francisco, 2003.

Frank, Anne. *The Definitive Edition, Diary of a Young Girl*. Edited by Otto H. Frank and Mirjam Pressler. New York: Bantam Books, 1997.

Freud, Sigmund. *Moses and Monotheism*. Translated from the German by Katherine Jones. New York: Vintage Books, 1967.

Friedman, Samuel. *Jew vs. Jew—The Struggle for the Soul of American Jewry*. New York: Simon and Schuster, 2000.

Geiger, Abraham. *Judaism and Islam*. New York: Ktav, 1970.

Gil, Moshe. *A History of Palestine, 634–1099*. New York: Cambridge University Press, 1992.

Gilbert, Martin. *The Arab-Israeli Conflict—Its History in Maps*. London: Weidenfeld and Nicolson, 1976.

———. *Jerusalem—Rebirth of a City*. London: Chatto and Windus, 1985.

Goldberg, J. J. *Jewish Power—Inside the American Jewish Establishment*. New York: Addison-Wesley, 1996.

Goldhagen, Daniel. *Hitler's Willing Executioners: Ordinary Germans and the Holocaust*. New York: Knopf, 1996.

———. *A Moral Reckoning—The Role of the Catholic Church in the Holocaust and Its Unfulfilled Duty of Repair*. New York: Knopf, 2002.

Goldmann, Nachum. *Autobiography: Sixty Years of Jewish Life*. New York: Holt, Rinehart, and Winston, 1969.

Gross, John. *Shylock—A Legend & Its Legacy*. New York: Touchstone, 1992.

Halevi, Jonathan D. "Al-Qaeda's Intellectual Legacy: New Radical Islamic Thinking Justifying the Genocide of Infidels." *Jerusalem Viewpoint*, December 1, 2003, Jerusalem Center for Public Affairs.

Halevi, Judah. *The Kuzari—An Argument for the Faith of Israel*. Jerusalem: Sefer Va Sefel, 2003.

Hay, Malcolm. *Europe and the Jews*. Boston: Beacon, 1961.

Heer, Friedrich. *God's First Love*. New York: Weybright and Talley, 1967.

Herford, R. Travers. *Judaism in the New Testament Period*. London: Lindsey, 1928.

Hertzberg, Arthur. *The Jews in America*. New York: Simon and Schuster, 1989.

———. *The Zionist Idea*. Garden City, NY: Doubleday, 1959.

Hertzberg, Arthur, and Aron Hirt-Manheimer. *Jews—The Essence and Character of a People*. San Francisco: Harper and Row, 1998.

Herzog, Yaacov. *A People That Dwells Alone*. London: Weidenfeld and Nicolson, 1975.

Heschel, Susannah. *Abraham Geiger and the Jewish Jesus*. Chicago: University of Chicago Press, 1998.

Hibbert, Christopher. *Disraeli and His World*. London: Thames and Hudson, 1978.

Hirsch, Rabbi Samson Raphael. *Commentary to the Siddur* [Commentary to the Prayer Book]. Jerusalem: Rabbi Kook Institute, 1992.

Hitler, Adolf. *Mein Kampf* [My Struggle]. New York: Houghton Mifflin and Hutchison, 1969.

Horovitz, David. *Still Life With Bombers—Israel in the Age of Terrorism*. New York: Knopf, 2004.

Huntington, Samuel P. *The Clash of Civilizations and the Remaking of World Order*. New York: Simon and Schuster, 1996.

International Catholic-Jewish Liaison Committee, *Fifteen Years of Catholic-Jewish Dialogue 1970–1985*. Rome: Libreria Editrice Vaticana, 1988.

Katsh, Abraham I. *Judaism and Islam—Biblical and Talmudic Background of the Koran and its Commentaries*. Jerusalem: Kiryat Sepher, 1957.

Katz, David S., and Richard H. Popkin. *Messianic Revolution*. London: Penguin, 1999.

Kaufman, Michael. *Soros—The Life and Times of a Messianic Billionaire*. New York: Vintage Books, 2003.

Kertzer, David I. *The Popes Against the Jews—The Vatican's Role in the Rise of Modern Anti-Semitism*. New York: Vintage Books, 2001.

John Paul II. *Crossing the Threshold of Hope*. New York: Knopf, 1994.

Johnson, Paul. *A History of the Jews*. New York: Harper and Row, 1987.

Kaplan, Mordechai. *The Future of the American Jew*. New York: Reconstructionist, 1948.

Karpin, Michael. *The Bomb in the Basement—How Israel Went Nuclear and What That Means for the World*. New York: Simon and Schuster, 2006.

Keller, Sharon R., ed. *The Jews—In Literature and Art*. New York: Konemann, 1992.

Kohler, Kaufman. *Backwards or Forwards? A Series of Discourses on Reform Judaism*. New York: Congregation Beth El, 1885.

———. *Hebrew Union College and Other Addresses*. Cincinnati, OH: Ark, 1916.

———. *Jewish Theology, Systematically and Historically Considered*. New York: Macmillan, 1928.

Kraeling, Emil G. *The Old Testament Since the Reformation*. London: Luttewortt, 1955.

Krey, August. *The First Crusade: The Accounts of Eye-Witness and Participants*. Princeton, NJ: Princeton University Press, 1921.

Laquer, Walter, ed. *The Holocaust Encyclopedia*. New Haven, CT: Yale University Press, 2001.

Lacquer, Walter, and Barry Rubin, eds. *The Israel-Arab Reader: A Documentary History of the Middle East Conflict*. London: Weidenfeld and Nicolson, 1964.

Lazaruz, Chava Yafe. *Olamot Shzurim* [In Hebrew]. Jerusalem: Bialik, 1998.

Lewis, Bernard. *The Crisis of Islam—Holy War and Unholy Terror*. New York: Modern Library, 2003.

———. *The Jews of Islam*. Princeton, NJ: Princeton University Press, 1987.

———. *Semites and Anti-Semites*. London: Phoenix Giant, 1997.

Maghen, Zeev. *After Hardship Come Ease: The Jews As Backdrop for Muslim Moderation.* Berlin: Walter De Gruyter, 2006.

Maimonides. *The Guide of the Perplexed.* Translated by Shlomo Pines. Chicago: University of Chicago Press, 1963.

Malachy, Yona. *American Fundamentalism and Israel.* Jerusalem: Institute of Contemporary World Jewry, 1978.

Maybaum, Ignaz. *The Jewish Mission.* London: James Clarke, 1949.

Mendes-Flohr, Paul, and Yehuda Reinharz, eds. *The Jew in the Modern World.* New York: Oxford University Press, 1995.

Mergui, Raphael, and Philippe Simonnot. *Israel's Ayatollahs: Meir Kahane and the Far Right in Israel.* London: Saqi, 1987.

Minerbi, Sergio I. *The Vatican and Zionism—Conflict in the Holy Land 1895–1925.* New York: Oxford University Press, 1990.

Mollov, M. Benjamin. *Power and Transcendence—Hans Morgenthau and the Jewish Experience.* New York: Lexington Books, 2002.

Montesquieu, Charles Louis de Secondat. *De L'Esprit Des Lois* [The Spirit of Laws]. London: G. Bell & Sons, 1914.

Narkiss, Uzi. *One Jerusalem* [In Hebrew]. Tel-Aviv: Am Oved, 1969.

Nietzsche, Friedrich. *Complete Works.* Stanford, CA: Stanford University Press, 1995.

Novak, David. *The Election of Israel: The Idea of the Chosen People.* Cambridge: Cambridge University Press, 1995.

O'Brien, Conor Cruise. *God Land—Reflections on Religion and Nationalism.* Cambridge, MA: Harvard University Press, 1988.

———. *The Siege.* London: Weidenfeld and Nicolson, 1986.

Oesterreicher, John M., and Anne Sinai. *Jerusalem.* New York: John Day, 1974.

Ohana, David. *Messianism and Sovereignty—Ben Gurion and the Intellectuals: Between Political Vision and Political Theology* [In Hebrew]. Sdeh Boker, Israel: Ben Gurion University Press, 2003.

Oren, Michael. *Power, Faith, and Fantasy—America in the Middle East 1776 to the Present.* New York: W. W. Norton, 2007.

Parkes, James. *Prelude to Dialogue: Jewish-Christian Relationship.* London: Vallentine Mitchell, 1969.

Patai, Raphael, ed. *The Complete Diaries of Thedor Herzl.* Vol. 4. New York: Herzl, 1960.

———. *Ignaz Goldziher and His Oriental Diary.* Detroit: Wayne State University Press, 1987.

Pearlman, Moshe. *The Capture of Adolf Eichmann.* London: Wiedenfeld and Nicolson, 1961.

Peter the Venerable. *Sermones tres.* Edited by Giles Constable. Cambridge, MA: Harvard University Press, 1967.

Pogrebin, Abigail. *Stars of David—Prominent Jews Talk About Being Jewish.* New York: Broadway Books, 2005.

Poliakov, Leon. *Harvest of Hate—The Nazi Program for the Destruction of the Jews of Europe.* Philadelphia: Jewish Publication Society, 1954.

Porath, Yehoshua. *The Emergence of the Palestinian-Arab National Movement 1918–1929.* London: Frank Cass, 1974.

Potok, Chaim. *Wanderings—History of the Jews.* New York: Fawcett Books, 1978.

Power, Samantha. *A Problem From Hell: America and the Age of Genocide.* New York: Basic Books, 2002.

Prawer, Joshua. *The Latin Kingdom of Jerusalem: European Colonialism in the Middle Ages*. London: Oxford University Press, 1972.

*The Protocols of the Learned Elders of Zion*. Translated by Victor E. Marsden. London: Briton, 1923.

Rauschning, Hermann. *Hitler Speaks—A Series of Political Conversations with Adolf Hitler on His Real Aims*. London: Thornton Butterworth, 1940.

Rawidowicz, Simon. *The Writings of Nachman Krochmal*. London: Ararat, 1961.

Riley-Smith, Jonathan. *The First Crusade and the Idea of Crusading*. London: Athlone, 1986.

Rose, N. A. *The Gentile Zionist—A Study in Anglo-Zionist Diplomacy, 1929–1939*. London: Frank Cass, 1973.

Rose, Paul Lawrence. *Revolutionary Anti-Semitism in Germany from Kant to Wagner*. Princeton, NJ: Princeton University Press, 1990.

Rosenbaum, Ron, ed. *Those Who Forget the Past: The Question of Anti-Semitism*. New York: Random House, 2004.

Ross, Dennis. *The Missing Peace*. New York: Farrar, Straus, and Giroux, 2004.

Roth, Cecil. *Benjamin Disareli—Earl of Beaconsfield*. New York: Philosophical Library, 1952.

Ruether, Rosemary. *Faith and Fratricide*. San Francisco: Seabury, 1974.

Sachar, Howard M. *Diaspora—An Inquiry into the Contemporary Jewish World*. New York: Harper & Row, 1985.

Samuel, Maurice. *The Professor and the Fossil*. New York: Knopf, 1956.

Saramago, Jose. *The Gospel According to Jesus Christ*. New York: Harcourt Brace, 1994.

Sarna, Jonathan D. *Jacksonian Jews: The Two Worlds of Mordecai Noah*. New York: Holmes & Meir, 1981.

Sartre, Jean Paul. *Anti-Semite and Jew*. New York: Schocken Books, 1965. Originally published in French in 1946.

Schaffer, Peter. *Judeophobia—Attitudes toward the Jews in the Ancient World*. Cambridge, MA: Harvard University Press, 1977.

Schindler, Pesah. *Hasidic Responses to the Holocaust in the Light of Hasidic Thought*. Jersey City, NJ Ktav, 1990.

Schlink, M. Basilea. *Israel My Chosen People—A German Confession Before God and the Jews*. London: Faith, 1963.

Schoenfeld, Gabriel. *The Return of Anti-Semitism*. New York: Encounter Books, 2004.

Schreckenberg, Heinz. *The Jews in Christian Art*. New York: Continuum 1996.

Shakespeare, William. *The Merchant of Venice*. Leipzig: Bernh Tauchnitz, 1943.

Shapira, Anita. *Berl* [In Hebrew]. Tel-Aviv: Am Oved, 1980.

Sharett, Moshe. *At the Nation's Gate, 1946–1949* [In Hebrew]. Tel-Aviv: Am Oved, 1966.

Shragai, Nadav. *The Temple Mount Conflict* [In Hebrew]. Jerusalem: Keter, 1995.

Silberman, Charles. *A Certain People*. New York: Summit Books, 1985.

Silver, Rabbi Hillel. *Where Judaism Differed*. New York: Macmillan, 1956.

Simon, M. *Jerry Falwell and the Jews*. New York: Middle Village, 1984.

Sivan, Emmanuel. *Radical Islam: Medieval Theology and Modern Politics*. New Haven, CT: Yale University Press, 1985.

Smith, Paul. *Disraeli—A Brief Life*. Cambridge: Cambridge University Press 1999.

Sombart, Werner. *The Jews and Modern Capitalism*. Edison, NJ: Transaction, 1982. First published in Germany in 1911.

Spiegel, Shalom. *Hebrew Reborn*. New York: Macmillan, 1930.

Spinoza, Baruch. *The Theological-Political Essay*. Jerusalem: Hebrew University, 1962.
————. *Theological-Political Treatise*. Chapter 3 translated by Samuel Shirley. Leiden: E. J. Brill, 1991.
Sprinzak, Ehud. *The Ascendance of Israel's Far Right*. New York: Oxford University Press, 1991.
Steiner, George. *Errata: An Examined Life*. London: Weidenfeld and Nicolson, 1997.
Stillman, Norman. *The Jews of Arab Lands: A History and Source Book*. Philadelphia: Jewish Publication Society, 1979.
Stone, Julius. *Israel and Palestine: Assault on the Law of Nations*. Baltimore: Johns Hopkins University Press, 1981.
Tal, Eliyahu. *Whose Jerusalem*. Jerusalem: International Forum, 1994.
Timmerman, Kenneth R. *Preachers of Hate—Islam and the War on America*. New York: Crown Forum, 2003.
Toynbee, Arnold J. *A Study of History—Reconsiderations*. New York: Oxford University Press, 1964.
Twain, Mark. *The Innocents Abroad*. New York: Oxford University Press, 1966.
Urbach, Ephraim. *The World of the Sages* [In Hebrew]. Jerusalem: Magnes, 1988.
Van Pelt, Robert Jan, and Deborah Dwork. *Auschwitz, 1270 to the Present*. New Haven, CT: Yale University Press, 1996.
Vincent, John. *Disraeli*. New York: Oxford University Press, 1990.
Walzer, Michael et al., eds. *The Jewish Political Tradition*. New Haven, CT: Yale University Press, 2003.
Wasserstein, Bernard. *Vanishing Diaspora—The Jews in Europe Since 1945*. London: Hamish Hamilton, 1996.
Watson, F. *Paul, Judaism and the Gentiles—A Sociological Approach*. Cambridge: Cambridge University Press, 1986.
Wedgewood, J. C. *The Seventh Dominion*. London: Labour, 1928.
Weintraub, Stanley. *Disraeli: A Biography*. New York: Truman Talley Books, 1993.
Wertheimer, Jack. *A People Divided*. New York: Basic, 1993.
Wigoder, Geoffrey. *Jewish-Christian Interfaith Relations*. Policy Forum no. 14. Jerusalem: World Jewish Congress, 1988.
Wills, Garry. *Papal Sin: Structures of Deceit*. New York: Doubleday, 2000.
Wistrich, Robert. *The Longest Hatred*. New York: Pantheon Books, 1991.
Wheatcroft, Geoffrey. *The Controversy of Zion*. New York: Addison-Wesley, 1996.
Wyman, David S., ed. *The World Reacts to the Holocaust*. Baltimore: Johns Hopkins University Press, 1996.
Yuval, Israel Jacob. *Two Nations in Your Womb—Perceptions of Jews and Christians* [In Hebrew]. Tel-Aviv: Am Oved, 2000.
Zangwill, Israel. *Chosen Peoples: The Hebraic Ideal Versus the Teutonic*. New York: Macmillan, 1919.
Zrubavel, Yael. *Recovered Roots, Collective Memory and the Making of Israeli National Tradition*. Chicago: Chicago University Press, 1995.

## Religious Sources, Encyclopedias, and Documents

Bacya, Rabbeinu. *Cad Hakemah, Jerusalem: Mosad Harav Koock, 1970* [In Hebrew].
Chambers Encyclopedia. New York: Collier, 1882.
*The Chumash* [The Pentateuch]. Stone edition, by ArtScroll. New York: Mesorti, 2001.

*Divrei HaKnesset* [In Hebrew]. Protocols of the Israeli Parliament, Jerusalem, 1948.

*Documents on the Holocaust.* Jerusalem: Yad Vashem, 1999.

*Encyclopedia Judaica.* Jerusalem: Keter, 1971.

Gospel of Barnabas, http://barnabas.net/lifebarnabas.htm.

*Hebrew Encyclopedia.* Jerusalem: Masada, 1970.

The Jewish Bible [The Old Testament]. Philadelphia: Jewish Publication Society, 1917. Artscroll edition, New York: Masorti, 2001.

Maimonides (Rambam). *Epistle to the Jews of Yemen.* Translated by Boaz Cohen, http://enwikisource.org/orgwiki/Epistle to Yemen/

———. *Mishne Torah—Hilchot Melachim* [In Hebrew]. Mamre Institute, http://www.mechon-mamre.org/index.htm.

Mishna. *Ethics of the Fathers.* http://www.chabad.org/library/article_cdo/aid/2019/jewish/.

The New Testament. The New American Bible, http://www.usccb.org/nab/bible/.

*New York Times Almanac.* New York: Penguin, 2003.

The Quran. The King Fahd's Holy Koran. Saudi Arabia: The Royal Palace, 2000.

*Sabbath Prayerbook.* New York: Jewish Reconstructionist Foundation, 1945.

*Song of Songs.* ArtScroll, New York: Mesorah, 1977.

Talmud. ArtScroll editions, Brooklyn, New York. Steinzalt edition, Jerusalem.

*United Nations, General Assembly Official Records*, www.un.org.

*U.S. Congressional Record.* Washington, DC, http://thomas.loc.gov/home/cr_help.htm.

Vatican, "Notes for Preaching and Teaching," June 1985.


## Articles

Adang, Camilla. "Ibn Hazm's Criticism of Some 'Judaizing' Tendencies among the Malikites." In *Medieval and Modern Perspectives of Muslim-Jewish Relations*, edited by Ronald L. Nettler. Oxford: Harwood Academic, 1995.

Adler, Stephen. "The Jerusalem Law: Origin and Effects." In *Jerusalem: Aspects of Law*, edited by Ora Ahimeir, xxv–xxxviii. Jerusalem: Jerusalem Institute, 1983.

Ammerman, Nancy T. "North American Protestant Fundamentalism." In *Fundamentalism Observed*, edited by Martin E. Marty and R. Scott Appleby, 1–65. Chicago: University of Chicago, 1991.

Anderson, Douglas. "The Old Testament Presence in the Merchant of Venice." *Journal of English Literary History* 52, no. 89:119–32.

Avi-Yonah, Michael. "The Roman Period and Byzantine Jerusalem." In *Jerusalem*, 40–52. Jerusalem: Jerusalem Pocket Library, 1973.

Bauer, Yehuda. *Post-Holocaust and Anti-Semitism*, December 3, 2002, Jerusalem Center for Public Affairs.

———. "In Search of Definition of Anti-Semitism." In *Approaches to Anti-Semitism-Context and Curriculum*, edited by Yehudah Bauer, 10–23. New York: American Jewish Committee and the International Center for University Teaching of Jewish Civilization, 1994.

Beker, Avi. "Choosing to Remain a 'Forced Convert.'" *Ha'aretz*, October 9, 2006, B1.

———. "Christian Donations Welcome Here." *Ha'aretz*, May 31, 2005.

———. "The Christmas/Hanukkah Story." *Ha'aretz*, December 23, 2004.

———. "Giving Up Normalcy." *Ha'aretz*, July 13, 2004.

———. "Guardians of the Fence." *Ha'aretz*, August 28, 2005.

————. "A Regional NPT for the Middle East." In *Security or Armageddon—Israel's Nuclear Strategy*, edited by Louis Rene Beres, 120–32. Lexington, MA: Lexington Books, 1985.

————. "Unmasking National Myths—Europeans Challenge Their History." In *The Plunder of Jewish Property During the Holocaust—Confronting European History*, edited by Avi Beker. London: Palgrave, 2001.

————. "We Saw the Signs Already in 1994." *Ha'aretz*, September 7, 2004.

Bell, Daniel. "A Parable of Alienation." *Jewish Frontier* 13, no. 11 (November 1946): 12–17.

Berman, Paul. "Bigotry in Prin." *Forward* (New York weekly), May 24, 2002.

Blackstone, William. "May the United States Intercede for the Jews." Originally published in 1891. In *Christian Protaginists for Jewish Restoration*, edited by Joseph Celleni, 13–14. New York: Arno, 1977.

Boyer, Peter J. "The Jesus War." *New Yorker*, September 15, 2003, 58–71.

Brikner, Menahem. "The End of Zionism? Thoughts on the Wages of Success." *Dissent* 32, no. 1 (Winter 1985): 77–82.

Buchanan, Pat. "Whose War?" *American Conservative*, March 24, 2003.

Dubios, Yves. "Orthodox Liturgy and Judaism." *Common Ground* 1 (1996).

Edward, Alexander. "George Eliot's Rabbi." *Commentary* 92 (July 1991): 28–32.

Einstein, Albert. "Why Do They Hate the Jews?" In *Out of My Later Years*, by Albert Einstein, 245–56. New York: Citadel, 1995.

Ettinger, Shmuel. "Moscovite Russia and Its Attitude to the Jews" [In Hebrew]. *Zion* 18 (1953): 161–68.

Feinstein, Israel. "Early and Middle Nineteen-Century British Opinion on the Restoration of the Jews: Contrasts with America." In *With Eyes Toward Zion-II*, edited by Moshe Davis, 78–100. New York: Praeger, 1986.

Finkielkraut, Alain. "In The Name of the Other: Reflections on the Coming Anti-Semitism." *Azure* 18 (2004): 21–33.

Fisher, Eugene. "The Holy See and the State of Israel: The Evolution of Attitudes and Policies." *Journal of Ecumenical Studies* 24, no. 2 (Spring 1987): 191–97.

Fraser, Giles. "Crucified by Empire" *Guardian*, February 7, 2004.

Gottschalk, Yehiel Alfred. *Ahad Ha-ham and the Jewish National Spirit*. Jerusalem: WZO, 1992.

Greenberg, Moses. "Fundamentalists, Israel and Theological Openness." *Christian Jewish Relations*, no. 19 (1986): 27–33.

Grynberg, Henryk. "Appropriation of the Holocaust." *Commentary*, November 1982.

Joffe, Josef. "The Axis of Envy—Why Israel and the United States Both Strike the Same European Nerve." *Foreign Policy* 132 (September–October 2002): 68–69.

Interview with Mikis Theodorakis. *Jerusalem Post*, November 11, 2003.

Kaplan, Yossef. "Jews and Judaism in Political and Social Thought of Spain in the Sixteenth and Seventeenth Centuries." In *The Hatred of Israel Throughout the Ages* [In Hebrew], edited by Shmuel Almog, 173–80. Jerusalem: Shazar Center, 1980.

Kolitz, Zvi. "Yossel Rakover's Appeal to God" in *Out of the Whirl-Wind*, edited by Albert H. Friedlander, 390–99. New York: Union of American Hebrew Congregations, 1968.

Lewalski, Barbara K. "Biblical Allusion and Allegory in *The Merchant of Venice*." *Shakespeare Quarterly* 13 (1962): 327–43.

Lewis, Bernard. "The Roots of Islamic Rage." *New Yorker*, November 2001.

Liebman, S.Charles. "Reconstructionism in American Jewish Life." *American Jewish Year Book* 71 (1970): 3–99.

Mead, Walter Russell. "God's Country?" *Foreign Affairs* 85, no. 5 (September/October 2006).

———. "Review Essay: Why Do They Hate Us?" *Foreign Affairs* 82, no. 2 (March/April 2003): 139–42.

Milson, Menahem. *Countering Arab Antisemitism.* Jerusalem: Institute of the WJC, Policy Forum, 2003.

Minerbi, Sergio. "The Church: Friend or Foe?" *Jerusalem Post*, January 24, 2003.

———. "Neo-Anti-Semitism in today's Italy." *Jewish Political Studies Review* 15 (Fall 2003): 3–4.

Morgenthau, Hans J. *The Tragedy of German-Jewish Liberalism.* New York: Leo Baeck Institute, 1962.

Murray, Charles. "Jewish Genius." *Commentary*, April 2007, 29–35.

Niehoff, Maren R. "Circumcision as a Marker of Identity." *Jewish Studies Quarterly* 10, no. 2 (2003): 89–123.

Oz, Amos. "The Meaning of Homeland." In *Zionism: The Sequence.* New York: Hadassah, 1998.

Palazzi, Abdul Hadi. *The Jewish-Moslem Dialogue and the Question of Jerusalem.* Policy Study No. 7. Jerusalem: World Jewish Congress Institute, 1997.

Piggott, Leanne. "Judges Ruling Rewrites UN Charter on Self-Defence." *Australian*, September, 7, 2004.

Prat, Naphtali. "Nikolai Berdiaev and the Jews." *Shvut* 3, no. 19 (1996): 5–25.

Rausch, David A. "Evangelical Protestants Americans." In *With Eyes Toward Zion-II*, edited by Moshe Davis, 318–33. New York: Praeger, 1986.

Reiter, Yitzhak. "All of Palestine is Holy Muslim *Waqf* Land—A Myth and Its Roots." In *Law, Custom, and Statute in the Muslim World*, edited by Ron Shaham, 173–97. Boston: Brill, 2007.

Rieff, Philip. "Disraeli: The Chosen of History." *Commentary*, January 1952, 30–40.

Roston, Murray. "Sacred and Secular in *The Merchant of Venice*." In *Sacred and Secular in Medieval and Early Modern Cultures*, edited by Lawrence Besserman, 83–98. New York: Palgrave, 2006.

Roth, Cecil. "The Economic History of the Jews." *Economic History Review* 19, 2nd series (August 1961): 131–35.

Sa'ab, Hassan. *Zionism and Racism.* Palestine Essays No. 2. Beirut: Research Center, Palestine Liberation Organization, December 1965.

Schriver, Nico J. "Responding to International Terrorism: Moving the Frontiers of International Law for 'Enduring Freedom'?" *Netherlands International Law Review* 271 (2001): 271–91.

Stillman, Norman A. "The Story of Cain & Abel in the Qur'ân and the Muslim Commentators: Some Observations." *Journal of Semitic Studies* 19 (1974).

Strauss, Mark. "Antiglobalism's Jewish Problem." *Foreign Policy* (November–December 2003): 58–67.

Talmon, Jacob L. "Uniqueness and Universality in Jewish History." *Commentary*, July 1957, 5–20.

Toynbee, Arnold. "Is there a Jewish Future in the Diaspora?" and response by Trude Weiss-Rosmarin, "Is Toynbee Penitent?" *World Jewry*, April and May 1959, World Jewish Congress, London, 22–32.

Twain, Mark. "Concerning the Jews." In *Mark Twain on the Damned Human Race*, edited by Janet Smith, 176–77. New York: Hill and Wang, 1962. Originally published in *Harper's Magazine* in September 1899.

Weinbaum, Laurence. "The Struggle for Memory in Poland—Auschwitz, Jedwabne and Beyond." WJC Policy Study no. 20. Jerusalem: Institute of the World Jewish Congress, 2002.

Wiesel, Elie. "Art and Culture after the Holocaust." In *Auschwitz: Beginning of a New Era?* edited by Eva Fleischner, 403–15. New York: Ktav, 1977.

———. "Jewish Values in the Post-Holocaust Future: A Symposium." *Judaism* 16, no. 3 (Summer 1967): 281–82.

Wigoder, Geoffrey. *Jewish-Christian Interfaith Relations—Agenda for Tomorrow.* Policy Forum no. 14. Jerusalem: WJC Institute, 1998.

Vinocur, John. "A Most Special Cardinal." *New York Times Magazine*, March 20, 1983, 28–55.

Yaalon, Moshe et al. "Iran, Hizbullah, Hamas and the Global Jihad: A New Conflict Paradigm for the West." Jerusalem: Jerusalem Center for Public Affairs, 2007.

Zeiger, Arthur. "Emma Lazarus and Pre-Herzlian Zionism." In *American Jewish Women and the Zionist Enterprise*, edited by Shulamit Reinharz and Mark A. Raider. Waltham, MA: Brandeis University Press, 2004.

## Newspapers and News Agencies

*Aftenposten* (Norway)
*Agence France-Presse*
*Al Hayat Al-Jadeeda*
*Al-Jundi Al-Muslim*
*Al-Sharq Al-Awsat*
*American Conservative*
*Associated Press*
*Australian*
*Daily Telegraph* (London)
*Economist*
*El Pais* (Spain)
*Ethnos* (Greece)
*Europe*
*Forward*
*Guardian*
*Ha'aretz*
*Isna* (Iran)
*Jerusalem Post*
*Jerusalem Report*
*Le Monde*
*Los Angeles Times*
*Macedonian Press Agency*
*Mahanaim* [In Hebrew]
*Newsweek*
*New York Magazine*
*New Yorker*
*New York Review of Books*

*New York Times*
*New York Times Magazine*
*Observer*
*Reuters*
*Syrian News Agency*
*Time*
*Wall Street Journal*
*Washington Post*

## Web Sites

Age of Islam, http://www.ageofislam.com/
Christian and Jewish Relations, Boston College, www.bc.edu/research/cjl/cjrelations/news.html
CNN, www.cnn.com
"'Dabru Emet': A Jewish Statement about Christianity," Religioustolerance.org, http://www.religioustolerance.org/jud_chrr.htm
"Epistle to Yemen II," Wikipedia.org, http://en.wikisource.org/wiki/Epistle_to_Yemen/II
International Court of Justice, http://www.icj-cij.com
Library of Congress, http://www.loc.gov
Middle East Media Research Institute, http://www.memri.org
Pope Pius XII, Mystici Corporis Christi, http://www.vatican.va/holy_father/pius_xii/encyclicals/documents/hf_p-xii_enc_29061943_mystici-corporis-christi_en.html
Realm of The Chosen One: My Islam, My perfect Religion, http://realmofthechosenone.blogspot.com/2006/12/my-islam-my-perfect-religion.html
The True Religion, http://www.islamworld.net/true.html
Time, http://www.time.com

# Index

Song of Solomon (Song of Songs), 35–37, 176

Sophronius, 162–63, 173

Soviet Union, collapse of, 149, 184

Spain, 1, 25, 32, 52, 70, 71, 90–91, 186–87, 191

Spanish Inquisition, xi

Spinelli, Barbara, 94

Spinoza, Baruch, 34, 99, 117

Stanley, Lord, 86

Steiner, George, 22, 71

Stillman, Norman A., 56

Stockholm Conference, 128

Strong, Josiah, 102

*Study of History* (Toynbee), 64

*Succot* (Tabernacles), 29–30

Sudayyis, Sheikh Abd Al-Rahaman Al-, 59

suffering, theology of, 110–13

Sundram, Jomo K., 7

"supersession complex," 55

supersession doctrine (displacement theology), xii, 6–7, 92, 122, 164; American Founding Fathers and, 24; " blood guilt" and, 7; of Catholicism, 11, 60–63, 147–49; of Christianity, 10–12, 26, 43–49, 62, 105–6, 113, 144–45, 161, 181–82; of Islam, 10–11, 26–27, 50–51, 55, 57, 163–64, 173, 184; Nazi, 116; in *The Passion of Christ*, 6; in Quran, 10–11, 50–51, 184; Spain and, 90; of Theodorakis, 93. *See also* displacement theology

Sweden, 76, 110, 128–29

Switzerland, 76, 126–27

*Sybil* (Disraeli), 85

symbiosis, German-Jewish, 117

Syria, 5, 151, 165, 187

Takeyama, Michio, 119

Talmon, Jacob, 65

Talmud, xi, xii, 15, 27, 111; anti-Semitism and, 44, 46, 102, 186, 192; censorship of, 46; on charity, 31, 69; chosenness and, 9, 10, 17, 18–23, 46; on destruction of the Temple, 170; as evidence of Judaism's development, 65; *hevlehi mashiah* in, 113; on Jewish dispersion, 69, 71;

love allegory in, 37–38; Quran's use of, 52–56; on Rabbi Akiva, 161; Rashi on, 133; as "subversive doctrines," 102; used as propaganda by Soviets, 97

*Tancred* (Disraeli), 82–85, 177

Telhaug, Inge, 5

*Tell Ye Your Children*, 128

Temple Mount, 158–59, 162–63, 169–74

Ten Commandments, 9, 17, 22, 30, 78, 95, 187

Ten Lost Tribes of Israel, 83, 102, 118

terrorism, 27, 60, 125, 138–39, 153–56, 180, 183, 187, 190, 192. *See also* September 11, 2001, terrorist attacks of

Theodorakis, Mikos, x, 4, 91–92, 94, 182

*tikkun olam* (repairing the world), ix, 3, 20

Titus, 42, 158

Torah, xi, xii, 15–25, 28, 30, 34–37, 131–33; denial of authenticity of, 10, 170–73, 186–87; Toynbee on, 39, 64

Toynbee, Arnold, x, 39, 63–67, 98, 178, 180

Travers-Herford, R., 20

True Cross, 162

Truman, Harry S., 138

Twain, Mark, 66–67, 143, 180

uniqueness of the Jews, 17, 26, 34, 66, 73–77, 135; anti-Semitism and, 3, 95; Ben Gurion on, 135–38; chosen-ness and, 3–4, 21, 61; dietary laws and, 79–81; Disraeli on, 84, 85; Gentiles' understanding of, 140, 164; Haggadah on, 31; Holocaust and, 3, 8, 94, 109, 111, 114, 121, 122, 129; Israel and, 81–82, 140, 165; Johnson on, 26; Maimonides on, 34, 177; Passover and, 30; Song of Songs and, 36–37; suffering and, 3, 165

United Nations: 1947 resolution (partition of Palestine), 138, 148, 155, 168–69, 183; 1975 Resolution 3379 (equating Zionism with racism), 137–39, 155, 183; Arafat invited to speak at, 155; attitude toward Israel, 137–39; Genocide